M E M O I R S

Books by Arthur Krock

IN THE NATION 1932–1966
MEMOIRS

ARTHUR KROCK

MEMOIRS

SIXTY YEARS
ON THE
FIRING LINE

Funk & Wagnalls NEW YORK

LIBRARY OF CONGRESS CATALOG CARD NUMBER: 68–26106
PUBLISHED BY FUNK & WAGNALLS,
A Division of READER'S DIGEST BOOKS, INC.

Second Printing

PRINTED IN THE UNITED STATES OF AMERICA

To my wife,
MARTHA GRANGER KROCK

Because it would require thousands of citations from the published record to supply the bibliography of sources from which this book is derived, I have limited the identification of these sources to (1) memoranda I made regularly over the years; (2) such uses of correspondence with individuals as the law allows and seemed to me to be within the bounds of propriety; (3) documents that have been specifically released by those concerned.

I am deeply indebted also to others for indispensable help in the preparation of this book. But in listing them as follows, I absolve them of any responsibility for its contents, particularly statements of my political point of view and my appraisal of the public persons who figure in the narrative:

JAMES SAYLER. For his devoted efforts as collector and assembler of this material; his abiding belief that it had value as an account of recent political events; and his skill and wisdom as copy-reader and as editor.

LAURA WALTZ. With constructive criticism, and with patience and industry immeasurably beyond the call of duty as my secretary, she typed, retyped, and reretyped these pages. My thanks to her are profound.

COL. CHARLES J. V. MURPHY (U.S.A.F.R.). This brilliant reporter —for *Life* and *Fortune*—of the major events of war, semi-war, and comparative peace in our time volunteered his services as a reader at the most critical period of the preparation of the book. His favorable opinion lent me the impetus to go ahead that I sorely needed.

JOHN LORD O'BRIAN. He is the leader and dean of the Bar of the Supreme Court and the nation; a public servant extraordinary who in two declared and two undeclared wars lent his wisdom, learning, and professional eminence to serve the national interest; the most authentic liberal in the classic tradition I have ever known. Were it not for the fact that he completely exemplifies "a passion for anonymity," Mr. O'Brian would be mentioned prominently and often in this account of the major events of the twentieth century and the men who created, exploited, or contended with them. Of all those who more or less urgently suggested that I write this personal memoir, Mr. O'Brian was the earliest and most encouraging, rising grandly above the inconsistency implicit in his refusal to write his own.

ARTHUR KROCK

CONTENTS

CONTENTS

FOREWORD

NEXT to the excellence and wide distribution of American plumbing and orthodontal skills, the people of this nation are disposed to boast that theirs is a "government of laws, not of men." Ideally and theoretically this is true of the constitutional system established at Philadelphia in 1787 and ratified in 1789. But as I have observed the operations of the system over six decades, most of them in Washington at first hand, the government of the United States, no less than others—democratic or autocratic—is primarily and practically a government of men.

The purpose of this book is to portray some of these men as I have known them in the context of great events—by watching them at work from a close point of vantage, and through intimate association. These experiences I promptly recorded in the detailed memoranda from which the following narrative is derived. It is in broad outline the story of the revolutionary transformation of the American system of government in my time, an account of certain activities by the principal shakers and movers of this transformation, and a set of profiles of these personages.

There are, I hope, as many lights as shadows in this composite. For dealing as the book principally does with the human factors that largely effected this transformation, the innate human traits and qualities inevitably appear as in ordinary daily life—the gaiety, wit, and humor of these individuals in their exercises of governmental power. Therefore, both bright and somber colors are interchanged in the portrait of the era as I see it.

It is drawn with full realization that the radical changes which have occurred in the political, social, and economic structure of the United States appear to suit the majority. Only when excesses in the use of their powers by the special pressure groups become intolerable does this diffused majority unite in a mood of resentment for the invasion of individual rights and physical security.

These changes are inherent in the chapters in which the Presidents and other major politicians who were chiefly responsible for the transformation, or who resisted it, are the central characters. But I have reserved to a final chapter a specific list of the changes that seem to me fundamental; also a personal appraisal of their immediate and ultimate consequences.

Because of the fortuitous fact that my span as a reporter and commentator was unusually long, the cast of characters encountered at first hand add up to a large number. And because I spent these years in the field of politics, which is government, the members of the cast range from Theodore Roosevelt to Lyndon B. Johnson.

The degree to which heredity and environment shape the actions, reactions, and opinions of human beings can never be accurately measured. But whatever this degree may be, I attribute my viewpoint and its concerns largely to my experience as a first-hand observer of the men and events that have reshaped our political system for the worse in the name of a "liberalism" both spurious of ancestry and destructive in practice.

This experience is the source of such conclusions. Because until the reshaping began to take form and to expand from the First into the Second New Deal, I was an enthusiastic supporter of the reforms pressed by the two Roosevelts and Woodrow Wilson to excise the ruthless abuses of power and of individual rights and liberties by the entrepreneurs of the American Industrial Age.

So far as one can put an accurate label on his own political philosophy, I am today the same Democratic liberal I was when I first took stock of my political inclinations. This estimate I believe to be supported by documentary evidence of an effort to attain objectivity despite my dim view of the stewardship of those to whom the American people have entrusted the institutions of democracy—Presidents, Congresses, and Supreme Court justices. For examples:

Although I was and remain opposed to the concept of the Big Brother, centralized welfare state to which John F. Kennedy became a sudden convert by pledging full support of the platform of the 1960 Democratic National Convention, I strongly endorsed his stand against the collusive price increases in the steel industry after it had exploited the prestige of the Presidential office to induce steel labor to scale down its original demands in negotiating a new contract. The industry had given him every reason to believe it welcomed and would not take advantage of the easier terms evoked by the Presidential intervention. To me the price increases were a breach of good faith by the industry and an affront to the President of the United States himself. To vociferous critics (largely self-styled conservatives) the increases merely were the assertion of a right inherent in the free-enterprise system.

And I was at least among the promptest of newspaper commentators to praise President Johnson for openly enlisting the Federal government in the birth-control campaign of private organizations. I immediately wrote an article pointing out that he was the first President to show the courage and the statesmanship to attack a condition that is the gravest of threats against the survival of the human race.

I cite these incidents among others that could be summoned to my purpose. That purpose is, with full consciousness of the sharp limitations that invest all personal testaments, to challenge the merits of the prevailing semantics that divides all private thinking and public expressions on the policies and acts of government into permanently separate compartments—liberal, moderate, progressive, conservative, hawks, and doves.

The license of gifted satire is not abused—but I think at least the facts are—in W. S. Gilbert's lines in *Iolanthe*:

Every boy and every girl
That's born into this world alive
Is either a little Liberal
Or else a little Con-serv-a-tive.

Among those of public spirit and good will to all humanity, this just isn't so.

The extent to which my political philosophy has been formed by environment and first-hand observations of the processes and processors of government in this country is a matter for determination by the readers of the accounts of these observations that follow. But in the view of many, a third determining factor is heredity; wherefore the following:

I am of the fourth American generation from immigrants who came to this country from German-ruled or congenitally German principalities: Prussia and Bavaria on the maternal side, Alsace, Silesia, and Posen on the paternal. They were all country or small-town people of what is called Jewish descent (when other Caucasians feel this euphemism is more considerate than the harsh three-letter word). In physiognomy, coloration, and physical mannerisms these immigrants ranged from various European to Mediterranean types, produced by the racial mixtures after the Diaspora. And in the mixed sphere of theology they ranged from the orthodox to the agnostic and the atheistic.

My father, with paternal approval, was a "freethinker," as many agnostics called themselves in his day. My mother's connection with ancestral faith was a seldom-observed formality. Her father's first wife was of the pioneer Kentucky Anglo-Saxon stock; and her brothers, half-brothers, and a half-sister married into the same community. In consequence of all this, I was brought up to make free choice of any creed or none. And, following my uninhibited inclination from earliest remembrances, I chose none.

MEMOIRS

1

EARLY YEARS

I WAS born without incident. No fairy godmothers or witches were seen on the premises. I was puny, and my first two months on earth would have been my last had it not been for my grandmother's discovery of a survival diet. This was oatmeal—I couldn't retain anything else. By my first birthday I was a healthy child. The intuition that led her to find the one infant food on which I could be nourished was typical of her natural gift for healing.

I grew up in the house of my mother's parents. This was in direct consequence of the facts that my birth had afflicted my mother with blindness for five years thereafter, and my father, who was a bookkeeper in small business, had left Kentucky with her for Chicago for a better job and access to a specialist who eventually restored her sight.

New York City, where my paternal grandparents lived (he was a cartographer, and one of my earliest recollections is of a detailed map of Java and Sumatra which I was told was his handiwork), was far away; and the death of my mother's father when I was five or six years old imposed on my grandmother somewhat reduced circumstances—at least they allowed no surplus for non-imperative travel.

[3]

Moreover, my mother had imbued me with her strong opinion that my paternal relatives in New York had always underrated my father. Hence, because of this and because of my grandmother's loving care and the devotion and admiration for her that I shared with the entire community, white and black alike, I felt no impulse to alter the situation in which I remained a stranger to my father's kin and they to me.

Probably, to allow full weight to the factor of heredity in any assessment of its influence on my bent of mind, I should add a few words about my mother's parents.

We did not have a Red Cross chapter, but my grandmother was its uncertified embodiment. Our section of Kentucky was a border cockpit in the War Between the States. She nursed the sick, tended the wounded, and concealed and fed the stray from the battlefields. When yellow fever epidemics struck the regions to the south of us, she opened her large house to refugees and provided shelter and medical care for those who were, or were thought to be, already infected.

She was repeatedly called on by the doctors of our town to help them with the delivery of children, white or colored, in rural families unable to afford or without access to regular medical service. I recall very well on a number of occasions being awakened in the middle of the night in my little room over the front portico of the house by the jingling of bridles and the creaking of saddles. I would look out and see three horses departing, on one of which sat Dr. Jepson, our family doctor, on another my grandmother, and on the third a Negro groom, to serve as needed. Sometimes a farm wife was in critical labor; sometimes the farmer had fallen ill or was injured. Black or white, it made no difference: with her mounted groom riding beside her, or a passenger in the doctor's buggy, my grandmother was practicing her concept of a normal neighborly duty.

For different aspects of the same nobility of character her husband, my grandfather, had the same standing in the community. He had made his way up the great river from New Orleans to Southern Kentucky, leaving his father's home at eighteen with a dollar and a silver watch in his breeches and a peddler's pack on his back. His goods must have been what the pioneer settlers wanted; perhaps also they were pleased by the courtly, strong six-foot youth. At any rate, his *ad valarum* had multiplied sufficiently en route for him to open a general store on his arrival in Metcalfe County, marry Marinda Nevil Turner, and begin the begetting of his eventual fifteen children.

Removing to Glasgow, a growingly important railhead that was the seat of the neighboring County of Barren, he enlarged his scope as a merchant; engaged in banking, farming, and raising cattle on widening lands; became Chairman of the Fiscal Court (thereby director and conservator of the county's economy and entitled to be addressed as "Squire" Morris—as invariably he was).

A considerable time before Fort Sumter he voluntarily set free his slaves (my grandmother told me "he just couldn't longer abide being any part of the system of owning human beings as chattels"). They, of course, continued in his service as before, provided with food, clothing, and shelter (as were their descendants, who were my playmates), but now they got wages, too. I knew him well enough to be sure that what it cost him in money was repaid in spiritual values.

Like most elderly people, I remember much better what I read or heard in childhood than in the years between. Accordingly, I distinctly recall the following things he told me as, in his old age and afflicted with the malady that killed him, we sat together under the huge maples on the lawn while he drank, slowly and appreciatively, one of the three daily toddies— bourbon, water, "and a leetle sugar in the gourd"—to which he was rationed.

A loyal Jefferson-Jackson Southerner, finding much substance in the regional grievances against the North, but, like the great Virginians, opposed to Secession, he believed that only Lincoln, his fellow-Kentuckian, could save the Union. In those days the voting was *viva voce*, or in the open courthouse square, indicated by raising the hand.

The Barren County voters in 1860 were strongly for the rump-Democratic, Secessionist Breckinridge-Bell ticket; their principal spokesman was Joseph E. Lewis, later the commander of the Confederate Army unit known as the Orphan Brigade because all Lewis' predecessors fell in battle. It took great personal courage and conviction to raise a hand for Lincoln. But my grandfather did, alone.

"Drop your hand," warned Lewis, "or, dear friend as you are, I'll shoot you down where you stand."

"If you do," replied my grandfather, "there'll be maybe a hundred hands to rise where mine has fallen."

That ended the incident, except that my grandfather discovered in due course that he had erred in his belief that the election of Lincoln would preserve the Union.

He must have been thinking of this with particular ruefulness when, already a man of middle age, he suffered the wound and exposure that, I was given to understand, ultimately accounted for the agonizing nature of his terminal illness. He sustained these injuries when, with the Confederate home guard of the town, he had been driven into the woods by an invasion in force of the infamous guerrillas led by Quantrill, whose mission was looting and pillage and who rendered fealty to neither the Confederacy nor the Union.

My mother and her half-sisters had been to what would pass for finishing schools now, and all three attended the annual music festival in Cincinnati, the cultural center of our part of the United States. They also had "graduated" from the secondary-school seminary in Glasgow that was called Liberty College; so they were considered in their time to be cultivated young women. Their brothers had attended various institutions of higher learning—the Naval Academy, the University of Virginia, Vanderbilt University, and Bethel College in neighboring Russellville, for examples.

My mother was a gentle, sweet, tiny woman. She had been brought up like all Southern girls of her class to do nothing, to learn little in scholarly depth. She couldn't cook. She couldn't sew. She played the piano and sang, and though her mother was a practical woman who could do all these things, she did not require this particular daughter, who was the youngest child, to learn anything except to be a period young lady. She rode horseback well enough to stay aboard. I know she did very little walking; her feet were so small that she wore triple A, No. 1 shoes, which were the smallest manufactured.

Before she married, my mother kept a record of the names of

her callers in a volume I believe was called a chap book. The rate of a Southern girl's popularity was determined by the number of male "callers" she received on Sunday. Her rate was above the average.

One day I noticed with filial pride that, about 1884, one of her callers had signed himself "F. Bret Harte." There were other names, including a governor or two, of whom invariably my mother would say, "I danced with him at his inaugural ball."

But though her mother was highly skilled in all the details of housekeeping and its budgeting—and on a very large scale—my mother was aware of money, for instance, only to the extent that there seemed to be enough of it to go around. Colored servants were plentiful, one of whom always was her personal maid. And because she was attractively petite and the youngest sister, the brothers called her "Dolly"—after the then current fictional heroine of *Barnaby Rudge*.

My mother's name was Caroline. Her sisters' names—also of princesses of Britain—were Cornelia Belle and Victoria Regina. I never understood what the attraction of the House of Hanover was for my grandparents.

After she married a man who never earned much more than just subsistence wages, she did her best to adjust to requirements for which she had no training at all. Among my tributes to her effort to give me advantages she could not give, the highest is that she never complained.

My father, who was born in 1859, was handsome when young. I lived long into his life—in fact, when he died, I was in my thirties. Like others of his generation, which grew up amid the devastation of the War Between the States, he hadn't much schooling. But he had literary and philosophical impulses. He wrote letters to the newspapers—especially *The Louisville Courier-Journal*—and essays and poems. But he never projected these inclinations toward the literary form, because they never completely came off as such. And his introspective type of mind made it hard for him to express his thought with full clarity.

Subjected to scholastic training or endowed with a true literary gift, he might have been much more than what he was all his life: an accountant or bookkeeper. He might have written significantly for a broader audience. He was highly intelligent, eloquent in a vague articulation of brilliant fancy, well read in standard literature. He held and expressed strong political opinions and judgments of public men. But he encouraged me to independent thinking. As I recall his political philosophy, it was a mixture of Jeffersonian and Hamiltonian, his radicalism taking form largely in his certainty that most politicians in power were mercenarily disposed to betray their public trust. But I cannot recall when I did not feel myself to be a Jeffersonian Democrat, after I had read enough political history to make a choice.

Since my father was a free thinker, no religious instruction or attendance was ever required of me, though I was exposed early to Baptist and Methodist camp meetings, Negro and white. I occasionally went to church in Glasgow according to the communion of the girl I happened to be with. Before my teens I found myself with no creed, the mere thought of creed being totally unacceptable. I was an early agnostic and have remained that way.

My birthplace was a settlement in south-central Kentucky, close to the Tennessee line, seat of the County of Barren—so named because its soil was harsher to the plough than the lush, open grazing places encountered by Virginians and Carolinians as they moved westward from the Bluegrass to the new frontier. About twenty-five hundred people lived in Glasgow during my childhood. It was a community that strongly reflected its Virginia ancestry, which was direct, the town having been named for Glasgow in Rockbridge County, Virginia. It was a graceful town, with many large houses surrounded by large lawns.

As was usual in those times and places the center of Glasgow was the Square, in which the courthouse stood. Around the courthouse was a picket fence to which the country folk who came into town on County Court Day tethered their mules, horses, and wagons. The Day occurred on a date certain in each month, when the country people could transact legal business that might have arisen and also buy such supplies as they needed from the merchants around the Square.

The town thrived on mercantile activities, being as aforesaid the railhead of a very large rural section. This area grew lumber, tobacco, and legumes. And a few miles away from Glasgow prospectors had struck oil.

The familiar propensity of oilmen to mix play with their work was only one reason things were very lively on Saturday nights in Glasgow. The indigenous population made the larger contribution to roistering. This tended to develop into violence because while the county was dry even before legalized state and national prohibition (and remains dry as far as I know), there were always ways of getting whisky. And one of the attributes of the Kentuckian, of the Southerner in general, is an inclination to become belligerent with the intake of whisky.

This was grievously emphasized by a tragedy involving five brothers who were great friends of mine. They were artisans. One had a monkey I was fond of, and its owner's special place in my affections was assured because as he passed our gate on his way into town every morning, he would allow me to play with his simian companion.

But kind and peaceful as the brothers were by day, Town Marshal Winston Collins, the only law officer the town had or needed, found it necessary to kill three of them (I think) because of the Saturday night frenzy that seized them when they got drunk. Though we boys were not supposed to see or know about the weekend violence, we did manage to creep up into the Square occasionally, and hence I was a shocked spectator on one of these tragic occasions.

Unlike the Kentucky mountaineers, the brothers were not the kind of people to start feuds—in this instance with Town Marshal Collins. And they were aware of how whisky transformed them into outlaws. Not one of the survivors after sobering up but conceded of his fallen brother, "He had it coming to him."

This wholesale instance of justifiable homicide was not unusual in the South of my boyhood. Its source, the dangerous combination of the Southerner and whisky, was a major reason these communities voted dry and were—as many remain—steadfast advocates of national prohibition.

However, it must have been at this time and in these circumstances that I developed a lifelong disbelief in the right or efficacy of sumptuary or other compulsory legislation to make all mankind conform to the moral concepts of a ruling few.

The accent of our region was Southern but of the Virginia Tidewater. This cadence is not as thick as it is in the Gulf States, nor does it draw out vowels, as in that area, to the point where they resemble the bleat of a goat: for example, "m-aaa-n" for "man." Nearly all our "rs" were slurred or leap-frogged, but some were pronounced as firmly as in the Midwest—by a selective formula that defies specification. In my part of Kentucky, as in the flat or rolling Virginia lands, we gave full value to the "r" at the end of "customer" but none to the terminal "r" of "tiger," which came out "ta-gaah."

Proper names, too, were subject to regional rules of pronunciation. Not until I went North did I discover that Evans was not invariably uttered as "Ivins," Jordan as "Jerdan," Rousseau as "Rue-saw," Coombes as "Combs," Morton as "Mo'ton." That any was not "inny" on every tongue. And that names of German-Jewish origin were elsewhere pronounced phonetically, whereas to us Kohn was "Khan," Khan was "Kann," Kaufmann was "Koffman," Straus was "Straws," and so on.

But moving about the world hardens the consonants and narrows the vowels. And when I listen to myself talking over some electronic medium, I realize that this is what has happened to me.

Our last house in the community—which now shelters the offices of the Barren County Board of Education—had fifteen or more rooms. The Negro servants, household helpers, and field hands occupied quarters well to the rear of the house that were clean, well built, and whitewashed.

In this house there was a room nobody used except for company. It was known as "The Parlor" and was furnished with pieces of heavy, strong mahogany, red damask curtains and red carpets, and a locally famous silver mantel. Over this mantel were silver candelabra and a large mirror framed in silver. The parlor was generally off bounds, even in very hot weather, though it was the coolest room in the house because it was kept shuttered. One exception allowed was Sunday, when, by custom, young men called on young ladies, and my mother, before she married, "sat for company" in the parlor. Since from twenty to thirty young men usually appeared, though the only refreshments were ice-cream, cake and tea or coffee, she was rated as "popular," a most desirable Nielson among the young women and their mothers in our town.

The parlor also had an old-fashioned horsehair-covered sofa, which I could slide down with great ease on the seat of my pants, and I sometimes sneaked into the parlor for this particular exercise. If I was detected, it was serious; but if, as usually, I wasn't, it was one of the pleasures of my childhood I remember fondly.

My grandfather had gone broke when Kentucky became a battleground in the War Between the States, and I daresay he had a trunkful of Confederate money by the time its purchasing power had vanished forever. But though in my childhood we seemed to have little legal tender, this was balanced by the fact that our place was largely self-sustaining. For example, we had a lye-hopper, to make the lye for soap, and other necessities of daily living. We had large vegetable, watermelon, and cantaloupe patches, bought meat only because to kill our own was uneconomical; poultry was most plentiful. A familiar sight was my grandmother at the wheel where she span cloth for her large family.

My Grandfather Morris was a great believer in education. Considering the circumstances of his youth and the devastating wartime of his maturity, his formal education couldn't have been much. But he spoke the language of a cultivated man. And it was his library that led me into writing as a profession, because in those bookcases were standard works of great modern and ancient authors.

In this room I read, book by book and page by page, Thackeray and Dickens and MacDonald, Dumas, George Eliot, Trollope and Matthew Arnold, Spenser, Shakespeare, Pope, Dryden, Spencer and Darwin, Kipling and Hardy, and a host of others. I had learned my letters at about four; by seven I had developed a greed for reading greater than my healthy appetite for the succulent viands that, on the testimony of my palate then and now, only Southern cooks know how to prepare.

In time I came to regret the preference of a bookish youth that I indulged in at the expense of the sinews produced by the proficiency in sports enjoyed by my contemporaries. But thus far a good constitution has kept the expense at a tolerable level.

Notwithstanding, the physical environment of my childhood was happy for growing boys—most of my companions had ample room for play on my family's property, called "a place" as distinguished from a plantation or estate. One edge of this "place" bordered the south fork of Beaver Creek, a large stream where my friends and I swam. And in rare instances when the winter was cold, we skated on the ice in the creek, and fished and showed off to one another what the Romans called "*abilitas*."

As for my own personal situation, in addition to being a member of a family so large that rarely did fewer than fourteen sit down to table, there were a number of dogs I considered my personal property. They were of a breed of St. Bernard that had excellent lines, so much so that one of my elder uncles took one—"Kaintuck"—to London, where he won the blue ribbon in his class.

Among our St. Bernards was a bitch named Princess, and I chose her for my own. I used to hitch her to a chair laid on its back, and she would pull me around the lawn like a horse, to the great satisfaction of myself and the annoyance of my elders. She also would obey me implicitly. For example, one evening, when I was still a year or so short of my teens, I went into town to attend a Confederate reunion. As I closed the gate I said to her, "Sit and stay until I get back." At the command she lay down, and about three hours later when I returned she hadn't budged.

We had a few cows and several horses. My grandfather was particularly proud of his Arab, a thoroughbred stud named Selim. He was beautiful: short-coupled with arched neck and flashing black eyes—actually a charger. I tried to make friends with him, but the one thing Selim knew better than anything else was that he didn't like me. I would offer him food through the fence around the paddock and invariably he would try to bite my hand off. I could tell what he was going to do by the way his eyes would change. They narrowed menacingly as I slowly extended an ear of corn, and then I would prudently drop it inside.

I always wanted to ride Selim but was never allowed to. He died at the ripe old age of twenty without our having attained friendship. But we did have other horses, and I would ride them to town in the summer. Summer is hot in those parts. Charley was one horse I rode for a long time. I'd go to town to Raubold's confectionary—one of those stores that draw children to it because of the aroma of candy and cake. It also had an icehouse, and my practice—when our own icehouse was empty—was to buy a hundred pounds, have it wrapped around with twine, and hitch it to a loop around Charley's rump. Of course, by the time we got home on a hot summer day, a hundred pounds of ice had shrunk distressingly.

One of the real agonies of my childhood concerned clothes. The boy of fashion was dressed in kilts of a plaid that had some real or imaginary relationship to one's family. Mine reflected the fact that my grandfather (first wife) and uncles had married girls of the Anglo-Celtic pioneer families of that area. At any rate, kilts it was for me, with long black stockings. In this outfit I circulated until I was about six years old.

I recall, in my kilted period, making a stick-horse from a long broom handle topped by a horse's head. You put the stick-horse between your legs and galloped around the Square. A great friend of mine, Frank McQuown, and I did this at least once a day.

After I graduated to short pants I was obliged to wear what was called the Little Lord Fauntleroy costume, the most hateful and poisonous habiliment ever forced on a child. My mother outfitted me like the rest of the boys my age, with Fauntleroy's tight velvet pants, his velvet coat with a huge lace Eton collar, strong, sturdy black shoes, and a frilled shirt. After emerging from the kilt era, I retained only the thick long black stockings.

I hated this costume, and, hoping to win a concession, I

insisted that my curls, which I still wore at the age of six (they were red-gold, *mirabile dictu!*), be sheared as the price for appearing in public as an ersatz Little Lord Fauntleroy. My mother refused the concession, but an uncle took pity on me. One day, without notifying my mother, he took me to the barbershop and ordered my curls cut off. But I was still obliged to wear the ghastly plumage for another couple of years.

In Kentucky in my youth we didn't shoot off fireworks on the Fourth of July. We did that on Christmas. But I had read in the papers that on the Fourth of July the boys in the North shot off firecrackers and guns. So, assuming the town pioneer role that I later would in football, I decided, on a certain Fourth of July, to make patriotic noises.

I couldn't find firecrackers—nobody used them at this season. Accordingly, I went behind the house to the cabin of my good friend Dan Smiley. Dan was out on some chore, but his shotgun was leaning against the wall. I peered down into the barrel and pulled the trigger: that I still live is incredible. Nothing happening, I decided to see if I could make that gun work.

I took it outside the cabin—within, say, thirty or forty yards from our house—when there approached me from the left my year-old cousin Frank Morris and his Mammy; she was holding him in her arms. I raised the gun and pointed it in the direction of my cousin, not realizing the potential consequences, though I had often seen guns in action. But it never occurred to me this one could be loaded: I thought I had tested that. At any rate, I again pulled the trigger, missing nurse and infant but scaring them to death. Taken into the house by my alarmed mother, I explained that my act was in honor of the Fourth of July. But this did not save me from being soundly disciplined in a rear-guard action.

The relations between the white and Negro communities in my town and throughout the state were courteous and considerate. We were sternly forbidden to use the word "nigger." Kentucky had not been much of a slave state and slaves there had been well treated. Very rarely had families been separated or sold down the river (despite Mrs. Harriet Beecher Stowe), and I grew up with Negro boys until the social convention required us to part.

It may be surprising to many that in our town Negroes served effectively to keep growing white boys in line. There was a Negro in Glasgow named Felix Duncan, an amiable man, but he consented to frighten boys into being good at the request of their white parents. He cooperated in establishing the legend that he was to be feared. One's parents would say to the offender, "All right, I'm going to take you to Felix Duncan," and if you casually encountered him, as frequently you did in the town square, you were very careful to assume a cherubic expression to avert the dread prospect that he would frown and say, "I hear you been cuttin' up some."

Another unforgettable colored citizen was Felix's Fidus Achates by the name of Sonk Cake—I don't know why that "Sonk"—who was a wonderful tap-dancer. We would flock around him whenever we went to town for the entertainment he provided gratis. He loved children and we loved him.

During my infancy, since my mother had been blinded in childbirth, I was nourished by a black woman known as "Aunt" Courtney. I was suckled at her breast, and throughout her lifetime she treated me as her own child. I was always able to count on her protection from painful disciplines I had merited.

We had a few bad Negro characters as well as white. Except when, as in the case of my family, they lived in cabins on the "place," Negroes lived in a segregated part of the town known as the "Kingdom." There I spent many of my happiest hours, with baby chickens to play with and wonderful food for my lofty partaking.

Among my dearest friends were "Uncle" Perry and "Aunt" Easter Wells. He owned and tilled the land my grandfather had, without interest, lent him the money to buy. I went happily to their house by frequent invitation, knowing I would be fed like a hog destined for the market, and there I sat alone at the table with her children looking on. Regardless of these semi-feudal relations, there was no resentment between the social orders.

Segregation was accepted as the natural outgrowth of the situation that had brought, largely to the South, a race markedly alien in appearance and culture to the Caucasian. But in our town segregation incited no difficulty. The only one I recall was a lynching. A young Negro who had been a janitor at Liberty College was caught in an attempt to rape a young schoolmistress, and the sheriff brought him to the Glasgow jail to protect him from a mob. But the mob was large and strong and its feeling was so intense that it broke into the jail, took the keys from the jailer, and pinioned the sheriff's arms before he could draw his gun. Then the mob hanged the Negro from a tree in front of the jail.

Realizing what was impending, I and another boy (from whom I had a letter about twenty years ago reminding me of this) hid in a shed on the property of one of my aunts and watched the lynching through a knothole. It was a traumatic experience, and luckily I never saw, nor in our town was there, another.

There was very little political activity among the Negroes in the town. They voted freely, if legally qualified, when they appeared at the polls. But sometimes, when an election concerned an issue that had aroused to gunpoint the enmity between white factions, the Negroes stayed away. On such occasions—there were two or three—one of my uncles who was city attorney would go to the "Kingdom" to see leaders whom he knew, and say, "I believe there's going to be trouble at the polls tomorrow. The sheriff's going to have a hard time handling it, and if you all come there and vote, it's just going to anger the factions involved. So if I were you, I'd go fishing." And fishing they would go.

It was desperately unfair, since Negroes are here through no fault of their own and the white man has exploited their labor and despoiled their women.

A fundamental reason for the resistance of the South to total equality of Negroes and whites is the concern about maintaining bloodlines, whether of animals or people. This concern, now rapidly becoming a dead issue in the North, affected white families as well. When a young man in one family proposed to the daughter of another, their ethnic origin was a matter of serious consideration to the parents of both.

Under the Federal compulsions of integration under law I fear that ultimately the reaction that caused the great race wars of the past will rise again, this time centering in the North, violently terminating the effort to enforce total integration between white and black.

My family circle included a man of all talents in Dan Smiley, colored, who taught me as much as I would learn of the lore of the outdoors that all boys should know. Among other things the correct handling of dogs, of which, at times, we had twenty-two.

Dan Smiley would organize moonlight coon-hunting expeditions in which, with the Kentucky type of fox hunting, I was happy to participate. Our fox hunting was not the elegant pink-coated affair of Virginia. When foxes became pests around the chicken coops, one of my uncles, who wrote a number of fox-hunting stories, and a few friends would make up a fox-hunting posse.

Our county was one of the original breeding areas of the American (Walker) foxhound. The hunt was composed of a group on horseback followed by these hounds. The riders would proceed at night to a small elevation commanding a narrow valley where the foxes were sure to run at moonrise. The hounds remained at the foot of this elevation with their keepers, though I don't think we ever called them that. When a fox appeared, the kennel men would release them and off they would speed in full cry, while we others would lounge on our plateau. The adults would drink whisky and talk and listen to the hounds yelping around and around the valley, and identify each by his or her "bugle" (voice). Sometimes the pack would run down a fox. But after a reasonable length of time, when the moon went down, everybody went home.

There was one fox that evoked a legend in which my uncle firmly believed, and which he chronicled in the local press and *The Louisville Courier Journal*. This animal was known far and wide as "Old Baldy." He was reputed to have lived for more than thirty years and to have eluded every pitfall and trap set for him. He would lure the hounds to a stone escarpment and disappear. According to my uncle, "Old Baldy" died laughing at the frustration of the hunters and the hounds.

The leading citizen of our town, Col. Haiden Trigg, an ardent fox hunter, developed the Trigg-Walker foxhound, the seed-stock of the great American species. When my grandfather died and my grandmother was obliged to curtail our household, Dan Smiley became the keeper of Colonel Trigg's foxhounds. But Dan Smiley and I kept in touch with each other. His letter writing was primitive, but we maintained a correspondence until his death. I never attended a funeral of more poignant sorrow to me.

No one was ever dearer to me than Dan Smiley, yet our association was of the limited kind that normally existed between the white man and the black man in our community who were truly friends. He never felt I was patronizing him, but he did not expect the unrealistic total egalitarianism that is now the object of the extremist civil rights movement in this country.

I grew up in the shadow of the Lost Cause. Confederate and Union veterans of the War Between the States were plentiful and most of them still able-bodied. They dominated politics and business. The abolition of Negro slavery had been the basic issue in the Deep South of the hand-to-hand conflict they had fought, Secession being merely the occasion. But in our Negro community, as throughout the South, their kindest and most understanding fellow citizens were the former Confederates.

Inspired by the record of their heroism in the bloodiest battles in the history of the nation and ignorant of the factors that made Secession intolerable to the manifest destiny of the United States, I looked upon the Confederate veterans as my boyhood heroes. It was an ever present wonder how these, the gentlest as well as the most constructive of our citizens, could have been the youths who fought with such ferocity at Pittsburgh Landing, Gettysburg, and in the Wilderness. Unconsciously I sought to emulate their conduct by my own, a principle that, though I have often faltered and failed in serving it, has abided with me throughout my life.

Joseph E. Lewis of Glasgow was the last commander of the Confederate Army's Orphan Brigade. We all called him "Judge," because after the War he became a Justice of the State Court of Appeals, the highest court in Kentucky. In consequence of Judge Lewis's residence there, Glasgow was the center of the annual Orphan Brigade reunion, and thereby I met a number of distinguished Confederates, one of whom was Gen. Simon Bolivar Buckner, a resident of the neighboring county of Hart. General Buckner, a veteran of the Mexican War, had been the final Confederate commander at Fort Donelson, which Grant captured after Buckner had been left alone to defend it by his superior officers, Generals Floyd and Pillow. General Buckner also was famous as the Vice-Presidential candidate on the gold Democratic independent ticket headed by General Palmer, a Union veteran, in 1896.

General Buckner physically and spiritually was a perfect symbol of a lost cause. His character and standards were as lofty as his stature: an erect six feet four inches. To the end of his life he regularly sent me one of the corncob pipes of his own making, a hobby of his old age.

In Louisville, I had the privilege of the friendship of two other distinguished veterans of the War Between the States— Col. Andrew Cowan, who served the Union battery on Little Round Top at Gettysburg, and Maj. John B. Castleman, C.S.A., who had raided Ohio with Gen. John Morgan and was under sentence of death until reprieved by President Lincoln.

When everyone was home, which was frequent, the evenings were spent around the piano. My mother played and sang, and her brothers joined in the songs—mostly sad—that were popular at that time.

I don't know why so many of them were sad. Maybe their choice was a reflex from the South's loss of the war, whose traces were still visible in education and in the local economy. A number were laments brought to this country by the Irish immigrants, such as "Kathleen Mavourneen" and the songs of

Tom Moore. This Celtic repertory included Scottish ballads, warlike and romantic, appropriate to a community in which the pioneer stock was almost wholly British.

But some Irish songs, like "Pat Malloy" and "Off to Philadelphia," were gay. American songwriters at that time were also writing such dismal stories of heartbreak as "After the Ball," "Only a Bird in a Gilded Cage," and so on. My elders sang them all, with the result that often—at age five or six—I retreated to weep under the piano stool at my mother's feet, overcome by the lugubriousness of the current offering. She sang a few in French, with bad pronunciation; I don't recall hearing any in German other than "Lorelei." This despite the fact that all my first American ancestors had migrated from one or another German-speaking province.

There were Confederate War songs, like "Dixie" and "Lee's Sword" and "The Bonnie Blue Flag." But the family concerts also included songs of the Union, "Tenting Tonight," for example, but never "Marching through Georgia" or "The Battle Hymn of The Republic."

When my mother played and one or more of her brothers sang the mournful songs in which people delighted in that period of American history, my retirement under the piano, drenched in tears and clamant with sobs, evoked the amusement of the younger kinfolk, but did not interrupt the solos and duets. Of these, several cling precisely in the memory as follows:

> Nita, Juanita,
> Ask thy soul if we should part,
> Nita, Juanita, lean thou on my heart . . .
> In thy dark eyes' splendor
> Where the lovelight longs to dwell,
> Thoughts both sweet and tender
> Gleam a last farewell.
>
> —
>
> 'Twas just one year ago tonight
> That I remember well
> I sat down by poor Nellie's grave
> And my tale of love did tell.

'Twas of a poor, unhappy slave—
Thank God she now is free.
Disturb her not, but let her rest
'Way down in Tenn-ess-ee.

—

A bonny laddie there lived o'er the lea,
A laddie both tender and noble and gay,
Who loved a lassie as noble as he,
The bonnie sweet Bessie, the Maid o' Dundee.

(They got married and were happy until):

But sorrow came to her heart one day
When her dear darling laddie was ta-ken away,
And O how sad and lone was she,
The bonnie sweet Bessie, the Maid o' Dundee.

(Now came the closing stanza, with the accompaniment of my sobs and tears from under the piano):

And when in the ground her laddie was laid,
Her heart then broke and she fer-vent-ly prayed
"O God in heaven, let me—ee go too,
"And be with my laddie sae gude and true."

Typical of the romantic songs dear to the era was a duet, sung by my mother and her brother Fred. Part of it was:

(She)   O! how could a poor gypsy maiden like me
Ever hope the proud bride of a noble to be,
Or fear not by him would her love be betrayed
And leave her forsaken, a poor gypsy maid,
And leave her forsaken, a po-oo-r gypsy maid.

(He)   I have lands and fair dwellings
And all shall be thine
And a coronet, Zilla, thy brow shall entwine,
Thou wilt nev-er have reason
My faith to upbraid,
For a countess I'll wed thee, my own gypsy maid.
Then fly with me now.

(She)   Can I tru-ust to thy vow?

(He)   Yes, yes, come away

(She)   Will thou nev-er-er betray?

(Both)   No never by (me) (him) will (my) (thy) trust be
              betrayed,
          And a countess (I'll) (he'll) wed (thee) (me)
          (My) (This) poor gypsy maid.
                    (Repeated crescendo)

But my recollection is that despair never seized me more
firmly, while I listened to the sad songs in my mother's reper-
toire, than when she sang a tale of lost love entitled "Ruby."
Perhaps precocity, at the age of five or six, had vaguely forecast for me the pangs of bereft lovers. As I remember the lyric,
which was accompanied by a slow, mournful musical composition, it was this:

          I opened the leaves of a book last night,
          The dust on its covers was deep and brown,
          As I held it to-ward the wa-ning light,
          A withered floweret came drifting down.

          It was only the wraith of a woodland flower
          That was plucked in the dear, dead days of old,
              [lines omitted for loss of memory]
          How well I remember the deep-fringed eyes
          Bent over the Tasso upon her knee,
          And the dear face looking in sweet surprise
          At the passionate pleading that rose from me.

          O Ruby, my darling, the slim, pale hand
          That gathered the hare-bell was never mine own,
          But faded and passed to a far-off land
          Ere the tale of my love could yet be told.

          A memory sweet, but as sad as sweet,
          Still covers mine eyes with resentful tears

That the angel Death, when he gathered the sheaves,
Left me sad and alone 'till our meeting there.
(Repeat last line an excruciating number of times)

During this early period of my first schooling and my child-hood up to my middle teens, I went to the town schools. The primary school was primitive by modern standards—a frame house with two or maybe three teachers to give us the rudi-ments of education. That education so well served me that I had no difficulty getting into high school and graduating. We learned the Three Rs mainly by memory, through repetition, and by the study of related textbooks. With respect to English, history, and arithmetic we depended greatly on the McGuffey Readers.

I was read to so much—I must have been about eight years old before I started to attend Miss Bybee's primary-school classes. A little later on I attended the same secondary school, proudly misnamed Liberty College, from which my mother had graduated. By this time I was twelve years old. My father meanwhile had established himself and my mother in Chicago. I finished high school there, but I could hardly wait for the summer recess to return with my mother to Glasgow and live with my grandmother in her big house. One such journey was especially exciting because of the bloody Pullman strike of 1894. I remember that the train was guarded by armed troops called out by President Cleveland over the protest of Governor Altgeld of Illinois to protect the United States Mails as well as the passengers from the violence threatened by the union strikers, some of whom were armed.

After finishing high school in Chicago, I took the college boards and was admitted to Princeton. Normally I would have picked the University of Virginia, where most of my uncles had gone. In addition, Virginia attracted me because in the family album was a photograph of one of my elder uncles at his fraternity banquet in a dress-suit with white tie and tails—the first I had ever seen even by camera—and a copy of the toast he had delivered.

But Princeton appealed to me because I had become addicted to football, which was fairly new in Glasgow though Vanderbilt University in Nashville, a few miles away, had played the game for a long time. I acquired a football and assembled two teams. This, with my newspaper reading, apprised me of the Poe family, the great football dynasty at Princeton. And the university's Tiger symbol was most alluring—I thought it more wonderful to be a "Tiger" than any collegiate counterpart. Also, it was a favorite university for Southerners.

One rainy night in Washington many years afterward I was walking my dog when I encountered Mrs. Ella Burling, a friend. She is tiny, and I noticed that her escort was not much taller than she and was as slender. He had a hat pulled down over his eyes, and Ella said to me, "You know my father, don't you?"

I took off my hat and said, "Mr. Arthur Poe, for better or for worse you are responsible for my having gone to Princeton."

And he said, "Oh, you mean that ninety-five-yard run with a broken ankle? My ankle wasn't broken at all, just sprained a little."

"But," I asked, "how about that dropkick of sixty yards that also beat Yale the next year?"

And he said, "An accident; it hit the side of my foot." That was the beginning and the end of my acquaintance with the Poe brothers.

I matriculated at Princeton University with the class of 1908, largely relying, unwisely as matters eventuated, on the promise of a loan from a relative to see me through. When I got to Princeton, I looked for the cheapest possible way to live and found it off campus in a rooming house at 2 Nassau Street. My expenses had been paid for the first semester, but by the time it became necessary to provide for the long-range financing, my father advised me that the guarantee couldn't be met. I decided that mine would be a very grim effort to carry on, and I had best try to get a college degree where the cost would be self-liquidating, and then go to work at a paying job. I could, had I had the fortitude, have supported myself at Princeton by hard work as David Lawrence did in the class of 1910. But I was too proud to wait on the tables in Commons and too indolent to seek some other means of self-support at Princeton.

A classmate told me that if I would go to Chicago to Lewis Institute, a small but very high-grade institution that gave respected college degrees, I could maintain myself by assisting professors and working on the college yearbook. All this was borne out by the events, and I encountered one of the richest experiences of my life by attracting the favor of Dr. Edwin Herbert Lewis (the Institute was not named for him). He thought I was a promising student in his subject, English, and hired me to help grade the papers of his classes and take over a small freshman class in English poetry. I acquired the degree of Associate in Arts in 1906, the year my class at Princeton became juniors, and took the first train I could get to Louisville with a newspaper job as my objective.

Through Dr. Lewis I had become acquainted with the general attorney of the Chicago and Eastern Illinois Railroads who gave me a pass for my journey. I lacked the spare $2 for a Pullman upper berth and sat up all night in a coach before reaching Henderson, Kentucky. At Henderson the C. and E.I. connected with the Illinois Central. This in turn took me to Guthrie, Kentucky, where I transferred to the Louisville and Nashville Railroad that bore me to my native town of Glasgow, where, in my grandmother's house, I could begin, cost-free, my negotiations for a job in Louisville.

In Glasgow I acquired a three-day stake for a visit to Louisville and eventually got a salaried job on *The Herald* that began my newspaper career.

2

KENTUCKY NEWSPAPERS

I HAD always been influenced toward newspaper work by belonging to a family that read newspapers aloud, and by a natural inclination. So, when I went back to Kentucky from Princeton and Chicago in 1906, I applied for a job on *The Louisville Herald*. In Louisville, *The Herald* was second to the *The Courier-Journal*, but I chose *The Herald* because my chances were better there.

In those days the "cub" system prevailed. You were hired as a reportorial trainee, working for nothing for several months to establish whether you could learn the craft. I hadn't the capital to support myself in Louisville in this period. Also, the managing editor of *The Courier-Journal* knew me and my family, and was aware that I had no newspaper experience. Therefore, in order to get the job on *The Herald*, I feloniously pretended to be a seasoned reporter. I went on the payroll at $15 a week.

I recall knowing so little about the operation that when the time came for me to write my first news story, I looked at my deskmate to see how he had begun his and noted that at the upper-left-hand corner of the page he had typed his name. It was "Moore," and he began it with a small "m." I imitated him by starting mine with a small "k."

I got along pretty well at first in my fraudulent role, picking up a number of human-interest stories. Since we worked on a six-day, or it may even have been a seven-day, basis I was usually on Sunday duty. One Sunday I turned in a feature about a man who had risked his life to avert the wreck of a passenger train but whose subsequent failing fortunes had brought him to the estate of a derelict on the Ohio River-front. This earned the commendation of the city editor, and all went smoothly until one night I was sent to cover a fire.

To cover a fire requires an expertise in reporting that cannot be supplied except by training, in proof of which I missed the real news. For instance, I hadn't got a list of the fire-engine companies that were summoned or an itemized account of the insurance on the property. I was blank on eye-witnesses to how and where the fire had begun. I also failed to learn that a well-known bachelor had jumped out of a lady's apartment on the second floor, where it would have been very inconvenient for him to have been found.

The city editor, when I came back without these essential elements, said, "Kid, you've really never been a reporter before, have you?"

And I said, "No, sir."

He said, "Well, you've tried hard, you've done pretty well, so forget it. You can keep your job and I'll raise you to $18 a week." Sometimes crime *does* pay.

In due course I became a correspondent throughout the state, traveling to places whose local news was of statewide interest—the advent of the Night Riders, for example, and a typical election in Breathitt County.

The Night Riders were a social and economic product of the same troubled times. In the depression of 1907–1908 the price of Kentucky's principal crop—burley tobacco, light and dark —had fallen below a subsistence level, and a movement spread among the growers to keep tobacco off the market as a pressure tactic to advance the price. This movement, beginning with farm-to-farm solicitation, rose to violent reprisals against those growers who refused to cooperate, the reprisals principally

taking the form of burning the barns in which their tobacco
was stored.

The violence led to gun battles, especially in the black burley area of western Kentucky, and the state fell into the extreme and violent disorder of a limited civil war.

As a reporter for *The Louisville Herald*, both before and
after the Governor sent troops to protect the dissenters' property and to keep order for the people at large, I covered a
number of these battles. The sentiment against the Governor,
the militia, and the dissenters became so unfavorable that some
Kentucky politicians led processions of Night Riders into the
towns on their speaking days. Once I saw Representative (later
Senator) Ollie M. James, one of the most influential members
of Congress—later a national figure in the Wilson Administration—ride proudly and openly in a victoria through the streets
of Cadiz, the seat of Trigg County, at the head of a group of
mounted, armed men who, everyone knew, had been burning
barns and destroying tobacco crops the night before.

As the depression righted itself and reasonable prosperity
was restored, the violence began to subside. Tobacco moved
toward the level of a subsistence crop. But prices continued to
be low until the 1920s—except for the price boom accompanying the First World War—and the oncoming depression of
1921 threatened a return of the outlawry in Kentucky.

I was by that time familiar with Bernard M. Baruch and a
plan he had for forming grower cooperatives—a plan he had
once personally put into effect by underwriting the entire cotton crop of his native state of South Carolina to insure reasonable prices. At the instance of Robert W. Bingham, the new
owner of *The Courier-Journal*, and at the urging of several of
the large tobacco growers in the state, I approached Baruch for
assistance in forming *The Courier-Journal* project—I had become Managing Editor of that newspaper—that became the
highly successful Kentucky Tobacco Growers Cooperative Association; Bingham agreed to serve as its president.

A young attorney from Maysville who was a member of the
Kentucky House of Representatives took charge of the essential state legislation, and in time became assistant general counsel for the Cooperative. I recall, as treasurer of the association,

signing the monthly checks for the indispensable and successful services of this young attorney. He rose to be the Solicitor-General of the United States and an Associate Justice of the United States Supreme Court. His name was and is Stanley F. Reed.

The Cooperative attained its objective, and I think maintains it still. The night riding was never repeated.

Breathitt County was nicknamed "Bloody" just after the War Between the States because of the violent feuds that broke out among returning Confederate and Union army veterans to that section of our then almost evenly divided state.

There was rarely an election in Breathitt County without a killing or two or three or four. The violence of the 1909 local election, though not of any particular or special consequence, was, however, responsive to the turbulent social conditions of the times that had produced the Night Riders in the western section of Kentucky.

When I got to Jackson, the county seat of Breathitt, the tension in the air was palpable. On the day before the election two events affecting me provided a clue as to the extent of this tension.

First, I was strolling around town and saw a very pretty young girl (an unusual number of Kentucky women are pretty and even beautiful). She looked friendly and I spoke to her. The result was that I bought her a soda and she suggested that I walk her home, a little outside the town. As we proceeded I noticed a youth circling us. His movements suggested that he was stalking prey. In response to my inquiry this conversation ensued:

"That's my beau."

"What does he want?"

"He doesn't want you walking with me."

"Well, that's absolutely all right."

So I went up to her beau, who wore a side arm, and said, "Look, I just was walking this young lady home, but I'm going right back to town."

He grimly indicated that this was a good idea, and I departed with a lively but fortunately unsubstantiated apprehension that I might get shot in the back at any moment.

Second, that night, the night before the elections, the Kentucky National Guard company from Cynthiana, in the Blue Grass, was sent to Jackson to maintain order. Meanwhile, citizens of Breathitt rode in from the country on their horses and mules to hold pre-election rallies for their various candidates. It didn't take long for them to discover that the Cynthiana Company had been given rifles but no ammunition. Thereupon these rural citizens of "Bloody Breathitt" began to circle the troopers like Indians around a wagon train, firing at their feet to make them dance. And dance they did.

The afternoon of the elections I was told that a man named Moss Hart (Moss is a Kentucky mountain abbreviation of Demosthenes) had been killed at the Greasy Creek precinct in a row with a son of County Circuit Judge Blanton; and that if I went to the Blanton house in Jackson, I would find this son and the reason for the gunfight, both Blanton boys having been watchers at the polls. I found, lying wounded on a bed, a handsome, tall young man. I was inexperienced enough of the Spartan mountain folk to be shocked by the rude language with which he ordered his solicitously hovering mother out of the room before consenting to be interviewed about the shooting.

He said that Moss Hart had pulled a gun and wounded him; that in self-defense he had killed Hart; that he had drawn and fired last. Not until several days later did I learn that the man lying on the bed was not the killer; it was his elder brother, and he had been putting on an act to give his brother time to flee into the hills and away. Such was the clan spirit of these people.

After the polls had closed, but before the ballots were counted, I was having coffee at the residence of County Attorney Pollard, who had been active in trying to stamp out violence and enforce the law against the offenders in the community. Also present were Mrs. Pollard and two other women, the wives of engineers who were building a plant on the other side of the Kentucky River. We sat around an old-fashioned Franklin stove. The room was lighted by two oil lamps.

Suddenly, a bullet crashed through the front window, knocking out one lamp and barely missing us. As we sank to the floor another bullet extinguished the other lantern. This was obviously no place for the two women from across the river or for me, and I volunteered, not wholly in the role of hero, to get them back to their camp. A railway trestle, which was certainly two hundred feet high, bridged the river gorge. With a lighted hand lantern I got from Pollard and put on the end of a stick, I led our small group to the trestle and we started across.

My lantern must have attracted the attention of the citizens on the river bottomland who were still celebrating the election, even though they did not yet know how it had come out. The lantern was a perfect target for them to demonstrate the fine marksmanship of the Kentucky mountaineer. Halfway across the trestle a shot from the bottomland destroyed the lantern. It was now pitch dark and I was scared to death.

I said, "Let's get down on all fours, crawl across, and hope they can't see us." The darkness had ended the target practice, and we made our way to the other side in safety. Dubious hero that I was, I lay down on the ground and, strictly from fear, developed an acute attack of appendicitis.

In the course of reporting the Breathitt County election for the Associated Press (which I had joined after leaving *The Louisville Herald*), I got in touch with Ed Callahan, High Sheriff of the county, whose candidacy for re-election had created a dangerous feudal situation all its own. His clan had been feuding with another for years. He lived in a settlement called Crockettsville, about twenty miles out of Jackson. I arranged by telephone to interview Callahan. The phone was on a party line; many country folk shared it, and they all were anti-Callahan. On my saying, "Sheriff, when can I come out to see you tomorrow?" a voice broke in with "Editor, don't believe him. He's lying to you. He don't even live there. He'll shoot you if you try to come."

I managed to arrange an engagement, and the day after the election I did ride out there, on a mule. But though my coming was well known by this time to everybody who had listened in on the conversation, I made it to Callahan's store and got my interview.

This same Callahan's life was perpetually in danger. In front of his store at a crossroads he had built a diagonal fence leading to his house across the highway, leaving a narrow gap for traffic. The structure enabled him to make the transit in reasonable cover from the sharpshooters of the other clan who, every day, all day, were hiding in the laurel on the hills commanding the highway.

For some years he had managed to clear this traffic gap without being shot, though he had been fired on. Eventually, he wearied of this ordeal and decided to move West—to Wyoming, I think it was. In order to get safely to the railhead at Jackson, he rode with his little granddaughter before him in the saddle. The Kentucky feudist will not endanger a child, especially a female child; hence, Callahan negotiated the journey without drawing fire. He held the child in his arms when he got off his mule at the railway station and while he mounted the steps of the train, avoiding windows when he got inside the coach.

But these mountain people love their habitat with deep devotion. They are unhappy anywhere but in their hills and valleys. Consequently, Ed Callahan returned to Breathitt after some years, practicing the same defense strategy when he detrained and as he mounted his mule. But ultimately his various security provisions failed him. One day he was making his usual dash across the gap in the fence and in that twenty feet he was shot fatally by the permanent watchers in the laurel.

Another example of the fierce passions of these people was provided by the Hargis family, a feudal clan whose chief was a judge and a state senator. He had a wild son called "Beach," an abbreviation of Beauchamp (pronounced "Beecham"). One evening the father called his son to the store to reprove him for violent misbehavior. In the ensuing quarrel Beach Hargis shot and killed his father and stamped on his body.

But while still on *The Herald*, my regular assignment was to cover a section of Louisville called the East End, keeping track of murders, deaths, assaults, and all the other aspects of district police reporting.

The area was large and the means of public transportation were limited, particularly after nightfall. I solved that problem by borrowing a horse from No. 5 Engine Company, and became the only urban equestrian reporter I ever have heard of. But the horse, of course, was unavailable when his hook-and-ladder equipment was fighting fires; and it was on one such night the desk informed me of a murder in a very desolate slum area of the city. Lacking my steed, I was obliged to proceed by streetcar to the scene of the crime. This turned out to be fortunate, for on the streetcar I met the county coroner en route to the same place.

This adventitious encounter led me to a couple of essential beats that eventually disclosed the murderer. He had killed his wife when she found him sexually molesting their daughter, a not uncommon situation in families of the sort commonly spoken of as "white trash."

I was an accredited professional when *The Herald*, which was a starving newspaper, was struck by an economy wave. The owner had ordered expenses to be cut a certain percentage, and a number of people were to be dismissed from the staff. Being unmarried, with light living expenses, I asked that my name be substituted for that of a married, older reporter on the "death list." My offer was accepted with disturbing alacrity, leaving me with no occupation. But this happened at a very opportune time.

The Court of Appeals, the highest court in the State of Kentucky, had decreed a special election in Louisville for mayor and all other city and county elective officers because the regular election the preceding November was proved to have been won by Democratic voting frauds. For example, in the Twelfth Ward it was discovered not only that all the eligible voters miraculously had come to the polls but also that they had voted unanimously for the Democratic ticket in precise alphabetical order.

Alexander Scott Bullitt, a friend and fellow-Princetonian, had been appointed by the court as sheriff of the county *ad interim*. He assembled a group of young men animated by high

moral purpose against corruption in politics, and we set out in
the role of deputy sheriffs to assure a clean special election.
This we did successfully. (Incidentally, the *ad-interim* mayor
was the Robert W. Bingham to whom I later sold *The Courier-Journal* and *The Louisville Times*.)

We deputies filled in our time before the special election by
searching for such minor and locally approved infractions of
the law as betting in poolrooms on the horse races. As I led the
raiders into one of these poolrooms I saw, to my great unhappiness, the famously colossal form of a Western Kentucky congressman who was engaged in trying to climb out of a window.
I looked hastily away, because exposure would have been disproportionate in damage to the offense, and he escaped without
getting his name in the papers and duly became a celebrated
United States Senator and national Democratic orator.

When the time arrived to turn in my badge, the new administration having been installed, the Louisville correspondent of
the Associated Press offered me a job as night editor, and for a
couple of contented years I worked the 8 P.M.–5 A.M. shift.
However, in the course of my service on *The Herald*, I had
attracted the favorable attention of the leading political reporter in our state, John D. Wakefield. He had drafted me to
act as his legman at the first national conventions I ever covered, the Democratic and Republican gatherings of 1908.

By a lucky chance, because luck plays a large part in newspaper beats, I got one such story at the Democratic Convention
at Denver. It concerned the ouster by the West Virginia delegation of its national committeeman. This established me as a
political reporter, so that when I did leave *The Herald* as the
result of the economy wave, I had qualified for the field.

But also at the convention in Denver I met Gen. W. B.
Haldeman, one of the owners of *The Courier-Journal* and *The
Times* and the editor-in-chief of *The Times*. He introduced me
to his family, including his youngest daughter. The outcome of
that association was that we were engaged to be married when
she died suddenly in Paris in the autumn of 1908.

The nexus that grew from the desolation felt by the family
of this lovely young woman and by me was never broken

during the lifetimes of General and Mrs. Haldeman. And it was responsible for my transfer from the AP to the Haldeman-Watterson newspapers that began with a telephone call from General Haldeman one night when I felt especially lonely and bereaved.

When the phone rang, I was working in the AP office on my job, which was to condense the incoming product of four wires from Chicago into a report that could be carried on two wires to Southern and Mexican newspapers. "Would you like to go to Washington as the correspondent of *The Louisville Times?*" the General inquired. It took me no time at all to say yes, and I arrived in Washington in that capacity early in the year 1909, midway in the Taft Administration.

I had served about a year as the Washington correspondent of *The Louisville Times* when the Washington bureaus of the *Times* and *Courier-Journal* were merged under my direction and I first met Henry Watterson, the world-famous editor of the latter newspaper. The meeting was at Mansfield, Watterson's country place near Louisville, and he asked me (this was in the pre-election period of 1910), "How do you plan to write about the politics of this campaign?"

"I spoke to General Haldeman about that," I answered, "suggesting a field survey in various crucial states, so that our readers will have some idea of what to expect in the election returns."

Watterson approved. In the company of Frank R. Kent of *The Baltimore Sun*—its Washington correspondent and one of the most distinguished political writers in the country—I surveyed the prospects of the 1910 election in those states, interviewing the party bosses, the candidates, and the local newspaper oracles. When the campaign was over, it was perfectly obvious that the Republican Progressives were bent on splitting the party as the overture to controlling it. The Republican opposition to Taft had become so great, for example, that the Chairman of the House Appropriations Committee, Representative James A. Tawney of Minnesota, was defeated for renomination. He had backed the reactionary Payne-Aldrich Tariff Bill, the principal conservative-liberal issue in the Congressional campaign.

The mood of the country was apparent, even in Washington. In the Senate, LaFollette of Wisconsin, Dolliver and Cummins of Iowa, Clapp of Minnesota, and other Republicans had already fought the Administration bitterly over the tariff act, and the fatal split of the Republican Party was on its way. The Democrats, having nominated Bryan for the third time and lost, were on their way back. They had put history aside, including Bryan, and started recovery of power with the successful candidacy for the governorship in New Jersey of Woodrow Wilson, who had left the presidency of Princeton to run on a reform ticket.

The election forecasts I supplied *The Courier-Journal* in 1910 pleased Watterson, and he adopted me as his professional protégé. From that time forward we were close, personally and professionally. I spent many weekends with him at Mansfield —so did my first wife, who died in 1938, and my young son.

Hence, it was no surprise to me in 1915 that when the papers were beginning to run into the red, I was chosen by the ownership to return to Louisville as managing editor of the two newspapers and to consolidate their new operations.

Watterson, who had the minority share of the ownership, was long the outstanding editor in American journalism for numerous reasons. One was the place of his birth. Born in 1840 in Washington, D.C., he was the son of a congressman from Tennessee. He was a child of three or four when his father began to take him onto the floor of the House of Representatives, a practice common among Congressional fathers in those days. The boy attracted the friendly notice of ex-President John Quincy Adams, who was a member in this era, and he brought the child books from the House Library. As a privilege of his Tennessee birthright young Watterson also knew Andrew Jackson, who still was the elder statesman of the Democratic Party, counseling it from his estate near Nashville, the Hermitage, where Watterson told me he often had sat on Old Hickory's knee. Hence, when Watterson died in 1921, he had personally known every President of the United States from

John Quincy Adams to Franklin D. Roosevelt (the last as an official of the Wilson Administration).

Watterson began his journalistic career on a second-string newspaper in Washington. When Lincoln was inaugurated he was there as a reporter, and, he said, he held the President's plug hat during the ceremonies. When the war broke out, Watterson served for a while in Forrest's cavalry. But he had lost an eye in childhood and left the service to edit a behind-the-lines Confederate newspaper in Chattanooga, Tennessee. The newspaper, called *The Rebel*, followed the Confederate Army until further operation became impossible.

When the war was over, seeing no journalistic prospects in this country, he took his lovely young bride, Rebecca Ewing of Nashville—the last *grande dame* of the antebellum South I have known—to London, where he had been offered a job in Fleet Street. Watterson had only one introduction to a British subject. After a polite interval, he sent the letter around and was invited by return note to pay a call. Many years later Watterson described to me the background of this correspondence and its sequel as follows:

When Montgomery, Alabama, was the capital of the Confederacy, and I was a working journalist there, I had lodgings at the house of a gentlewomen of British birth. We became great personal friends, and she, foreseeing the eventual defeat of the Confederacy, suggested that in this event I might try my fortunes abroad, in which case she had a brother in London who might be of service. The note introducing me to this brother I had preserved throughout the war; and so, when I found myself in London, I put it in the mails.

Invited to call, I went to the address in Jermyn Street, finding it to be that of a boys' private school. As I entered, down a broad staircase came a charming middle-aged gentleman with side-whiskers. He received me most cordially, and in the course of a conversation suggested that I and my bride—I had told him of our recent marriage and that she accompanied me to London—dine with him and a few friends that evening.

A few friends indeed! They included Charles Darwin, Her-

*bert Spencer and Prof. Tyndall—not so astonishing, as it
turned out, in view of the fact that my host was Prof. Thomas
Huxley, the great English biologist, zoölogist and educator.
We passed a most pleasant evening, and the company was
delighted when, yielding to its entreaties, my young wife
played and sang a series of Southern melodies in which
Spencer enthusiastically joined.*

In his memoirs Watterson has related some of the benefits of
this remarkable accidental connection that he and Mrs. Watterson enjoyed during what proved to be a short tour of duty in
Fleet Street before he returned to newspaper work in the
United States. But it is typical of the kind destiny that watched
over him throughout his long career that his first acquaintances
abroad should have been this group of some of the greatest
creative thinkers of the nineteenth century.

I was reporting the Peace Conference in Paris, 1918–1919,
when Watterson reached his fiftieth anniversary as Editor of
The Courier-Journal, and the paper was preparing a special
edition, a Watterson edition, collecting tributes all over the
world from statesmen and soldiers. I asked President Wilson if
he would contribute. His response was a letter of declination,
saying in effect: "I would like very much to do as you ask. But
there are certain things that I cannot say in truth. They would
be hypocritical. Our rift was very deep at one time and it has
been only bridged over."

This was the Calvinist side of Wilson. He knew the things
one was supposed to say in that kind of context, but he didn't
feel them. He always resented some of Watterson's more extreme attacks. For instance, Watterson's comment, after his
break with Wilson in early 1912, "*The Courier-Journal* has
found that Woodrow Wilson is a schoolmaster rather than a
statesman."

Watterson was in Congress during the time of the stolen
1876 election, and he acted as spokesman of the Democratic
Presidential candidate, Governor Samuel J. Tilden of New
York, on the floor of the House in the proceedings that led to
the choice of an electoral commission. This packed commission
contrived to make Rutherford B. Hayes President by throwing

out the electoral votes won by Tilden in Florida and a couple of other Southern states. As spokesman Watterson played a large part in the effort in Congress to have Tilden declared the winner of the electoral as he had been of the popular vote. And this he supplemented with editorials and public speeches, in both of which Watterson most vehemently, and at times in a very inflammatory way, denounced the electoral commission and its "solution" of the contest. It was in this connection that he called through *The Courier-Journal* for a march on Washington of "ten thousand unarmed Kentuckians." That was a paradox, because an unarmed Kentuckian in the current political atmosphere was a contradiction in terms.

Tilden, alarmed at the very real prospect of another Civil War, called Watterson to New York to inform him that he would accept the decision of the commission. Even though it was a Republican-loaded panel, Tilden's attitude was that he did not want to be responsible, or be held responsible, for the obviously perilous consequences of non-acceptance. His representatives followed suit.

Eight years later Watterson supported the Democratic candidacy of Grover Cleveland with his usual vigor. He was Chairman of the Resolutions Committee at the convention in 1884. But soon afterward something that has never been quite explained happened to sever their personal relations.

The gossip was that Cleveland felt Watterson, who was a very dashing fellow, had been a "little too Southern" in manifesting his admiration of Mrs. Cleveland. Watterson always denied this, stating that he and Cleveland had come to disagreement on matters of party policy.

This, however, did not preclude Watterson's support of Cleveland for renomination in 1888, when Harrison defeated Cleveland. But by 1892, at the convention that chose Cleveland for the third time, Watterson bitterly opposed the renomination and said to the convention, "If the Democratic Party renominates Grover Cleveland, it will be marching through a slaughterhouse into an open grave."

Yet during Cleveland's second term, when many members of his party turned against him, Watterson played a principal role in supporting the President. He perceived that Bryan and other free silver advocates were seeking dominance of the monetary policy in the Democratic Party in the interest of "free silver" and at the sacrifice of the gold standard. He resumed his former alliance with Cleveland throughout the second administration and, like Cleveland, opposed the nomination of Bryan in 1896. He also supported the gold Democratic ticket of John M. Palmer and Simon Bolivar Buckner that was partly responsible for McKinley's election in 1896.

These are among innumerable demonstrations that Watterson was a thoroughly independent editor. He was not influenced by protests from advertisers or subscribers if he decided that his position was in the national interest. That was best exemplified by his slogan for *The Courier-Journal* in 1896: "No Compromise with Dishonor!" Watterson knew perfectly well that the sentiment of the Democratic majority in Kentucky was for free silver and Bryan. But he felt free silver to be an irresponsible monetary policy that would impair the value of the currency in a disastrous and dishonorable way.

The result was that *The Courier-Journal* almost folded under the opposition of the Democrats in Kentucky, especially the farmers, who resented the newspaper's part in the formation of the gold Democratic ticket of Palmer and Buckner. Bundles of *The Courier-Journal*, dropped at the stations of the Illinois Central and the Louisville & Nashville railroads, were burned throughout the state.

I remember another instance of Watterson's fierce editorial integrity. During the Wilson Administration, the Fourth Deputy Postmaster General, a former Missouri Governor and Congressman named Dockery, sent a letter to *The Courier-Journal* inquiring if there was any relation between its liquor advertising and its opposition to prohibition. This infuriated Watterson, who telephoned me in Washington and told me to hand his reply to Dockery in person. It ran something like this: "Anyone who dares suggest that *The Courier-Journal*'s opinions and beliefs and policies are influenced by any material consideration is a scoundrel." The frightened bureaucrat withdrew his letter, and that was the end of the matter.

The gossip about the cause of the rift with Cleveland was

credited the more because Watterson was highly appreciative of the charms of women. In his memoirs, *Marse Henry*, there is a chapter on the American theater, which he knew very well; among his close friends were many actors and actresses, and as a patron of the theater he helped importantly to start on her fabulous career the great Kentucky actress Mary Anderson. When I read this chapter in manuscript, I said to Watterson, "Marse Henry, you have made no mention here of the greatest actress of her time, Clara Morris."

"Well," he said, "Miss Rebecca [his wife, then nearly eighty] wouldn't like it."

But to those who consider that indulging in poker, champagne, and beer (his favorite tipple) are vices, he had them all. He seems, however, seldom to have lost more at cards (or abroad at roulette) than he could afford, though at times he may have been temporarily embarrassed. But IOUs are legal tender among gambling gentlemen. One Saturday evening Watterson apparently decided that the time for redemption of some of his had come. On his way to the Louisville Hotel, Watterson tarried a bit at the cash register, whose proceeds had not yet been audited for the day. Therein, after discreetly waiting for Watterson to pass on, the cashier checked to see what had happened in that fleeting moment. He found the box empty except for this memorandum: "All. H.W." Watterson was the only one who knew what "all" amounted to. But he made restitution, of course, and none doubted it was to the penny. And the impression was that he had won enough also to redeem his IOUs—such was his demeanor on the following day.

Watterson's knowledge of men and matters is partly accounted for by his love of travel abroad. In his later years he wintered in Florida, but previously he ranged Europe for a period of every year. In Louisville, however, he was at the office every night and part of every day, and he worked long stretches without holidays.

During the Republican and Democratic Conventions of 1916, which I covered, he required me to wire him each night a synopsis of the news developments. On this information, on night duty at almost seventy-five years of age, he based and wrote a first-page column headed "The Situation" in time for the current editions.

It is my good fortune to have been associated with gentlemen in all of the several executive posts I have held on the five newspapers by which I have been employed. Without exception my superiors and those who worked on my level possessed and practiced the qualities of character and demeanor that fit my concept of what it is to be a gentleman.

In a business association, as contrasted with wholly social relationships, this quality does not—indeed it cannot—preclude certain underhand maneuvers by management with the design of displacing top-level executives who, for any reason found sufficient by management, have become difficult partners in policy or administration. Twice during my professional career I was the object of this covert method of making my job untenable.

But those who were thus engaged were merely exercising their fair prerogative to attain the executive unanimity they considered essential to their concept of how a newspaper should be produced. They chose the method as the most considerate of the several at their disposal. Hence, I freely include in the statement (that I have always been associated with gentlemen) two of my employers who used this covert means: Robert W. Bingham, whose ownership of *The Courier-Journal* and *Louisville Times* derived directly from my choice of him as the purchaser; and Ralph Pulitzer, Publisher of *The World*. Bingham, because I opposed certain of his policies and standards; Pulitzer, because my fellow executives on *The World* resented my assigned function, as his assistant, to provide him with a daily appraisal of their professional performance.

When I started in journalism at the reportorial level, my first managing editor—a brilliant Canadian and as a journalist a Bayard sans reproche—was A. T. Macdonald of the now defunct *Louisville Herald*.

As the Washington correspondent and later the editorial

manager of *The Courier-Journal* and *The Louisville Times* (a joint ownership operation), I worked under the direction of Watterson, Gen. (Kentucky National Guard) William Birch Haldeman, his brother Bruce Haldeman, and, ultimately, Bingham.

On *The World* in New York my principal associates were Ralph Pulitzer, Frank I. Cobb, Herbert Bayard Swope, John O'Hara Cosgrave, Walter Lippmann, Florence D. White, John Breshanhan, and John H. Tennant.

On *The New York Times* they were Adolph S. Ochs, Arthur Hays Sulzberger, Rollo Ogden, Orvil E. Dryfoos, Arthur Ochs Sulzberger, Edwin L. James, Turner Catledge, Lester Markel, Louis Wiley, and my successors as the Washington correspondent of *The Times*, James Reston and Thomas G. Wicker.

The train of events that led to my over-all editorial management of *The Courier-Journal* and *The Louisville Times* and eventually to my total separation from that connection begins with a visit I paid one morning in early 1917 to the office of Bruce Haldeman, president and publisher of the joint operation.

The population of Louisville—though Protestants of Anglo-Saxon stock composed its ethnic majority—included a large group of German descent that was the wealthiest segment of the industrial complex and influential in the political activities of the community. With the outbreak of the First World War this group revealed an atavistic devotion to the cause of Kaiser Wilhelm II that manifested itself in the organization of passionately pro-German "Bunds."

These expressed their opposition to the Allies in public demonstrations and through private pressures that—as the prospect of the involvement of the United States in the war grew nearer with the rising interference of the German Navy with American merchant vessels on the high seas—persuaded *The Courier-Journal* that its obligation to the community required a direct attack on the local Bund and its sympathizers as alien subversives of the interests of the United States.

These attacks, from Watterson's pen, had long since become a matter of concern to Bruce Haldeman as the business manager of the enterprise, because of losses in advertising and circulation that were the effect of reprisals by the pro-German element, hitherto an important source of *The Courier-Journal*'s prosperity and broad readership.

When the business office's concern was brought to Mr. Watterson's attention, he spurned it, in the best journalistic tradition, as a basis of consideration in determining editorial policy. His attacks on the patriotism of the pro-German Bunds and their supporters were intensified with what he conceived to be the mounting peril of their activities to national security. When he went to Florida in late 1916 for his annual working vacation, he continued to forward articles that reflected this judgment with increasing forcefulness.

As editorial manager of the two papers I was instructed by Watterson to relay these editorials to the composing room and see that they were published immediately.

But I was subject to another instruction from another of the owners. Bruce Haldeman had concluded that there was some basis for the resentment of the pro-German citizens over the mounting intensity and extremism of Watterson's editorial attacks. Accordingly, he directed me to submit to him (before sending it to the composing room) any Watterson editorial that in my judgment would expand the conflagration; thus, he could pass on its justification and general policy soundness.

"In my judgment!" What a position for the faithful discharge of my duty to both the Publisher and the Editor-in-Chief! But one morning in 1917 a Watterson editorial from Florida arrived on my desk that clearly fit the description of the kind of article the publisher had directed me to show him before processing.

He read it carefully, and then, with a calmness which gave no indication that he realized the fateful potential consequences quite as much as I did, said, "Leave this with me, please. We shan't run it. I will return it to Mr. Watterson explaining why."

The consequence was as dire as I, at least, had anticipated. Watterson, in protesting the publisher's censorship, denied his right to impose it on *The Courier-Journal*'s supreme editorial authority—and a co-owner at that. General Haldeman, the publisher's elder brother, supported Watterson. So did Gen. (his rank derived from the office he held in the Confederate veterans' organization) Bennett H. Young, representative of the stock interests of the widow of John Haldeman, the third brother and co-heir to the properties.

When Watterson returned from Florida in May, 1917, this trio, who accounted for two thirds of the ownership, thereupon deeply abridged and diluted the functions of Bruce Haldeman and removed him as president and publisher. He sued on the grounds that in 1912 he had been invested with these posts and the authority that went with them by a contract made with the co-owners and irrevocable by them. In response to Watterson's deposition that he had neither signed nor even was aware of this contract, Bruce Haldeman repudiated the deposition. Watterson viewed this as an implication of perjury and so informed the court.

The dispute was carried to the State Court of Appeals, which affirmed the power of the owners representing two-thirds of the stock to take the action against Bruce Haldeman and to have elected Watterson in his place. Until Bruce Haldeman eventually sold his one-third share to the new owner of the papers, he devoted his activities as a director to dissenting to virtually every managerial decision.

This family fight weakened the operation—already beset by an economic decline that was due in part to war-imposed shortages of pulp paper and manpower—to such a degree that I soon concluded a sale was necessary if the papers were to survive. As a member of the board of directors by virtue of my post as editorial manager I was in a position to offer this judgment, although I was well under thirty, for the serious consideration of a board on which three of the other four members wore in their lapels the silver button that signified service in the Confederate Army. (The fourth, Bruce Haldeman, was too young to have served during that conflict.)

When I proposed a sale to the three Confederate veterans, W. B. Haldeman, Bennett H. Young, and Henry Watterson, they directed me to find a new owner worthy of the great journalistic heritage and to suggest a figure for the transaction. The following letter from Mr. Watterson records the functions thereby entrusted to me:

NEW YORK, APRIL 8, 1919

MY DEAR ARTHUR:

FOR THE PURPOSES OF THE RECORD IT GIVES ME PLEASURE TO STATE THAT THE SUBJECT OF DISPOSING OF THE STOCK IN THE COURIER-JOURNAL AND THE TIMES, HELD BY W. B. HALDE- MAN, ISABEL HALDEMAN AND MYSELF, TO JUDGE R. W. BINGHAM, WAS FIRST BROACHED BY YOU; THAT THE STOCK AMOUNTED TO SOMETHING OVER TWO-THIRDS AND CARRIED WITH IT CONTROL OF THE PROPERTIES; THAT YOU STATED YOU HAD SUGGESTED THE PURCHASE TO JUDGE BINGHAM AND THAT HE WAS FAVORABLY INCLINED TO IT; THAT YOU NAMED A TENTATIVE VALUE FOR THE NEWSPAPERS ON WHICH BASIS THE DEAL WAS FINALLY MADE; AND THAT YOU, THROUGHOUT THE PROGRESS OF THE NEGOTIATION, MADE THE ARGUMENTS AND RENDERED THE SERVICES WITHOUT WHICH THERE WOULD HAVE BEEN NO TRANSACTION WITH JUDGE BINGHAM. IN BRIEF, YOU ACTED AS HIS AGENT WITH US AND OUR AGENT WITH HIM, AND TO YOUR ORIGINAL SUGGESTION AND SUBSE- QUENT SERVICE THE SALE OF THE NEWSPAPERS CAN BE AS- CRIBED.

HENRY WATTERSON

After the transfer of two-thirds ownership to Bingham, he asked me, in July, 1918, to continue as editorial manager of the two papers. In that capacity I sailed to France toward the end of the war under the new owner's assignment, and to cover the Versailles Peace Conference of 1918–1919.

My choice of Bingham arose from a combination of a de- liberate selection and a chance encounter. The deliberate selec- tion was the outgrowth of several circumstances. As an attor- ney he had been co-counsel to W. B. Haldeman, to Young (representing Isabel Haldeman), and to Watterson in the liti- gation initiated by Bruce Haldeman. Bingham was a Democrat who, I believed (mistakenly as it later proved), subscribed to the Jeffersonian political philosophy that Watterson had consistently expounded in *The Courier-Journal* and W. B. Haldeman in *The Times*.

Finally, he and I were personal friends. And with the sudden death of his second wife—the widow and heiress of Henry M. Flagler—he had inherited a fortune sufficient to finance the restoration of the economic stability of the papers.

But had I not encountered him in the context of my commission to arrange the sale, as I did one day in the Pendennis Club, I probably would have followed through my thought of offering the properties to James M. Cox, Governor of Ohio. Cox was well and favorably known to me as a legislator and politician during his service in Congress; I was also familiar with his professional skill and integrity as publisher of *The Dayton News;* and I greatly admired him for rigid separation of his policies as an editor from his political interests.

The circumstances of the Pendennis Club encounter that turned my considerations to Bingham were these: I was alone in the library, well before my usual time for luncheon, redeeming a long-unkept intention to read Somerset Maugham's *Of Human Bondage*, a novel that had been widely praised at the time of its publication several years earlier. While I was reading the book another club member entered. But instead of going to the shelves, he walked to a window and stood looking out, the droop in his shoulders contrasting totally with the normal military erectness of his posture. I saw that my companion was Bingham, and when he turned, the dispirit indicated by his bowed figure at the window was matched by the expression on his face.

"You seem troubled," I said.

"I have been rejected for military service," he replied, "and abstention from it in wartime is alien to the tradition of my family. Also, I don't know of anything useful to my country in its need that is available to me to do."

"Wouldn't you be performing a great public service as the owner and publisher of the *Courier-Journal* and *Times?*" I asked.

It took a minute for him to recover from his astonishment.

"Are they for sale, and could I buy them?" he asked incredulously.

"I think so," I said. "Shall I explore the prospects?" On his enthusiastic reaction to the question, I initiated the proceedings by which the sale and transfer were made.

I first reported the conversation to Watterson, who was recovering from a minor illness in St. Joseph's Infirmary, and gave my reasons for favoring Bingham among the potential purchasers of the two-thirds ownership and control. These included William Randolph Hearst, Sr., who had gathered that the sale was a possibility.

In Watterson's weary state of mind (which I could only attribute to his temporary illness and the ordeal of the litigation with Bruce Haldeman), his impulsive reaction was that Hearst, whose journalism and political ambition he had often publicly arraigned, had the instant cash and facilities requisite to the promptest and most lucrative sale. It proved very easy to talk him out of this incredible idea and to get instead his sanction of Bingham as the purchaser; this was quickly persuasive with the owners of the remaining two thirds.

As the negotiations were moving toward the transfer, and after it was concluded, Bingham reiterated a wish that I should continue as editorial manager, even laying on the flattering unction that this was a vital factor in deciding him whether he could successfully undertake a venture for which he had no training at all. He made the same point to Robert E. Hughes, at that time the general business manager of the papers.

But once proprietor, Bingham made an appointment that, as was soon demonstrated, presaged a purpose to limit my authority as editorial manager, particularly of *The Courier-Journal*, and put the restrictive pressures on Robert E. Hughes that soon accomplished their design of making the latter's position untenable. The appointment was that of Wallace T. Hughes, a former city editor of *The Courier-Journal* who was then an attorney in Chicago for the Rock Island Railroad and a close lifelong personal friend of the new owner. His assignment as executive assistant was to act as Bingham's deputy in supervising both the editorial and business activities of the papers.

This arrangement was beginning to prove onerous to me

before I sailed to France, and even more so to Hughes. But though I recognized the appointment as a clear manifestation that Bingham intended to check the free hand he originally had assured me, I did not then suspect him of a design to remove that hand from the morning paper altogether. Or that during my absence, and without notice until my return, he had charted the reorganization by which I ceased to be editorial manager of the two papers and became Editor-in-Chief of *The Times* instead. The only connection I retained with *The Courier-Journal* was as a member of a new body—the Executive Committee, which was that in name only.

It was the covert, underhanded procedure by which the reorganization was made—such as my assignment abroad so that the transfer could be worked out without my suspecting it—that I considered unfair and unsavory. For Bingham was not the first novice, nor will he be the last, with the money to buy a newspaper who has found that an inherited professional executive is an obstacle to his desire to change or abolish its policies and practices.

Before I was conveniently thus removed from direct editorial management of *The Courier-Journal*, Bingham and I had twice come into basic conflict: first, when, despite his assurances to me of maintaining the fundamental attitudes of the papers, he editorially endorsed Watterson's blackest bêtes noires: national prohibition and unlimited women's suffrage; second, when he proposed actively associating with the management, as political adviser, the head of one of the two factions by which the Democratic Party in Kentucky had been long and bitterly rent.

This latter plan I had successfully, though temporarily as it proved, opposed by declining to consult a professional politician on political policy either made or under consideration. But I could do no more than protest the change of attitude on the national issues from those firmly identified by Watterson as a fixed position of *The Courier-Journal*.

My basic mistake was in appraising Bingham as the most likely among other potential purchasers to continue the major policies of the newspapers. He had expressed this to me as his firm intention, but I was foolish to rely on this as confidently as

I did, for I was aware from many examples that intent of continuity by new ownership, however sincere, is more subject to reversible pressures in the newspaper field than in any other.

A newspaper is peculiarly a property that invests a new owner with the desire to run it as he sees fit. And the more often he encounters resistance, especially on historic grounds and from inherited chiefs of staff, the more intense this desire becomes and the quicker its execution.

Bingham's most important break with a major *Courier-Journal* tradition was when he advised me that the papers would support national prohibition and instructed me to allow its critics no more representation than minimally required by the general obligation to the press to print the news. I looked for an opportunity to make the order ridiculous by blind conformity, and a letter to the editor soon provided me with the means to accomplish this small treason.

Letters to the Editor of *The Courier-Journal* were selected for publication by the late Ralph Coghlan, a special favorite of Wallace Hughes whose professional merits and courage eventually won him the editorship of the editorial page of *The St. Louis Post-Dispatch*.

I awaited an opportunity to demonstrate the vulnerability of Bingham's directive. It came one day when a letter arrived that was an authoritative and closely reasoned survey of the legal and social aspects of prohibition signed by a citizen of consequence. Deliberately encouraging Coghlan to decide on his own that the intent of the order could not conceivably cover such a communication, I stood aside, and Coghlan sent it to the composing room for publication.

When the letter appeared, I called it to Bingham's attention, with the deliberately loaded inquiry as to whether its publication was a breach of his instructions. Coghlan was promptly fired, an action deeply and openly resented by the staff. In expiation for my use of Coghlan as the guinea pig for demonstrating the lunacy of the directive, I promptly recommended him for a job as an editorial writer on *The Post-Dispatch*, having just been asked for a nominee by Joseph Pulitzer, Jr. He got the job, and I his forgiveness—and the undeserved reward of a close lifelong friendship.

Before leaving the Louisville part of my life, I should make some mention of what happened when I reported the conference in Europe that prepared the formal conclusion of World War One (then the most disastrous in history) and laid the basis for World War Two.

The assignment to report the 1918–1919 Peace Conference at Paris and Versailles broadened my professional horizon, but it certainly did not make me an authority on international affairs. I witnessed in review and at close hand the array of the world problems at that time—they are in essence still the same —and in varying degree knew the principals who were futilely engaged in trying to solve them by establishing a durable peace. As in all such matters before and since, the practical factors of nationalism and the characters of statesmen have frustrated the idealists, of whom Wilson was the only one among the Big Four that was constituted of himself, Prime Minister David Lloyd George of the United Kingdom, and Premiers Vittorio Emanuele Orlando of Italy and Georges Clemenceau of France.

But there were incidents, grave and gay, in my purview that come from the mint where the small change of history (*la petite histoire*) is coined, and may serve to recreate a sector of the atmosphere of the Peace Conference:

. . . *The magnificent entrance of Swope into the reportorial corps.* With Percy Hammond and John McCutcheon of the Chicago *Tribune*, I was on my way to a restaurant, where, it was reputed, butter was available to diners. This establishment was the Brasserie des Pyramides, in the Place Régina, and Samuel G. Blythe, the famous correspondent of the *Saturday Evening Post*, directed us to it as follows: "You know the Place Régina? You know the statue of Joan of Arc there? Well, draw an imaginary plumb line from Joan of Arc's horse's ass and it will lead you into the Brasserie des Pyramides."

On our way we were groping past the Ritz in the Place Vendôme (Paris was still largely blacked out) when, under a single, pallid green streetlamp appeared the great Swope in evening dress, his white shirt effulgent in the gloom, accompanied by the *World's* brilliant managing editor Charles M. Lincoln, soon to yield his place to his imperial companion. "Welcome to Paris," thundered Swope, who to most of us was a Johnny-come-lately. But somehow his voice and manner dissipated the drabness of the environment; and in our crumpled day clothes we moved on to the *brasserie* with uplifted spirits.

. . . *The uprising of the newspaper correspondents that opened the plenary sessions of the Conference to the public.* The Big Four having agreed to keep these and all other sessions private, the correspondents, nation by nation, gathered to frame a protest, and each group chose three delegates to join in composing the *démarche*. The three from the United States were Swope, John Nevin of the Hearst press, and myself.

We held an evening meeting at the Ritz that lasted until the early hours of the morning from which we produced the general request for open plenary sessions, to be presented to President Wilson for transmission to the other members of the Big Four. When representatives of the French press demurred on the firm phraseology of the request, I made the observation that the French press was notoriously dominated by the Foreign Office. Whereupon one of the French delegates—my memory is that he was the Marquis de St. Brice—challenged me to a duel. Somehow I managed to crawl out of that fix; the text of the protest was agreed on; and the Big Four, on the urging of Wilson, opened the plenary sessions to the public.

Among the distinguished correspondents present was Luigi Barzini, Sr., of the *Corriere della Sera* of Milan. His descriptions of German atrocities in Belgium in the early phase of the First World War had been an important means by which the Italian government moved that nation into the war on the Allied side. He had a joke with which he entertained all the provincial American reporters, of whom I definitely was one. The joke was that the familiar anteroom signs in French rooms of assembly catered to three nationalities—the English, the Spanish, and the French: "Lavabo," he solemnly explained, was the office of "Señor Lavabo," a Spanish grandee; "Vestiare" was the residence of the lovely and celebrated Frenchwoman "Madame Vestiare"; and "W. C. Bains" was the nameplate of the Englishman in the trio.

. . . *The affectionate and trusting relations among the Allies.* I once made a trip through the sewers of Paris to follow the lines of electronic communications between the American mission in the Hotel Crillon and President Wilson's residence, the Palace Murat. My guide was the famous Col. John Carty, in peacetime a high official of the A. T. & T. Company. Observing that he was inspecting the cables very closely and testing them in some mysterious fashion, I asked what he was looking for. "The constant attempts of our loving allies," he said, "to tap these lines."

. . . *My first meeting with Bernard M. Baruch.* Under the booming escortage of Swope, I was taken to the Ritz to be introduced to this distinguished financier and American citizen, to extract from him some words of wisdom and publish them in the *Courier-Journal*, to be picked up by the Associated Press if it so desired. We were shown into a sumptuous apartment overlooking the Ritz gardens. There a magnificent human creature, clad in a purple dressing gown, arose from a reclining chair to his lean height of six feet five or so and greeted me with an aristocratic charm that recalled what Claire Sheridan, the beautiful Irish sculptor and author, had said to Baruch on meeting him: "When you were a king in Babylon/ And I was a Christian slave."

Our introduction over—grandly conducted by Swope—the Babylonian king sank back into his reclining chair and the minions resumed their operations: a pretty girl manicured his nails, a barber shaved his face and trimmed his hair, a chasseur shined his boots, while over him hovered his valet, Lacy, to perform any final touches to Baruch's toilet that might be indicated.

"Have you any message for the American people," I asked, having been prompted by Swope to frame this question, "now that they have saved democracy in Europe and the world?"

"Yes," replied Baruch through a mask of scented lather, "they must work and save."

I burst into laughter in which Baruch—sensing the incongruity between this platitude and the environment in which it was uttered—quickly joined. But it was good advice nonetheless, and in the decades afterward—during which the American people profited from his wisdom to the extent that its product was employed by the powers in Washington, and I profited from his company and friendship—I found this counsel precisely applicable to many critical situations into which politics and official pride of opinion had led the United States.

. . . *An incident that would have embarrassed anyone but its creator.* Now fully captivated by Swope, his junior partner in getting and writing the news of the Conference and the object of his desire that I should know "the important people," I was swept one day into the Ritz lobby in the jet stream of his flying coattails. There, seeing a small group in one corner, Swope rushed to join it, I following humbly in his wake. As I recall it, the group was composed of Lord Reading, Lord Northcliffe (publisher of *The Times* of London), a Lady Johnson (who seemed to be a sort of Diana of the Crossways), and Philip Kerr (later the Marquess of Lothian and British Ambassador to Washington).

Disposing as usual of my presence by muttering the preposterous statement, "Of course, you all know Arthur Krock," Swope took over the conversation and led it into an analysis of the Conference record thus far. As he pursued his discourse, which had become a monologue, a young man appeared behind the group and poked his head through the shoulder spaces. He wore a bowler and his gaudy apparel, though obviously the work of the best London tailors, might not have been considered by connoisseurs of such matters to be in the best of taste. Pausing in his oration, Swope exclaimed, "Who is that dreadful young man?"

Whereupon Lord Reading, peering at the interloper, said, "I'm sure you don't mean my son, Lord Airleigh" (for his son and heir it was).

"Oh, no," cried Swope, looking in another direction and pointing his finger at an innocent Ritz denizen on his way somewhere else. And, without a trace of embarrassment, reboarded his gilded train of thought.

. . . *The plight of Secretary of State Robert Lansing.* We correspondents, on President Wilson's order after our successful protest against the secrecy of the Conference sessions, were periodically received by the United States mission composed of Lansing, Ambassador Henry White, Gen. Tasker H. Bliss, and Col. Edward M. House, Wilson's confidential adviser. On one occasion Lansing was beginning to phrase a reply to a reporter's question when House cut in to give it. This was only one instance of the open denigration of the Secretary of State that was derived from House's peculiar but powerful relations with Wilson. I do not believe that Wilson realized this until the damage was done.

. . . *Among those of us in the American colony* who had been in France before the Armistice, and for one reason or another lingered on, was Capt. Monroe Douglas Robinson, A.E.F. A son of Theodore Roosevelt's dynamic sister, Corinne, "Mose" Robinson, as he was known, was equally dynamic, but in a different way. Relaxing after a gallant military record, Mose employed his extraordinary talent for hell raising in doing just that in Paris.

One day he had an encounter that especially enriched his life. As Mose described it, he had met "the only private in the American Red Cross," and they had become fast friends and inseparable companions in destructive funmaking. The destructive element was made more effective by the third member of the firm, a beautiful but ferocious Alsatian bitch named Bella.

Perhaps the most celebrated act of Mose, the Only Private in the Red Cross, and Bella was performed in front of the austere banking house of Morgan, Harjes et Cie. in the Boulevard Haussmann. It occurred to Mose that the bank and its passers-by needed a little excitement. So, with the aid of his two-footed and four-footed companions, he set up a soapbox in front of the institution and proceeded to auction it off. This drew an unusual number of Parisians, who are always prone to assemble at any active scene.

The affair was going well. The bids had risen above 100 francs under the stimulus of Mose's auctioneering, when he espied the approach of the only person of whom he stood in awe, his mother. It was the matter of but a few moments for the three to flee the premises. When asked by Mrs. Robinson later whether she had not seen her son on the boulevard that morning, Mose assured her it was a case of mistaken identity.

. . . *There were several kings* and their counterparts in Paris during the Peace Conference. I encountered only two at first hand, but the circumstances were unusual.

My first king—not yet in possession of his royal estate—was the Emir Feisal. I was summoned by Lawrence of Arabia to be introduced to Feisal at a sitting-on-the-floor tea party. Lawrence and the eventual King of Iraq made their propaganda pitch; and though my recollection of Feisal, a bearded desert Arab who looked like all the other members of his family, has grown somewhat indistinct, I shall never forget the lean hawk of Britain who paved the way for Field Marshal Allenby's investment of Jerusalem and Damascus.

Lawrence was to end his mysterious life as "Air Craftsman Shaw" in a motorcycle accident along a rural, peaceful English country road. But that day he was in garb, in complexion and bearing as much a desert Arab as Feisal himself. And he spoke with such majesty that I and the two or three correspondents who also were present came away in the spell of the impression that, through some inexplicable switch of North Sea and ancient Semitic genes, we had been in the company of a reincarnated Saracen of the times of Suleiman the Magnificent.

My other king was Alexander of Serbia, who also was yet to advance from Crown Prince to the ultimate royal estate. The elevator service at the Continental was erratic, so that I was accustomed to press the bell several times while waiting. Unaware that I had given the royal Serbian signal, I did not particularly notice the occupants of the elevator that stopped for me, except that they were resplendent in uniform and clinking with medals.

One was short and slender, the other tall and huge. The latter, employing French, which I sufficiently understood, bawled me out for both summoning and entering the lift, with the scowling explanation that it was reserved for "His Royal Highness," and making clear that the reference was to the other passenger. That personage, neither by word nor expression, gave the slightest indication that he knew of my presence. In this state of humility I debouched on the ground floor, third (naturally) in the procession. When Alexander was assassinated early in his short reign, I felt a pang of regret that inadvertently on my part, our relations had not been of the best.

My professional partnership with Swope was mutually advantageous because at his suggestion we pooled each correspondent's nightly allowance of four hundred words for wireless transmission to his respective newspaper, which gave us eight hundred words apiece. Although no other correspondent could fault Swope's arithmetic—that a pooled dispatch by two reporters with a separate allotment of four hundred words produced a dispatch of eight hundred words—*The New York Times*'s London representative, Charles Selden, composed a protest charging foul play, signed it, and put it on the bulletin board at press headquarters, 4 Place de la Concorde, for others to sign.

Shortly thereafter Swope stalked in, perceived the manifesto on the board and promptly added his name to Selden's. By such audacity the protest was killed at birth: there were no other signatories.

Most of the time we faithfully shared each other's gist of the news. I typed it for publication, the content being the work of both. But now and then Swope would not appear to contribute his part of the dispatch. And when it developed that on these occasions he usually had acquired news on which he wanted a clean beat and had sent it exclusively to the *World*, I decided to try to do the same if I could—at least once.

Through my acquaintance with the late Col. Bentley Mott, the liaison between the United States military arm and those of our allies, I managed to get the one interview that Marshal Ferdinand Foch, the Supreme Allied Commander, consented to give during the Peace Conference. This I sent exclusively to *The Courier-Journal*, and it was carried back by the Associated Press to the Paris morning newspaper *Le Matin*.

Next day, very early for Swope, he was on the telephone reproaching me for the betrayal (he had read *Le Matin*) until I cited the several of his that provoked it. There were no similar acts of treachery on either part.

The news Swope got through his close connections with great personages in Paris, and shared with me, sufficiently rewarded me for the humble legwork and typing. Through Lord Northcliffe, the proprietor of the *London Times*, and particularly Lord Reading, Swope had access to what Prime Minister Lloyd George was thinking and doing. Through Baruch he had similar and more direct access to Premier Clemenceau. My pipelines to Lloyd George's activities were good but indirect: Philip Kerr, later, as the Marquess of Lothian, the British Ambassador to Washington; and George Mair of the information division of the Foreign Office.

But once Baruch took me along to dine with Clemenceau at the famous flat in the Rue Franklin. This unforgettable privilege, and a couple of private interviews with President Wilson that his Naval aide and physician Rear Admiral Cary Grayson arranged, constituted my closest approximation to Swope's galaxy of top-level news sources.

When Baruch and I dined with Clemenceau, I went resolved to ask him if he was really the author of a famous cynical comment on French politics. "To be successful," the quotation ran, "a French politician must have three possessions not necessarily valued in the order of their mention—his dog, his mistress, and his newspaper." (In *L'Homme Enchâiné*, renamed *L'Homme Libre*, the Premier owned the last of these items.)

But in the awesome presence of the great statesman I lost my nerve.

I remember Clemenceau as a man looking much older than his years, sallow of skin where it was not yellow on his bald head, with ferocious white eyebrows and piercing eyes, a remarkably resonant voice, and a large, muscular English vocabulary.

In public during the Conference it suited the Premier to pretend a deficiency in English, but once he forgot the pretense. This happened at a plenary session when Prime Minister Hughes of Australia, whom The Tiger clearly disliked, arose to make again his repetitious inquiry whether "the small nations were to have their day in court." Before the interpreter could begin putting the inquiry into French, Clemenceau, banging down the gavel in his perpetually gray-gloved hands, exclaimed "wixout any kes-*tion*." And the deception was over for those few who did not already know that Clemenceau had acquired a generous speaking and writing acquaintance with English while living in Brooklyn as a doctor of medicine.

There were a number of dramatic incidents during the Conference, but the one I recall best was contributed by Michael McWhite, a devoted Sinn Feiner who was to become Eire's first diplomatic envoy to Washington. McWhite served in the war with the French forces, and one morning he appeared in uniform at the steps of the Quai d'Orsai where the Big Four entered the building. He carried a rolled-up document that, when Clemenceau appeared, he presented to the Premier, who, seeing it in the hands of a French officer, naturally accepted it. Whereupon the officer ran to a waiting automobile, hopped into it, and, as I learned afterward, was instantly sped away to the border.

It soon developed that the document was the plea of the Irish Republicans to the Big Four for nationhood. Lloyd George had served notice on his colleagues that if such a presentation were officially received, the United Kingdom would withdraw from the Conference. Yet there it was in Clemenceau's hands!

But Lloyd George was not required to make good his threat because Clemenceau, as soon as he discovered what the document was, consigned it in perpetuity to whatever passed for an ashcan in the Quai d'Orsai.

3

THE NEW YORK
WORLD

WHEN it became evident that my breach with Bingham over the administrative methods and the policies of *The Courier-Journal* and *The Louisville Times* was inevitably moving to the point of no return, I decided to explore several prospects of entering New York City journalism that had, from time to time, been tentatively suggested. But the immature status of these prospects required me to transfer my base to New York for effective exploration.

Having insufficient capital to make this survey without an interim paying job, I informed my old friend, Will H. Hays, former Chairman of the Republican National Committee, that I was available, temporarily, for employment he had proposed to me with the Motion Picture Producers' Association of which he was President. He responded favorably, and in February, 1923, I terminated my newspaper connections in Louisville and moved with my wife and small son to New York City, where, as one of Hays's assistants, I performed a number of duties on an understanding I would be free to leave the organization in six months.

There were three New York journalists with whom I had been more or less closely associated professionally and personally—Frank I. Cobb, the great Editor of *The World;* Swope, then *The World*'s City Editor; and Percy Hammond, the eminent drama critic of the *Herald Tribune.* I advised them of my change of base, and Watterson added a generous commendation of my newspaper qualifications to Frank A. Munsey, at that time the proprietor of *The Herald* and *The Sun.* (Munsey interviewed me, but, as with William R. Hearst at a later date, we amicably agreed on my incompatibility with his concept of journalism.)

A couple of years earlier Cobb had paid me the compliment of proposing that if he could carry out his design to buy *The New York Evening Post*, with himself as Editor and Publisher, I should join him as its managing editor. As previously related, Swope and I had worked as a reportorial team at the Versailles Peace Conference, and Hammond had been my Continental Hotel roommate in Paris during the same event.

The first material result of my "adsum" in New York City was an invitation from Cobb to contribute editorials to *The World* during my off-hours, as at least a physical replacement for Walter Lippmann, who was on a three-months' leave for the purpose of writing a book. So at lunchtime every day, for a considerable period, I went downtown to *The World*, where I wrote an editorial on a subject assigned by Cobb. A typical example of Cobb's assignment method was this:

. . . When I entered his office one day in July, 1923, he looked up and said: "Charles Evans Hughes, fresh from shaking the bloody hand of the Turk at Lausanne—huh, huh?" And on that lead I turned out an article critical of the Sevres peace treaty with Turkey signed three years previously.

After a couple of months of these contributions, Lippmann returned to duty as second to Cobb, and I to spending my lunch period at the Manhattan Club. But shortly afterward Cobb sent for me again. He said he had suggested to Ralph Pulitzer that the post of Assistant to the Publisher be created for me, and that Pulitzer had responded favorably. The prompt sequel was that I was tendered the job, and I accepted it and the duties, inherent in its title, of critical observer and follower-up for the publisher of the daily product of *The World*, morning, evening, and Sunday. But Cobb also volunteered the terrifying information that what Pulitzer principally wanted and expected of me was to "ride herd on Herbert Swope!"

To "ride herd" on Swope developed into a tough job, particularly because whenever I raised an issue of Swope's conduct of the news department in his capacity as Managing Editor, Swope either roared me down or managed to disparage my qualfication to evaluate what he was doing. And Pulitzer not only valued Swope's tremendous journalistic abilities, but was also awed by the impact of Swope's personality and character, and by his determination to run the news wholly as he saw fit.

My presence in that particular job was also distasteful to Walter Lippmann, who on Cobb's death had succeeded as editor of the editorial page. My situation was also not entirely popular with Florence D. White, the general manager, a gifted Irishman who was justly one of Pulitzer's favorite employees; nor with the very talented Managing Editor of *The Evening World*, John H. Tennant, over whom and which I had been assigned broad supervision by Pulitzer.

The struggle grew more and more unequal as time went on because of Pulitzer's unwillingness to enter into a controversy with these distinguished and very forceful newspapermen. After about three years of this, Pulitzer demoted me—a move cloaked in lavish praise—to a minor executive position, and changed my office from the symbolically important location in the Golden Dome to one on the floor below the news department.

One particular experience can serve as an example of the difficulty of occupying a post on *The World* that thrust me between the Publisher and the other chief executives. Among my personal friends in New York were Morton L. and Charles Schwartz, who were financial entrepreneurs. They were commissioned by Clarence Dillon, chairman of Dillon, Read & Co., to buy the Dodge Company from the widows of the brothers Dodge, a transaction later consummated at a cash price of $156 million, the largest sum, up to then, for a single deal ever paid for with a personal check, Dillon's.

The Schwartz brothers, at the suggestion of Baruch, and in the course of their efforts to buy the company for Dillon against the equally ardent efforts of J. P. Morgan & Co. to do the same, occasionally asked me for private counsel on a matter of public relations. I complied on a friendly basis whenever the request in no way infringed on any professional obligation or involved *The World*.

Except Pulitzer, I was *ex officio* the only member of the executive boards of both the evening and morning papers known as "The Council." (This bears on what followed in the matter of the Schwartzes.) One day Lippmann, who opposed certain details of the sales agreement between Dillon and the Dodges, read to the morning paper Council an editorial designed for publication the next day criticizing these details. The editorial duly appeared, and at about eleven o'clock that morning Charles Schwartz telephoned me to complain about it. I made some such reply as, "Well, the editorial's public now, and you and Dillon must deal with it as best you can. *The World* is not going to take it back, you can be sure of that."

About two days later Pulitzer summoned me. He said that he had been informed that *before* the editorial was published, I had apprised Charles Schwartz of the details and when it was to appear; also that as a result Schwartz had exerted pressure to try to prevent publication. With considerable effort I persuaded Pulitzer to tell me the source of his information, and he named Lippmann, whose office adjoined mine.

I promptly sought out Lippmann, and in opening our conversation, which was amicable, I asked the source of his report. He replied that, by chance, when passing my door, he had overheard me talking on the phone, realized whom I was talking to and that the subject was the editorial—on the day *before* it appeared.

The time element being vital, I produced sufficient evidence to convince Lippmann that his recollection of the timing was wrong, that the conversation with Schwartz occurred on the day the editorial was published.

But I think the incident had a certain influence on Pulitzer; he concluded that if any associate could believe me capable of such misconduct, there was always bound to be dissension of a

disagreeable kind between my fellow executives and me; and
that even though I had committed no fault *vis-à-vis* Lippmann,
Swope, Tennant, and White, I was the one who was dispensi-
ble.

Doubtless he was also influenced to sacrificing his leanest
lamb because in assigning me to "ride herd on Swope," he had
given me only the saddle. Swope had the horse and had locked
it up, and Pulitzer had no stomach for the scene that would be
evoked by a demand to surrender the key. Already Swope had
telephoned me every once in a while to say "Keep your goddam
hands off my department," and I had replied, "It's my business
to keep my hands *on*."

The consequences grew more and more unpleasant; hence, I
was surprised and relieved to learn—though much later—that
while our dispute was growing over whether the job of assistant to the publisher was tenable on *The World*, Swope had
proposed that I go to Washington to write an editorial column.
For it is strange but true that this is exactly what I wound up
doing for *The Times*, and I have never enjoyed anything more.

If I had known of Swope's idea at the time, I might have
stayed with *The World* until it folded and then, perhaps, I
might have established a reputation that would have brought
me to *The Times* in that very capacity. But perhaps also the
spell of the metropolis was still too strong to have induced me
to return to Washington for *The World*. I don't know, and
never shall.

I didn't enjoy my new duties downstairs from the Golden
Dome, so one day when Bernard Baruch told me that Adolph
S. Ochs was interested in me in the event I was looking for a
change, I said I was. He arranged an interview with Ochs,
who, following a discussion of whatever qualifications I might
have for *The New York Times*, turned me over for a deeper
inquiry to his son-in-law and assistant, Arthur Hays Sulzberger. Sulzberger was apparently satisfied with his investigation,
and I was invited to join *The Times* as a member of the
editorial board, writing editorials and serving as a consultant
on other editorials and on *The Times*'s news problems. I joined
the paper on May 1, 1927.

But I can't leave *The World* at this point in my narration

without an effort to depict what an extraordinary paper it was. Swope had made a remarkable contribution to American journalism by establishing what is now known as the "op. ed. [opposite editorial] page." He had assembled as special writers a galaxy of great stars. And never, even in the heyday of Fleet Street, was a more fascinating and gifted company assembled. My office on the fourteenth floor, in the Golden Dome, was flanked by Cobb's and Lippmann's on the right, Pulitzer's on the left; rounding out the circle were the cubicles occupied by editorial writers John L. Heaton, E. R. Paulin, and Maxwell Anderson. On the floor above were, or during my time became, the workrooms of Laurence Stallings, Rollin Kirby, James M. Cain, and Allen Nevins.

The pleasure of association with this company was raised to an even higher level at lunchtime, when it was augmented by the gifted characters who occupied the floors just below the Dome. These more or less regularly included Franklin P. Adams, the fabulously witty "F.P.A." of "The Conning Tower" column; Heywood Broun, the brilliance and subject-matter of whose column set the Hudson afire almost every day; John O'Hara Cosgrave, the erudite Sunday editor; his coruscating and usually harassing assistants (and in time successors), Paul Palmer and Louis Weitzenkorn; Morris Markey, who was to gain fame as the first of *The New Yorker*'s "Reporters At Large"; and such occasional drop-ins as Wells Root, Deems Taylor, and William Bolitho (the literary stylist and prescient thinker, on leave from the Paris Bureau of *The Guardian* of Manchester).

The food in the lunchroom on the thirteenth floor was probably the worst in all New York City (at least it received that unanimous accolade from these patrons). But if the menu had actually been composed of the sawdust and ditch water that the group swore were its daily ingredients, this patronage would still have been preserved in full measure by the lure of the table talk. It was largely composed of banter, the sting of whose barbs was assuaged by the balm of admiration for their craftsmanship. The arsenal of wit and satire was free for all, and always open. So, those who didn't one day set the table in a roar, except for the victim, were pretty sure to do it the next.

To illustrate the roughness as well as the hilarity that prevailed, my mind returns particularly to a remark made by Cain. Stallings, as befitted a man born in Macon and brought up in Atlanta, spoke in the rich brogue of those parts. This was a constant irritant to Cain, a Marylander, who appeared convinced that any Southern accent beyond the slight tinge in the speech of the natives of the Free State was put on.

One day the group was joined by Markey, a Virginian whom I had placed, on the recommendation of Stallings, as a reporter for the *Evening World*, and whose idolatry of Stallings, Cain concluded after listening to Markey a while, included a devout effort to imitate Stallings' Georgian slurrings. Whereupon, the future author of *The Postman Always Rings Twice*, among others, arose from the table, and, departing, announced, "I *have* to listen to Stallings, but not to his stand-in on a road show!"

Cain had come to *The World* from *The Baltimore Sun* on a letter of recommendation addressed to me by Henry L. Mencken. Its estimate of his journalistic abilities soon proved to have been one of Henry's rare understatements. Cain was first assigned by *The Evening World*, at my suggestion, to introduce into the news columns of the New York press a fast-fading sense of the contiguity of the Atlantic Ocean and of the ships and crews it delivered to the greatest port in the two hemispheres.

After a brilliant tour of this duty, Cain advised me that the legwork involved threatened a return of an earlier attack of tuberculosis, and requested another assignment.

"What else do you know?" I asked.

"A little about music," he replied.

This turned out to be an understatement comparable to Mencken's, for Cain's critiques soon invited reader comparison with those of the great Joseph Huneker in the days of the elder Pulitzer. But when one of these critiques included a passing judgment that Beethoven was the most overrated of composers, the reader protests poured in in such volume that another assignment for Cain seemed the judicious course to pursue.

This coincided with a quest by Lippman for a writer of what is known in the trade as "light editorials." In that area of production Cain was brilliantly successful, and the page glowed with the radiance of his essays until he left to become Managing Editor of *The New Yorker*. His subsequent career as a writer of scenarios in Hollywood and as a novelist has cast an abiding light on two categories of American literature.

Laurence Stallings was already established as the *Wunder-kind* of *The World* staff when I joined it. He had lost a leg at Belleau Wood as a combat Marine in the First World War, and written an autobiographical first novel, *Plumes*, whose high promise had failed to be reflected by sales. When covering Broadway on the theater news run produced a series of abscesses on the stump to which his wooden leg was fitted, Stalling's talent was diverted, first to editorial writing and then to the daily book reviews that added greatly to the distinction of *The World*'s op. ed. page under the heading "The First Reader."

It was on *The World* that his association in editorial writing with Maxwell Anderson began, climaxed in the overwhelming success of their play *What Price Glory?*. When Cobb was obliged, by the inexorable progress of a cancerous condition, to forego coming to the office, I assigned this team to stop by his house every morning and bring in his editorial instructions and ideas. This was another period when Lippmann was away on leave, and I was in general responsible for light supervision of the page. Stallings and Anderson continued these visits until Mrs. Cobb advised me they would have to be discontinued.

One morning thereafter, when as usual the team appeared at the office, I told them Cobb was dead. "This," said Stallings, "is the worst blow to American journalism since the birth of Frank A. Munsey." The comment, made without a second's hesitation, was only one of the many that disclosed his great gift of enclosing ironic wit in a capsule of basic truth.

The World group was much given to gambling—poker, dice, and at the racetracks. These diversions also greatly appealed to our employer, Ralph Pulitzer, and to his brother Joseph, the publisher of *The St. Louis Post-Dispatch*. An important difference was that unlike the brothers but like Swope (though never in his class for daring), we enjoyed the game

especially because of the ever present risk of gambling beyond
our means.

Consequently, I was not surprised one Monday morning
when Stallings walked into my office and said, "What do you
do when you lose $500 you haven't got to your boss's brother?"

"You pay it," said I.

This resulted in a transaction between Stallings and my
friends at the Chemical National Bank, a note for $750 which I
co-signed. In addition to this endorsement I telephoned the
bank's president—my fellow Kentuckian, Percy H. Johnston
—and predicted that the time was near when Stallings would
become one of the best and most profitable of his clients. I
based this on a pre-reading of the play Stallings had just
completed with Anderson. The blazing triumph of *What Price
Glory?* that soon followed lucked me out of this venture at
prophecy in the most undependable of all commercial activities,
producing a play. (I never took the risk again.)

The fact that I had personally arranged the loan with the
president of the bank made Stallings and me potential multi-
millionaires, temporarily. Johnston's secretary, assuming he
could not conceivably be concerned with a note for $750, made
the sum "$750,000" in the memorandum Johnston dictated to a
lesser official. When Stallings reported this to me, plus the
astonishment of this official at my acceptability as guarantor of
such a loan, this colloquy ensued:

"Did you get it?"

"No, I told him the amount was only $750."

"If you hadn't, we could have hit the bull market for millions."

Of course, this was spoken in jest, because the error of the
Johnston memorandum to his subordinate was obvious on its
face. But for a while thereafter Stallings and I held mock
funerals over our pot of fool's gold, agreeing, however, that we
probably would have lost it all in the stock market crash of
October, 1929.

This was the period when the Thanatopsis Literary and
Inside Straight Club held regular poker sessions at the Algonquin Hotel Round Table; for high stakes, devastating dia-
logue, rapid and coruscating repartee these sessions were the

most famous and potentially bruising assemblies of the intelligentsia of American journalism, literature, and the stage. Its name, one of F.P.A.'s jests, set the spirit of the occasions. My sporting blood was not rich enough for competition in this company, either in the financial or humor departments. But F.P.A., Broun, Swope, Alexander Woollcott, and a couple of others from *The World* formed its nucleus. They also sharpened their skills and their tongues in the minor poker games the rest of us held regularly.

These began in late afternoons in a private room of a tavern on Mulberry Street. The proprietor of this restaurant was "Papa" Moneta. And though the fare and wines at "21," the Colony, and Voisin were more celebrated, our common verdict was that none was superior, and—in the matter of pressed duck and Italian dishes—none was comparable.

I recall these occasions, one in particular, with a delight that the passing of many years has not diminished. Our game, interrupted only by dinner, had progressed to about the hour when *The World*'s op. ed. page was in type and ready for plating and printing. There burst in upon us a head office-boy whose usual imperturbability had clearly given way to frantic distress.

Two factors accounted for this. He had used up the time in locating us that the reason for his search made highly precious. The reason was that several articles already in type for the op. ed. page had suddenly been found to be obsolete: Stallings had reviewed a book the publishers had withdrawn. Broun had reviewed a play whose premiere had been incontinently canceled, and I forget whether another disaster had overtaken a concert of which Deems Taylor had written an advance critique.

Anyhow, the op. ed. page was in ruins, and the night managing editor was desperately searching for substitute material of a relatively timely nature. A rush back to *The World* office, and the reviewers of non-events somehow provided it. Except for the facts that this op. ed. page was debased in quality by what are known as "fillers," the first edition was an hour or so late, and Swope was in a state approaching apoplexy, no damages to the paper were incurred by this unforeseeable contretemps.

Several of the regular participants in the Algonquin Hotel poker games, where their wit was on perpetual display, also joined us of the lower echelon for play at the residences of Raoul Fleischmann, founder and publisher of *The New Yorker*, Mrs. Eleanor ("Cissy") Patterson, Condé Nast—the publisher of *Vogue* and *Vanity Fair*—and others. Without attempting to pinpoint the locus of the japes that I especially remember, here are a few:

Harold Ross, the Editor of *The New Yorker*, and Broun were the only players left in a pot. Ross had drawn three cards, Broun none. Concluding that Broun's pat hand was a bluff, Ross called his raise every time. After a number of these calls Broun tossed his hand into the deck, excusing this violation of the rule that a called hand must be shown by murmuring, "I have been tray-deuced." The pun was clarified when a snatch of Broun's cards from the pile disclosed only a pair each of deuces and trays, to which the fifth card lent no assistance. Ross won with the three fives he had started with.

One evening Prince Bibesco, the Rumanian Minister to the United States, inadvertently broke a rule set down in Hoyle. "Boy," shouted Swope to no one in particular, "the Prince's hat and cuffs!"

Looking around the table, Gerald Brooks, who though a mere stockbroker was admitted to the Algonquin circle by its haughty potentates, once pretended he had fallen into low company. "I don't think any of you has a family tree," he said. "For example, my ancestor Sir Bedevere Brooks fought in the Crusades."

"So did mine, Sir Roderick," replied George S. Kaufman, and instantly added, "He went as a spy."

It was not often that the charter members of this particular elite encountered the challenge of a wit that matched, and sometimes excelled, their own. The venture was too precarious. But there were such occasions, and my favorite example is a riposte during a poker game at Fleischmann's.

Henry Wise Miller, the husband of the poet-novelist Alice Duer Miller, was a stockbroker and thus a certified alien in the group. Moreover, he was of the old Massachusetts Puritan stock and the brand of Harvard was deeply imprinted upon him. So, while his credentials as a delightful companion were fully established, his parity with "the first wits of their time" was not, until the following occurred:

A certain pot had been growing steadily by calls and raises around the table in the course of which Ross, commenting on Miller's black hair, fierce blue eyes, and hawk nose, offered the suggestion that he was actually an Arab. "My grandmother was an Arab," replied Miller with the gravity custom demands of a statement that is patently untrue; and tossing his hand into the discard, he quickly added, "I fold. I am a folding Bedouin."

One Sunday afternoon at Swope's country house, when he was living at Great Neck, Long Island, and had not yet progressed to the magnificence of "Kewaydin" at Sands Point, Swope was unsuccessfully attempting to arouse his guests from a post-luncheon languor that had overtaken all except F.P.A. and Alice Miller, who were playing cribbage in a corner.

In an effort to evoke general conversation Swope, seizing a copy of *The New York Times Book Review* that led with an article about modern German poets, blared out, "Who was Suderman?" (No answer). "Who was Koerner?" (No answer). "Who was Hauptmann?" (No answer, then desperately), "Who was Kleist?"

Looking up for a moment from the cribbage board, F.P.A. said, "The Chinese Messiah."

One day Broun appeared on the group's winter croquet ground, not far from the Central Park Zoo, his vast form clad in a coat that must have cost the lives of every raccoon in Connecticut. After a brief inspection of this garment, Kaufman offered him a piece of advice: "Don't," he said, "bend over in Central Park."

In addition to Miller, others who held their own with these masters of banter when so disposed were Paul Palmer, then *The World*'s Sunday Editor, now a senior editor of the *Reader's Digest;* Arthur H. Samuels, who at Princeton wrote the musical scores of the Triangle shows and later in New York some of the songs for *Poppy* of which W. C. Fields was the star; Louis Weitzenkorn, who shifted from journalism to playwriting in the sudden cloud of glory that enveloped the premiere of *Five-Star Final;* Russell Crouse, Herman Mankowitz, Richard Rodgers, and Robert E. Sherwood.

The Algonquin center and its concentric circles shone also in the studio of Neysa McMein. Because of her greatness as a human being; her radiant beauty, intelligence, and charm; her uncanny ability to perceive latent talent in the many unknowns to whom she opened the gates of opportunity, this studio was a salon in the eighteenth-century French tradition but with the informality of the twentieth.

It was the seed-bed of the now prevalent parlor games that test the imagination, intellect, quick recall, and informational scope of the players. And it was the only place where in a single evening one might hear Sherwood's gravely ludicrous rendition of "When the Red, Red Robin Goes Bob, Bob, Bobbin' Along"; Heifetz burlesquing the graduating solo of a boy violinist; Father Duffy singing old Irish songs; and Ring Lardner spinning such of his fantastic tales as "The Tridget of Greva" with the impassivity of expression found only on the faces of cigar-store Indians.

Such were among the privileges and pleasures of life in the New York I knew from the early twenties to the mid-thirties. And living there was made more agreeable by the fact that the great city was still able to provide prompt and efficient facilities for its population.

Taxicabs were available. Headwaiters and their minions were polite. The crossways that lead to the theaters and the docks were passable. The people, from those encountered on Fifth Avenue to those seen roosting on the fire escapes of the tenements in hot weather, showed few traces of the cancerous urban malaise that now infests the city. And both women and men could walk the streets or stroll in Central Park at night without looking fearfully over their shoulders and with certainty that the police and the courts would deal swiftly and effectively with any violation of laws against the person.

On the North Shore of Long Island, where I rented one house or another each summer, fresh air, green spaces, good company, and good manners were in abundance. And one did not have to be rich, famous, or listed in any other category of the elect.

It is to my connection with *The World* that I owe the opportunity of savoring the life and company I have described. But the greatest increment of this opportunity was access to the joyous atmosphere that enveloped the daily business of producing *The World*.

It was joyous, because we who were so engaged found the highest satisfaction a newspaper worker can experience in the knowledge that the paper was aggressively independent of the outside pressures that advertisers, civic notables, and public officials are prone, often successfully, to summon to influence the content and presentation of news and commentary. It was joyous, because any day some member of the staff was likely to score a master stroke of journalism, and because color and ingenuity were not edited out unless they clearly transgressed the elder Pulitzer's dictate of "accuracy, terseness, accuracy."

To be able to say, "I'm from *The World*" was a point of special pride, because somehow the paper managed to effect a combination that appealed equally to the mass of urban readers in its area, to those in and outside academic circles with special interest in the serious concerns of mankind, and to members of the newspaper profession everywhere.

Yet as I read back over the daily critiques of *The World* in which I carried out the assignment from Ralph Pulitzer to compare it with the other New York newspapers, I see that in my expressed judgment our competitors—*The Times* in particular—regularly gave better coverage of certain prime news, and (after Cobb's death) sounder and/or more timely editorial comment. These analyses, being one man's opinion, were of course vulnerable to the dissent of the executives concerned. And this created an *ex-officio* hostility toward my job that eventually and inevitably made it untenable. But any who take the trouble to examine these critiques (now in the library of Princeton University, alongside the issues of the newspapers they concern) will find that I generally supported my evaluations with what I conceived to be documentary evidence.

Nevertheless, in the common estimate of the professional and the reading public that I enthusiastically shared and share, *The World* was a great newspaper; a compassionate and constructive force in the public interest; a lethal enemy of official sham and officially inspired misinformation, a literary product of the first rank in the essential categories of journalism on its highest level. Much of the credit for sensing and fostering these qualities belongs to Ralph Pulitzer.

The eldest son of the blinded genius who reconstructed Jay Gould's *World* from a prostitute newspaper to the brilliant daily chronicle in which no exterior influence could add or excise a single word, Ralph Pulitzer labored all his life under the burden of paternal underrating. The will in which Joseph Pulitzer, Sr., bequeathed the largest ownership portion to his youngest son, Herbert (who was eleven years old when his father died), with control of *The World* passing automatically into his hands when he reached thirty, is bleak corroboration of the elder Pulitzer's faulty evaluation of Ralph's qualifications—a misjudgment that eventually extended to Joseph, Jr., the second of the three sons.

But a consequence was that Ralph Pulitzer succeeded to the direction of *The World* with the sense of being on probation, his term—however competent he might prove for the task—always dependent on whether Herbert would decide to take over at the time appointed in the will. This feeling of abiding insecurity induced R. P. to take too much counsel, first from the business and editorial department executives chosen by and inherited from his father; then from their successors chosen by himself. (These were all on the editorial side, since Florence D. White, the elder Pulitzer's selection as a business executive, was General Manager throughout the remainder of *The World*'s existence.)

Yet in the three years during which I served as Ralph Pulitzer's assistant as Publisher of *The World*, I formed what became my fixed conclusion: the restraint imposed on him by the dead hand of his father was a contributory reason to the death of a fine newspaper that otherwise might be shining brightly today in the firmament of American journalism. For Ralph Pulitzer, as I intimately observed him from my post, had all the qualifications—character, courage, insight, and professional instinct—required to direct *The World* toward ever increasing excellence and financial stability. This was forestalled only by the power of the ghostly inhibition.

He was tall, slender and charming of voice and demeanor. Having been brought up to do well the things expected of a person of quality, he was an accomplished horseman, a sportsmanlike participant in high-stake games of chance, a fine conversationalist, a talented writer of both sinewy prose and light verse, an excellent shot, and endowed with the caliber of courage that equally invests the moral, mental, physical, and spiritual compartments of those who possess it. He had a gift for personal friendships that was revealed in relationships with men and women that endured from his school days at St. Mark's and Harvard to his death, and is fixed in the memories of those friends who have survived him. He had the greater gift of subordinating his friendships to his high concept of professional duty when the two came into conflict (as ever they must in an honorable journalistic career), without loss to the one or the other.

Of the executives of *The World* at the death of the senior Pulitzer, three in particular played the most influential parts in Ralph's tutelage. They were the Editor, Frank Irving Cobb; the Managing Editor, Charles M. Lincoln; and the General Manager, Florence D. White (responsible for expenditures and receipts).

White's influence over the entire operation naturally ascended in proportion to the growth of *The World*'s economic difficulties in the 1920s. For example, it was his counsel that prevailed with Ralph Pulitzer over the opposition of at least some of the other executives when, alone among the New York newspapers, *The World* increased the price of the daily from two to three cents. To this step I trace in part the beginning of the decline in revenue and readership volume that proved fatal six years afterward.

The World's policies were decided by Ralph Pulitzer after discussions of alternatives in The Council. In the matter of raising the price, two of its members were actively opposed to White's recommendation: Herbert Bayard Swope, then Executive Editor, and myself.

From the minutes of the Council meetings and my own personal impressions and experiences with Ralph Pulitzer, I believe his instinct was to veto a step that, while it might temporarily bring revenue and expenses nearer to balance, would—as we contended and it proved—inevitably diminish the circulation of *The World* among the general group of newspaper readers that was the basic source of its influence on public policies.

In an economic prospect even as alarming as that described by White at the time, I have no doubt that Ralph would have sided with the vociferously dissident two if the general manager, in addition to his endowment of much ability, integrity, and charm, had not carried the awesome credentials of having been the last survivor of his father's elect.

Surrounded as he was by one of the most brilliant galaxies of talent ever gathered into a newspaper, Ralph Pulitzer was eclipsed by its radiance only in the perception of the general public. This was deliberate obscuration, partly impelled by natural shyness, partly by the underevaluation of his qualities by the titan who begot him. For when he chose—in either professional or social relationships with members of the group of Olympians in his employ—he could match them at their favorite game of vying in the exhibition of wit or intellectuality, and without their predilection for showing off.

He was deferential to these Olympians up to a point, the point being where it became an inescapable duty to assert his responsibility and authority. This he always did reluctantly; he abhorred "scenes" evolving from a conflict of wills, or from the abuse of the liberty that it was *World* policy to accord to its news executives, editors, and commentators.

But when confronted with this necessity, Ralph Pulitzer accepted it firmly and uncompromisingly. The most noted example was the firing of Heywood Broun, who had progressively expanded into the area of license the vast scope of the liberty accorded him to write as he pleased. He climaxed that by referring to the residence of President A. Lawrence Lowell at Harvard as "Hangman's House"—in bitter comment on Lowell's attitude in the Saccho-Vanzetti controversy.

The dominant personality of Swope, often reflected in conducting the news department of *The World* as his own and imperial domain, was another aspect of the paper with which Pulitzer was loath to grapple. His hesitation was not so much because this would surely produce one of those "scenes" for which he had such strong distaste. It arose principally because, as he once said to me, "the eagle must have altitude or he ceases to be an eagle."

In profusion, rapidity, and accuracy on target, the wit of Pulitzer's staff bore comparison with the clothyard arrows launched by the English archers at Agincourt. But as one demonstration that the boss could hold his own among them, there was this exchange in a poker game:

"If you wanted to insult me to the Queen's taste," acidly inquired a participant whom Pulitzer had bluffed out of a pot, "what would you call me?"

"The King," was the instant response of the winner as he gathered the chips.

4

THE
NEW YORK
TIMES

ON *The Times* I began by writing political editorials for Rollo
Ogden, who ranks with Cobb as one of the great editors in the
history of American journalism, but who by his personal
preference was anonymous insofar as the readers of the paper
were concerned. He was a superb writer as well.

In addition to making editorial contributions I was assigned
by Ochs (as a test of my executive ability) to organize a group
of correspondents throughout the United States. They were to
supply weekly articles dealing with their localities which were
to be embodied in a new Sunday section named the "Watch-
tower." Under Sunday Editor Lester Markel it developed into
the famous Section 4, "The News of the Week," that is one of
the great features of American journalism.

My new associations on *The Times* were happy. I had resolved to stay in New York. Like all Southern country boys, I
loved the big town and was received into it with the special
consideration it appears to give immigrants from the South. I

knew the headwaiters and—more importantly—they knew me; I had tickets to the opening nights at the theaters, and attended the big boxing matches at ringside. In that period the people encountered on the streets were agreeable, the subways ran, and strikes that interfered with the collection of garbage or with hospital care were not tolerated. Therefore, at the end of 1931, when *The Times*'s Washington correspondent died suddenly and Arthur Sulzberger asked me if I would take over the job, I tried to elude it. I suggested substitutes, but vainly, and much against my inclination and expectation I returned to Washington in January, 1932, as the head of *The Times* Bureau whose elegant title was and is "The Washington Correspondent."

But I continued so indisposed to live and work in Washington again that I arranged to stay at my post only during the sessions of Congress. It worked well enough, which gives an idea of how different and much less voluminous were the activities of the Federal government in those days. Between sessions I returned to New York to write editorials and perform such other duties as were assigned. But two years of this division of time and function convinced me that this was a poor arrangement, and though I kept an apartment in New York, I moved my family to Washington as a permanent base and worked there for *The Times* until my retirement on October 1, 1966.

The position of The Washington Correspondent of *The Times* is a very important one. It confers high professional and social prestige, and these provide opportunities for getting important news that is denied to reporters who may be better ones, and often have been. I believe that in the twenty-one years I occupied this post I made a good record in publishing exclusive and important information. Under the indispensible guidance of Neil MacNeil, Assistant Managing Editor, I reorganized the Bureau, on the pattern it now follows, to form at least the nucleus of what now is, I think, the best news bureau of any in journalism.

The principle of this reorganization was to transform a group of loosely directed reporters into a unified news-gathering establishment. For two reasons this coordination had not been effected up to that time: First, the desire of the news editors in New York to make the most of the professional eminence, industry, and immediate access to high policy-making officials of the chief correspondent, Richard V. Oulahan; second, the drain on his time in covering the principal first-page news stories that prevented him from administering the work of his staff.

In consequence, the copy desk, manned by a staff man who lacked the authority required of the job, served as a mere channel to New York for the flow of copy from the staff. Left in considerable degree to choose their own assignments, *The Times*'s Washington reporters, once Oulahan had decided what news story or stories of the day he would cover personally, often duplicated each other's efforts and made their own evaluation of the volume of their wordage. On occasion two or even three *Times* reporters would interview the same official on the same news story, evoking his annoyance at the levy on his time.

The reorganized Bureau was given a copy editor, who, under the general supervision and with the approval of "The Washington Correspondent," had the authority to make individual assignments and set the volume of wordage of every news story. It was difficult to reconcile some of the free-wheeling veterans to this mechanization of the report. But it was accomplished, and the procedure has since been maintained.

During the four and a half years in which I worked entirely as a member of the Editorial Board in New York, my happy associations with the high command were more or less fractured in only two instances.

The first was a difference of interpretation with Ochs over whether the general 10 per cent salary cut, made mandatory by the Depression, should apply to an annual bonus he had granted me in addition to my salary. I lost that argument when, in his kindly but impressive way, he asked me if I thought an expense to *The Times* of $2,500 a year was a more important consideration in his decision with respect to my earnings than the principle of fairness to all employees on which it was based.

The second brush I had with my superiors was the consequence of what Ogden viewed as excess zeal on my part, but what I viewed as the application of a sound rule in the production of a newspaper. One night when I was in charge of putting the editorial page to bed—a rotating duty—Representative Fiorello LaGuardia announced his candidacy for Mayor about half an hour before closing time for the page in the first edition. As a managing editor I had operated on the maxim that the duty of the man on the job was to deal with the unexpected as seemed best to him when there was no time for consultation. ("You can't," as Watterson expressed it to me, "tell a locomotive engineer exactly what to do if a cow wanders onto the track when the train is running at eighty miles an hour.")

Acting on this precept, I eliminated enough editorial matter to make room for a short leader welcoming a candidacy committed to reforming the New York City government. This got me a rebuke from Ogden for the first and only time during my association with the great *Times* editor. While I had not committed the paper to LaGuardia's support, I had certainly laid down a basis for it without consulting higher authority. And Ogden's point was that in so doing, I had exceeded my authority, even though lack of time for consultation was the cause. In this circumstance, he admonished me, an editorial comment could and should have been withheld. But he absolved me from any larger sin than excess of zeal in keeping the editorial page wholly abreast of the news. And until illness incident to his age —high in the eighties—obliged him to lay down his pen, he steadily expanded the latitude he allowed me as his unofficial second in command.

This latitude was directly encouraged by Ochs in the annual periods, after I had become The Washington Correspondent, that I spent in the New York office. Before the Publisher died, he had encouraged me to hope for eventual appointment as editor of the editorial page, assuring me that the prospect would not be diminished by any risk of being forgotten as a result of my general transfer to Washington. And for some time after his death Arthur Hays Sulzberger, Ochs's successor as Publisher, and Julius Ochs Adler, a nephew of Ochs who had taken over the business management, both maintained my informal status and encouraged the prospect Ochs had suggested as something more than a possibility.

It was in this situation that Sulzberger assigned me to draft the *Times* editorial "America's Aloofness," which urged abandonment of the national policy of neutrality in the forming European war crisis created by Adolf Hitler. This editorial, suggested to me by Secretary of State Cordell Hull as vital to Congressional support of President Roosevelt's still-secret decision to seek repeal of the Neutrality Act, was the pioneer publication that organized the forces for repeal and produced repercussions in the chancelleries and the press of the world.

But this was the closest I came to becoming the editorial spokesman of *The New York Times*. When *The World* ceased publication, I had commended to Ochs the employment by *The Times* of two members of *The World* staff, Charles Merz and William L. Laurence. And with my duties in Washington requiring my permanent removal thereto, Sulzberger found in Merz not only great abilities as an editorial writer but a man of like mind with whom he felt he could work more harmoniously than with me as spokesman of the views of *The Times*. The soundness of his judgment was justified by the sequel.

Accordingly, in November, 1938, with high praise of my services in Washington, he informed me that he had chosen Merz as head of the editorial page and I was to remain permanently in the capital. It was a decision, despite immediate disappointment, for which I soon became thankful and have been thankful ever since. *The Times* editorial policies on which Sulzberger and Merz were ever after harmoniously united conflicted more and more with those I would have advocated as editor; but the Publisher generously allowed me full liberty to express my own in my Washington column "In the Nation," painful though these often were to him.

But not until the Presidential campaign of 1944 did this liberty become onerous to Sulzberger, although he refrained from any expression of this until I had completed the coverage of the campaign and had written, as was the *ex-officio* function of The Washington Correspondent and as I had done quadrennially since 1928, the lead news story of the results of the national election. Sulzberger wrote me a letter, which he delivered in person, after the lead story of the 1944 results appeared, that in substance was as follows:

. . . *The Times* had "sweat blood" before deciding to support President Roosevelt for a fourth term—in 1940 we supported Willkie in opposition to a third—and had not concealed its difficulty in reaching a decision that was entirely based on approval of Roosevelt's international policies. He wished I had, in my pre-election commentaries, been "guided a bit more by similar consideration" and better protected my desire to be deemed "an objective reporter." Though I wrote as such in my lead story on the election, Sulzberger felt some of my columns had made it more difficult to convince *Times* readers that I had not lost some of my objectivity.

. . . It was not, he wrote me, in the "best interest" of *The Times* or of myself to have "answered its editorials" in my columns: better to have written independently of the editorial page than in its refutation. We would "talk this over" when he returned from a journey through the Pacific war zone on which he was about to embark.

These statements did not come as a surprise to me, as witness the fact that before Sulzberger handed me his letter, I had written him the following earlier that day, before the votes were counted:

. . . "IF THE ORACLES AND STRAW-VOTE TAKERS ARE RIGHT, THE PRESIDENT WILL BE ELECTED TODAY TO A FOURTH TERM. . . . IF THE EVENT PROPHESIED COMES TO PASS, IT OCCURS TO ME YOU WILL FEEL *The Times* SHOULD HAVE AS THE HEAD OF ITS WASHINGTON BUREAU SOMEONE OTHER THAN ME. I AM *persona non grata* AT THE WHITE HOUSE, WHICH THE PRESIDENT HAS OFTEN EMPHASIZED BY ATTENTIONS TO OTHER *Times* EXECUTIVES AND WRITERS, AND HIS ELECTION TO A FOURTH TERM WILL MEAN THE *non* IN THAT PHRASE WILL ASSUME CAPITAL LETTERS. . . . I FELT IT MY DUTY TO YOU AND *The Times* TO OPEN THIS SUBJECT MYSELF AND THUS MAKE IT EASIER FOR YOU TO DISPOSE OF THE PROBLEM BEFORE YOU LEAVE. . . . I HAVE NO FEAR THAT WE SHALL BE UNABLE TO GET THE NEWS, AND CONTINUE TO BE RATED AS THE SOURCE OF THE MOST COMPREHENSIVE AND FAIREST NEWS REPORT OUT OF WASHINGTON, IF ARRANGEMENTS CONTINUE AS THEY ARE. BUT YOU MAY THINK OTHERWISE, AND I KNOW I HAVE BEEN UNDER HEAVY FIRE FROM SOME OF YOUR CLOSEST FRIENDS."

After I had written my election lead, and we had exchanged our letters at my desk, we had a conversation in which he told me he did not wish to avail himself of my offer. But our talk was so brief that I sent him another letter, to San Francisco, from which port he was about to embark for the Pacific war zone, requesting that he give me a direct answer to the question whether "his confidence in me was unimpaired." He replied by telegram that it was; that "matters stand as you and I would wish"; and he confirmed this in a last letter.

That episode was the first and last of its kind in the many years I had the privilege of working directly under this generous, high-minded, considerate, and very, very able exemplar of managing journalism on its top level. Arthur Sulzberger inherited an already great newspaper when he succeeded his father-in-law as Publisher of *The New York Times*. But he made it greater, strengthening its firm foundations, broadening to global dimensions its coverage of the news, and protecting the freedom of the press within the obligatory limits of the responsibility this freedom imposes on management and staff alike.

He fixed more firmly the pattern that was the brilliant inspiration of his predecessor. And he chose as his own successor Orvil E. Dryfoos, a young man who most thoroughly comprehended and pursued the practical ideals of Ochs and Arthur Sulzberger. Dryfoos, before his untimely death, had totally established a true professional inheritance. As for Arthur Ochs Sulzberger, who succeeded Dryfoos, the proof of his choice awaits, not a demonstration of high capacity in the business end of *The Times* operation—he made this mark from the outset of his succession. It awaits, at this writing, proof that he can avert the complacency that too much power and too little competition instill in news and editorial executives, and proof that he can stem the seepage of editorial attitudes into the news columns that his father and Dryfoos vigilantly excluded.

This seepage historically is the usual result—unconsciously, I believe, in the case of *The Times*—of policy-making by a group imbued with the same doctrinal approach to public issues on which there is sound basis for constructive dissent. In this instance, the self-styled "liberalism" that has asserted in behalf of its thinking a monopoly on the complimentary nouns, verbs, and adverbs in the dictionary: for examples, "moderates" and "progressive."

A news-story lead and a concurrent editorial in *The Times* of May 25, 1967, are typical of both this "liberal" supererogation of what are the more admirable terms in the language and the seepage to which I have referred:

. . . The news-story lead:
Moderate Republicans [in this state] and the party leadership in this city which have given [name of city] a progressive image . . . have been defeated in an attempt to nominate an urban Roman Catholic for the governorship.

. . . The concurrent editorial:
Clean politics and progressive Republicanism have both suffered a sharp setback in [name of state] gubernatorial primary. . . .

Small wonder if the news leads appear infected by the editorial position to the many readers of *The Times* who define "moderate" and "progressive" as not factually exclusive of the millions of excellent citizens to whom these terms are denied.

When Arthur Sulzberger made the journey to the Pacific war zone, after the Presidential election of 1944 and our exchange of letters previously described, he took a companion along. He was Turner Catledge, then Assistant to the Publisher. The attendant circumstances and the subsequent emergence of Catledge as a major executive of the newspaper, deeply involved in its mounting success, are sufficiently remarkable in themselves to merit inclusion in this account of my own experiences on *The Times*.

Not long after I took over the Washington Bureau, in January, 1932, I found myself particularly impressed with the personality and professional promise of Catledge, then one of the younger reporters. So much so that one evening, still hopeful that I might return to duty in the New York office after a few years, I invited this reporter to my apartment to explore his future as potentially important to *The New York Times*.

I told him I would groom him for my job if he so desired. He did, and I proceeded to give him such opportunities as I fairly could, with reference to the others on the Washington staff, all of which opportunities he grasped with the competence I had anticipated. But as the prospect of my being recalled to New York as editor of the editorial page diminished to the vanishing point in 1938, his restlessness at his own prospect of remaining a subordinate without date grew in inverse proportion.

As a form of encouragement, after a number of salary increases, I created for him the title of National News Correspondent. The prestige this gained for him—in a city where ratings (social, political, and professional) are equated with titles—calmed his restlessness for the time being. And at this point President Roosevelt unintentionally furnished me with an assist.

The Times, at my request, had carried a notice of Catledge's new title, and Mr. Roosevelt used it as a hopeful occasion to injure my professional standing. He called Catledge to the White House "to congratulate" him, but also, as it proved, to undermine me. The President's offer, in effect, was this: he would see that Catledge got full and exclusive access to important Administration news from which I would be excluded. Catledge politely but immediately took pains to leave the President with no impression he would be a consenting partner to such an arrangement, which he at once reported to me. But the offer, as it was bound to do, opened his mind to delightful vistas of what his career could be if, as Archibald MacLeish put it to me at the time, Catledge could be freed from "the shadow of my reputation."

Sensing this, I encouraged Catledge's desire to test temporarily whether he would enjoy and flourish in a severance from *The Times:* specifically, an offer from Marshall Field III to become Foreign Editor of the *Chicago Sun-Times*.

"You'll want to return," I told Catledge. "I am so certain of this I will try to build a bridge for you to use when that happens." I informed Arthur Sulzberger of this conversation, with the result that when, after a year, Catledge informed me he would like to "cross that bridge if it was available," Sulzberger appointed him as his assistant in New York.

The association between the two grew steadily closer. In a year or so Sulzberger installed Catledge as Assistant Managing Editor against the day when the post of Managing Editor would be vacant. This was held, with much distinction, by

Edwin L. James, but he was already entering the shadow of the illness that cost him his life and opened the succession to Catledge. Meanwhile, Sulzberger, also finding the pleasure in Catledge's company that has been the general experience of those who have shared it, chose him as his companion on such expeditions as that of 1944 to the Pacific war zone.

The Times, with Catledge at the helm of the news, mounted higher rungs on the ladder of success. Eventually Catledge became the first *Times* Executive Editor, with jurisdiction over the Managing Editor and the Sunday edition as well, the most important and powerful position a member of the news or editorial staff of the newspaper can attain.

I came to *The Times* too late—1927—to see in action one of the great news editors in the history of journalism, and a protean genius as well, Carr V. Van Anda. Histories of journalism, which this is not, abound with accounts of his fabulous news sense in practice: basically, the sure anticipation of events that invariably followed, equipping *The Times* in advance with plans for dealing with these events that made their coverage the most comprehensive on record; the wide range of technical knowledge that enabled Van Anda not only to fathom Einstein's Theory of Relativity, but also to correct an error by its propounder; the detachment of Van Anda on the job from any personal distraction or human association.

My only immediate contact with this genius came about when Ochs, seeking to make certain my appreciation of the greatness and durability of the institution I was being invited to join, arranged for Van Anda to expound these factors to me. Needing no such persuasion, I recall only the cold mastery of his exposition.

But I was in a position to be directly aware of the high quality of Van Anda's hand-trained successor, Frederick M. Birchall. Birchall was untitled, directing the news machine in the capacity of Acting Managing Editor because he declined to surrender his British citizenship in exchange for the title itself. And Ochs believed that the publicly certified Managing Editor of the most important American newspaper should necessarily be a citizen of the United States, owing not even a formal allegiance to another country.

This was primarily a concept of public relations, because Birchall was in every way a craftsman competent for the difficult task assigned to him, and he administered it brilliantly. In proof of his all-round competence, his dispatches from abroad, when he moved from his tripod into the foreign reportorial field, were high expressions of the quality that for many years has made outstanding *The Times*'s coverage of news all over the world.

My translation from the Editorial Board to the post of The Washington Correspondent automatically made me a member of the news staff. In this capacity I served on the team that was headed by Birchall's duly titled successor, Edwin L. James. In all the years I have spent on newspapers I have not encountered James's superior as a managing editor or worked under a supervision more harmonious and intelligent, or one with better understanding of the inherent problems of a correspondent with the large responsibilities, which, in war-and-peace reporting in the foreign field, he himself had met, and notably discharged during and just after the First World War.

In my numerous controversies with officials, principally Franklin D. Roosevelt, over the handling of Washington news while I was in charge of the Bureau, James was ever the protector of my belief that the Washington staff was better qualified than distant editors and executives, including himself, to decide on the evaluation and presentation of the run of the news within its purview, instead of being managed in detail from the New York office, as has steadily increased since James's time and mine.

He reserved, and now and then employed, the final authority that is the obligation and the necessity of his function when some fundamental difference arose between the Washington staff and the news editors in New York. But these occasions were rare, and James's reasons were invariably supported by sound basic principles of *Times* journalism, foremost among which is to trust the man on the job until and unless he clearly proves unworthy or inadequate.

An example was a suggestion James made to Ochs when President Roosevelt couched a letter of complaint (about a Washington dispatch I had written) in terms that amounted to

a proposal that I be relieved of my post. The President wrote
Ochs that this dispatch, reporting an adverse sentiment among
the foreign-policymakers of his Administration toward the
British Foreign Secretary, Sir John Simon, not only was untrue
but was a deliberate disservice to essential Anglo-American
relations. "Let Krock draft your reply," said James to Ochs,
and the suggestion was adopted.

James had an outward cynicism, disguising a deep sense of
tolerance and compassion, that often annoyed associates who,
like Ochs, were partial to the verbal amenities. Disturbed one
day by a succession of observations by James to the effect that
working on *The Times* was not in itself the *summum bonum* of
all journalistic aspiration, Ochs expressed the view that perhaps James underrated the connection. "Mr. Ochs," James
replied, "you and I are even every payday." Yet between the
two men ran a deep tide of mutual respect, admiration, and
affection that endured to the day of Ochs's death. And so far as
I and most of James's fellow employees are concerned, the
same endured to the day of *his* death, and abides in the memory.

I found *The Times* a very different place to work in than
The World. Its stars, too, were scintillating, but they were
scattered across a wider firmament. And unlike *The World*,
companionship was much more limited to the working day.
When that was done, *Times* men went their several ways:
there was, for instance, no floating poker game or other common diversion after hours in the years when I frequented the
news room.

The perpetual weekend house parties of Pulitzer and Swope,
which the stars of *The World* regularly illuminated, had no
Times counterparts, though Arthur Sulzberger's hospitality
was generous and frequent. *Times* men did not make the same
constant use of the office restaurant that *World* men did; they
dispersed instead to a variety of favorite public taverns, thereby
depriving one another of an association that also could have
been sparkling.

Only a high echelon of *The Times*'s executives regularly
lunched together in the private dining room. And though they
were not lacking in the capabilities of entertaining conversation, there was small scope for this because the group nearly

always included a guest invited to discuss an important public issue seriously and with authority. This necessarily held light conversation to a minimum. But when it broke through, the wit and humor would probably have been a most surprising revelation to the readers of *The Times*.

It has been years since I was a regular member of this executive luncheon group. But I do not doubt that Catledge, Lester Markel, Clifton Daniel, Harding Bancroft, Irving Viet, and the young Publisher are leavening the heavy talk as deftly as did Arthur Sulzberger, James, Ogden, Charles Merz, Dr. John H. Finley, and Markel himself in that earlier time.

I have mentioned Dr. Finley, but he merits more than that because for a number of years he was the incarnation of *The Times* to the public that attends banquets, listens to baccalaureate addresses, lunches at the regular feasts of civic clubs and associations, and participates in the meetings of learned societies. He was by profession an educator (he had been President of Knox College in Galesburg, Illinois, and the City College of New York); by personal endowment a poet and writer of quiet, cultivated journalistic prose; by physical compulsion a noted and incessant pedestrian. For example, once a year he faithfully traversed on foot the entire perimeter of Manhattan Island. And it was not unusual for him to meet an engagement at Princeton, New Jersey, by walking overnight to that community from New York. Since the philosophic mind seems in some degree to be generated or enlarged by long and solitary walks, this may account for the fact that Dr. Finley was also a deep and gentle philosopher.

In addition to his appointed function as *The New York Times*'s Public Presence, Dr. Finley wrote editorials as part of the arrangement by which his services were retained by Ochs. These were mostly on cultural subjects. But in the year after Ogden's death, during which, in deference to his distinction in the community, this good and kindly gentleman was given the title of Editor by Arthur Sulzberger, he sometimes wrote the paper's more generalized leading articles. Typical of his modesty was the fact that before sending these to the printer, he would submit them for suggestions to members of his staff whom he considered better qualified for the task. Of those suggestions with which I am familiar, I recall none he did not graciously adopt.

For many years before I joined the paper, and for some years afterward, its Public Presence was Louis Wiley, the Business Manager. An early associate of Ochs in the rebuilding of the flaccid newspaper he bought in 1895, Wiley had established himself as a finder of revenue beyond prior comparison. Just about five feet tall with a bonhomie that disguised a steely decisiveness and boldness in venture, Wiley was also a master in the art of public relations—his own and that of *The Times*.

Though harmless vanity accounted to some degree for his propensity to organize and preside over dining clubs (like the Society of the Genessee), make banquet speeches all over the place, and collect an outstanding number of honorary collegiate degrees, Wiley did much to humanize *The Times* in the public consciousness. He became so publicly and favorably identified with the paper as to give the impression—which he did not discourage—that he was its final source of authority.

This amused Ochs as much as it did *Times* associates on or near Wiley's own level. And since Wiley was also unmarried, it made him for years the favorite extra man of the dowagers who ruled what then really qualified as the "Society" that now is in the last stages of dissolution at Newport, Bar Harbor, Southampton, and along Fifth and Park Avenues in New York City.

This social prestige, which was a fulfillment of Wiley's youthful aspiration, he came in time to take lightly and as a matter of course. Witness a conversation between him and Sumner Gerard one day after a stately luncheon party at the home of Mrs. Harrison McK. Twombley, a puissant and Vanderbilt-connected queen among the dowagers:

"Louie," said Gerard (an elderly flower of the Knickerbocker aristocracy), "why do we still go to these things? When also, as in your case, it fritters away time you need at your desk?"

"I don't know why *you* still do it," said Wiley. "But I think I know why *I* do. I came to New York from Rochester, a skinny youth of eighteen, to work on the lowest level of the advertising department of *The New York Sun*. Look at me now—fat, old, and bald—and fancy what I looked like in those days in my one ten-dollar suit. Well, to save expenses, I shared a hall bedroom with another clerk, and the only recreation we could afford was to ride a Fifth Avenue bus on Sundays. My companion was a born New Yorker, and as we passed the great mansions, he would point them out to me: Whitney's, Gould's, Astor's, or Vanderbilt's, and so on. 'An ugly little Jew like you,' he said, 'will never see the inside of any of them.' 'Oh, won't I?' I retorted. . . . Sumner, I think I have contracted the habit of still proving that I can."

The extraordinary talent and integrity in newspaper-making that suffused *The Times*, in the many years I was intimately familiar with the staff, was so general that there is no room in this chronicle to single out more than a few others. But there were Merz, a clear and positive thinker and fine stylist, who became editor in fact after Finley's retirement; Simeon Strunsky, whose "Topics of The Times" was a sustained flow of the finest light essays on the news that ever, I believe, appeared in American journalism; N. M. Kingsbury, whose editorial felicity Charles Lamb could have envied; William L. Laurence, who combined an uncanny grasp of applied sciences that impelled the United States government to choose him as the sole journalistic witness of the first atomic bomb explosion on the Western sands; and Meyer Berger, the gifted reporter of news events, which, large or small, he touched with the brush of true genius.

The roster of these talented daily creators of a responsible newspaper is necessarily incomplete. But it would be glaringly so were I to omit the contribution of a brilliant journalist who came to Washington under my jurisdiction when young and lent a special distinction to the news content that has grown steadily with the years. This is James Reston.

One morning, after the reorganized Washington Bureau, in my judgment and that of my masters, was operating smoothly and at a high potential, I dropped in to discuss an improvement in its coverage with Charles M. Lincoln, the ranking Assistant Managing Editor under James. He was famous as former top director of the news-gathering machines of *The Herald* and *The World*.

The Bureau needed, I believed, a reporter who would concentrate on the postwar foreign-policy-making sector of the government and the diplomatic corps in Washington. I inquired of Lincoln which *Times* reporter, in his judgment, had done the outstanding work in the current year. "A kid in the London Bureau named Scotty Reston," he replied. And when he joined the Washington staff, it was not long before Reston completely demonstrated that Lincoln had accurately detected his capacity to find, develop, and clarify the news.

I remember Reston on first professional and personal acquaintance as young, good-looking, eager, and gifted with personality, intelligence, charm, and an instinct for asking the right questions of the right people that induced every news source he dealt with, however highly placed or reticent with the press, to tell him what he wanted to know. I remember him as the possessor of an uncanny "nose for news"—the quality that renders a reporter the gestator as well as the chronicler of news before it officially happens. And as endowed with a talent for pithy phrasemaking that conveys to the reader of the news the essential factor of perspective.

Very soon I invested Reston with the title Diplomatic Correspondent. And by 1953 he had made himself, in my opinion, so essential a member of *The Times* staff that when he was tempted by the prospect of much more money and greater personal publicity by *The Washington Post*, I offered to recommend him for the position I had occupied for twenty-one years —The Washington Correspondent.

My proposal was agreeable to the management. It was agreeable to me, since it would enable me to concentrate on my daily and weekly editorial column and dispense with the cares of administration. And, of course, it was agreeable to Reston, fulfilling as it did an ambition of his of which I had long been aware. Since then, under a *Times* management that has fortified its admiration of Reston's abilities in increasingly substantial ways, he has moved from strength to strength, as the litany has it in quite a different context. And by the unflagging professional interest, industry, and instinct that have propelled him to areas in which news is breaking, or about to break, all over the world, to gatherings of other newspaper workers, and to college communities, Reston in his fifties has become foremost among those Americans who are admired personally and respected professionally in their own land and abroad. He has been an active promoter of promising young newspaper people. Outstanding among these as a reporter and commentator is Tom Wicker, whom Reston, after eleven years as chief of *The Times*'s Washington staff, and on becoming Associate Editor of the paper, recommended as his successor in the former post.

The list of great *Times* professionals is so long and distinguished that I cannot attempt to do more than a few the equal justice of mention in this chronicle. But they all have been vital in the creation of the mighty product whose like, I think, has never existed in the journalism of any country.

To the American people who now are providing more than $80 billions annually for the military establishment, the facts attendant on its allotment, its uses, and the relative competence of the disbursing civil and military authorities have for years been indispensably and exclusively disclosed by Hanson W. Baldwin. Because of the vigilance and integrity of those reporters who, like Baldwin, daily collect the news of their areas—the nation and the world—the readers of *The Times* are better informed of events and their meaning than any popular group in the history of journalism.

But with the growth in scope, size, and capability of this extraordinary news-collecting medium—and in the huge gross revenues that have accrued from the patronage of its community—certain disquieting changes seem to me to have been the consequences. Among these are over-organization; the second-guessing treatment applied to highly qualified reporters by a growing horde of editors in the New York office; a mechanization of the personal relations between management and staff on which depend the pride of individual and devoted achievement; and the self-satisfaction of successful management that is fostered, more than by anything else, by the excess of power that attends the lack of competition.

Over-organization drains away the spirit that makes a working force approach its daily task happily and with the determination to do its best that derives importantly from the certainty
of appreciation. Where there is a plethora of generals, there is
an excess of dull drill for the privates.

Where remote second-guessing of competent reporters is
rampant, so is there mounting resentment in the ranks of the
able reporters who are, in essence, the real creators of a newspaper.

Where the news report is successively filtered by echelon
after echelon of rising authority, the pace and firmness of final
decision are slowed toward the points of wavering judgment
and long inaction in a profession in which the opposite attitudes mark the difference between what is interesting and what
is dull.

Hence, the chief casualty of these changes, as I perceive
them, in the production of *The Times* is the walling-off of the
staff from the editors. There was a warm benevolence that is
now missing in the personal relationships of *Times* people with
one another when the management was conducted in the pa-
triarchial spirit invoked by Ochs and maintained by Arthur
Sulzberger and Orvil Dryfoos.

The sudden death of Dryfoos thrust on Arthur Ochs Sulzberger the responsibility of a publisher that, at the outset, is
primarily economic. But if the complicated managerial machinery of the news and editorial departments are ever to return to
the simplified and humanized status that the temperament of
newspaper people acutely requires, the young Publisher and
Reston, his new Executive Editor, must restore them.

To do this, they must forsake the mounting policy of standing by while there proceeds, by chain reaction, the dehu-
manizing and bureaucratic centralization of the news and editorial operation in which the warmth that infused the patriar-
chy has, in my opinion, been dispersed.

Of Adolph S. Ochs, the patriarch himself, a full appreciation
of his genius as a publisher is yet to be written. Swope, conceding the gift but baffled by the fact that it operated behind a
thoroughly pedestrian exterior, characterized Ochs as a "sub-
caliber genius." But close daily association with Ochs for some

years persuaded me that this rating was as superficial as the evidence on which it was based. He certainly was not an intellectual. Osmosis, not textbooks or distinguished professorial lectures, accounted for his education. Often in council he would offer ideas that seemed puerile and impractical to his associates, and they were. But Ochs was quite as aware of this as the others. The purpose of these trial-balloons, and he generally achieved it, was to generate a good idea about the project in hand or to stimulate the production of one by demonstrating that his associates had none at all.

After Ochs assumed the tremendous task of restoring the element of vitality in *The New York Times* and making it dominant in the metropolitan field, he continued, as have his successors, the ownership and over-all operation of *The Chattanooga Times*. But this was an expression of loyalty to the paper and the community, the ladders on which he rose.

For some years he also owned and operated *The Public Ledger* of Philadelphia. But the Philadelphia newspaper operation involved no distraction from or conflict of interest with *The Times*. I do not believe he would ever have acquired that near monopoly of the metropolitan field, with its inevitable diffusion of the energies and talents of *The Times* management, by publishing a second New York City newspaper—a project that, when *The Herald Tribune Journal* closed down, was seriously surveyed by *The Times* executives.

The wisdom of all the sages and the virtues of all the saints could well be concentrated in the task of making *The New York Times* ever more responsive to its great public obligation. As an instance of Ochs's reaction when a New York newspaper died—the very opposite of an impulse to exploit it in the interest of a *Times* monopoly of the field—the following minute I made of a *Times* council meeting is most revealing:

. . . No member of the Editorial Council could possibly forget today's meeting [March 16, 1931]. It was the first at which Mr. Ochs has been present since the sale of the Pulitzer newspaper properties in New York. He has rarely been so animated in discussing anything. He began by saying that probably he had been spared another very weighty responsibility, but one which he would have been eager to assume, by not having been in New York when *The World* was sold. He said it was deplorable that this property had been allowed to pass out of existence. On one occasion during the negotiation of the Pulitzers for the sale, he had sent word to Herbert Pulitzer and to the business heads of *The World* that if they would permit the property to pass into the hands of the employees, he would make a very substantial contribution. No official response had ever come to this offer. He added, and Sulzberger confirmed the statement (because it was Sulzberger who had carried the message to Herbert Pulitzer), that the latter had shown no interest whatever in the idea.

Had Mr. Ochs been in New York during the hearings before the Surrogate, he said he would have entered the case as an expert witness. He would have testified that the newspapers had enormous value. He would have agreed to raise $5,000,000, which is several millions more than the actual sum paid by Scripps-Howard, to finance a cooperative employees project. He would have testified that personally he would raise enough money to finance the papers until problems of management and economics had been met. Mr. Ochs said it would have been possible to have saved annually from a million to two million dollars in the operating expense, for example, cutting out many columns of useless financial news, which *The Times* and *The Herald-Tribune* covered sufficiently for the professional population downtown, and eliminating the Sunday Magazine. He would have told the Surrogate that in his opinion as a publisher a newspaper patterned along the lines of *The Daily Mail* would be both useful and successful in New York. He would have found competent management in the ranks of the employees of the Pulitzer papers, arranging that for, say, 25 per cent of their salaries they would be given stock and be afforded further opportunities to participate in the earnings of the properties. The community would have supported such a project with enthusiasm, and the employees themselves would not only have worked to the top of their bent in producing good newspapers, but would have been able to exert strong and legitimate influence on advertisers. "If I had testified to these things," said Mr. Ochs, "the Surrogate would have had a different question before him. It would not have simply been whether the heirs might sell to whom they pleased, thus leaving them no option but to proceed to the execution of their contract with Scripps-Howard."

Mr. Ochs, who seemed more like thirty-three than seventy-three in his enthusiasm and vigor, said that this course of his might have hurt *The Times* somewhat, but it would have been justified by the good it would have accomplished for the profession of journalism and for the community. Now, he said, he anticipates that *The Times* will gain about seventy-five thousand daily and a hundred thousand Sunday from the sale of the Pulitzer properties, and this without putting up any money except that used in circulation promotion.

He cited as a fact of interest and significance that of all the morning papers which were flourishing in New York when he came up from Chattanooga and bought the wreck which was *The New York Times* there remain only two, and these have required the expenditure of vast outside sums to prolong their existence; *The Tribune* by purchase and merger, *The American* by steady artificial nourishment.

Perhaps never in all their many amazing, endearing, and illuminating contacts with the publisher have the members of the Editorial Council been more impressed with his courage, his compassion, and his great professional abilities.

Without Ochs there would have been no *New York Times* as it now exists. It rests on the foundations he laid and will survive no longer than they do.

5

HAYES

THIS account of certain of my relationships with notable public persons—the occupational consequences of reporting national politics—may as well begin with the first meeting that I am aware of between a President of the United States and any member of my family.

This involved a series of disagreeable incidents, which advanced steadily to a painful scene in the White House in the year 1877. Frederick Morris, my maternal grandfather's second son, had been appointed to the Naval Academy at Annapolis; and his father decided to escort him on the journey from Glasgow, Kentucky. The sequence of unfortunate events and ill omens was as follows.

As the pair was waiting for the train to Washington in the L. & N. Louisville terminal (we called railway stations "*dee-pos*"), my grandfather's plug hat blew off and started rolling along the platform. Instead of chasing it or joining the chase, a filial duty to which he had been reared, the youth gave way to a fit of laughter that overcame him entirely when his progenitor went sprinting in hot pursuit.

What discipline was administered I don't know, though I am certain it was a chastened midshipman-not-to-be (he failed the eye test) who boarded the steam cars. But the lapse of good manners could hardly have prepared my grandfather for the painful climax.

With his son in tow, and at the suggestion of the current Senator from Kentucky who had given the boy the appointment to Annapolis, my grandfather proceeded to the White House to "pay his respects" to the President. They had been received with the graciousness characteristic of this bearded chief of state, who, after shaking hands with the father, extended the friendly gesture to the boy. Whereupon my Uncle Fred, firmly joining his hands behind his back, compounded the rude gesture: "I decline," he said, "to shake hands with the man who stole the election from Tilden."

However deeply this may have shocked Rutherford B. Hayes, a devoutly religious man, it was nothing compared to the humiliation of my grandfather that a son of his should feel it incumbent to demonstrate in such insolent fashion his fealty to the Democratic Party and to the existing bitterness over the Republican resort to *force majeure* by which Governor Tilden was deprived of the Presidency to which he had been elected by the popular majority.

In the performance of what I conceived to be my journalistic duty I have earned the abiding displeasure of Presidents—at the expense of close friendships with three of them—and in my case the printed page has been the impersonal source of these severances. Yet on each occasion I have recalled the deplorable incident of 1877 and pondered whether a tendency to expect a President to rise above the politics that put him in the White House may not run in the family.

6

THEODORE ROOSEVELT

IN ONE way or another I have known eleven presidents of the United States, ten during their incumbency. The eleventh was Theodore Roosevelt. Once I encountered him at first hand after he had left office; twice I was witness to events pertinent to his career.

The only time I met Theodore Roosevelt alone was after he had returned from Africa toward the end of President William Howard Taft's Administration. A committee of the House of Representatives headed by Representative A. O. Stanley of Kentucky was conducting an investigation of the U.S. Steel Corporation. This necessarily included a review of the circumstances by which U.S. Steel had acquired control of the Tennessee Coal and Iron Company—circumstances that eventually involved the huge industrial complexes called "trusts" in litigation that terminated with the Supreme Court's separation of some of their affiliates from the parent companies.

Since Representative Stanley was a Kentuckian, and I the correspondent in Washington of *The Louisville Courier-Journal* and *Times*, I knew him very well. A consequence was that when his investigation reached the point of review of the Tennessee Coal and Iron deal, he sought my assistance in arranging for the appearance before his committee of the most important witness on the record. This was Theodore Roosevelt, whose opposition while President to Big Steel's acquisition of Tennessee was a dramatic chapter in the history of the trust-busting he had initiated as administration policy.

Stanley asked me to serve as his intermediary in arranging for Colonel Roosevelt's appearance before the House committee. He gave me a letter of introduction, investing me with "plenary power" to agree to whatever conditions the ex-President might impose. I went to New York and made a telephone call to T. R. at the office of *The Outlook*, the magazine of which he was Contributing Editor.

He was away, at his home in Oyster Bay. When I explained what my errand was, *The Outlook* conveyed the information to Colonel Roosevelt, and he rang me up. In that conversation I suggested a meeting at his residence on Long Island. I remember his reply very distinctly. "There are always a lot of reporters hanging around here," he said, "watching for any news that might be indicated by the people I see. They might deduce what you came to see me about, and since I don't know precisely what it is or what I'm going to do about it, I have another suggestion for our meeting place. Tomorrow morning at nine forty-five I will board the Hudson River ferryboat from Twenty-third Street to the Jersey terminal, where I have a compartment on a West Coast train [he was traveling to Cornwall, New York, to visit Dr. Lyman Abbott]. You be on that ferry, but don't seem to recognize me and I will do likewise. Follow me from the ferry onto the train and into my compartment, and then we'll have this conversation."

I followed the instructions very carefully. The Colonel had his shoes shined aboard the ferry, and I neither looked at nor spoke to him. At the terminal on the New Jersey shore he marched vigorously off the ferry. I followed him into the train and into the compartment. He closed the door and said, "Sit down. Now, what is it?"

"Mr. President," I said, "Representative Stanley would like

to have you testify on the Tennessee Coal and Iron deal as a witness before the House committee investigating the U.S. Steel Corporation."

He promptly replied, "I'll be glad to do that, but on assurance of no advance publicity. I assume Congressman Stanley is a gentleman."

"At least he was brought up to be one," I said.

"All right," said the Colonel. "You tell Congressman Stanley to assemble his committee in the City Hall in New York next week [I forget the day he named] and have a witness on the stand some time prior to ten A.M. I will enter the committee room through the double doors. When Representative Stanley sees me, he is to ask the witness to step down temporarily. I will then take the stand and answer the questions the Congressman wants me to answer insofar as I am able or feel privileged to do so."

This program was followed exactly as the Colonel prescribed. I explained to Stanley that there must be no leak of any kind because obviously T. R. wanted to make a dramatic appearance. He was already running for the Republican nomination in 1912, and this was to be the formal overture. It was bound to get enormous publicity on the first pages all over the United States, and it did. Painful as it was to me professionally, to know of great news and be unable to reveal it, I kept my word and Stanley kept his.

As I recall it, on the morning appointed at precisely ten o'clock the President of the U.S. Steel Corporation was on the witness stand. The double doors flew open and Theodore Roosevelt strode in. Stanley said, "Just a moment, Mr. Witness, please step down. Colonel Roosevelt, would you honor the committee by testifying in this case?"

"By all means," said the former President. He took the witness stand, answered the questions, and the big story broke. A wildly excited group of reporters got to the wires as fast as they could. I was in the Senate press gallery in Washington waiting for this break when the flash came over the wire: "THEODORE ROOSEVELT IS TESTIFYING BEFORE THE STANLEY COMMITTEE IN NEW YORK CITY."

My most vivid experience connected with T. R. occurred during the Republican National Convention in 1912 at which Taft was renominated over the opposition of Colonel Roosevelt and the new Republican Progressives. To everyone's astonishment, early in the convention week, when Taft's renomination appeared to be a certainty, Colonel Roosevelt reversed a previous position and decided to go to Chicago. When he appeared on Michigan Avenue, on the way from the New York Central station to the Congress Hotel, the street was lined with cheering hundreds of thousands, and no sooner had the Colonel reached his hotel suite than he summoned what is now called a press conference, but was then described as "seeing the newspapermen." We entered his suite in line, most of us expecting little more than the courtesy of a greeting. There were no questions from us and he volunteered no statement that generated any. He just said he was glad to see us all again.

But when Edward B. Clark, the correspondent of the *Chicago Evening Post* came to Mr. Roosevelt in the line, the Colonel took him aside and they had a long whispered conversation, arousing everyone's curiosity. What, we wondered, was he telling Ed Clark? After this conversation ended, the line continued to pass in review, and that was that.

Immediately on the breakup we surrounded Clark, pleading for an explanation. "Well," he said, "you'll hardly believe this, but it's true. T. R. knows I am an amateur ornithologist, as he is. It seems that yesterday morning at Sagamore Hill, his house in Oyster Bay, he saw what he believes to be a hermit thrush, and he wanted my opinion whether it could have been. He described the bird in detail."

Clark reported he had told T. R. it might have been a hermit thrush, but he doubted very much it was. This in the midst of one of the fiercest political battles in American history. And there was another incident in the line that led to the biggest story of the convention, which I had the good fortune to share with two other reporters.

In the line as it passed T. R. that day was George Miller, the Washington correspondent and later the Editor-in-Chief of the *Detroit News*. Colonel Roosevelt slapped him on the back and said in a loud voice, "I never was able to fool this old boy!" The intimacy thus certified soon served most importantly.

The Roosevelt forces had failed to "purge the roll" of Taft delegates with the argument that they had been illegally chosen. If T. R. had won that motion, he would have defeated Taft for renomination. But Elihu Root, (T. R. afterward referred to him as "the head devil"), the permanent chairman of the convention, his famous bangs quivering above his equally famous eyebrows, gaveled down every motion to purge. A real steamroller flattened the Roosevelt forces, so we naturally expected Colonel Roosevelt to take the next train to Oyster Bay.

To our surprise he did not, and the word spread that he was going to address his delegates in the Florentine Room of the Congress Hotel that evening. He stood on a low platform, his face flushed, the veins on his brow inflated, his manner and gestures characteristically emphatic and vigorous, and made the speech that clearly prefaced the formation of the Bull Moose Party and his independent candidacy on that ticket.

But before he spoke to his delegates in the Florentine Room, three of us who were working together asked George Miller, who was in the group, if he would try to find out why Roosevelt was staying in Chicago after his cause was totally lost.

The product was stunning. "I asked him the question," Miller told us, "and this was his reply: 'I'm remaining in Chicago to make sure Mr. Taft is nominated.'"

This was the declaration of war that crushed the Republican Party. Ths was the action that led directly to the election of Woodrow Wilson as President of the United States.

T. R. was an extremely forceful man. He also demonstrated in my only meeting with him that he was a great public-relations expert. He was intensely vigorous physically. He spoke with great decisiveness, both impulsively and after deliberation. He was a determined man with a set of definite percepts of government that he strongly enforced.

He was not a tall man, but sturdily built. He often seemed to be peering—his glasses were thick. His mustache was not of the guardsman type like Dean Acheson's. But like Acheson's, it bristled when he felt bristly. He moved with extraordinary vigor. I recall that when he left the ferry for the railway train that morning, he walked so fast that I had trouble maintaining the distance between us that he had prescribed.

T. R.'s forcefulness was obnoxious to many of those who disagreed with him. He was disposed toward a feudal relationship with opponents. He quarreled with Congress and other characters in public life. He had strong views about historical persons, once dismissing Tom Paine as "a filthy little atheist." He aroused hostility and returned it with interest.

7

TAFT

MY NEXT Presidential acquaintance in any degree was with President Taft. I was a new boy in town when I came to Washington midway in his Administration, and I saw him alone or in company only once or twice. This was about the usual experience of the representative of an interior newspaper in those days. The correspondents of the great metropolitan papers, Richard V. Oulahan in particular, saw him more often and more intimately. We small fry were invited once a year to a Congressional reception, and once I called on Taft with a message from Watterson. I forget what the message was. But I remember finding Taft an affable and charming gentleman; and after I had answered affirmatively his inquiry as to whether I was a native Kentuckian, his comment followed, to this general effect:

"When I was a boy I used to lie on a hill in Cincinnati overlooking the Ohio River to watch for the coming of spring. It arrived on the Kentucky side a week or so before it crossed the river, and I rejoiced at the sight of the apple and peach trees coming into bloom."

In those days Taft was certainly entitled to any agreeable memory he could summon. He was already plagued by the split among the Republicans over the Payne-Aldrich tariff bill, and by the growing evidence that Colonel Roosevelt intended to challenge him for the leadership of the party. And there were plain signs that Taft was baffled and angered by the opposition that in due course would make him a one-term President. He was pierced by the irony implicit in the fact that though his first nomination was imposed on the Republican Party by his predecessor, Colonel Roosevelt, it was Roosevelt who was heading the movement to prevent his renomination or, failing that, his re-election.

This must have had an extra trace of bitterness for Taft, because I think if he had shaped his own career, he would have moved directly, instead of after a bitter political interval, from the secondary Federal judiciary to the Supreme Court, escaping the miseries that can overbalance the splendors of elective politics. He was thrust into that arena because T. R. believed Taft would carry out his own policies to the letter, and he was eliminated by the thumbs-down of the same hand. In this respect Taft's political career is unique, at least in the Republican Party.

8

WILSON

AT PRINCETON, in my time, Woodrow Wilson lectured on government, and I had the privilege of being a listener in McCosh Hall. I was too obscure to have known him personally, but after he entered politics as the Governor of New Jersey in 1910, I began to see him with some regularity in my capacity as a Washington correspondent. *The Courier-Journal* welcomed his advent to politics, and despite the interruption of the "Manhattan Club Incident" in 1911,* resumed its support of Wilson in the Presidential campaign of 1912. When he became President, I attended his news conferences—the first Presidential exposure to questions from the press that is now standard procedure. I saw him frequently until I returned to Louisville in 1915 before the end of his first Administration.

In Paris as a reporter of the 1918–1919 Peace Conference, I

---

* Wilson in a meeting at the club with Editor George Harvey (with Watterson indignantly present) replied in the affirmative to a query from Harvey as to whether Harvey's support was "embarrassing" Wilson. This was in late 1911 while Wilson was the Governor of New Jersey. Harvey at this time published a national magazine with strong backing by large corporate Wall Street interests, which interests he editorially reflected. Later, Harvey was President Harding's Ambassador to the Court of St. James's.

visited Wilson a couple of times at his residence, the Palais
Murat in Parc Monceau—a special privilege made possible
because Rear Admiral Cary Grayson, his personal physician,
Naval aide, and close friend and counselor, was my generous
friend.

In the last week of 1918, after the Armistice, I was among
the newspaper reporters who accompanied President Wilson to
Italy. He spoke to a multitude in Rome, and in Milan hundreds
of thousands of people sank to their knees to hail him as the
savior of Italy.

I remember thinking that Wilson lost his head there because
when the band burst into patriotic airs, he picked up a baton
somebody handed him and conducted the music. But the applause and hero-worship of the vast throng in the Piazza del
Duomo would have tested the resolve of any statesman to keep
his *ex-officio* dignity intact.

Another of my recollections is an incident at Turin. When
our party arrived there, I was in the room with Wilson in the
ducal palace, and a mob was gathered outside, cheering him
and demanding his appearance. Turning to me he asked, "How
do you say 'Long live Italy'?"

I said, "I think you say *'Eviva l'Italia.'* "

"I hope that's right," he said, and went onto the balcony,
raised his hand, and took the chance.

On the Presidential train that left Turin for Paris there was
one special car reserved for newspapermen. The train made a
routine stop at Modena, on the Italian-French border. I walked
along the platform to wait for the change of crews, and while
passing the President's car, I saw a French telegraph messen-
ger enter it with a telegram and deliver it to the President's
valet, whose name, I think, was Arthur Brooks.

I watched him as he entered the compartment where Wilson
was sitting in plain view, and I watched the President as he
opened and read the telegram. The first expression on his face
struck me as extraordinary. As I reconstructed this (after I
learned what the message was—that Colonel Roosevelt was
dead), Wilson's first expression was that of anyone at news
that his most powerful adversary has forever left the lists: a

kind of spontaneous relaxation. But Wilson's next expression
was distinctly a sad one. I was unable to understand and reconcile the facial reactions until after Admiral Grayson, whom I
called to the platform, told me the contents of the telegram.

I immediately carried the news to colleagues who, like me,
were strolling about the station. Thereupon Richard V. Oulahan, the eminent Washington Correspondent of *The New
York Times* (whom I succeeded in that post years later), rose
fitly, as always, to the occasion. We followed him to a little
boite across the way from the railway station and there proposed and drank a toast to the memory of a great American.

My relations with the President in that period can be exemplified by the fact that when he decided to return briefly to
Washington for the adjournment of the current session of
Congress, Grayson brought me word that if I so desired, the
President would take me along on the U.S. liner *George Washington*. But shortly after this Grayson informed me that because other American reporters in Paris had learned of the
passenger list, and one who was intimately and favorably
known to Wilson from Princeton days was among those who
had asked to join the ship's company, the President had concluded that if he took me, he would have to take the other, and
hence was obliged to withdraw my invitation.

Not until Wilson returned to private life did I see him again.
The last time was in the library of his house on S Street N. W.
in Washington. I was shocked by the unmistakable mark of the
moribund on his face—as years later I would be the last time I
saw Franklin D. Roosevelt. But Wilson's mind was unimpaired, and he gave it full play in wholly uninhibited comment
on the heads of state with whom he had contended at the Peace
Conference.

I was planning shortly to visit the Ruhr to report the situation that had arisen there between France and Germany. When
I told him of my plans, he warned me not to expect the truth
from the French government. "Its information policy," he said,
"like every other, is set by Premier Poincaré," a politician
whom he said he had found congenitally unreliable in word and
deed.

He was unresponsive when I tried to sound out his prefer-
ences for the 1924 Democratic Presidential nomination. Therefore, I was unprepared for the vehement opposition he later
revealed to the renomination of James M. Cox.

As the party nominee in 1920 Cox had been the uncompro-
mising defender of Wilson's long reliance on unpreparedness
and neutrality to keep the United States out of the First World
War; and had held high the banner of the Covenant of Paris
that established the League of Nations—though Cox was fully
aware of the current unpopularity of both positions. Yet Wilson was so disposed against Cox's renomination that in 1923,
when his faithful former White House secretary, Joseph P.
Tumulty, urged this on the party at a speech at Tammany
dinner in New York, Wilson felt constrained to issue a repudiation of any impression the speech might have created that
Tumulty was projecting Wilson's view.

I shared the surprise at this manifestation with many other
steadfast Wilsonians, and in a telegram to the former President from Louisville (where I was still associated with *The
Courier-Journal* and *The Times*) I asked him in effect what we
were to make of his statement of repudiation. Replying by
letter, he wrote merely that there was a concerted effort by
certain leaders of Democratic city organizations to stack the
1924 convention for Cox, that he believed this would be a
"serious mistake" and accordingly had issued the statement to
dispel any other inference.

Reverting to this last meeting with Wilson, which he pro-
longed beyond my expectations, I recall the contrast between
his enfeebled physique, as he sat shawled in a wheelchair, one
arm hanging loosely at his side, and the strength and clarity of
his enunciation. I was halfway down the stairs on my way out
when I heard him call, loud and clear, "Of course, you'll treat
this as off the record."

Only by chance, and almost forty-five years later, I discovered that after this meeting Wilson wrote letters to two public
men abroad in whom he had confidence, informing each that he
had advised me to call on him and commending me professionally and personally in terms far beyond my merits or expecta-

tions. One of these letters turned up when a Columbia University candidate for a doctorate in history was researching the papers of A. G. Gardiner, the famous British editor.

I cite this only as evidence that contrary to the impression hostile critics sought arduously to create, Wilson was perceptively kind and thoughtful in what must have been hundreds of instances of which the beneficiaries were as unaware as I was of this one.

To me Wilson was a great man and a great President. Two examples fortify this appraisal. One was his order for the industrial mobilization that helped so decisively to hurry Allied victory in the First World War; and his inspired choice of Baruch to take charge, with undeviating Presidential support. The other was his foresight that only a League of Nations in which all the great powers would participate with all the small nations—the victors as well as the vanquished—could hope to institute on earth an orderly and durable peace. He succeeded in the one and he failed in the other. If we had joined the League, he might have triumphed doubly. Since his international peace formula has never been fully invoked, who can deny with assurance that if in 1919 it had been, subsequent wars would have been limited and brief? Certainly, it might conceivably have prevented the rise of Mussolini, Hitler, and the Japanese war party.

The incidents of error that plague humanity, even among the greatest, mount in proportion to the possession of vast power and high official place, and from this equation Wilson was not immune. But I have always thought that history would hold him directly responsible for only four basic errors—though necessarily the quotient of their damage was enormous.

The first, I think, was his long resistance to rebuilding the military power of the United States when his information and the reports from government intelligence agencies should have persuaded him that German military strategy would inevitably draw us into war. He accepted that prospect and purpose in 1917; hence not too late to raise the United States military-industrial complex to overpowering strength from the state of weakness it was in and would have continued to be in had Wilson maintained that year his policy of absolute neutrality and non-preparation. For in 1917 Wilson asked Congress to give him authority to arm U.S. merchant ships engaged in the supply of munitions and other auxiliaries of offense and defense to the Allies.

By the time Wilson reversed his policy, he had been relieved of the presence in his Cabinet of Bryan, who was urging pacifism. Bryan soundly conceived that the end of neutrality would inevitably draw the U.S. into the First World War.

Wilson's second mistake, as I appraise it, was his failure to include Republicans of great political influence in the Peace Mission he took with him to Paris—for example, Taft, Elihu Root, and at least one Republican senator. Had these been associated with Wilson officially in his struggle over the reparations and the territorial exactions in the Treaty, I doubt that Senate bipartisan coalition would have been able to reject the Treaty, even though the Covenant of the League might have been less precise as a military peacekeeping body.

Mistake number three was his decision to attend the Peace Conference in person. I thought he should have been represented at Paris by his Secretary of State and an American mission including Taft and Root.

I base this view on the fact that his presence obliged him to agree to compromises he could have rejected in the aura that surrounds the Presidency in Washington as nowhere else. But once he formed the Big Four, he had to keep it together. This automatically generated an atmosphere of negotiation, of give-and-take, and Lloyd George, Clemenceau, and Orlando were as skilled in this maneuvering as Wilson was not.

The incidence of Wilson's physical presence led also, as I see it, to mistake number four—his total refusal to compromise on the text of the Covenant, including Article 10. Having personally committed himself to his colleagues in Paris, he felt honor-bound not to yield a syllable of the text. On this vulnerable ground defeat was foreordained by the inexorable play of domestic politics.

Reverting to the brighter days of Wilson's earlier and happier administrative period, I am impressed in retrospect with its similarity to the accession of Franklin D. Roosevelt. Like Roosevelt, Wilson brought to Washington a legislative pro-

gram of economic and social reform that paralleled the one he
had instituted when he became Governor of his state. Much of
this reform was along the same line Theodore Roosevelt had
been advocating, with the exception of the latter's most radical
aspect—the recall of judicial decisions by popular referendum.
Wilson, too, was a liberal. But his liberalism was of the classic
variety that made such a proposition unthinkable.

He was a pragmatic radical, however, as demonstrated by
his transfer of national monetary and fiscal management from
Wall Street to Washington. Examples of this are the Federal
Reserve Act, the establishment of the Federal Trade Commission, and the enlightened regulation of the hours and working
conditions of labor. In the Adamson and Clayton Acts the
eight-hour day and the suppression of corporate monopolies
and corporate malpractices became realities. Labor was elevated toward the status of an equal negotiating element in
industry. And it is interesting that except for Bryan's proposal
of government ownership of the railroads and of national prohibition of the manufacture, sale, and transport of intoxicating
spirits, almost everything Bryan advocated—and a great seg-
men of T. Roosevelt's reforms—were enacted into law in the
Wilson and F. D. Roosevelt Administrations.

With the added stimulus against stand-pat conservatism inherent in the large vote cast for the independent Bull Moose
ticket in 1912, Wilson came to office on a popular wave for
these reforms. One significant difference in the spirit Franklin
Roosevelt brought to Washington twenty years later was that
Wilson's reforms were not projected in an atmosphere of national economic disaster. FDR's first Congress assembled in
the presence of acute depression, when businessmen, bankers,
and citizens of all kinds were streaming in and out of the
White House, begging Roosevelt to assume the powers of a
dictator. Wilson's first Presidential environment was a surge
for *procedural* reform.

Another difference between the Wilson and Roosevelt records was that except after the Senate had resisted Wilson's
abrupt abandonment of neutrality, Wilson did not twist the
arm of Congress, as Roosevelt did, after Congress ceased

blindly to follow his leadership. So intense was this follow-the-leader attitude of Congress in FDR's first year that once Senator Robinson, the Democratic Majority Leader, got approval as legislation of a piece of paper on which not a word of the legislative text appeared—for the good reason that it had not yet been drafted. There was no such urgency or haste in any year of Wilson's first Administration.

He approached Congress as both the leader of the nation and the leader of the party in power. He did that with great dignity and firmness. But not until his second Administration was he confronted with the problem of whether to try to ram legislation through by the usual Presidential pressures that include political deals and promises. Even when the unavoidable necessity arose, Wilson shrank from the latter. He long accepted and practiced his concept of the constitutional intent that the President proposes and Congress disposes. But this was in the period when Congress disposed as he proposed, and he had the popular support that helped assure this. Later, as I have indicated, things were different.

Franklin Roosevelt's original experience with Congress was the same. But it came to earlier and more violent change. It was not until the two Republican wings merged in 1916 that Wilson no longer merely had to wave his wand of office. The Republican split to which he owed his 1912 election (by a popular minority) was bridged at the national convention that nominated Charles Evans Hughes as Wilson's opponent in 1916. His honeymoon was also shortened by the fact that by this time he had become embroiled with Theodore Roosevelt over neutrality, a dispute that expanded to cover Wilson's conduct of the war. And the end of the honeymoon was hastened by another alienation—of Wilson from the anti-war and anti-League Senate Democrats whose spokesmen were William J. Stone, Chairman of the Foreign Relations Committee, James A. Reed (both of Missouri), and Burton Wheeler of Montana.

But comparisons between the first Democratic Presidents after Cleveland fall short in other particulars. Wilson was austere. FDR was one of the most congenial of people. Wilson was a President with a definite political philosophy. Franklin

Roosevelt was an opportunist as far as political philosophy was concerned, but the one he made his own laid the foundations of urgent and long-neglected social and economic reforms.

Roosevelt had some basic views. But he was ready to change or compromise or even abandon them under certain pressures, whereas Wilson was firmly identified with one school of political philosophy, Jefferson's, as opposed to another, Hamilton's, an example being his unremitting hostility to national prohibition. And while both Democratic Presidents were effective public speakers, Wilson was a greater natural orator than Roosevelt and far better educated.

Roosevelt's oratory was persuasive and literate, and it appealed to the people because of the cultivated accent and smooth elocution that were among its popular characteristics since it is to these that so many Americans secretly aspire. But Wilson's was literature itself, and his delivery was Periclean.

9

HARDING
&
COOLIDGE

OF the next two Republican Presidents who came after Taft, I first knew Harding as a Senator from Ohio. He was a handsome man: no one ever looked more a President than he did. He was genial, he was easygoing, as a Senator he took no part in legislation. I can recall none attached to his name.

In the spring before the 1920 convention Harry M. Daugherty, who was managing Harding's campaign for the Presidential nomination as Ohio's favorite son—to whom no one gave a chance—brought Harding to my room in the Willard Hotel for a pre-dinner drink before the Gridiron Club dinner. I had imported a couple of bottles of rare prewar bourbon from Kentucky and, as I recall, the Senator from Ohio drank almost a pint by himself. However, he showed it not at all. He held his liquor well.

The events of his nomination and Presidency are very well known. He was the victim of his good nature and his faulty judgment of character. He was imposed on by corrupt friends and he died discredited, largely for the trait his father attributed to him when he said, "Warren, it's a lucky thing you were not born a girl because you can't say no." Harding often told the story himself.

When Harding died suddenly and unexpectedly in San Francisco after a trip to Alaska in 1923 and his Vice-President, Calvin Coolidge, succeeded him, the factory of poisonous rumors that is always in operation in these circumstances emitted its usual product. In this instance, that Mrs. Harding had been jealous of her husband because of certain alleged escapades— even intimations that she was somehow personally involved in his taking-off. There appears to have been substance in the rumor that the President had given her cause for unhappiness with respect to his personal behavior. But none that his death was attributable to other than natural causes. He contracted pneumonia and his system was unable to resist. Medical science had not yet found a sure cure for that disease.

Coolidge had been nominated for Vice-President by the Republican Convention of 1920 because, as Governor of Massachusetts, he had suppressed the Boston police strike. In so doing, he forcefully asserted the great democratic principle that no public servant, particularly one assigned to maintain public order and the daily economy, had the right to strike against the government. And he enforced that principle so completely to break the back of the strike that he emerged as the most eligible nominee for Vice-President.

I met Coolidge for the first time during the Boston police strike, having gone to have a look at the situation in which the principal clearly was a politician who was going to attract national attention. I talked with him only a few minutes, but my impressions were distinct. Of a reticent, aloof man who had nevertheless managed to be successful in a gregarious trade. Of a laconic man, but one whose few words carried an indirect thrust of wit and satire. A sufficient example is the story of his comment on a sermon he heard at church during his Presidency. When he returned to the White House for luncheon, a guest asked him what the sermon was about. "Sin," the President said. And, after a pause, "He was agin it."

Though he never seemed to be influenced in his acts or policies by forethought of the factor of public relations, Coolidge nevertheless proved himself an expert in what now are current Madison Avenue techniques. He immediately dramatized the contrast with Harding that he embodied in manner, act, and speech, and thereby supplied the Republicans with their major campaign issue when he sought the Presidency in his own right in 1924: the man of character and stability, archetype of the old New England virtues.

On this issue Coolidge arrested the demoralization of the Republican Party produced by the scandals in his predecessor's Administration. And I can think of no other Republican who could have done this at the time, especially since the Democrats, in nominating John W. Davis as his opponent, had chosen a man of great distinction and impeccable private and public record in high office and at the bar.

In 1924 the Republican was still the majority party, as a result of the abiding effect of the backwash of World War I. But its disintegration as a result of the scandals in the Harding Administration would, in my judgment, have been irreparable in 1924 had Coolidge not understood and incarnated the public-relations technique of contrast with his predecessor.

I lived in Kentucky during his time in the White House, but I went to Washington frequently and on those occasions I sometimes saw him. He was a very interesting man. He liked to pretend a lack of the sense of humor that yet was inherent in his dry, dead-pan comment on men and events, and he was perhaps the greatest practical joker among the occupants of the White House. He would create situations he knew would alarm the Secret Service or embarrass pompous bureaucrats, and then pretend innocence of any forethought to that purpose.

The method was a paradox, because he used pretense to deflate the pretentious, whom he innately despised. This strategy required him to give the impression of being cold and unsociable, whereas he was really very friendly and rather garrulous. One example of this pixie prompting was at the expense of a solemn popular illusion about the Presidency itself.

President Coolidge had a group of guests on the Presidential yacht cruising the Potomac. As he stood alone at the rail, looking out at the expanse of water, someone exclaimed, "Look at that slight and slender figure! Look at that head, bowed over the rail! What thoughts are in the mind of this man, burdened by the problems of the nation?"

Finally, Coolidge turned around, and joined the others, saying, "See that sea gull over there? Been watching it for twenty minutes. Hasn't moved. I think he's dead!"

The strategy of studied paradox, however, eventually cost him what I believe was his heart's desire—to be nominated in 1928 to run for a second term. He was the victim of his own technique that was inherent in his careful choice of words in the famous statement, "I do not choose to run in 1928." If Coolidge had said this prior to the time when many Republican leaders, during his long silence, had committed themselves to the candidacy of Herbert Hoover, I firmly believe they would have put the accent of that phrase on *run*, as I think the President hoped they would and intended they should. In effect, this would say that while he would do nothing to gain the renomination, he would be a willing recipient.

But by that time it was too late for Yankee subtlety, as Secretary of the Treasury Andrew Mellon discovered on the train bearing the Republican delegation from Pennsylvania to the convention at Kansas City. The Philadelphia party boss, William S. Vare, easily overrode Mellon's effort to register the delegation in favor of renominating Coolidge.

Coolidge was, however, essentially a philosopher as well as a trained professional politician. So I accept the evidence that he lost no sleep over the misfire of his strategy (if this, as I firmly believe, it was); and found a contentment in private life that deepened with the growing harvest of political and economic disaster his successor was fated to reap from the evil seeds planted by the Republican Party in the 1918–1928 decade.

Coolidge realized, I am sure, that he had been magnificiently rewarded for the one conspicuous act of courage in the public interest by which he broke the Boston police strike. For courage, like candor, is not a sure road to high political office. And the American voters are basically responsible for the low standards that exist in the political trade. Except in the case of a national hero, such as Eisenhower, they do not reward these qualities that are considered indispensable in private individuals. As a result the professional politicians, as a species, are largely those who compromise principle, who avoid candor, and who renege on the solemn pledges of the platforms on which they stand for election.

One of the finest political reporters in the history of American journalism, a man of the highest principle in person and profession, was Frank R. Kent of the *Baltimore Sun*. It was the maxim of his experience that a newspaperman should always "look down" at a professional politician—a blown-up figure of speech, but one with which I generally agree.

One evening at a Washington dinner party given by Mrs. Dwight W. Davis, the wife of a former Secretary of War (also the donor of the Davis Cup), Senator Key Pittman of Nevada, Chairman of the Foreign Relations Committee, was among the guests. So was Kent. He had been writing very critical articles about the Democratic leadership in the Senate.

"Frank," said Pittman to Kent, "you are grieving your friends in the Senate."

To which Kent replied, "Who ever said I wanted friends in the Senate?"

For it is true that in most instances the price of friendship with a politician is too great for any reputable newspaper man to pay.

10

HERBERT HOOVER

A MAN came to dinner at my house in Washington one evening in the late 1950s, and his private personality was a stunning revelation to a company that had assumed the truth of most of the cruel criticisms that had been published about him. It was a sophisticated company, including diplomats, politicians in office and their wives. But nearly all had come to Washington after this particular guest's official tenure had ended.

He was very relaxed that night, allowing full exposure to a high degree of social grace, anecdotal humor and wit, a keen analytical talent in assaying history, men, and measures, an unusual knowledge of remote places—yet all this with a dignity of bearing both innate and impressive.

When he left, the wife of a Senator (who had furthered the false legend of a President who lacked the imagination and resolution to meet the acute problems of his time in office) exclaimed, "That just can't be Herbert Hoover." But it was.

Herbert Hoover was swept into office in 1928 in an atmosphere of euphoria and a belief that an ever-soaring condition of national prosperity was not an economic possibility or probability, but an established fact; that somehow or other the perpetual and rising affluence of the large minority would, by the mystical operations of an unwritten law of economic physics, and because of the good will toward all that was accepted as basic in the American character, percolate to the bottom of the economic vessel.

An end to poverty. A garage for everybody. Two automobiles in every garage. Two chickens in every pot.

These were not only the commonly accepted prospects of a few years. They were encouraged by the tenor of Hoover's inaugural speech and statements he made from time to time until the roof fell in on Wall Street in the autumn of 1929.

The President and his party were swept from office in 1932, after a twelve-year tenure, by a voting deluge that registered an unusually rapid reversal of public opinion. Three years of business stagnation, farm foreclosures, an appalling rate of unemployment, widespread bank failures, and indignation over the monotonous Republican chant that things "could have been worse" and were as bad as they were because of the lack of cooperation with the President and the Democratic House elected in 1930—such were the primary sources of the political tragedy of Herbert Hoover.

He had promised too much, however sincerely, and in his time this was still certain to evoke a crushing political repudiation. "In his time," because with the creation of the Welfare State that began under his Democratic successors, with Federal handouts the opiate of the people, the fact of extravagant and unfulfilled Presidential promises is no longer tantamount to the defeat of the party leader and party in power.

For example, the coincidence of a war emergency or war itself, and the favoritism of Executive acts and policies in serving the special interests of minority pressure groups over that of the country as a whole, salvaged a third term for Roosevelt in 1940 (after the New Deal had proved both unable and incompetent to redeem its promises).

I remember listening to Hoover's inaugural and reading the subsequent rosy predictions with total disbelief. A recent personal experience was somewhat responsible for my extreme dubiety. In the spring of 1928 I had conceived a new formula for another morning newspaper in New York City, and a group of wealthy friends had tentatively pledged investments in the project sufficient to give it a start. The formula was new in that it contemplated a morning tabloid devoid of the sex-and-murder stress then prevalent in tabloids.

It was to employ the largest copy desk in the journalism of that time, so that the important news of the day could be presented comprehensively but with brevity. It would publish cartoons and editorials only when they contributed significantly to public opinion; devote all of page one to a news account or news photograph when warranted; hire outstanding commentators on the drama, music, financial matters, politics, and sports; and omit such statistical matter as the stock market prices which were already provided *in extenso* by the existing New York City press.

When I submitted this idea to my employer, Adolph S. Ochs, the Publisher of *The New York Times*, he encouraged me to pursue the project, observing that it could be self-sustaining by reason of its content and a page-dimension convenient for subway reading. I proceed to make up a rough prototype, known in the trade as a "dummy" or "mockup." And among those with whom I had kept in close touch during my planning was Bernard M. Baruch, who had tentatively agreed to join substantially in financing the launching of the enterprise.

One morning, shortly after I had told him of my conversation with Ochs, he telephoned me to inquire how long I thought it would require in time and money to test whether the new newspaper would be a success. "A couple of years," I said, "during which I would be free of any pressure of any kind from its backers; and three to five million dollars."

"I don't like the look of this crazy bull market," he said. "There is a strong probability of a break before you got really going that would dry up your sources of revenue—pledges, circulation, and advertising alike."

I heeded his counsel, threw away the dummy, abandoned the project, and in October, 1929, with even greater respect for Baruch's business judgment, watched the market fall to pieces and signal the economic crash that took form in the subsequent long depression.

Thus it was that on March 4, 1929, with Baruch's warning strongly in mind, I listened with total disbelief to Hoover's inaugural portrait of mounting prosperity "just around the corner." This disbelief recurred in reverse when the Democrats managed, in 1930 and 1932, to make Hoover the goat for the collapse of these prophesies.

For I continue to believe that a full-length study of Hoover's public career will convince history that he deserves a far higher place than contemporary judgment has granted him. Long since, even in that judgment, Hoover has been acquitted of the accusation that his political opponents, especially Franklin D. Roosevelt, exploited so thoroughly that it assured defeat of his bid for re-election in 1932. This charge was that the Great Depression in the United States was a direct and avoidable consequence of his failure to use the tools at Presidential command by which the disaster could have been averted.

In public appearances this most delightful and witty of companions was dour. His speech delivery was monotonous. He could not profitably assign the economy's disastrous state to the immediately previous Administrations, because they too were Republican; he had been a ranking member of both, and he felt in honor bound not to disclose the efforts he had made in that capacity to cushion the calamitous economic nature of the consequences of official policies that he had foreseen.

These consequences were supplemented by a political one that was not in reasonable prospect when Hoover was overwhelmingly elected in 1928: the loss of Congress to the Democrats in the mid-term polls of 1930. And there was still another —the incessant, organized "smear Hoover" outpouring of the Democratic National Committee's mimeograph machine—that doomed his effort to persuade the voters in 1932 of his main contention. This contention was that if the political reversal of 1930 had not prevented him from free use of the tools of economic recovery he had fashioned (the most effective of which were later employed by his Democratic successor), he could have stemmed the Great Depression and moved the economy toward steady recovery.

The Committee's "smear Hoover" machinery had been supremely well oiled by financial contributions obtained by National Chairman John J. Raskob and put in the charge of one of the ablest political propagandists since the days of Andrew Jackson's pamphleteers and journalists, Charles Michaelson, formerly of *The World*. The daily output of personal attacks on Hoover's Presidential capacity—including a deluge of ghost-written speeches for Democratic spokesmen—fixed as a fact in the American mind the thesis that Hoover's Presidential incapacity was to blame for the outbreak and prolongation of the Depression.

A particularly impressive testimonial was uttered by Eleanor Roosevelt in her newspaper column in the summer of 1948. She wrote flatly that the accusation was without merit on the record.

In this connection there is a story, current at the time but perhaps new to middle-aged and young readers of this account of Hoover's ill-starred Administration. The story is that, one day, after Hoover had initiated major Federal Reserve loans to commercial banks and other recovery programs, former President Coolidge called on his successor at the White House. Hoover, enumerating his efforts, said he could not understand why their efforts were as yet so disappointing, and his critics growing in number and vociferousness.

"You can't expect to see calves running in the field," said Coolidge, "the day after you put the bull to the cows."

"No," replied Hoover, "but I would expect to see contented cows."

Among the basic relief measures that Hoover either conceived or supported, outstanding examples were the establishment of the Reconstruction Finance Corporation (providing emergency financing for agriculture, commerce, and industry) and the Glass-Steigall Act (modifying the eligibility requirements for loans sought from Federal Reserve banks and thereby reducing the drain on our dwindling gold supply). Moreover, in Fiscal 1932, truncated by the popular verdict in the Presidential election in which Hoover was defeated in his bid for a second term, the Federal deficit was only $2.7 billion (revenue received $1.9 billion, expenditures $4.6 billion).

With an enormously larger deficit, plus a mounting imbalance of international payments and ever-rising inflation, the Democrats nevertheless have won six of eight Presidential elections and controlled fourteen of the sixteen Congresses since 1932. But the mass handouts and group subsidies of the Welfare State have only begun to foreshadow their disastrous consequences to individual Americans. And when these consequences arrive, as inevitably they will if the spending for the Great Society is not sharply adjusted to fiscal realities, and self-reliance and acceptance of personal responsibility for good citizenship are not restored, the punishment brought home to the individual will produce the same blind mass reprisal against those in power. Also, as was not the fact in 1932, blind mass reprisal may unintentionally include among its political victims progressive citizens who are trying to restore the fundamental social order, already imperiled by widespread disrespect for the law and the craven governmental breakdown of enforcement of the public order.

I did not meet Hoover until his humanitarian labor during the First World War had been successfully accomplished—a sound program of conserving food in the United States and feeding the victims of the war abroad. This meeting was in Paris, shortly after the Armistice, and the medium of our introduction was Bernard M. Baruch, who had accompanied President Wilson to the Peace Conference. On a subsequent visit to Belgium I saw at first hand the nature and success of Hoover's labors for that people.

Later, when Hoover had ended a period of partisan indecision by finally and formally aligning himself with the Republican Party and had become the object of the amateurish effort to have him chosen as the Republican Presidential nominee in 1920, I reported the Chicago convention at which this effort came to its insignificant conclusion—a handful of delegates. The lack of interest in Hoover's candidacy among the leaders of that convention was also tangibly displayed in his headquarters, whose unpopulated space brought this comment from the celebrated humorist, Irvin S. Cobb, momentarily engaged in writing special articles for the press: "If I wanted to commit the perfect murder, I would do it, and leave the corpus delicti in the Hoover headquarters—where it would never be found."

During the Harding-Coolidge Administration, when Hoover was Secretary of Commerce, I was an editor in Louisville, and saw Hoover only on one or two of the occasions when I visited Washington. But in January, 1932, when I returned to the capital as The Washington Correspondent of *The New York Times*, he was the President of the United States. From that time until his death we had a growing professional and personal relationship, the latter developing after his Presidency into what was as much of a personal friendship as can exist between a reporter and an active participant in public affairs.

But I never encountered anyone, particularly anyone committed by public office to engage in the activist politics that was foreign to his nature, who could so totally "freeze" when a visitor's remark seemed to him to denigrate the dignity of the Presidency. This happened, among other places, at White House news conferences. And it was usually a "double freeze," because it congealed the offender as solidly as it had Hoover himself. On rare occasions this reaction can be of political benefit. But as in Hoover's case, it becomes a political liability by usage.

Inadvertently on the President's part and mine, the professional phase of our relationship led to my rift with Franklin D. Roosevelt that constantly narrowed and widened, according to Roosevelt's concept of the value to him of giving special information to The Washington Correspondent of *The New York Times*. On January 12, 1933, after Roosevelt had become the President-elect, Hoover sent for me to deliver a private message to Roosevelt. He explained that he had selected me because of his understanding that I was particularly and favorably known to Roosevelt, whose aspiration to the Democratic Presidential nomination in 1932 I had warmly supported in the cool atmosphere toward it that prevailed in the *Times* councils.

The subject on Hoover's mind was the pending measure for granting immediate independence to the Philippines. He regarded this as inimical to the immediate national interest. Since, he said, the Senate might and the House probably would override his veto of the bill, the prospect could be averted if Roosevelt would convey directly to Democratic Senate the opposition to the bill that Hoover understood to be Roosevelt's attitude.

Impressed with the President's account of the national security fears that led him to veto the bill, I felt obliged to deliver the message he requested. This I did to Roosevelt in person, by telephone to Campobello. He received it without comment, and did nothing about Hoover's request. But later I learned that Louis M. Howe, Roosevelt's most intimate adviser, had expressed the opinion to the President-elect that he should disregard the message as derived solely from Hoover's political interest, and that I was a "Hoover agent."

For some months thereafter, lasting through much of the Hundred Days after Roosevelt entered the White House, I encountered various kinds of evidence that I was far from a Presidential favorite. This status varied upward and downward for the next twelve years. But I believe that the process definitely began with my relay of the message about the Philippines bill, although on a later occasion Roosevelt assured me to the contrary.

Many years afterward, in April, 1952, I wrote a note of thanks to Hoover—for a copy of his memoirs covering the period 1920–1933—in which for the first time I informed him of my impression that Roosevelt was receptive to Howe's 1933 comment that I was a "Hoover agent." Hoover's reply to this is a good example of the wry humor that the solemnity and even dourness of his public presence so unfortunately concealed from the American people throughout his lifetime. "I knew," he wrote, "that Roosevelt made some evil remarks about you, but none so low as you mention. What you both [*sic*] do not understand is that a conscientious political leper must be careful not to infect his friends."

Yet FDR himself was an enthusiastic supporter of the proposal that Hoover should be elected to the Presidency in 1920. This was in 1919, just after the ending of the First World War. Roosevelt wrote a letter to Hugh Gibson, Ambassador to Poland during the Wilson Administration, which included the following comment:

I HAD SOME NICE TALKS WITH HERBERT HOOVER BEFORE HE WENT WEST FOR CHRISTMAS. HE IS CERTAINLY A WONDER, AND I WISH WE COULD MAKE HIM A PRESIDENT OF THE UNITED STATES. THERE COULD NOT BE A BETTER ONE.

Moreover, FDR was thirty-seven years old when he wrote this, an age of maturity for most politicians. The letter was shown to me by Gibson, with the remark that, "of course, Roosevelt didn't always feel this way about the Chief."

To every age its burdens seem the greatest, the most complex, the most exasperating and insoluble. This is one reason the American public submits to the evasions and excesses of politicians, and leaves problems for settlement by "posterity."

Every politician and the cliché-ridden American press proclaim each oncoming election as "the most important in our history," though all involve decisions on which the shape of the future more or less depends.

Thus, though the burdens of the age on President Johnson appear superficially to be the heaviest ever borne by a White House incumbent, many of them were even more painfully encountered by Hoover in his Presidency. His biggest problem, of course, was keeping a nation—perhaps even a civilization—intact while it appeared to be entering a modern Dark Age. And this one enormous problem was made up of an incredible number of smaller but crucial troubles, of which the following list names but a few: The Allied debts (still unpaid) contracted to the United States by most nations during the First World War. The development of technology, especially with respect to fiber and food production, in backward, crowded, lazy, and/or dogma-ridden nations. A hostile Congressional majority in his last two Presidential years. The disrespect for law and law enforcement and the existence of the gangster state that in his time were engendered by national prohibition (Hoover's most beleaguered phrase was to describe it as "a noble experiment") of the manufacture, use, and transport of spirituous liquors. A shattered national and world economy. The still unfulfilled quest for means to restore and maintain a peaceful world order.

The problems of nation and world continued to press on Hoover after his tenure: The disorganized waste of the Federal governing system that President Truman assigned Hoover, by then a private citizen, to check and eliminate. And the global human suffering that Truman delegated Private Citizen Hoover, in his old age, the task of trying to alleviate.

In many conversations I had with Hoover, as President, as his own party's reject, and as Presidential plenipotentiary, he discussed all or most of these problems with the penetration that was high in his superb mental equipment, a wit dry in the sense that the finest champagne is dry, and a vocabulary that evoked the reminder that, after all, this Quaker had bossed miners all over the world.

He had been less than nine months in office when the economic earthquake struck, hence the subject of recovery came up very often. On March 1, 1932, the President's mind was focused on how to dissolve the hard core of unemployment and on what he considered the more effective attack that could be made through private industry. The Democrats, he said, had a "hell of a way" of showing cooperation with him; for example, after assuring the House Republicans that the majority would bring up nothing important while the minority was off speech-making, Speaker John Nance Garner had suddenly sent artificial jobmaking legislation to the floor.

This was a bill providing $132 million for road construction, a helter-skelter, leaf-raking affair, since there then existed no national highway program. Why, said Hoover, "with all that money" only fifty-four thousand jobs would be created, directly and indirectly. Whereas a shop just opened by the Nickel Plate Railroad in Ohio put more men to essentially productive work in that state than the road-building legislation would. And when it came to creating "direct employment," Henry Ford had materialized a better idea by adding twenty-five thousand jobs to his operation.

. . . He would veto the $132 million bill, of course, but with Republican Congressmen in the "scared state they are in" a veto conceivably would be overridden. Especially since his critics in the press did not carry consistency to the point of riddling the measure in advance, which would be indicated by any analysis.

Jobs and other forms of recovery were uppermost in his mind a couple of months later (April 30). His mail and official statistics, said the President, showed that business was "looking up" under the stimulus of the Reconstruction Finance Corporation and the Glass-Stiegal Act. He smiled sourly in quoting the Congressional label put on these items—"Democratic legislation"—saying he had been obliged to "argue the Democrats" into adopting both concepts. The business stagnation after February, said Hoover, was due to the House Democratic flight from a Federal sales tax and to the agitation over a "veterans' bonus" which culminated in the pitiful encampment of jobless veterans in Washington and their rout by the military under Gen. Douglas MacArthur ("which MacArthur ordered on his own"—implying a personal disclaimer?). Now, said the President, he "had no idea" what to hope for in the way of business recovery. . . .

In the same conversation Hoover established his credentials as a prophet, though without honor, in discussing the monetary problem.

. . . If there is runaway inflation, he said, we shall go off the gold standard immediately, because foreign governments will demand their gold; and foreign investors in our securities, with gold payments guaranteed, will ask for their money. This will involve repudiation of our obligations abroad and a 30 per cent premium on gold. Ever since the 1896 Bryan campaign, bonds and mortgages in this country promised payment in gold.

. . . But scorning Keynsian theory as he did and lacking the imagination to foresee the New Deal ingenuities, his gift of prophesy deserted him at this point. For, he said, when the United States abandons the gold standard, the equities in nearly everything held by the American people will disappear, every railroad will go into receivership, "there will be a revolution shortly thereafter." With assets in currency and liabilities in gold the citizen will be pauperized. Only stockholders in banks will profit by the change. It may require—the President said he wasn't sure—an act of Congress to take us off the gold standard legally. But inflation would bring it automatically. He will bend every energy to prevent that.

. . . In December, said the President, we were within thirty days of going off the gold standard. It was then that Senator Glass was induced to abandon his original bill (for the Glass-Steigall measure). The United States is peculiarly the country that must, for the safety of its citizens, maintain the gold standard. The British obligations, for example, are payable in sterling . . .

(However, one of Roosevelt's first acts was to cancel the gold-guarantee clause in government obligations, by Executive action, taking the nation off the gold standard, with a hands-off *—noli tangere—*decision by the Supreme Court.)

. . . The President noted that he was getting more offers of support than for some time past. But businessmen are very unreasonable about Federal economy. Here is this new school of economics, which believes in balancing the budget by simultaneously reducing taxes and government costs. If an effort were made to balance the budget through economies alone, the government would not be able to perform any of its functions; even the Army and the Navy would have to disband. The President realized, he said, that the Democrats wanted to legislate an Army-Navy merger in the hope he would veto the whole so-called pending "economic" measure; although he had repeatedly told them of a way to make more savings than the merger would accomplish and still preserve the integrity of each department.

In the clearer light of hindsight Hoover's references to the "effort to balance the budget through economies alone" illustrate one of the grossest inconsistencies in the history of issues between the two major parties. After the Democrats carried Congress in 1930, and for Roosevelt's Hundred Days, it was they, not the Republicans, who made balancing the budget the basic consideration in recovery measures. The following account of Speaker Garner's dramatic gesture (with respect to budget balancing) emphasizes the paradox that was created when, after the Hundred Days, Roosevelt—emulated by his Democratic successors—buried this fiscal principle of government under a pile of recovery and social-reform spending measures.

Garner, who died recently at the age of ninety-eight, was a short, stocky man with a grizzled face, an earthy vocabulary, and sharp blue eyes under bristling white thatches. This frontal feature he shared with a party adversary in the House, over whom he scored a notable and humiliating triumph on one occasion but who was later to occupy the Speaker's chair that Garner vacated for Vice-President's. The adversary was Repre-

sentative Joseph W. Byrnes of Nashville, Tennessee, an early
and consistent advocate of the Federal anti-depression spending toward which Garner only temporarily relaxed.

The occasion of the Garner-Byrnes clash was on the issue of
balancing the budget that Garner submitted to the House in
the Seventy-second Congress. The Democrats had taken control of the House from the Republicans in the 1930 elections,
choosing Garner as Speaker and Byrnes, his unsuccessful opponent, as Majority Leader. On March 29, 1932, with the
House in revolt against the imposing of new taxes, the Speaker
took the floor in a speech whose climax was his call: "Those in
favor of balancing the budget please stand." Slowly but surely
the House rose, with the notable exception of Byrnes. But as he
looked about him at the throng that had risen to the Speaker's
bidding Byrnes began slowly to rise and was on his feet at the
climax. And when Garner, pressing his triumph, asked that all
who opposed balancing the budget come to their feet, none
responded.

That afternoon, as often I did, I visited the Speaker in his
hideaway. Certain members went there by invitation every day
to "strike a blow for liberty"—Garner's euphemism for imbib-
ing bourbon and water. The Speaker was jubilant over
Byrnes's reluctant and embarrassing submission, which he described in a Texas idiom that concerns the befouling of its own
hocks by a hooved animal. This, said Garner to me, "Old Joe
Byrnes" had certainly done that day.

When I talked with President Hoover after his defeat for
re-election on December 14, 1932, he seemed unconcerned with
his electoral fate. Instead, he said, he was worried about the
Allied debts to the United States from the First World War. It
was characteristic of him that in the moments when his country
was rejecting him, he spoke of ways of aiding it.

Moreover, Hoover felt that the Depression was economic,
even technical, in cause and substance. And since it showed no
sign of abating, neither did his interest in it. He was especially
concerned with the World War One debts America's Allies

owed her—because in his opinion, which was widely shared, the payment of the debts represented a way of easing American economic troubles. The money would certainly come in handy.

But Hoover was in a dilemma, because Europe was becoming as bankrupt as the U.S., and would not pay. It was ironic that he had made major efforts to save the Allies by proposing a moratorium on the payment of the debts in the spring of 1931—a move designed to keep intact the rapidly collapsing structure of international exchange and trade. But his 1931 effort was ineffectual in the long run, merely marking the last time the U.S. stood a chance of having the major Western European nations pay those debts. Nevertheless, in 1932 Hoover was still interested in revising the moratorium in the hopes of salvaging something of value for the United States.

He sought in vain to communicate his knowledge and fears to Roosevelt. Perhaps it was a case of an engineer meeting with a politician, and finding nothing in common to talk about. Some of the specific points that Hoover made in our December 14th talk follow:

. . . The President said he would "put the whole matter [the Allied war debts] up to Congress, which should do something but won't. [President-elect] Roosevelt will be obliged to act because default is practically certain in June if no revision has been undertaken. From Roosevelt's statement, after the White House conference, it is possible to assume that Roosevelt favors executive negotiation with the several debtors through diplomatic instead of Congressional agencies. This implies the making of a treaty, to be submitted to the Senate, and therefore excluding the House. But the House prepares the appropriation budget and, in this, the war-debt payments figure. If it is constitutionally possible for the President to make a treaty arrangement with our debtors, through Executive and Senate action, the House could and would balk it through the appropriations weapon it holds." So, said Hoover, he was in doubt as to just how Roosevelt proposed to proceed.

(By shelving the issue, as it turned out.)

. . . Hoover noted one omission in a then recent economic speech of (Premier of France Édouard) Herriot. The Premier never mentioned capacity to pay. Hoover said there must be such a yardstick, though it may frequently be remeasured. France used capacity to pay in fixing the German reparations and later, at Lausanne, in reducing them. Why should we not use it in measuring payments legally due us?

. . . Revision could not be unilateral. The important thing to do was to stabilize foreign currencies. Unless this was done there could be no rise in commodity prices, and until that happened there could be no recovery. Except for our gold, that held in the world by governments was deliberately immobilized. Since gold, for our generation at least, was the standard of value, gold must be mobilized if currencies are to be stabilized. Hoover said there must be reduction of armament, and we must be given some material concession in exchange for revising the debts downward. All this was for the agenda of an international conference, which cannot be avoided if any recovery is to come.

(This conference, in London, May, 1933, was torpedoed by the FDR telegram reverting U.S. policy stresses to domestic affairs.)

. . . These background matters of economics settled in the conferences, we could then take up debt revision separately with our debtors.

. . . The British behaved admirably in the debt business and deserve all sympathy. They have shown their sporting spirit, for they alone find real difficulty in paying. The reason they have seemed less adroit than usual is because they had to make a secret compact with France to stand with her in order to induce France to go along on reparations at Lausanne. (Prime Minister Ramsay) Macdonald authorized the compact. Of course, if a new Prime Minister came in, the arrangement may not stand.

(Herriot had not fallen when I talked with the President, but I assumed then he would consider the Anglo-French front broken, and Britain able to proceed separately.)

. . . He [Hoover] had tried his best to persuade the press not to use the word "moratorium" in June, 1931. Hoover had heard nothing but that word since then about every kind of debt and will continue to hear it. It implied suspension. He would have preferred the words "deferred payment."

. . . Roosevelt at the White House [post-election 1933] conference showed no grasp of the debt question. Apparently he had
given only a few hours study to it. The President [Hoover] did not
accuse Roosevelt of having implied full agreement. If FDR had
been fully acquainted with the issue, Hoover would have thought
so. But Roosevelt obviously wasn't clear as to what the President's
policy was.

(Party politics did not interest Hoover as such; he was surely no
professional. But he brought up the subject on December 14,
1932, commenting that Republicans had mentioned fourteen persons to him as national chairman to reorganize the party.)

. . . He was willing to sit back and watch the struggle between
the Old Guard and such Progressives as Hiram Johnson.
[Senators] Moses and Watson both wanted to be chairman. As for
[Laurence] Richey [Hoover's Secretary], that story was foolish.
Richey was wanted . . . to install a new office-management system
for the committee. Anyone who knew Richey must have realized
that he was no managing politician. He was just a fine fellow who
did things for people all the time.

Hoover's philosophical adjustment to his defeat and the collapse of his ideas on how the economy could be revived was
implicit in a talk I had with him in his New York City apartment, September 28, 1937. His statements were firm but
moderate. He looked well, laughed a good deal, and used some
of the vigorous language to which he resorted in private conversation. I noted with interest that twice he referred to the
1936 standard bearer of his party, as "poor Landon." Among
the statements made by Hoover on this occasion were:

. . . There must be erected an opposition to the New Deal. If
the Republicans don't soon attempt to formulate a set of general
ideas for those opposed to the Administration the party will disappear, "as the Whigs did—the parallel is remarkable," and become
only a small tail to an opposition kite under another name.

. . . The Republican strategy of silence on the Supreme Court
fight [over FDR's packing plan] was disgraceful. Also, it was not
effective, for it was not strategy but destiny that killed Senator
Robinson. His exertions for FDR's bill, which might have been
successful, proved fatal to him on the eve of the Senate showdown.
And his death ended all chance for Congressional approval of the

program. If the Republicans will meet and formulate a set of general ideas, one may be sure that anti-New Deal Democrats will soon do the same; and in a meeting and blending a definite opposition will arise. "I am indifferent to the matter of the name [of the combination]," said Hoover.

. . . He said that returns from the "grass roots" show overwhelming support of his idea of a regular Presidential mid-term conference among Republican county chairmen. He said also that "several millions of people, I don't know how many, look to me for guidance and support me in this plan. The conference will be held, whether [John W.] Hamilton [the Republican National Chairman] and Landon like it or not. The National Committee is not at all representative of outstanding Republicanism. They are machinists and organizers." At the end of the "pitiable 1936 campaign" all was confusion among Republicans, and the Party offered them then, as now, nothing by way of a program.

. . . Hoover saw the nation heading for an economic cataclysm; he can't call the year, but it will come, in his opinion, unless the New Deal is checked or checks itself. Business [whose high executives had in 1933 appealed to Roosevelt to become a dictator] now completely lacked confidence in the President. Yet a few simple steps could alter the nation's course and prevent disaster, largely through modification and repeal of inequitable taxation features and the end of punitive threats to legitimate business and finance.

. . . Hoover said he did not believe Roosevelt deliberately intended to change our form of government; he took no stock in the dictator talk; but he thought the effect might be much the same. Meanwhile, Hoover expected a good upturn in business soon, after "a dull period." Rising costs [due to the wage-pressure tactics of the CIO] and falling prices were responsible for the then present condition.

. . . He reviewed his efforts to get statements of cooperation from the President [-elect] in the winter of 1933; said it was "nonsense" to say [a Democratic charge] that he knew nothing of the Trading-with-the-Enemy Act until René Léon [a monetary expert] mentioned it to [Treasury Secretary] Ogden Mills in May, 1932; that Attorney General Mitchell had given him a memorandum about it in February, 1932, "when we almost went off the gold standard." He had warned Carter Glass in February, 1933, that Roosevelt would devalue, and advised him to find out about it before accepting the Treasury portfolio. Glass couldn't get a denial from Roosevelt, and therefore refused to serve. If the President had cooperated [with Hoover after the 1932 election] on the war debts, said Hoover, the payments would never have stopped. Now they are ended "forever."

. . . "Some politicians will never believe me when I say that I will never stand for President again," he said, "but it is true." As a former President he intended to furnish ideas and offer guidance to "the several millions who look to me for it." He modestly agreed to my suggestion that because of the combination of his defeat, his failure to be renominated, and his unpopularity with certain powerful Republican leaders, the President [Roosevelt] is the only really national leader just now.

. . . He did not doubt at all, said Hoover, that the President had a following in the country far more than a majority of the voters, and that such a following was not to be lost on the Supreme Court issue as such.

Some of the misconceptions, encouraged by partisan propaganda, of Hoover's ideas about the conduct of the Second World War and the eventual peacemaking, are evident in the following account of communications I received from him on both subjects. He was wrongly accused of favoring a return to isolationism and "Fortress America."

. . . [Summary of a letter dated June 22, 1942] There has been a general misunderstanding of the relations between proposals made by Under Secretary of State Sumner Welles on the one hand and Hoover and ex-Ambassador Hugh Gibson [in a book] on the other. Welles used the word "armistice." Hoover-Gibson is no such concept. What it proposed was instant peace, covering [Second World War] enemy disarmament, the fixing of temporary boundaries of the *de facto* governments, restored economic relations—the latter by postwar commercial treaties. Hoover-Gibson also envisages separate commissions for the longer-view problems listed: these "could be settled in any way the victorious nations wanted at any time, since these nations" would remain under arms "to some extent"—with the "minimum forces required to maintain order in the world." If that were delayed it would be unlikely ever to take place. The "armistice" period in the First World War "was one of total degeneration all over the planet": the Hoover-Gibson formula is designed to "avoid this and the confusion of such assemblies as Versailles."

. . . [In a letter dated June 17, 1942] As a result of Roosevelt's wartime metals production program, zinc, lead, and copper ore output is declining . . . "under the same chaos that affects food." Though Hoover and certain governors have made alternative proposals, FDR's "opposition is congenital." But events will "crowd him"—diminished food supplies, increased black markets, rising prices, and "hell itself may break loose in our seaboard cities before another year is over," weakening the whole war effort on the home front.

. . . [From a letter dated September 20, 1943] The manpower situation is much worse than Washington admits, or even the survey made by [Bernard M.] Baruch for the President discloses. The shortages of labor in almost every essential industry total at least 1.5 million. Railroad maintenance and food supply are imperiled, the latter because the adequate number engaged in production is greatly composed of old men and boys. How can the Administration propose to move 1.5 million men into industry and simultaneously increase the armed forces by 1.2 million by the year's end? Why, in view of the continued shipping bottlenecks, is an increase to 7.5 million servicemen abroad from the present 2.5 million necessary by January 1?

. . . Then there are the trade-union restrictions on labor in the war plants, reducing production capacity by 20 per cent; also employer hoarding and waste of labor through cost-plus contracts; and 6 to 10 million men engaged in the lend-lease program alone. "It all raises the question whether or not we are running so fast that we will get out of breath on the home front." Germany, with 6 million of imported labor and prisoners, and 4 million more in the occupied countries, has no lend-lease obligation, and requires only short hauls for materials.

. . . [From a letter, dated April 2, 1945] The proposals at Dumbarton Oaks [preliminary to the formation of the United Nations at San Francisco] "are steadily drifting closer to the pattern of the League of Nations." Why haven't the conferees included "at least one man" experienced in the weaknesses that killed the League, or arranged to take such a man—"Felix Morley, for instance"—to San Francisco? As for the "old mandates question" that is arising again: these are fixed parts of the French and British empires. It would therefore be best to give the United States the Japanese mandated islands in the Pacific, Italian North Africa back to Egypt [then under British domination] "from which most of it was taken," and consign "the older ones to be developed for war refugees."

In May, 1954, I thought that Hoover's protean official activities, his foresight on continuing problems as revealed above, and the Presidential experience of Harry S. Truman, could be utilized to the great benefit of President Dwight D. Eisenhower in a joint interview. Truman was willing when I proposed the idea; and so was Hoover, I thought, until, seeking confirmation, I got the following note from him dated May 15: "The prospects of that meeting are pretty dim." I never knew the basis of his statement, since I had informed him of Truman's cooperative attitude. And I still don't know.

When Hoover died, I supplied *The New York Times* and its radio station, WQXR, with an appraisal of his public career and personal attributes. Two or more years later I have nothing to add or to subtract. It follows:

> The career of a great man is often a record of paradoxes. Perhaps there never was a better example of this than the career of Herbert Hoover.
>
> The Republican Party management wanted no more to nominate him for President in 1928 than they did in 1920. In 1920 they treated his candidacy as a joke. Hoover, they said, had just made up his mind which party he belonged to, and now, look, he wants to be President. . . . But by 1928 Herbert Hoover was so dominantly the choice of the Republican rank and file that the professionals were obliged to give way to a popular demand. The strength of this was conclusively demonstrated by his subsequent overwhelming election as President.
>
> In 1932 the party leaders were obliged to renominate Hoover because, though the downward plunge in the economy made his defeat a probability, rejection by his party would have made the defeat of the party's national, state, and local ticket a certainty. The paradox here was that the very popular preference which thrust him into the highest and most powerful office in the gift of the American electorate deposed him from it four years afterward. Thus, he was the only President for whose nomination, election, and repudia-

tion after one term the American people, and not the party
leaders, were wholly responsible.

Another paradox of his career was that, while his achievements in non-political fields, not personality or political party
strategy, elevated him to the Presidency, the latter were important causes of his failure to be re-elected.

Warm, witty, and forceful in his private exposure, Herbert
Hoover was cold, heavy, and alternately too blunt or uncertain in his public exposure. Masterly in his grasp of the facts
and portents of issues as he expounded them in executive
sessions, and with a brilliance of mentality rarely matched in
our history, his public presentations were usually somber,
complex, and pedestrian. Not until the American people in
later years read his memoirs, and brief occasional speeches on
topics far above the purely partisan conflict, did they realize
the warmth, wit, forcefulness, and brilliance familiar to the
few who really knew Herbert Hoover.

But there was a third cause of his defeat for re-election to
the Presidency in 1932. Had this not materialized, the handi-
caps of public personality and professional incompetence in
politics might have been overcome. This third cause was hard
luck. When a President of the United States has hard luck,
even proved ability to make great contributions to his country
and his times is futile to survive the blows of fate. Napoleon
recognized this cruel but abiding truth when he dismissed
generals and marshals, not because they were incompetent,
but because they were unlucky. And such was the political
destiny of Herbert Hoover.

His hard luck was the arrival of the economic disaster
before he had been two years in the White House. It was the
product of world factors, the bad seed sown in the First
World War and its settlements, fertilized by statesmen, industrial managers, and greedy human beings, all blind to the
consequences of acts and policies that were animated by
vaunting personal ambition, avarice, and the trampling down
of moral values.

But Herbert Hoover was President when came the whirl-
wind that was the harvest of the evil seeding. This timing
presented the Democrats with the opportunity to lay the principal blame for the economic disaster on the incumbent of the
White House. In doing this, they far exceeded the limits of
legitimate partisanship. But the Republicans had done the

same with like opportunities. And though Hoover initiated sound measures to arrest the decline, and might if re-elected have succeeded earlier and better than his successor did, his political power and official prestige were hopelessly crippled by the Democratic attack and by his inability to convey to the people the humanitarian qualities and understanding of their plight which were essential in the desperate circumstances.

He possessed these qualities in full. But congenitally he was unable to project them, especially under the handicap of the great damage already wrought to his political power and official prestige.

Yet he made contributions to the relief of the miseries of mankind that were greater and more durable than any in his time, and over a longer period. These are his public services, which earned him the shining place in the annals of the human race that his political failure cannot obscure.

He was a great American, a great citizen of the world. On these high and solid pedestals Herbert Hoover takes his place in history.

11

FRANKLIN DELANO ROOSEVELT

THINKING back now on my relations with Franklin D. Roosevelt and his Administration—which covered a large segment of my professional life—they take form as a sort of cat-and-dog affair. Not that of animals strange to each other, but members loosely of the same household. They endure each other and for periods display affection and even admiration. But every so often nature asserts the innate conflicts of the species.

Nature, in this instance, was the built-in difference between the obligations of a reporter and the personal and public interests of a politician. My difference with Roosevelt was the more acute because I was the correspondent in Washington of the newspaper he had been reared on; and since he had the common distaste for criticism of men in office, his distaste for and resentment of mine had this added provocation.

It may also be that FDR's attitude became negative as my obligation moved more and more into critical analysis of his execution of the lofty, awesome responsibility of the leadership of the United States and the hope of men of good will throughout the world. In earlier years, however, I was persuaded that FDR somewhat reciprocated my personal liking and admiration for him.

After the many years in which Roosevelt was the center of my thoughts and professional activities, I set down a kind of balance sheet for clarification of my own judgment. This was in January, 1945, about four months before his death; perhaps my tally was prompted by a face-to-face meeting with the President (of which more later) from which I drew the conclusion that despite the public reassurances of his doctors to the contrary, he was moribund.

Here is the balance sheet I composed at the time, edited only slightly for the purpose of clarifying the phraseology:

. . . *The President's virtues and political assets.* A sincere devotion to the social uplift of the underprivileged and fairer economic distribution. Congenital bonhomie. A moderate, endeavoring to salvage the economic damage to the American System inflicted by the forces of reaction. The common touch, accentuated by a complete lack of what is called "side." Industrious absorption in his great tasks. A quick mind. Human compassion. A vivid interest in all the aspects of nature, especially the sea. Hatred of government systems built and maintained through armed force and other forms of oppression. Love of country and of family and friends. Quick and graceful adaptability to any environment, and a capacity of adjusting to events that often made retreat resemble standing fast. A very special charm in private and public behavior—or, as it is now called, charisma. A deep appreciation of articulate, literate and witty people. A quality of leadership rare in history.

The President's defects. Lack of intellectual depth. Too great a reliance, when thinking problems through got too tough, on what is clever and slick. A cynical approach to the trade of politics by which he ascended, notably by alliance with even more cynical city bosses. Fundamental weaknesses as an administrator. A callous or negligent reaction to the commercialization of his fame and office that some members of his family openly engage in. Too ready to persuade himself that the national interest justified glossing over or withholding the facts due the people. A disposition to view honest critics with personal prejudice, and often to punish them by questionable use of the great powers of the Presidency. Conceit and arrogance, particularly illustrated by his third-term ambition, in his estimate of his own talents as protean and absolutely indispensable to mankind. A shallow grounding in history, including that of the United States.

Superficial as this balance sheet is, and doubtless influenced in considerable degree by his several attempts to disparage my professional product—and, at least twice, my job—I continue to subscribe to its outlines.

But though my tally of 1945 attributed to him "conceit and arrogance," these traits did not manifest themselves until his election as President, and until he became aware of the great powers of the office and of his talent for evoking sweeping public approval for whatever daring use he chose to make of his powers. For example, while Roosevelt was still the Governor of New York, I got a letter from him in which he modestly mused on how he could best serve the American people in token of his gratitude for their growing preference. He wrote that a fortuneteller once told him that writing was his forte ("the first event in my life that has given me a really swelled head"). This was at a time when he could not foresee the power and glory of his future. Despite the humorous caveat, the letter indicated a feeling that the fortuneteller might have disclosed his basic and most useful endowment—an illusion that John F. Kennedy was later to share and reluctantly subordinate to politics. Men in Roosevelt's position at the time (afflicted as he was physically as a contender in the national forum) are wont to indulge in this kind of speculation. But as it developed, the "writing" talent Roosevelt had was largely a capacity to organize the content of a speech, to sublimate ponderous official rhetoric into simple and arresting phrases, not always his own, and to electrify routine campaign oratory with an extempore interpolation.

Of these last-minute interpolations, entirely his own, two are the most famous. In a foreign-policy speech at Chicago in 1937 Roosevelt inserted a call for "quarantining the aggressors"—Nazi Germany and Japan—that changed the cautious spirit of the text as prepared by the State Department and panicked the diplomatic bureaucracy. (Satisfied with the sensation he created, and the hint of a policy not yet in being, the President did not implement the policy until the inception of the lend-lease program in March, 1941.)

The second interpolation was a couple of inspired paragraphs in a 1944 campaign speech to the Teamsters Union. Not only was his written text the product of weeks of careful selection of topics by his ghostwriters, but the President had approved it and a White House press attaché (Thomas Dawes Blake) had drilled a Teamsters claque in advance so that at specified passages it would interrupt the delivery with thunderous applause.

But the prearranged effects of both this stage management and the prepared text itself were lost in the rapturous tumult of the audience (which spread to the voters at large) when Roosevelt, looking up from his written arraignment of Republican campaign attacks on his record, suddenly said:

> These Republican leaders have not been content with attacks on me, or on my wife, or on my sons—no, not content with that, they now include my little dog, Fala. Well, of course, I don't resent attacks, and my family doesn't resent attacks, but Fala does resent them. You know . . . Fala's Scotch, and being a Scottie, as soon as he learned that the Republican fiction writers in Congress and out had concocted a story that I had left him behind on an Aleutian island and had sent a destroyer back to find him—at a cost to the taxpayers of two or three or eight or twenty millions—his Scotch soul was furious. He has not been the same dog since.
>
> I am accustomed to hearing malicious falsehoods about myself—such as that old worm-eaten chestnut that I have represented myself as indispensable. But I think I have a right to resent, to object, to libelous statements about my dog!

Were this and other manifestations of genius as a politician the product of his unexpected public success after affliction presumably had retired him? I do not think so; the genius was inherent. Roosevelt's character, of course, had been redefined, but not changed, by two events: first, his triumph over his physical handicap, accompanied by greater concentration than before on reading and thinking; second, the difficult political and administrative problems that confronted him from the moment he became the Democratic nominee for Governor of New York in 1928.

He was chosen because his name was Roosevelt, because he was highly personable and an object of great public sympathy, and because by that time he had qualified himself sufficiently to conduct a public debate in an impressive manner. But thereafter every gift at the disposal of the public began to accrue to him. And thereby his character was refashioned, reshaped, developed, and expanded.

If, for instance, the official misfeasances of Mayor James J. Walker had not forced on Governor Roosevelt a decision to hold hearings on a reform movement for Walker's removal—which Walker, calling the hearings deliberately unfair, obviated by resigning—I am not sure that Roosevelt would have been elected President and thus been afforded the opportunity to show the superb qualities of leadership he disclosed. Furthermore, the Depression gave him the opportunity and the power to invoke dictatorial measures that his predecessor lacked—the bipartisan muscle to impose measures invoking the great reforms made necessary by the abuse of power on the part of the capitalist system—without which I question whether he would have become a President of such notability.

Finally, had the war that began in Europe in 1939 not occurred and had the Japanese not attacked Pearl Harbor—thus opening the way for the public support he desired, but still lacked, for declared, formal United States participation—I believe that Roosevelt would have been assessed at the end of two terms as a domestic reformer whose failure at social and economic experiments had forced him to go too far. Halfway through his second term, in 1938, he had already suffered great reverses in Congress. For unlike a predecessor, Thomas Jefferson, who was devious only when necessary, Roosevelt was often devious when it was not necessary. And only the war emergency (that was the source of his third-term election in 1940) and the involvement of the United States in the war in 1944 (that assured his election to a fourth term) forestalled, I think, a popular rebuke for this quality of deviousness for its own sake.

These impressions of one of the greatest human forces in American history, past, present, and continuous, make no claim as biography or psychological analysis. But some references to his family environment—in childhood, young manhood, and full maturity—are essential even to this modest design.

That he was born and grew up amid riches, the luxuries it brings, and in a matriarchy is a matter of ample record. So are the dominant personality and far-darting public activities of the woman he married until death did them part. Nevertheless, the family presence and political influence of Eleanor Roosevelt on her husband fall within the range of this narrative.

In the early part of the first Administration, I was occasionally asked by Mrs. Roosevelt to small family dinners at the White House. She was extremely gracious and friendly. Later on I was made aware of her disapproval of what I was writing about her husband's domestic programs. And this was important, because she was even more definitely motivated as a politician than the President was.

She had stronger convictions than he on the subjects of social welfare and social progress. She was also a very determined woman—determined not only to make a career for herself so that she would not be just the President's wife, but also to make a career that would in her opinion put pressure on her husband to pursue the path of social and economic reform that he was embarked upon. (Though I believe he wanted and intended to terminate this program before it led the nation into a welfare state.) An illustration of the President's consciousness of his wife's public status was provided by a story Roosevelt himself told me.

When the U.S. decided to recognize the U.S.S.R., and Foreign Commissar Maxim Litvinov was sent to Washington to conduct the negotiations, Mrs. Litvinov (Ivy, the Commissar's English wife) was also invited. Litvinov duly arrived, but alone, and the President said to him, "Mrs. Roosevelt and I regret so much that your wife couldn't accompany you."

Litvinov replied, "Oh, well, you know. Very active woman, career of her own, constantly traveling, making speeches. Impossible to interrupt what she was doing. Came alone because she is individual in politics just as I am."

Said Roosevelt, "I *think* I understand."

Once, defending me from the President's complaint about a dispatch of mine, Joseph P. Kennedy offered the estimate that I supported Roosevelt's programs "95 per cent." "Oh, but that other 5 per cent!" was the President's retort. From what I saw and heard, I strongly doubt that Mrs. Roosevelt would have even *seemed* to agree on that "95 per cent." She took such matters too seriously even to appear to accept a statement in order to rebut it with a wisecrack.

She was not capable of such tactical fencing. And I never detected in her what is commonly rated as a sense of humor (necessarily including the capacity to laugh at oneself). But except on those occasions when, in pretended unawareness of its obvious impact, she said or wrote something damaging about an individual, she was candid and straightforward. And at all times she was, in my judgment and observation, a great woman.

There was little more than the common name to unite the Hyde Park and the Oyster Bay Roosevelts, particularly after, as Frank Sullivan phrased it, "The Oyster Bay Roosevelts are out of season." But one exception was the President's distant cousin, my close friend and fellow worker on *The New York Times*, Nicholas Roosevelt. He shared none of the bitterness toward FDR of Theodore Roosevelt, Jr., Archibald Roosevelt, or Alice Roosevelt Longworth. In fact, he probably had as objective and detached an attitude as was possible in the circumstances of not approving of the political associations of Franklin Roosevelt, but still recognizing his qualities. As witness this letter about his fifth cousin, the President, written to me in 1933:

I WISH THAT MY VERY CHARMING NAMESAKE HAD A LITTLE MORE POLITICAL BALANCE THAN HE HAS. HOWEVER, SO LONG AS WE KEEP THE OFFICE IN THE FAMILY I SUPPOSE I SHOULDN'T COMPLAIN. HE'S A SWELL FELLER—PERSONALLY —I HAVE A GREAT ADMIRATION FOR HIS PERSONAL CHARACTER. BUT I THINK . . . THAT MUCH OF HIS POLITICAL PAST IS NOT AS I SHOULD LIKE. ALSO I DISTRUST THE GANG WHICH HE HAS ABOUT HIM—ALL OF YOUR FELLOW PARTISANS OF THE NORTHERN STATES, THOUGH NOT THOSE OF THE SOUTH. I WISH HIM SUCCESS, BUT WOULD HAVE VOTED FOR HOOVER HAD I BEEN IN AMERICA. [Nicholas Roosevelt was Hoover's minister to Hungary at that time.]

. . . INCIDENTALLY, HAVEN'T SOME OF MY RELATIVES BEHAVED LIKE WHATNOTS ABOUT FRANKLIN'S RELATIONSHIP? IS IT HIS FAULT—OR MINE—TO HAVE THE SAME NAME, ROOSEVELT? AND, HAVING IT, MUST WE KEEP OUT OF PUBLIC LIFE SO AS TO KEEP THE WAY CLEAR FOR AN HEIR APPARENT?

. . . JOIN ME IN MY PRAYER TO SAVE THE COUNTRY FROM SOME OF YOUR—AND FDR'S—FRIENDS. SHADES OF HARRY DAUGHTERY AND ALBERT FALL! [Daughtery had been Attorney General under President Harding, and Fall, Harding's Secretary of the Interior, had been a principal in the Teapot Dome Scandal. And the relatives Nicholas Roosevelt plainly had in mind were his cousins Ted and Alice. His relations with Ted were personally very friendly, but he and Alice certainly did not admire each other then or since.]

My first and very slight acquaintance with Franklin D. Roosevelt was when he was Assistant Secretary of the Navy in the Wilson Administration. This acquaintance expanded in 1920, when he was the Democratic nominee for Vice-President, the expansion arising from the fact that I was serving, at the request of James M. Cox, the Democratic Presidential nominee, as assistant to the Chairman of the Democratic National Committee, George White of Ohio. This was my only experience in active politics. My main task was to keep White, an old

Klondike sourdough, from blurting out embarrassing truths to the press about the dim prospects of the national ticket. But the intimate association, with its subsequent periodic cleavages when Roosevelt was displeased with my reporting, began when he became Governor of New York in 1929.

During the 1920 campaign the Republican National Committee broke a "scandal" alleging official toleration of perversions among those confined in the naval prison at Portsmouth, New Hampshire, while Roosevelt was Assistant Secretary of the Navy. FDR called on Chairman White for assistance in preparing his defense, and I was delegated to go to Hyde Park for that purpose. In the process of turning out something suitable by way of a reply, I was an overnight guest in the house. Vivid in my memory are the handsome, vigorous, enormously attractive Vice-Presidential nominee, the charming hospitality and personality of Mrs. Roosevelt, and their well-mannered and attractive brood.

The Vice-Presidential nomination of Roosevelt was a routine operation of the political formula on which these choices are generally based. Will a prospective running mate weaken the chances of the national ticket? Or will he improve them because he has no irrepressible, open difference on party policy with No. One? Is there anything vulnerable in his personal record? And does he have a name or fame that attracts votes on its own? In 1920 Roosevelt conspicuously met all these qualifications, especially the last. In 1938, in a most desirably forgettable biography of FDR, the German writer Emil Ludwig portrayed Roosevelt as surprised at, and the convention as totally unprepared for, the proposal of his name for the Vice-Presidential nomination; and Ludwig quoted FDR to this effect.

But the facts, being routine, were very different. The following true account was written by Edward Moore of Ohio, the successful manager of the movement to choose James M. Cox for the Presidential nomination, and was left among Moore's papers at his death:

. . . After Cox was nominated in San Francisco—at about dawn in Dayton, Ohio—Moore telephoned him to remind him that when the convention reassembled, the leaders and delegates would want to know his choice for Vice-President.

. . . "Naturally, I've been thinking about this a good deal," said Cox to Moore, "and my choice is young Roosevelt. His name is good, he's right geographically, and he's anti-Tammany. But, since we need a united front, go to see Charlie Murphy [the Tammany leader] and say we won't nominate Roosevelt if he objects. He can suggest other names."

. . . Murphy [wrote Moore] said, "This is the first decent treatment I've ever received from a Presidential candidate. Thank you. This young Roosevelt is no good, but if you want him, go ahead and we'll vote for him."

. . . The go-ahead was communicated by Moore to Roosevelt. So none of this was a surprise to him by the time his name was put in nomination.

. . . When I published the refutation of Ludwig's story, in *The New York Times* of January 6, 1938, Postmaster-General James A. Farley got me on the telephone. He knew Moore's account was true, he said. Moreover, "Cox has told it to me at least ten times."

I had no further contact with Roosevelt after the Hyde Park visit in 1920 until the Madison Square Garden Convention of 1924 where FDR, now permanently crippled by the disease that struck him at the height of his physical powers, made the "Happy Warrior" speech in which he nominated Governor Alfred E. Smith of New York for President on the Democratic ticket. Though his candidate was not chosen, the speech awakened the Democratic Party as a whole to the availability of Roosevelt for high public service and to his inherent popular appeal.

It is not unique in politics that the author and the subject of distinguished eulogies, like the "Happy Warrior" speech, emerge as rivals for the same office. And this happened to Roosevelt and Smith, whose relations were made more tenuous by the facts that in 1928 Smith was overwhelmingly defeated as the Democratic Presidential nominee and Roosevelt was elected Governor of the state of their common citizenship that Smith failed to carry.

In 1930 I began to expect an ultimate complete split when,

with his re-election as Governor, Roosevelt inevitably became formidably eligible for the 1932 Presidential nomination—now having an opportunity to retrieve the party disaster of 1928. Roosevelt was already launched on "liberal" philosophies and programs of which Smith disapproved. Moreover, Smith had some reasons to suspect private negotiations by Roosevelt, looking to the 1932 nomination, with New York Democratic leaders who had previously stood firmly under Smith's political banner.

Private conversations with Smith during this period readily disclosed that he regarded Roosevelt as an opportunist with few firm political principles. This developed into their rival status at the 1932 Democratic National Convention, the "Happy Warrior" eulogy now a matter of the dead past.

The climax came when—unable to prevent Roosevelt's nomination, and with his only convention triumph over Roosevelt the adoption of the platform plank advocating repeal of the Eighteenth (the national prohibition) Amendment to the Constitution—Smith announced that he was "going to take a walk" from the party and went home.

The breach between the two former friends eventually was healed, although Smith's public campaign greeting to Roosevelt, "Hello, you old potato," was a strictly limited gesture. The real reconciliation came about in pathetic circumstances when an aging Smith, beset with financial troubles as head of corporations through which his wealthy friends had sought to make him rich, was obliged to appeal to President Roosevelt for Federal assistance with respect to the growing loss of tenants of the Empire State Building.

One day, while I was lunching with Jesse H. Jones, the brilliant manager of the Reconstruction Finance Corporation (the most successful of the government agencies coping with rebuilding industry during the Depression), he showed me a communication from the President. It mentioned Smith's troubles as narrated by Smith to Roosevelt and ended with the President's inquiry as to whether purchase of the Empire State Building by the RFC might not be a sound investment. Jones told me he had taken the communication back to the President with the request that if he wished the transaction made, he initial the document "FDR." "I wasn't going to take the responsibility of using RFC funds as a matter of compassion, easing somebody's conscience, or whatever," Jones explained to me.

He did not get the communication initialed. But he agreed that the RFC could make good use of some of the space in the building. This, to the pleasure and relief of Roosevelt, was what Jones did. Then and now I shared Jones's grief that because of misguided rich friends, who took Smith out of character by trying to make him one of them, and because of the advent of the Depression, one of the ablest and most courageous of American statesmen and administrators had been brought to humble himself before the protégé who became his successful rival.

The last time I saw Al Smith—visibly made prematurely old by his unhappy experience in business and by the blow to his pride in having to appeal to Roosevelt for financial aid—was in Penn Station in New York as we both were leaving a train from Washington. He chatted with me in the familiar, winning, gay manner. But his shoulders were drooping as he walked, and so was my heart.

Among Roosevelt's authentic gifts was that of raconteur, and of this product I particularly remember two: one was an account of a memorable personal experience he had with President Wilson before the United States entered the First World War; the other was the kind of yarn he deeply enjoyed spinning.

First: One day, after the German threat to our freedom of the seas had reached the intensity of a *casus belli*, Roosevelt—Assistant Secretary of the Navy and Acting Secretary in the absence of Josephus Daniels—sought an interview with the President to propose that the fleet be mobilized at Guantanamo as a warning to Berlin of a militant reaction. After listening, Wilson said, coldly, firmly, and simply, "No!"

As his dejected subordinate reached the door of the Presidential office, Wilson called him back to the desk. He explained that it was not his intention to be abrupt. "But," said the President, "a hundred years or more from now some respected historian, maybe a German or a Chinese or whatever, will write the chronicle of these perilous times. I do not intend that, by any act of mine, he can put upon this government the onus of affirmatively expanding the war."

Second: In 1919, when Wilson temporarily left the Paris Peace Conference to dispose of the legislation passed up to him by Congress, he invited Assistant Secretary of the Navy Roosevelt to accompany him home aboard the USS *George Washington*. A few days before disembarking the President notified the skipper, Capt. Edward Macauley, U.S.N., that he wanted to make first port at Boston instead of New York as originally planned.

"To Eddie Macauley's consternation," as Roosevelt told the yarn, "he discovered he had no chart aboard for a Boston landfall, and would have to feel his way, with such assistance as I, who had long sailed the ocean off New England, could give him. I explained that this could be very slight, considering the difference between navigating a sailboat and an ocean liner. One night, in the course of Eddie's quandary, which was concealed from the President, I was awakened in my berth by a shuddering noise. Thinking the *George Washington* must be aground, I rushed to the bridge in my pajamas and bathrobe to discover that the ship's engines had been reversed and cut off—that was the noise—and that she lay between two jagged rocks, with little way between, facing a shoreline with a row of summer cottages.

"I recognized the settlement as Nahant, where I had frequently made port. And in a general way I was able to tell Eddie where he would find Boston harbor. He then gave the orders for backing the ship out of its perilous location, and proceeded safely to Boston. President Wilson, who had not been awakened as I was when the ship's engines were reversed, was never told of what had happened."

After Roosevelt became President, I asked Captain Macauley, by then retired and member of the War Shipping Board, how much truth there was in this yarn. "None," said he.

My files disclose that throughout Roosevelt's two terms as Governor, we exchanged in much correspondence and met with some frequency. The latter included visits to Albany and Hyde Park, on his motion. Consequently I became convinced that of all of the party's possible Presidential nominees in 1932 his qualifications were outstanding, the results of the 1928 national election having made it obvious (or so I believed) that Smith (though deserving and much more highly qualified as an administrator) could never be elected to the highest office in the land.

One such communication to me, dated July 3, 1931, offers special material for Roosevelt's biographers. It reveals how closely he followed the news and press comment about him, and also a sense of humor that later was strained and often broken by the stresses of the Presidency. The communication was in the form of a fable, evoked by an editorial in *The New York Times*, which, having previously criticized him for "dipping into national problems" when he had so much to do at Albany, now criticized him for not "dipping into" a current national problem.

The fable was a political satire. In summary, it was this: An "unfortunate individual," elected to be a state Governor, found generally that he had enough intrastate problems to deal with and hence refrained from comment on those of a wholly national character. One day, however, he "foolishly" did discuss a national problem because he thought it affected his state directly, and was rebuked for so doing by "an All-Wise Press," which directed him to stick to his knitting. He obeyed the injunction strictly, refraining therefore from commenting on an "excellent suggestion" the President of the United States had made with respect to a national problem. Whereupon the same "All-Wise Press" chided him for "not commenting on national and international affairs!"

I asked him to sign this on an assumption of its future biographical value. He did so, prefacing his signature with "Private and Personal for Arthur Krock."

The policy of informing the public about the President's health in exhaustive detail began with the first illness of Dwight D. Eisenhower at Denver, early in his Administration. Under the President's direction to his press secretary, James C. Hagerty, it was expanded in succeeding illnesses to virtually clinical reports. And the accuracy of each account was regularly proved by the event.

But it was Franklin D. Roosevelt himself who first recog-

nized in 1932—though impelled to do so as an act of political
self-defense—that present and prospective health in the context
of high office was a matter of legitimate public concern and
should be met in a way the people would accept as objective
and reliable. He was moved to entrust James A. Farley with
this assignment because of mounting whispers in public, political, and medical circles that the disease which made him a
lifetime cripple would incapacitate him for the burdens of the
Presidency he was then seeking to assume.

Farley brought the whispers into the open in a speech on
July 30. Accusing the Republicans as their originators, he
disclosed that on October 18, 1930, Governor Roosevelt had
applied to the Equitable Life Assurance Society for a $500,000
policy, with the Warm Springs Foundation as beneficiary; and
that the doctors of Equitable and companies associated in the
matter had examined him and approved the issuance of the
policy.

But Farley also disclosed that "more recently" (date not
specified) Roosevelt, by now an active candidate for the Democratic Presidential nomination, had submitted to a test by
"three of the country's leading diagnosticians" of his capacity
in every respect to execute the duties of office, and that the
three had certified to this, "however high the office." Their
evaluation of Roosevelt's lameness ("which was steadily growing better," said Farley) was that, in the circumstances, it was
of no more significance than "a glass eye or premature bald-
ness."

The panel of three, it developed, had been composed of
Doctors Evan Evans, Samuel Lambert, and Foster Kennedy,
all leaders in their fields—cardiology, internal medicine, and
psychiatry. And thereby hangs a tale that was told me by an
intimate friend of one of them.

"After agreeing on their findings," he said, "Dr. Kennedy
was commissioned to prepare the public statement that all
three were to sign. He did so; he and Evans signed promptly,
but Lambert, who disapproved heartily of Roosevelt's politics,
remained looking out of the window.

" 'Come on, Sam,' said the others, 'sign up and let's get
through.'

" 'All right,' replied Lambert, picking up the pen. 'But remember, so far as I am concerned this doesn't go for above the neck!' "

Spoken, of course, in oblique jest. Nevertheless, it gives a rough idea of the pervasiveness and depth of the impression that he was a "lightweight" that swirled around FDR from the time he re-entered public life after his recovery from the attack of polio that struck him down in the early 1920s.

Our relations had continued on a basis of friendly exchanges when Roosevelt took the Presidential oath. I did not suspect for some months thereafter that they might have been altered by my act in delivering to him, as President-elect, the message from President Hoover about the Philippine independence bill. He gave no intimation of a cooling-off even when, following the delivery of the Hoover message, I telephoned him with the suggestion that in announcing that Representative Lewis W. Douglas of Arizona would be his Director of the Budget, he specify the office be raised to Cabinet rank.

For taking Douglas from the House of Representatives had required Douglas' sacrifice of a future that was leading directly to at least the Speakership; it also deprived the oncoming Administration of a very effective spokesman in Congress. Roosevelt adopted the suggestion, nothing in his reception of it indicating a change in the old relationship.

But in the course of the Hundred Days, after Roosevelt became President, people began to relay certain critical Presidential comments about *Times* dispatches I had written or, as head of the Washington Bureau, was responsible for. And with an account, too detailed from the President's standpoint, of his acid reception of Douglas' notice in 1934 that he was resigning as Director of the Budget (on the factual ground that his commitment to government economy had been repudiated by Roosevelt's approval of a heavy Federal spending program), I learned positively, for the first time, that I was in the President's black book.

This lasted for some months. It was in this period that Roosevelt declined my request to come to see him for an exploration of his grievances, and wrote the letter of complaint to the Publisher of *The New York Times* that was virtually a suggestion I be replaced in Washington.

But this was also the period of changing policy, in repudiation of the platform on which Roosevelt was elected in 1932; and the period that forecast that the New Deal, even when the First was vastly expanded and socialized by the Second, would not solve the economic problems that had materialized during the Depression, prominent among them being the continued high rate of unemployment.

It required the threat of war and the subsequent involvement of the United States after Pearl Harbor to create the military-industrial complex by which the economy has been inflated and dominated ever since.

Notwithstanding Roosevelt's recurring disfavor, I had no great difficulty in reaching Administration news sources. The most satisfactory experience of a reporter is to come into possession of major news which, though its official makers attempt to defer the publication or suppress it, cannot be denied because it has reached the status of *fait accompli*. In that category was the choice of Cordell Hull by President-elect Roosevelt as Secretary of State.

Hull's name was the most prominent in the speculation as to whom Roosevelt would choose as the premier of his Cabinet when Hull was summoned to Warm Springs, Georgia, where the President-elect was selecting the occupants of the highest posts in his Administration. The then Senator from Tennessee had been infuriated by a Washington dispatch to a Nashville newspaper suggesting that he would be named Chairman of the Tariff Commission. He suspected that the dispatch was inspired to turn the mind of the President-elect to a post for him other than, and incidentally far below, that of Secretary of State. In telling me of his summons to Warm Springs, Hull angrily reflected this suspicion, assuring me that he would accept the Secretaryship or nothing.

He was living at the time in a modest family hotel, where he could not possibly have met the social obligations that go with the post. When I reminded him of these, he remarked in the most casual manner that since Mrs. Hull did not want to cope with a large house he thought that perhaps removal of his residence to a large hotel could solve this problem.

I sought out Hull immediately on his return from the conference with Roosevelt to try to learn its outcome, for the dispatches from Warm Springs had not conveyed this. He met me in the Senate antechamber known as "the President's Room." Scarcely giving me time to frame the inquiry he knew was coming, he said: "I am convinced the Carlton Hotel has the facilities to take care of that matter we were talking about the other day."

So, as soon as I could get to my typewriter I wrote a dispatch flatly stating that Senator Cordell Hull of Tennessee had been offered and had accepted the office of Secretary of State in the incoming Administration.

The New Deal began, I suppose, on a negative basis: the refusal of the President-elect, with the advice of Professor Raymond Moley, to cooperate with President Hoover on measures proposed at the pre-inaugural White House conferences that Hoover sought Roosevelt's assistance in attaining. But the positive side was initiated very promptly by the adoption of some of these very Hoover measures and by Roosevelt's association in the Bank Holiday first proclaimed by Governor Herbert Lehman of New York, the close friend and political protégé of the President-elect. And on March 8, 1933, four days after Roosevelt was inaugurated, he held a press conference, partly on and partly off the record, that supplied the details of the broad blueprint he had sketched in the Inaugural Address.

Prior to a general release of this historic document, which was to be withheld from publication until delivered, the President sent me what he said was the first copy off the White House mimeograph. I shall never know whether it was. But I took it as a thoughtful act of personal courtesy in the atmosphere of an old friendship that, so far as I was then aware, still endured.

At this news conference the President was emphatic on the

following points, the first of which, among others, was temporarily held off the record:

. . . There would be no Federal guarantee of bank deposits. A combination scrip-new currency medium of trade is being worked out, for use in the emergency, looking to a quick retirement of this government paper as business resumes. He planned to urge a managed currency as the permanent medium, but there will be no "flat money," no "starting of the printing presses." He planned also to ask Congress the next day for the broadest possible powers to deal with the emergency situation, also for authority to issue the temporary government paper as needed.

The reversal of some of these projects that ended the Hundred Days was so sharp that the following expansion of the President's press conference remarks is in order:

. . . He said it was impossible at that time, "or even by tomorrow," to draft a complete and permanent reorganization program. The situation was changing from day to day; hence details were in constant state of flux, and Congress would have all it could currently do to provide machinery to meet and deal with the situation. That is why he would have to ask for fairly broad powers. And he suggested that Congress recess after dealing with two or three emergency bills, returning in two or three weeks to work on a permanent reorganization plan.

. . . There undoubtedly were to be additional executive proclamations, chiefly for the maintenance of control on gold. He frankly admitted that he did not know for certain whether the United States was off the gold standard. He had read an article from the *New York Evening Post* that he said was an explanation of the gold standard as he understood it, and this article indicated to him that the U.S. was still on the gold standard so far as the basis of currency is concerned. As to the domestic liquidity and foreign exchange of money, he held little doubt that we were off the gold basis. His words were: "Use your own judgment."

. . . He professed very strong opposition to a bank deposit guarantee, now or in the future. He asked that this be used as strictly off the record, explaining that any announcement at this time of his opposition to a deposit guarantee might cause upheavals against the weaker banks when they resume payment. He said that some of the weaker ones surely would have to go, but held that "though we were practically out of circulating currency last Friday" a vast majority of the banks would resume operations and make good on every liability. He then suggested, and for a while tried to outline, a formula by which his opposition to the guarantee could be stated without giving new fears to depositors in smaller or weaker banks. But he came up with the conclusion that his views along this line had best be left temporarily undisclosed.

. . . He was vehement on the subject of managed currency. He said that a plan had to be evolved whereby the Federal government would have absolute control of the currency, and that the currency itself would be so readjusted as to make it capable of being expanded or contracted at the will of Federal authority.

. . . The foregoing was explained by the President as what he meant by "adequate currency" in his Inaugural Address. His idea of "sound currency," which he also sponsored in that address, was that it should be based on the unimpaired credit of the Federal government. That credit would stand before the world as incapable of being impaired, he said, when the government starts paying itself out of debt. He indicated unmistakably his belief that a balanced budget, including payments for retirement of the Federal debt, was the real standard upon which currency of this country should be based. [This belief lasted only for the Hundred Days.]

. . . The President said that undoubtedly the international problems involved in the present monetary crisis would be one of the subjects for discussion and probably for action at the coming world economic conference [in London in May, 1933]. He did not think, however, that any of our domestic difficulties properly could be made subjects for international conversations or negotiations. [This proved to be, though it was not realized at the time, a forecast of the action with which he torpedoed the London conference by excluding the fiscal and financial condition of the United States from the consideration of, and recommendations by, the London Conference. As someone described this momentous event, "FDR suddenly went native in the cosmos."]

According to my memorandum of a conversation on August 8, 1933, with James M. Cox, a member of the delegation, the United States delegation to the London Conference was under the President's instructions, when it sailed, to see that the subjects of international money stabilization, tariff, and trade treaties were on the agenda. When the delegation was about three days at sea, said Cox, the President gave notice that he had abandoned his plan to seek powers in the area of tariffs, "thus crippling the delegation in one important particular." This was no great surprise to Cox—he had felt before he left that the President was "weakening" on this point. But the shift "greatly depressed" Secretary of State Hull, the chairman of the delegation, because he had "confidently expected this grant of power" from Roosevelt to pursue his lifelong attack on international trade barriers. The gist of the remainder of Cox's statement to me was as follows:

. . . Cox and James P. Warburg, having been directed to effect international monetary stabilization, worked on the matter aboard ship. Cox, however, had not expected to find [as official fellow passengers on the *Olympic* and Presidential agents on the same matter] Professor O. M. W. Sprague, the Treasury's gold expert, and George L. Harrison of the Federal Reserve.

. . . Ten days before a stabilization agreement was in sight at London, Warburg cabled this fact and its details to the President; and receiving neither acknowledgment nor reply, he and Cox assumed Roosevelt's approval. [After returning to Washington from the conference, Warburg was told by the President that he had no recollection of having received the cable; but when Warburg produced it from the State Department files, Roosevelt recalled seeing it but said he had been so busy at the time that he hadn't paid much attention to it.]

. . . At any rate, this first stabilization agreement was repudiated by the President. With reference to the second stabilization agreement, which consisted of the issuance of a statement by the gold bloc and other powers, Cox said that he, Hull, and Warburg, having learned their lesson, decided to put the full responsibility for this on Professor Moley, the latter having by that time arrived in London with [Herbert Bayard] Swope. If another repudiation was coming, they wanted Moley to be the victim of it. So Cox, Moley, and some others had a conference, and they asked Moley what the President's monetary program was. Moley said he wasn't sure, but he believed it was outlined in John Maynard Keynes's book on the commodity dollar. "Which book?" asked Warburg. "He has written two which reverse each other."

. . . Cox then suggested that Moley get Keynes to write out a statement of monetary policy that would be satisfactory to the

President of the United States, in Moley's opinion. Moley could then, if it was agreeable to the other nations, approve it and transmit it to the President. Moley, Keynes, and Walter Lippmann then sat down and wrote the statement of July 1. It was relayed to the President, who suggested two or three slight revisions. The other nations agreed to it and so did the President's monetary advisers in the United States—Treasury Under Secretary Acheson, L. W. Douglas, and others. With Moley's approval, it was offered to the President for his, and he promptly repudiated it.

. . . There followed the President's repudiation message of July 3 to the conference, dated from the cruiser *Indianapolis* after a secret meeting with Henry Morgenthau, Jr. Upon its receipt in London, Ramsay MacDonald called Cox to 10 Downing Street. "The Prime Minister sat there looking at the message. 'How could he have sent such a message to me?' asked MacDonald. He said it was a rejection of every understanding he and the President had at Washington. He said further that he feared he would have to resign as a result of the blow. Later, in a meeting of the Monetary Commission, each delegate in turn accused the President of having gone back on his Washington understandings. MacDonald, speaking last, said he would not have mentioned the matter had others not, but he was forced to say that the criticism was justified by the facts."

. . . Secretary of State Hull said he had discovered, after Moley had left London, that he had, from the beginning of the conference, instituted a "regular spy system on all members of the American group." Credited by Hull as Moley's "chief spy" was his secretary, who sent cablegrams to a woman in Washington who delivered them to Moley. It was this as much as anything else that caused the Secretary to tell the President later in 1933 that he would not hold office if such things were allowed to go on.

. . . William C. Bullitt [first U.S. Ambassador to the U.S.S.R. and wartime envoy in Paris] "was another source of annoyance and humiliation to Cox and me [Hull]. He was constantly searching for dictaphones and spies and generally made himself offensive and ridiculous."

In his statement to me on the 1933 conference Cox said that the chief causes of the difficulties of the American delegation were the quick changes and repudiations from the President, and "his sufferance of Moley and Bullitt to plot against the prestige of Secretary Hull." But he thought also that the U.S.

selected its conference delegations poorly; that they should be composed, as the Europeans compose them, of men who have long been familiar with the subjects and who have repeatedly met the European experts on that ground. He also thought that no holder of an elective office should be a member of these delegations.

Cox predicted that "by early winter at the latest," the U.S. inflation policy would have been resolved by a 25-per-cent reduction of gold coverage and by a devaluation of the gold content of the dollar to about seventy-five cents. This, he thought, would be done "to save the NIRA experiment." (NIRA, better known as NRA, the National Recovery Administration, invoked under Gen. Hugh Johnson, was an unexampled set of private business controls in peacetime. The "experiment" collapsed when the Supreme Court found it unconstitutional).

This blow by Roosevelt to the hopes of the conference (an action which Henry Morgenthau, Jr., later Secretary of the Treasury, effectively and secretly labored) was opposed by some of the brightest intellectual lights in the Brain Trust, notably Professor Moley. This group, named by James Kieran, a *New York Times* reporter, was the most articulate ever collected in Washington until then. Consequently, their differences were expressed in emphatic terms, as witness their public airing between Harry L. Hopkins, Roosevelt's favorite troubleshooter and official anti-depression job manufacturer, and Harold L. Ickes, Secretary of the Interior.

Ickes was always busy trying to undermine Hopkins' influence with Roosevelt, and they finally reached a point where the two were personal enemies. The only thing that held them together was their common loyalty to the President. For undoubtedly the aim of each was to make Roosevelt a great and successful President.

Never, within the limits of the period when I was in a position to observe what went on in the inner circles of an Administration, was there a more interesting and able group assembled in Washington than those officials, high, medium, and lowly, who revolved around Roosevelt and took their light from him. Only a part of the satellite galaxy was the Brain Trust, largely émigrés from colleges and New York law firms who were recruited to join such pre-New Deal imports as Thomas G. Corcoran, Edward H. Foley, and Benjamin V. Cohen. The other group included Jesse H. Jones, the soundest and most brilliant restorer of the stricken industrial and financial economy; Henry A. Wallace, who came to the Department of Agriculture as Secretary with more practical information on his subject than any other Cabinet colleague had on his; Hopkins, who was to develop from an anti-depression jobmaker to a war- and foreign-policy-maker just below the President; Ickes, a difficult and controversial administrator of the public's natural resources, but devoted and very able; Dean Acheson, whose capacities have been as numerous as they have been brilliant; Francis Biddle, a firm believer in "adjusting" the Constitution to changed conditions, even when this broke both the letter of the national charter and the mold in which it was set; and Joseph P. Kennedy, unmatched for competence, imagination, and courage in the areas of fiscal and monetary economics.

The fame and visible influence on the President of these two groups had aroused such interest abroad that when Anthony Eden paid a visit to this country after resigning his Cabinet post in protest over the British appeasement of Hitler at Munich, and Kennedy (then Ambassador to London) asked me to meet Eden in New York and help him make good use of his time, I arranged a series of meetings with members of these groups at the British Embassy in Washington. He met most of them for the first time, with what effect on subsequent Anglo-American relations and the Tory Party I cannot say. But I believe that these sessions at the British Embassy contributed to the wartime cooperation between Roosevelt and Churchill, and to a better understanding of American politics and policies by the Tory Party that lasted until the Washington-London break over Suez during the Eisenhower Administration.

It may well be that the young lawyers and academics who were attracted to public service in Washington in 1932–1933 by the emergency whistled more gaily at their work than their predecessors or successors. In their spare time they turned the town, not into Kennedy's Camelot or Johnson's Texocratic capital, but a fiesta such as is held in Pamplona for the Running of the Bulls. And among their gaieties the practical joke was much favored.

Perhaps the most successful players of this game were Robert Lassiter of North Carolina and John Burling of Washington. Lassiter, a former Yale football captain, is a member of the celebrated Hanes family of Winston-Salem, North Carolina; Burling, now deceased, was the son of the head of the leading law firm of the capital, Covington & Burling. They especially delighted in making a target of Justice Louis D. Brandeis' law clerk Adrian ("Butch") Fisher, now gone to the high and rich echelons of the practice of law. And they had a standing bet with him (a law-school classmate) that they could mightily pull his leg.

In pursuance of this noble enterprise, Lassiter spent one entire evening at a party following Eugene Meyer around until he had mastered the voice, tone, inflection, and syntax of that puissant banker and eventual owner of *The Washington Post*. A few days later Fisher was summoned to the telephone by a person who introduced himself as Meyer and, by all indications, was. "I want to speak to the Justice," he said. The impressed Fisher promised, in breathlessly appropriate fashion, to put the Justice on immediately if not sooner.

A few seconds later Fisher returned to the phone to report that Brandeis was temporarily absent from his office but would surely reappear shortly and respond to the call. Whereupon "Eugene Meyer" musingly commented that he "wondered where the old s.o.b. could be."

Flushed with this victory, Lassister and Burling offered Fisher another bet to the same purpose, and it was accepted with the protest that it was like taking money from a baby. After the lapse of the usual few days, another character telephoned to request to visit Justice Brandeis.

Fisher was suspicious. But every accent and sentence construction finally convinced him that this was indeed the famous Zionist he claimed to be, and named a time and day for the engagement. Whereupon Lassiter resumed his natural voice and North Carolina accent, and the second deception was revealed.

Flushed with success, Lassiter and Burling never tried to hoax Fisher again. Being ahead, they rejected his piteous demands for one more chance.

Some members of the Brain Trust, Thomas G. Corcoran in particular, doubled as entertainers of Roosevelt in his leisure hours. As the result of an embarrassing contretemps, I was present within sight and earshot of one of these festive evenings, June 30, 1935. There follow extracts from a memorandum (dated July 1) of this strange experience that perhaps casts some added light on Roosevelt's private personality and the working atmosphere of the Administration at the time:

. . . I spent the weekend at Marwood, fourteen miles northwest of Washington, on the Potomac River, a large estate leased by Joseph P. Kennedy, Chairman of the Securities and Exchange Commission. It happened that in the previous few days I had felt obliged to write critically of the President's methods in trying to drive the wealth tax, so called, through Congress without hearings and in defiance of Constitutional procedure. Therefore, it was with a shock at noon Sunday that I learned from my host, Mr. Kennedy, that the President had decided to come out for late-afternoon drinks and dinner.

Clearly, my presence might be embarrassing to him and to me, since relaxation was his aim. Somewhat confused [by sudden notice of the impending visit] Mr. Kennedy had failed to mention that I was in the house. The day being intensely hot, I decided, instead of returning to town, to stay in my quarters upstairs, a voluntary prisoner. [Though this was at my host's polite suggestion, I should not have exposed him to the inherent possibility of FDR's discovery and displeasure—which, luckily, did not materialize—and I should have left Marwood shortly after lunch.] I was to be served my dinner on the second floor of this amazing château. The only other person present during this weekend, beside the servants, was Eddie [Edward M.] Moore, Mr. Kennedy's private secretary and companion.

At 7 P.M. I saw two White House cars coming up the drive and fled upstairs. Little did I realize how truly imprisoned I was to be.

Five Secret Service men accompanied the President, and since Mr. Kennedy had failed to mention that I was in the house, my escape would have been noticed by the cordon. This situation forced me—because of the design of the house—to be an involuntary eavesdropper on the [out-of-doors] fête. Although I moved, each time the party on the terrace moved, to the most distant room on my floor, it was impossible not to hear much of what went on.

The President was accompanied by his private secretary, Miss Marguerite LeHand; her assistant, Miss Grace Tully; John Burns, General Counsel of the Securities and Exchange Commission; and Corcoran, chief drafter of the utilities holding-company bill, which is to be voted on in Congress, amid great controversy, today and tomorrow. Mr. Roosevelt is striving to enforce the so-called "death sentence." [The "death sentence," a provision of the holding-company bill, was designed to dissolve any holding company that could not establish an economic reason for its existence—such companies having been alleged to be the source of much economic harm and little good. The bill became law two months after the Marwood incident, and unconstitutional by the end of 1935.]

The party soon became very merry. The President's laughter rang out over all, and was most frequent. After a reasonable number of mint juleps, which the President [when they were proposed] said would be "swell," they dined in the same mood. At dinner, though I was trying not to listen, the President said one thing so loudly it was impossible not to overhear him: "If I could," he said, "the way I'd handle [Senator] Huey Long would be physically. He's a physical coward. I've told my fellows up there that the way to deal with him is to frighten him. But they're more afraid of him than he is of them."

After dinner there was a movie on the law, *Ginger*, starring a child actress, Jane Withers. The President thought her excellent, and said the movie was one of the best in years.

Then Mr. Corcoran took out his accordion and the real merriment began. The President joined in all the songs, in a rather nice tenor-baritone, and finally he took the instrument and performed creditably for one unfamiliar with it.

"The night after the Chicago convention [of 1932]," the President said, "we decided we needed some campaign songs. After working all evening the only thing we turned out went 'The old GOP, it ain't what it uster be.'" This moved Mr. Corcoran to improvise: "Old George Huddleston, he ain't what he uster be" [a reference to a member of Congress from Alabama, a Democrat, who had recently defied the President on the "death sentence" provision]. The President, when this was concluded, burst out with "Old Carter Glass [the Virginia Senator who had opposed the pending measure], he ain't what he uster be," etc. No further inspiration coming, someone remarked, "Did you know [Representative Blank] once posted his wife for debt?" There were cries of horror from the ladies, and then the company turned back to the favorite song of the evening, Kipling's "Gentleman Rankers." On the repetitions of "Baa, baa, baa," the President's voice was remarkably distinguishable.

Mr. Roosevelt, as if without a care in the world, which continued to impress an unwilling but fascinated eavesdropper—for the President had been battered all week by Congress and the press— began telling stories of his college life, of his sailing adventures as a young man in which a number of dull-pated classmates [one, a Boston banker] figured in a series of amusing anecdotes. "Your taste in dumb cruisemates doesn't seem to have changed," said Mr. Kennedy, referring to the Nourmahal group with whom the President goes fishing every year—Vincent Astor, William Rhinelander Stewart, Milton Holden, and others. A hearty roar of Presidential laughter at this.

The favorite jest of the evening seemed to deal with the Yankee pronunciation of "boat." The President gave this as "bhutt." From that time on, whenever he said "boat" or "float" or any similar word, Miss LeHand would chime in with "bhutt" or "flutt." This must have happened twenty times. The President sometimes paid no attention to the interruption, which must have grown tiresome to him, but at times he conceded the jest with a laugh.

They discussed the holding-company bill briefly, and Mr. Corcoran at one point said, "I've never been drunk in my life, but if this amendment [the death sentence] goes through tomorrow, I'm going to get stinking." The President laughed heartily at this.

His stories of New England sailor-and-fisherfolk were very amusing, and very well told. He aped the Yankee accent impressively.

The singing and talk went on until well after midnight. About that time I fell asleep, pondering the paradoxes of the men who occupy the highest office in the land.

The New Deal immigrants from the colleges and prestigious law offices included some fascinating, even fabulous, characters. But it remained for the political community to supply the most fabulous of all—Senator Huey P. Long of Louisiana.

I first became acquainted with his forensic skill and his

intellectual quality at the Democratic National Convention of 1932, when Roosevelt was nominated for his first term. But in the development of a personal relationship that grew out of a strange set of unusual circumstances, I learned to know Long intimately.

At the Chicago convention he took the floor to press the claim of his (pro-Roosevelt) group of Louisiana delegates. Their credentials had been rejected by the National Committee, also by the convention committee that resolves such issues.

Long's speech, a gem of legal presentation, was also remarkable for the delicacy with which he overcame the hesitancy of politicians to unseat a woman delegate which was implicit in this case. The effect of this speech was a reversal by the convention of the findings of the two committees—to the great benefit of Roosevelt's prospect of nomination.

When these favorable appraisals of the convention speech were published under my byline in *The New York Times*, Long expressed to me his surprise at receiving objective treatment in the news columns of a journal that editorially was highly critical of his record as the ruthless political boss and tyrannical Governor of Louisiana. But once convinced that this was standard practice in *The Times*, he became a valuable and reliable news source of its Washington Bureau.

After the Senator fell out with Roosevelt in August, 1933, and embarked on his famous series of personal attacks on the President (Roosevelt, he said, was "a liar and a faker"), Long would bring me advance copies of these speeches, which had become prime news. That preference gave *The Times* an advantage over all other communications media, to which the speeches were not released until the time set for their delivery. Earlier there had been some leaks to the White House of what Long was planning to say. And the reason he gave for an act of favoritism that allowed us ample time to assess the newsworthy quality of his speeches was, "I know *you* won't tell Roosevelt."

By the time Long had become established as a national curiosity many of my friends who visited Washington, particularly those from the New York financial district, wanted to meet him. I used to invite them to my house with the Senator, knowing he would put on the colorful performance they were hoping for. And this he never failed to do.

His concept of the status of our personal terms was made known to me in a surprising manner during the Bank Holiday of 1933. I had gone to the Capitol to see another Senator and encountered Long in the antechamber while waiting for the other to appear.

"Do you need any money?" Long asked. In the course of my explanation that *The Times* was arranging to keep its employees and offices supplied with the cash necessary to continue their normal activities, he had pulled out of his pants pocket a large wallet, which seemed to be well-supplied with banknotes of high denominations.

"No thank you, Senator," I said, "but tell me, how do you happen to be so well-heeled? You first sold Bibles and other religious works, which couldn't have brought you in much more than you needed to get through Tulane Law School. Then you were State Railroad Commissioner at three thousand dollars a year, Governor at five thousand, now Senator at seventy-five hundred. Yet you maintain the family residence at Winfield, a fine apartment in New Orleans for your wife and son, and a big spread here in Washington."

"Well," he said, "you see, I am still a partner in a law firm down home; and the boys cut me in on the receipts. You know something else? There ain't a corporation doing business in Louisiana that will employ any law firm but ours, provided they can get us to represent them."

I now think he was engaging in his special form of cynical kidding because, though he was tainted with corruption, Long was a political idealist. But I was never entirely sure.

One day in the Senate, Long defended me from what he considered an attack by Senator Bennett Clark of Missouri on a dispatch of mine concerning the opposition of William Jennings Bryan to the nomination of Clark's father, the Speaker of the House, at the Democratic National Convention of 1912. Never a moderate in any view or undertaking, Long praised me and professed our friendship in extravagant terms. The result was that several diplomats who wanted to meet the Kingfish socially asked me to arrange it.

Among these diplomats was the longtime counselor of the

French Embassy in Washington, Jules Henry. National prohibition was still the law of the land when I conveyed Henry's aspiration to Long. His first reply was a question: "Do you reckon that Frenchman has some real champagne?" Being assured of this, Long selected a dinner date for what developed into an evening that will live in my memory, and did in Henry's to the day of his death.

To show his appreciation of the champagne that flowed bountifully, the Kingfish asked to use the telephone. The call he made was to Baton Rouge, and it soon became evident that the person on the other end of the line—who was getting the roughest reprimand I ever heard from one politician to another —was the Governor of Louisiana. After bloodcurdling threats by Long of what the Governor might expect—impeachment the minimum—if he obstructed a certain piece of legislation the Senator had initiated in the Louisiana Legislature, I informed the incredulous host of the identity of the party on the receiving end.

Both the Kingfish and Henry found the occasion so gratifying, each in his separate way, that a few weeks later Long asked me whether I thought "that Frenchman had any more of that champagne." On my assurance that he probably had, a second dinner was arranged—not so exciting as the first but featuring a marvelous and unbelievably candid account by the Kingfish of his activities, his likes and dislikes in national and state politics, and his transformation of the Louisiana government into a personally conducted police state.

My undesired reputation as Long's social entrepreneur brought me one day a request from two beautiful ladies—one even then a national political personage—to bring him to cocktails. Disregarding my warning that they might be giving the Senator a wrong impression of their interest, they insisted that I produce him. I don't know the details of his visit because I left the three together after a few minutes. But I can never forget the automobile trip from my office, where the Senator picked me up. We sat in the front seat of the car, the Kingfish driving. Two of his toughest bodyguards sat in the rear, shotguns on their laps. We ran through every red light, the Kingfish explaining that he never paid them any particular attention.

And when we entered the house, the armed bodyguards sat on the doorstep.

Apparently the cocktail party *à trois* was a great success, for the Kingfish informed me he had been reinvited, at his suggestion, to mix sazerac cocktails and cook a Creole dinner. But he must have been extra-ebullient on the second go-round because both ladies let the acquaintainceship drop at that point.

I believe that in the short but stormy era of his political ascendancy, before an assassin's bullet ended it in September, 1935, Long established himself as the first important architect on a nationwide scale of what Lyndon B. Johnson programmed thirty years later as "the Great Society."

His was the same Populist concept that is based on helping the underprivileged at the often ruinous expense of the prosperous, whether self-made or through heritage. Long used violent, demagogic, and corrupt means in pressing his proposals for a forced redistribution of wealth and generous subsidies for the elderly. But I credit him with sincerity generated by the desperate plight of farmers and certain urban groups that was wrought by the Depression. And the philosophy of his program to "soak the rich" with virtually confiscatory taxation was firmly based on the principle of government solvency.

He was way ahead of the New Deal and he had ample reason to feel that Roosevelt was fearful of the possible effects, on his renomination and on the Democratic Party, of the independent Presidential candidacy that Long was earnestly promoting at the time of his assassination in 1935. For Long's speeches, in and out of the Senate, had demonstrated a gift for oratory that put his opponents shakily on the defensive.

In all the years that Alben W. Barkley occupied the forefront of the political stage and was justly renowned for his ability to wither an adversary with a wondrous mixture of satire, humor, and serious argument, I saw him bested only once on the floor of the Senate—by Long.

Barkley had raked Long with all his guns, and sat down well satisfied with himself when the Kingfish rose to reply. After a palpably mocking account of the "veneration" he said he felt for his Senate party senior and of his sorrow at displeasing him, Long finished with a story. He once knew, he said, a Louisiana farmer whose piety, industry, and compassion were the model for the region in which the farmer lived. One day, when this noble character was ploughing the back forty, his wife in the farmhouse was aroused by loud groans. On investigation, she found her husband lying in a fence corner, bleeding from several ghastly wounds. He explained that while he was ploughing, the venerable farm billygoat, attracted by his posture, had gored him deeply from the rear.

"Don't take on so, honey," said the wife, as the Kingfish told the tale. "You have lived the good life and you know you are going straight to heaven and be received in full grace by God Almighty."

"Yes, wife, I know that," the dying man replied. "But I sure hate to be served up to God Almighty on the horns of a vicious old goat."

Barkley, whose gallant manner toward the opposite sex was well known to his colleagues, rose, opened his mouth, found nothing to say, and sat down.

In the early days of the New Deal, I was often a duly invited guest and participant in what were known to the insiders as "bull sessions." The participants discussed frankly, informatively and argumentatively everything that was going on in politics or government at the time. These sessions were held at the homes of individuals, and one of the most active hosts was Edmund Pavenstadt, who was in the Securities and Exchange Commission that had just been formed.

One bull session I particularly remember was held at Pavenstadt's house on the night of the day Louis D. Brandeis had retired from the Supreme Court. William O. Douglas had just announced that he was retiring as Chairman of the SEC and returning to the law faculty at Yale University.

Douglas lived beyond Alexandria, in the hills, and he had to leave early that evening. When he left the room I followed him. "Bill," I asked, "what is it about this law faculty at Yale that has drawn you back to it despite all your promise of advancement in public life and political affairs?"

"Security," he said.

"Is it more secure than any other position you think would be open to you?"

"Yes," he said. "The only way you could lose your job would be to rape the wife of the President of Yale University. But even then it would probably have to be on the campus at high noon."

I expressed the judgment that Douglas was especially qualified for "the vacancy on the Supreme Court."

"What vacancy?" he asked.

"Brandeis retired today."

"He did?"

"Yes, and I think it's within your range."

"Well, that hadn't occurred to me, but then I didn't know about the retirement."

I asked Douglas if he would object if I repeated our conversation to the Attorney General, Frank Murphy, the next day. It appeared he would not. Accordingly, I telephoned Murphy. He had a slow, soft-pitched way of speaking, and as I recounted how Douglas—an ardent New Dealer, a great favorite of the President, and a brilliant lawyer—would fit into the situation, Murphy kept saying, "That's a natural, that's a natural. . ." and then finally, "I'm going to submit that name to the President." Which he did.

Of course, there were a number of other names submitted, probably two or three by Murphy himself. But eventually Douglas was appointed to Brandeis's seat on the Supreme Court.

This was one of many experiences that grew out of bull sessions with the New Dealers. Others were very vigorous arguments about the trend and objectives of the New Deal. In those days, insofar as the objectives and most of the instruments of accomplishing them were concerned, I was generally in their favor of them. It was only after it became a habit for Roosevelt to assume and solicit autocratic powers—such as trying to control the Supreme Court by "packing" it—that I fell away from the New Deal and never returned. But in its earlier days I was its ardent supporter, as I had been of the nomination of Roosevelt.

Generally, the bull sessions were off-the-record surveys, by the people who were actually administering the government of the United States under the President, of what they had done or what they planned to do. From these I gained an insight of men, measures, motives, and ambitions in those times that otherwise I could not have attained.

A different gathering place, where the New Deal was likely to be under fire, was the 1925 F Street Club. This was established by Mrs. James (Laura) Curtis who later married John Gross of Bethlehem, Pennsylvania. She was, is, and until she dies will be, the real boss of the Club, especially in deciding who shall be admitted and who shall not.

One evening a memorable party was given there by former Representative ("Pood") Russell of Massachusetts for T. Jefferson Coolidge of Boston. The occasion was Coolidge's retirement as Under Secretary of the Treasury in the first Roosevelt Administration. Coolidge had fallen out with the New Deal fiscal and monetary policy and felt he could no longer remain in this job with dignity and propriety. In the speech he made that night he related the circumstances attending his retirement.

> When I concluded I could no longer conscientiously serve, I didn't want any argument with Henry Morgenthau [the Secretary of the Treasury]: for instance, that it was my duty to remain because of the interpretations that might be put upon it by the President's critics. So I just went in and said, "Henry, I'm resigning hereby as Under Secretary of the Treasury because I cannot support the President for a second term."
>
> Henry's face blanched. He went back with me to my office and practically helped me clean out my desk and put on my hat. The reason I gave, from which I said I could not be induced to withdraw, was enough to impel Morgenthau to get rid of me as fast as he could and almost physically assist in the process.

After a short silence Coolidge resumed.

> But it was very funny [eloquent pause]. As my successor they chose John W. Hanes [another pause] who had been unable to support Roosevelt for a *first* term!"

Dean Acheson followed with a bitingly witty speech. At that time he was on the outs with Roosevelt, who, in a show of resentment for Acheson's legal finding that the famous gold purchase plan was unconstitutional, had dismissed him as his first Under Secretary of the Treasury. According to Acheson, who spoke with deliberate hyperbole, the Administration's fiscal and monetary policy were occasionally decided by "Sistie" and "Buzzie," President Roosevelt's grandchildren, who in the mornings were wont to climb on the President's bed. Acheson had written a paper in opposition to the gold purchase plan, and it was leaked to the *Washington Post*, not by him but with the effect of making his job untenable.

A third incident of that evening was contributed by Senator Arthur Vandenberg. The election of 1936 was impending and Vandenberg was being pressed to accept the Republican Party's Vice-Presidential nomination. When this was mentioned to him, he replied that he wouldn't accept it, even if it were freely and unanimously offered. Of course, nobody believed him, myself in particular. So I bet him $10 that if the nomination were tendered, he would take it, and he bet me he wouldn't.

He kept his word at the subsequent Republican National Convention in Cleveland. There the leaders did agree on Vandenberg for Vice-President; and Col. Frank Knox, later Secretary of the Navy, who was proprietor of the *Chicago Daily News*, was assigned to go to see him in his penthouse suite and get his acceptance. Vandenberg, hearing about this, locked himself in his suite, cut off the telephone, and refused to answer the door; Knox never reached him. He absolutely absented himself from any contact until the convention had nominated somebody else. Invariably thereafter he claimed the real reason he had locked himself in was to make certain he would win the bet with me. (We had exchanged formal acknowledgments of the wager in which he referred to the parties as "A" [me] and "B" [Vandenberg].)

The 1925 F Street Club once most curiously entered a conversation I was having with FDR during one of those periods when I was in his reasonably good graces. On this occasion Roosevelt asked me why I didn't come to his news conferences anymore.

"Because," I replied, "I can't keep my objectivity when I'm

close to you and watching you in action. You charm me so much that when I go back to write a comment on the proceedings, I can't keep it in balance."

"Well," was his ironic retort, "that's very, very flattering."

"But," I said, "that's the reason. And, anyhow, *The New York Times* is quite well represented at your news conferences and I help to frame the questions asked you by the staff."

"But another thing," said FDR. "I understand you spend all your evenings at that club of Laura Curtis' where all my enemies gather."

"Mr. President, I do spend some evenings there, very enjoyably, but I would spend many more if I could make my way through the crowd of your children who are always present."

He laughed, and that ended one of my oddest encounters with FDR. For I realized not only that all manner of personal gossip was poured into the President's ear, but that he was highly receptive to it. In time I was to learn that the President even encouraged reports of the social relations of members of his Administration, down to the lower echelons, especially their relations with newspapermen.

This naturally made it more difficult for correspondents known to be in the President's disfavor to maintain liason with essential news sources. An instance of this, in my case, was provided in a conversation with Under Secretary of State Edward R. Stettinius on October 27, 1943.

Shortly after his appointment by Roosevelt, which had been sponsored by Harry L. Hopkins, I called on Stettinius, a close personal friend. "You know," he said, "we must not be seen here together because anything you write within a week afterward will be attributed to me. Bill Hassett [one of the President's secretaries] is on the Department payroll, and I feel sure he knows you are here now.

"I spent a weekend with the President at Thurmond [his Shangri-la in Maryland] recently," Stettinius continued, "and as we drove through the Blue Ridge I mentioned that General [George C.] Marshall, [Senator] Harry Byrd, and you had farms in the region. After talking about farming a bit, FDR suddenly reverted to this, saying, 'You must watch your step with Jimmy Dunn [European political adviser of the Secretary of State]. You know he and Arthur have long talks together all the time.' "

This was another facet of the tactics by which Roosevelt, except in recurring periods of friendly association, made private remarks to important policymaking officials that had the intended effect of eliminating as my news sources the more timid or self-serving among them. It was a variation from his earlier offer (previously described) to Turner Catledge of my staff to open to him channels of inside information that would be closed to me, with the result that Catledge would acquire the reputation among his Washington colleagues, and particularly with our superiors in New York, as being "well informed" when the head of the Bureau was not. Roosevelt also, to avert any complaint of official discrimination against *The Times* that I might make, took pains to include Mrs. Anne O'Hare McCormick, with whom I shared the commentary on *The Time*'s editorial page, in the small groups with whom he talked freely at intervals, and to be readily accessible to the Publisher, Arthur Hays Sulzberger.

Fortunately, by none of these devices was the President able to shut off any important information I sought that it was my *ex-officio* obligation and my business to obtain. Much of this, of course, I held in confidence. For example, through a slip of the tongue by one Administration official, a particular friend of mine, I knew well in advance the date fixed for Operation Torch, the North African invasion. And I learned, in similar accidental circumstances, of the U-2 probing flights over Soviet Union territory long before they became public knowledge by the shooting down of the U-2 piloted by Francis Gary Powers.

Some generalities concerning Roosevelt's dealings with and relations to the press can be ventured, with good support in the record. Like all his predecessors and successors—Jefferson and Jackson were publicly the patrons of journals primarily dedicated to serving their political interest—Roosevelt wanted the news of his Administration presented in the most favorable terms, and editorial comment and analysis predicated on acceptance of the official Executive line. But he did not strive for this with either the assiduousness (including intense social cultivation of reporters, editors, and columnists) of Kennedy or the abrasive, more obvious, and less candid and subtle approach of Lyndon B. Johnson. Harry S. Truman's attitude was take-it-or-leave it and Eisenhower was generally indifferent.

Roosevelt's only experience in collecting and presenting the news was as a reporter on *The Harvard Crimson*. Nevertheless, he often gave the impression that he understood these functions better than the lifetime professionals. If he was aware that his self-appraisal was deeply influenced by his clear interest in what was published about him and his Administration, he did not show it. Frequently, he would say to the White House group of reporters, "If I were writing this story, here is how I would write it." Or "If I were writing the heading on this story, here is how I would headline it." On each such occasion it was evident that he was slanting the facts to his purpose, which is easy for a President to identify with the national security.

Another example of Roosevelt's approaches to managing the news was his letter of protest in 1935 to Adolph S. Ochs, the Publisher of *The New York Times*, against my published report that Sir John Simon, the British Foreign Minister, was disliked and distrusted by the Administration in consequence of his tactics in dealing with the argument in London over future naval ratios among the United States, Great Britain, and Japan.

Previously, in May, 1933, Roosevelt had publicly singled out *The Times*'s Washington Bureau for presenting as facts "fabrications" or mere "speculations" with respect to matters of foreign policy. But in 1935, citing my dispatch about Simon, he made a direct approach to Ochs, more than broadly hinting that the international interest of the United States would be better and more factually served if someone other than myself were in charge of the Washington Bureau.

As recounted in a previous chapter, Ochs, at the suggestion of the Managing Editor, Edwin L. James, turned over the President's letter to me so that I could draft the reply. It included this sentence: "I am sure if you would discuss the article with Mr. Krock personally he could enlighten you with respect to other details" (the dispatch being based, as it was, on conversations with such high policymaking officials in the Administration as the Secretary of State).

The suggestion was not accepted at the time. But in a number of private talks I had with the President not long thereafter he failed to avail himself of the opportunity to revert to this particular complaint. And in September, 1936, I found myself an invited overnight guest at Hyde Park, listening to Roosevelt outline his "great design" for dissipating the gathering clouds of war over Europe that precipitated in blood and devastation in August, 1939. The only other person present was Miss LeHand. The account I wrote of this conversation, while it was fresh in my memory, follows in part:

. . . We talked over a wide range of subjects, but the President was concentrating on his hope to prevent a Second World War from beginning in Europe as a result of Hitler's emerging policies and ambitions. It was at that point that he told me of an idea forming in his mind—of meeting with the heads of the major states abroad. And he supposed, he said, that if he assembled the heads of these states he would have to have their premiers, too.

. . . Among the principals would be the Emperor of Japan, the Chancellor of the German Republic, the President of the French Republic, the King of Great Britain, and Stalin [if, which he doubted, he could get Stalin to sit down with Hitler]. But, emphasized Roosevelt, the plenary committee would be a "small one."

From that conversation came a dispatch I wrote a few days later in *The New York Times* that was published on page one, with pictures of some of the rulers Roosevelt had mentioned. Before publication, I informed the President through Miss LeHand of what I intended to write, on the understanding that he would not deny it, and the message I got back was to emphasize that what Roosevelt had in mind was only "a small committee." But after the article appeared the clamor mounted among my colleagues for the President to repudiate it as a fabrication. He kept our understanding to the extent of refusing any comment. But he did encourage Henry Wallace to say on his own, after a talk with the President, that in Wallace's judgment the story had no foundation. I wrote to Wallace, giving him the background, and in his reply he expressed regret for his intervention. But he wrote this to me in a private letter; to have expected him to make a public retraction was not to know his chief. As for the "great design," it died with the end of the President's re-election campaign, during which it was published.

I did not fare so well at Roosevelt's hands when, during the summer of 1938, I published a dispatch that the President had sent out "feelers" for a peacemaking conference with Hitler and Mussolini on the high seas and had been rebuffed. His public comment was that "the story was interesting and well-written, but just not so."

A few days later Frank Murphy, the Attorney General, remarked to Roosevelt that he thought the dispatch was "very useful to the President," reflecting as it did an incessant search for means to avert the war in Europe, and asked, "Mr. President, why did you deny it?" To which, according to Murphy's account to me, Roosevelt replied, "He had the timing wrong. It didn't happen when he said it did. It happened three months before."

The background of my dispatch, later confirmed by others, was as follows. One day, as always when he was in Washington, my old friend James V. Forrestal, later Secretary of the Navy and first Secretary of Defense, came to see me after talking to Roosevelt at the White House. With him was Paul Shields, a Wall Street investment banker. They said the President had told them he had sent out some feelers to see if he could arrange a meeting with the two dictators in the interest of preventing war, but he had been unsuccessful. Forrestal and Shields related this to me in the strictest confidence, which I accepted. I said to Shields, "When you get back to your office in New York, be sure you make a memorandum of this conversation, because it's historic." I think he said he would.

At any rate, about four or five days later Bernard M. Baruch and I were having lunch in Washington and he volunteered that Mrs. Roosevelt had told him a very fascinating story. It developed that the story was the same one the President had related to Forrestal and Shields. She said that the President had originated the idea, had made an effort to materialize it, and had been rebuffed. That released the news for me because Baruch was a new source, and his only stipulation—which I carried out—was not to associate him or Mrs. Roosevelt with the article in even the vaguest way.

Previously, in a letter dated November 9, 1936, I had proposed to Roosevelt that he follow through on his design (as related to me at Hyde Park) to meet with foreign statesmen if a critical situation should develop abroad, arguing that his advice would probably be sought in view of his recent landslide re-election. This letter also suggested that, for privacy, he meet the statesmen at sea, possibly in the Azores or in another haven between the United States and Europe that would be mutually convenient.

In reply, the President wrote that "the idea is perfectly pious and fascinating to ponder," but he doubted it could be executed; and that when he "dropped anchor in the harbor of X," he would find Washington reporters Robert Allen, Drew Pearson, Paul Mallon, and Walter Winchell appearing, "pencils in hand, from the mouth of a sea-going whale!" Only with the Marine Corps in charge, he wrote, could he feel safely isolated from the determined probing of the American press beneath the surface of the news.

Ultimately, the national emergency, arising from the war in Europe and then the attack on Pearl Harbor that assured American participation in the conflict on a global scale, produced a "voluntary" self-censorship by the press that in the natural interest of national security came to have the force of an imposed one. This heavy restriction on reporting and comment, in both the military and civilian areas of government activity, eased for Roosevelt the abiding Presidential problem posed by the obligation of the press to keep the people constantly informed. Behind this shield even Presidential subordinates claimed that national security made them immune from reports of such unofficial travels as Henry Morgenthau's weekend visits to his farm!

So the relationship with a probing press that had cost Roosevelt much time and trouble had become, from his standpoint, comfortably distant when he died at the outset of his fourth term. But highly pertinent to the longer period is a dissertation on their profession to the newspapermen at Hyde Park, on November 8, 1934. Here it is, as recorded by Charles B. Hurd, who was the member of *The Times*'s Washington Bureau on duty there:

> He [the President] said he thought this [interpretative newswriting] was over-done . . . , maintaining without citing examples that he frequently read reports of what was in his mind or what purported to be decisions by himself which were not so. Correspondents at the conference, principally [Ernest K.] Lindley and myself, challenged this statement in a good-humored conversation, drawing the reply from the President that what he meant to criticize most was the extreme of reporting such as that in the Daily Washington Merry-Go-Round [the daily column produced by Drew Pearson].
>
> When asked what type of reporting he thought should be engaged in he said he thought that retaining of the facts as announced would be sufficient, adding that he thought the public had enough intelligence to make its own interpretations.
>
> The news men reminded Mr. Roosevelt that such handling of the news would be little else than dissemination of Administration propaganda and, in addition, that material from other Government agencies combined with an informed background contribute to reports of Administration policies.
>
> As the upshot of the talk, the President explained that he had not meant to imply that White House correspondents were misrepresenting him but said he had been thinking mostly of the "dope" columns syndicated out of Washington, none of which was represented at this conference.
>
> Following this conference the correspondents of four press associations and of the *New York Times*, *Herald Tribune*, *Wall Street Journal* and the *Washington Post*—all who were present—carried out their work for that day by interpreting the President's reaction to the [Congressional] election results.

There were many evidences of the difficulties Roosevelt, in his Second New Deal, faced and did not overcome in his "pump-priming" efforts to establish a stable, managed economy —a failure reflected by the heavy Republican gains in Congress in the election of 1938. But one of the most illustrative episodes occurred on June 27–28 of that year.

Several days previously the United States Steel Corporation, because of deepening financial trouble, had announced a reduction in prices, and the President had commented favorably on this decision in a radio talk to the people. Though Edward R. Stettinius, then Chairman of Big Steel, had denied that the decision presaged another—that there would be no accompanying wage cuts—FDR had so construed the announcement. This interpretation greatly disturbed Thomas W. Lamont, the Morgan partner who handled the banking affairs of Big Steel, and Joseph P. Kennedy was called in by Roosevelt to try to postpone the evil hour when and if balancing wage cuts would be forthcoming.

Kennedy asked me to sit in on a talk with Lamont in Apartment C in the Waldorf-Astoria Hotel in New York City. The following are notes I made of the conversation and its sequel:

(June 27) . . . Lamont brought with him a letter from the President, written last Saturday, mentioning the denial [by Stettinius], pointing out he had not said no wage cuts *would* come, but adding that he hoped there would be none because that "would shake the confidence in which you and I are so interested." Lamont . . . commented that the corporation would go deeper in the red if it did not reduce wages, that John L. Lewis [then head of the CIO] understood its position, that the Corporation was planning conversations with Mr. Lewis after July 4. He feared Presidential reprisals. He was nervous.

Kennedy made him this proposal—have the corporation issue a statement to the effect that in order to give recovery every chance and to give proof of real cooperation with labor and government, it would try out the volume of business for ninety days under the new price schedules; if, after ninety days, the revenue loss was as great as expected and insolvency was threatened, the company would propose wage cuts to Lewis.

Kennedy then showed Lamont two memoranda, one written by T. G. Corcoran, one by Secretary Ickes, both with the President's approval. These documents proposed a way for the government to buy all its material from Big Steel if it cooperated by making no wage cuts. Corcoran's ground was that the government had a right, bids being about equal, to favor a company that was "playing ball," and, if its bids were somewhat higher, to call for new ones and give a friendly company a chance to get its business. Ickes's memorandum was more brazen and direct.

It also developed that, on Corcoran's suggestion, the President had instructed Chairman Stevens of the Tariff Commission to find some excuse for raising the tariff on iron ore. This was to strike at Bethlehem Steel, which imports its ore from Canada and isn't "playing ball."

Lamont turned pale. He said he would not ask the Steel Corporation to be a party to a deal of that sort. He said it was unfair and wrong. He asked what business was going to do in contention with a government holding such ideas.

Kennedy answered: "Tom, you are a respectable man. You can't understand these people. But you've got to. There they are. You don't have to be a party to any deal. I'm just telling you what you can expect if you hold off these wage cuts and follow my suggestion. But, forgetting the deal, my suggestion has greater value and some moral quality. Your statement will put the President in two holes. One, if business doesn't improve and you put on the wage cuts, there will be proof that the pump-priming has failed to work. Two, if you wait ninety days to see, he cannot again accuse business of failure to cooperate."

Lamont promised to discuss the proposal tomorrow morning with the steel operating heads and to meet that afternoon with Mr. Kennedy and Corcoran, whom the President was dispatching to discuss the proposal and make certain essential statements in return.

(June 28) . . . Corcoran failed to appear today in Kennedy's apartment at the Waldorf-Astoria. The explanation—since Corcoran gave none—is probably to be found in these incidents:

Last Saturday night in Washington Corcoran and two other administrative agents made direct to Stettinius the proposal that, in consideration of no wage cuts, the government would give its business to the U.S. Steel Corporation to the point of increasing that company's operations 50 per cent and reducing those of its opponents to 10 per cent. Yesterday Stettinius reported this to Lamont, who advised him to telephone to Washington [where Stettinius had been asked to appear on Wednesday, June 29, with

Big Steel's decision] that the proposal was impossible and wrong and could not be entertained. When he got through on the telephone the man to whom he spoke said: "That's all right. We've come to the same conclusion ourselves." [Nevertheless, the corporation followed Kennedy's advice not to cut wages for at least ninety days, and in the end did not cut wages at all.]

Franklin Roosevelt's Second New Deal measures produced one of those rare situations in American history in which the President and the Vice-President are fundamentally split over Administration policy. Throughout the First New Deal, particularly with respect to government regulations of the existing abuses of power in the fiscal and industrial sectors of the free enterprize system, FDR and Vice-President John Nance Garner operated as a team.

Up to the point at which Roosevelt's attack on the Depression developed into definite beginnings of the Welfare State, Garner was the President's powerful and like-minded agent in getting New Deal proposals through Congress. Garner, despite his total devotion to the principle of a balanced budget, even accepted the argument that in certain circumstances the principle be suspended temporarily.

Though Garner merely indicated in public his growing disagreement with the movement of the New Deal toward the Welfare State concept, throughout his tenure as Speaker and Vice-President this was made clearer in private ways.

For instance, whenever I wrote critically of this trend, I was likely to receive a copy of the publication from Garner with the overscrawl "good article today." And when the Vice-President reported to the President, after carrying out Roosevelt's request to scout the Senate's attitude toward the proposed packing of the Supreme Court to gain approval of New Deal legislation, I am reasonably certain that he found it pleasant to tell FDR, "Cap'n, you just haven't got the votes." (So far as I know, Garner was the only one who addressed the President as "Cap'n" in intimate sessions—a Texas metaphor for the highest command, I assume.)

John L. Lewis, both angered and alarmed over Garner's

effective opposition to organized labor's abuses of its power and legal privilege, once assailed the Vice-President as a "tobacco-chewing, whisky-drinking, poker-playing evil old man." True, he drank whisky and chewed tobacco, but not immoderately. True, he regularly played poker for high stakes with a select group of public personages in the years when Nicholas Longworth was majority leader and then Speaker of the House. Moreover, he *was* old—about Lewis's age—at the time the leader of the mine workers' union and the CIO uttered his harsh characterization.

But evil John Nance Garner was not—by any fair standard. His public service was distinguished, courageous, and honorable. He parted with Roosevelt strictly on principle. His private character, in family and other relationships, was unexceptionable. Summing up, it might be said of Garner what Schiller wrote of another:

> Heaven never meant him for that passive thing
> That can be struck and hammered out to suit
> Another's taste and fancy. He'll not dance
> To every tune of every minister.
> It goes against his nature—he can't do it.

The Vice-President was entirely willing to run with FDR for a second term in 1936 on a platform that was considerably to his left. But when, in the Second New Deal, Roosevelt steadily but vainly increased anti-depression spending to reduce unemployment to the classically tolerable level of 4 per cent, proposed a government reorganization plan that would vastly have increased the already huge powers of the Presidency, and sought to get judicial sanction for his programs by packing the Supreme Court—this was too much for Garner. And he left no doubt of his attitude with the President and his Congressional colleagues, though loyally making no public show of his basic dissent.

Garner also was opposed to a third Presidential term for the same reason Jefferson had implanted in the minds of the people so successfully that it remained unbroken for more than a hundred years. Garner's reasoning was that a third term would establish the President as a dictator, conceivably for life. This viewpoint alone made Garner unacceptable to FDR as his running mate in 1940.

But this was a superfluity, because Garner would not have accepted a third nomination in any event, even a "draft" by the Democratic National Convention. And so, being an organization man, with the precepts that go with it, he returned in silence to Uvalde, Texas—a silence concerning Democratic Presidents he maintained until he died, unless he had something complimentary to say.

The basic reason the United States was not adequately prepared for participation in the Second World War differs, of course, from the reason the same condition prevailed at our entrance into the First. Woodrow Wilson had too long hoped and firmly believed that this nation could remain a neutral in the war against the Kaiser, and he opposed rearming on what proved to have been this hollow ground. But Franklin Roosevelt anticipated for several years our role of belligerent in the Second World War that was irretrievably established when the Japanese attacked Pearl Harbor. In my opinion, third-term politics accounts for the restraint of Executive policy that was reflected in the inadequate state of our military in December, 1941.

By brilliantly skillful plays on public opinion after his re-election in 1936, Roosevelt gradually created the popular sentiment that belatedly rid him of the Neutrality Act and enabled him to make United States industry the prewar, seaborne source of Allied military supply. But to keep the people persuaded that he could achieve his stated resolve to maintain the status of non-belligerency, though he was privately persuaded to the exact contrary, was the fundamental strategy of his long-denied intention to seek a third term, a technique of which I was reminded by Governor Nelson A. Rockefeller's reiterated disavowals of any further Presidential ambition.

An essential part of Roosevelt's strategy was also to persuade the people that by the middle of 1940 the United States possessed military power strong enough to deter the Central Powers and Japan, if they were victors, from going to war with this country. Such was the purpose of his "on hand or on order" speech in May, 1940, from which the grim fact was omitted that the bulk of the deterrent was "on order" instead of "on hand," not capable of fulfillment for a long time. And this grim fact was fully exposed in the year that followed the Japanese attack on Pearl Harbor.

The inadequacy was well known to the military, and to the higher echelon of the industrialists whom the President had brought into the government after the national emergency created by the outbreak of the Second World War in Europe and the Far East. Also well known was the long hesitation of the Administration to set the industrial priorities on which depended both the establishment of an effective deterrent or an operating warmaking machine.

Baruch used to lament over both situations by the hour in private conversation, not only with the President but with reporters like myself. I reported his sound statistical evidence in a number of dispatches. But the public effect of this evidence was much diminished by the fact that Baruch would not authorize me to name him as their source. And as the President made plain to a number of callers, Baruch was boring him by repetitions of situations he knew all about, anyhow, but was dealing with in other considerations, among them his third-term strategy.

Of the numerous well-informed citizens, official and unofficial, who were factually aware of the misleading nature of the "on hand or on order" speech, none with whom I discussed it was more upset than Wendell L. Willkie. He had not yet been nominated as Roosevelt's third-term opponent, but he was already deeply engaged in the superb public-relations operation by which the nomination largely was won. And he was in the confidence of many members of the aforementioned well-informed group.

An experience, shared only by Turner Catledge, that I had with Willkie after he arrived on the convention scene at Philadelphia on June 23, 1940, would invite the suspicion that Willkie was not the political amateur he seemed were it not for the fact that neither by facial expression nor by temperament was he able to dissemble. Though I observed his behavior on occasions when dissembling was the prudent political action, his emotions and intentions always broke through.

For this reason both Catledge and I placed full faith and credit in Willkie's astounding show of political insouciance and even naïveté, of which shortly thereafter I wrote the following account:

. . . About last midnight Catledge and I set off from the Bellevue-Stratford Hotel to the Benjamin Franklin to see Alf. M. Landon [the Republican Presidential nominee in 1936]. We wanted to discover how he would eventually line up his support. As we reached the Benjamin Franklin corner we saw Willkie standing by a taxicab with Mrs. Willkie. He greeted us jovially, said he was going to another hotel to get some sleep (there was no room in his small headquarters, he had discovered), and asked us to come along so that we might talk things over.

We went to Chancellor Hall . . . where a sleepy night clerk told a sleepy bellboy (the only one) to show the party upstairs. Arrived there, Mrs. Willkie went into the bedroom to lie down. We knew she took off her shoes; we could see her small stockinged feet through an angle of the corridor between the living room and the bedroom.

I asked Willkie how things were going, a usual banality. He said he thought surprisingly well; he had many unexpected offers of support; it was a tough row to hoe; but now that he was in it he would see it through with everything he had.

I asked him if he had a floor leader. He didn't seem to know what I meant, and asked in turn if one was needed. Catledge and I, restraining our astonishment (already lively because of the smallness and amateur character of the headquarters, the stuffy little hotel, and the absence of any companions when the Willkies set out for their sleeping quarters), then explained the duties of a floor leader, and the necessity for one plus a strategy committee. We explained that since it was secondary support Willkie was seeking, and his task was to get more votes on each ballot—taken from his reserve strength after [Thomas E.] Dewey and Senator [Robert] Taft had had their "runs"—he must have a group that would manage the accessions, the rate of these accessions, etc. We described how it was necessary for him to have well-known politicians, being known (unlike himself) to the state leaders, to roam the floor, to say to this delegation that the other was about to "plump for Willkie," and regulate the pace of his bid when the time came to make it.

Willkie seemed surprised that so much organization was necessary, interested in the description of its workings and quick to understand them, though he gave the impression the plan was wholly new to him.

"Who would be a good floor leader?" he asked. I suggested Governor Baldwin of Connecticut, not dreaming the capture could be made. "He's very friendly with me," said Willkie. "I'll try to get him." Then he asked about Governor [Harold] Stassen of Minnesota. I said that as keynoter the Governor probably could not drop his neutrality. Catledge corrected me and said of course he could, as soon as his keynote was delivered; that keynoters always did. So Willkie said he'd "try" for Stassen, that he was very hopeful he could get him.

He seemed to us like a man who had set out on a mule to defeat a German Panzer division, confident of his star, sure that he needed nothing more to rout the mechanized political forces against him. If it's an act, it's a good one.

We suggested some other practical measures, none of which he seemed to have thought of previously, and he agreed to try them all. Meanwhile, the bar and room service being closed, he had sent out the bellboy for some Scotch and mineral water (no soda available); this was produced, and we made such highballs as we could, and drank them while Mrs. Willkie rested in the bedroom, and Philip Willkie, the son, lurked in the hall outside the suite, waiting to speak to his father about something that doubtless was important to him.

About two o'clock Catledge and I retired. As we walked away we expressed fear that so naïve and unprepared an attempt against the powerful professionals would not be able to recruit the natural strength for Mr. Willkie among the delegations. But we concluded that maybe this lack of organization and forethought was deliberate, and would be most effective in the end, since it showed [indicated] that little money had been used and that the one-man nominating bid was as real as it had been represented. Willkie told us he had spent from $3,000 to $4,000 in his quest; and that Russell Davenport and Oren Root, Jr., had spent another $23,000. That was all.

(Before leaving the discussion of the strategy board, I must add that Willkie at first seemed to think that Representative Charles A. Halleck of Indiana, who was to nominate him, was the only agent he needed in the convention and in the political dickering. We explained that Halleck was also a member of the Resolutions Committee and could not possibly look after everything.)

This afternoon Willkie telephoned me that he had acquired Governor Baldwin to assist him in the manner suggested, and that the Connecticut delegation would vote for Willkie on the first ballot. This curious crusade seems to be working out in a dashing manner; I had suggested Baldwin as an ideal, not a probable, recruit. Willkie added that he thought he would soon have Stassen in the harness. His headquarters are now manned by more volunteers, including beautiful girls from the fashionable world who are running the switchboard. The drive isn't at all professional yet, but it soon may be.

Before and after 1940 Willkie visited me regularly when in Washington. And in the retina of my memory is distinctly preserved a picture of him sitting across from me—intensely sparkling eyes under a bramble of black-brown hair, a face of unusual animation, large of stature, strong and resonant of voice, one long thick leg invariably draped over the arm of his chair.

In the 1940 Presidential campaign Willkie sought to establish two propositions with the voters. One was that, contrary to the "on hand and on order" speech, the nation's peacekeeping military deterrent was a shell that would be long in filling. The other proposition was that Roosevelt was pursuing policies favorable to the Allies that would make the United States a belligerent shortly after his re-election.

Among the builders of the American military defense in this period were two Republicans: Edward R. Stettinius, Jr., loaned by U.S. Steel, later made Secretary of State by the influence of Harry L. Hopkins; and William S. Knudsen, loaned by General Motors. To these Willkie vainly appealed for corroboration of his charges as to the immediate and prospective strength of this military defense, and also for corroboration of the lack of the priorities required by industry to supply it. They rejected his appeal, on the ground that what he asked would be a betrayal of their official trust. Often, in after years, Willkie expressed the judgment to me that this refusal by Stettinius and Knudsen in particular had cost him the 1940 election.

The Icarian nature of Willkie's rise in the Republican Party was grimly demonstrated at the GOP National Convention held in Chicago four years after its predecessor had nominated Willkie for President. Following his defeat by Thomas E. Dewey in the Wisconsin Presidential primary of 1944, Willkie had formally retired from further contest. But as the most recent Republican Presidential nominee, he normally would still have retained some conspicuous place in the Party councils. But since that place would have been that of a figurehead, Willkie kept away from the convention scene altogether.

One morning my telephone rang. Willkie was at the other end in New York. Could I get for his personal inspection a copy of the foreign-policy plank that was to be submitted to the convention later in the week?

"Can't you get it yourself?" I asked incredulously.

"No," he said. "You see the Republican is a very *private* party."

I relayed Willkie's request to Senator Warren Austin of Vermont to whom the writing of the plank had been assigned by the Committee on Resolutions. He gave me a copy on condition that I, as a reporter, would await its release and that Willkie would hold it in confidence. When I called Willkie back to read the plank, I explained the condition on which it had been made available to him. "Go ahead," he said, which I took to be an acceptance of the condition. During my reading Willkie made sounds over the telephone that indicated his displeasure with what he considered to be the party's neo-isolationist policy. But I was surprised, and Austin was indignant, when Willkie made a public statement critical of the plank in advance of its release by the Committee on Resolutions.

I note the incident not to pose an ethical issue involved, (conceivably he could have obtained the plank elsewhere, without restriction) but to point out that, like Icarus, the wings on which Willkie had ascended to the Party's height proved indeed to have been made of wax. In 1940 he was the enthusiastic choice of the Republican National Convention. In 1944 he was the Party nobody, on the outside looking in.

The number, proportions, and details of the immediate prewar and wartime events that must be classified as momentous and were centered in the Roosevelt Administration have already been recounted and analyzed in millions of words, with multimillions yet to come. A balance of judgment on these events must be left to historians in the distant future, if enough of the reputable archives survive incineration in the nuclear age.

For these reasons I shall limit accounts of these events, based on contemporary and necessarily narrow observations, to general outlines of things I saw or was authoritatively told. Since the American people's grant in 1940 of a third term to Roosevelt made him the principal figure in them all, I shall begin with two conversations I had with James A. Farley on this subject.

Farley, like Vice-President Garner, opposed a third term on principles he considered embedded in American democracy, and for a year or so before the 1940 Democratic Convention he fondly believed President Roosevelt shared his position. In this belief, his choice for the Democratic Presidential nominee in 1940 was Secretary of State Cordell Hull, and his personal ambition was to be Hull's running mate. In point are the conversations with Farley, the first on July 25, 1939.

Before embarking for a holiday to Europe that day, Farley called me on the telephone. "Just for your information," he said, "off the record, and it can't be written about in any way, my talk with the President at Hyde Park this weekend was very satisfactory from my standpoint. . . . I'll see you about it as soon as I get back."

"Did you," I inquired, "go frankly into everything on your mind?"

"Very frankly. And I might add that he doesn't want to get

very far away from me in the future. He wants us to work together as closely as possible."

"I presume he knows your position and what being close to it means."

"He does and you do," said Farley.

Very different indeed was our second conversation on the same subject at luncheon on March 3, 1940.

. . . Ernest K. Lindley, who had written an intimate biography of the Roosevelt Administration, had published as the President's opinion that Farley's nomination for national office, even for Vice-President, would raise the Catholic issue and perhaps bring about "another Al Smith debacle." Discussing this article, Farley said he was not sure it had been written with Roosevelt's knowledge and consent, though the political and press communities were confident of this. But Farley expressed surprise that the President had not repudiated the article, since it was widely taken as a stimulus to raising the religious issue against Farley. He said he would not bring up the subject with the President, but, if Roosevelt did, Farley would "go fully into the matter."

. . . Farley recalled that just before he left for Europe in 1939, Cardinal Mundelein of Chicago had sought him out. The Cardinal urged him not to break with the President "on anything"; advocated a third term for Roosevelt; and sought to persuade Farley that for him "the time was not ripe" to be a candidate for national office. Farley expressed the opinion that His Eminence "had been sent, presumably by the President." But never, said Farley, had he based a political action on a religious consideration, and never would he, and hence he intended to remain a candidate in the Presidential primaries in Massachusetts and New York.

. . . On one occasion, "now long past," said Farley, the President told him he would issue a statement, and named the date, taking himself out of consideration for renomination by the Party. But a little later, Farley recalled, Roosevelt had expressed annoyance and regret that Vice-President Garner had formulated his objection to a third term by becoming a Presidential candidate himself.

. . . Farley's answer was that Garner had quoted the President as saying he would be "going back to Hyde Park next January," whereupon Garner had said, "Then I'm going back to Uvalde." Garner had become a Presidential candidate, Farley said he had told Roosevelt, only "because Farley is convinced you have changed your mind" and that his candidacy was the best way to express and lead Party opposition to a third term.

. . . Our luncheon conversation of March 3, 1940, ended with Farley's acceptance that there would have to be a "showdown" one day between Roosevelt and himself at which he will "speak freely." But in public he would continue to do or say nothing, he said, to justify an accusation that he was disloyal to the President or "resentful over anything that has happened."

He kept his word, as always. But though in 1940 the evidence grew overwhelming that Roosevelt—whatever his attitude in 1939—was maneuvering for the third-term nomination, a handful of Farley delegates remained steadfast on the first ballot at the 1940 Democratic National Convention. The President wanted, and his managers used great pressure to obtain, his renomination by "acclamation"—requiring the first-ballot vote of every convention delegate. Instead, after registering their votes for Farley, they went along with making the renomination "unanimous" before the first-ballot count was officially announced. This conformed to Farley's undeviating principle of supporting the party ticket.

The foreign policy of the New Deal culminated in war, the aspect of the art that is enforced by guns and blood. Roosevelt's telegram that torpedoed the London Conference of 1933 marked the nation's retreat into the furthest corner of isolationism to which it had repaired after the First World War. Yet within a few years, in his second term, the President and his Secretary of State were privately and successfully maneuvering —with the indispensable assistance of Hitler in Central Europe and of Japan on the Asian mainland—for the repeal by Congress of the Neutrality Act.

But Roosevelt never in policy expanded the principle he expounded, in a 1937 speech, of "quarantining the aggressors" to the limitless bounds of world policing that was read into the Truman Doctrine, not by its author, but by his later Democratic successors. And though Roosevelt was late in setting up the priorities of the nation's industrial effort, we were not long involved in the global conflict that began in 1939 when he firmly announced that "Doctor New Deal" must temporarily yield to "Doctor Win-the-War."

In parallel with President Johnson's long insistence that despite ever-growing involvement in war in Southeast Asia, the nation could still have all the butter it wants and the armed forces all the armaments and men they require for victory, this marks the sharp contrast between the foreign-domestic policy combine of the New Deal, on the one hand, and that of the New Frontier and the Great Society on the other.

This transition of the New Deal foreign policy, after the concealments and the deceptions of consequences in Roosevelt's 1940 campaign oratory, was violently shattered by Pearl Harbor. This transition, and the subsequent conduct of the war, became, of course, the preoccupation of all Washington reporters.

In March, 1941, when Congress made law of Roosevelt's legislative proposal entitled "lend-lease," it appeared to many, including this reporter, that the only remaining question was the direction from which Nazi Germany and Japan would launch the attack that would make the United States a formal belligerent on the Allied side. Though the Administration and its spokesmen in Congress brazenly assured the American people that lend-lease was a program that would narrow the prospect of United States belligerency, it bore on its face the precisely opposite effect.

By engaging in lend-lease, with a starting appropriation of $7 billion, the Administration became the open supply source of the armaments desperately required by the Allies to continue their stand against the onrushing Hitler armies and Germany's brutal submarine warfare against the transport by sea of this material from the United States. And when Roosevelt authorized American merchant shipping to arm itself and "shoot back" at German warcraft endeavoring to sink American men and cargoes, this nation informally went to war in defense of the Allies. This was only a step in advance of Willkie's campaign prediction that if Roosevelt were re-elected, the troops

would be aboard the transports to the war zone within a few
months.

But before lend-lease could be demonstrated—beyond
official denials of its inevitable effect, this being the American
military intervention in the Second World War—the Administration needed more positive actions than the German submarine attacks on United States merchant shipping in the Atlantic
to solidify the American people in favor of formal belligerency.
This greater action, the assault on Pearl Harbor, was provided
by Japan under the stimulus to the war party that was furnished by the steadily widening and hardening United States
policy of economic embargoes.

An important factor in Japan's decision to bomb the Navy
base at Pearl Harbor was its knowledge that—on the President's order and over the protest of Admiral Joseph Richardson
—the Pacific fleet had been split, with part of it based on
California and the remainder positioned like sitting ducks in
Pearl Harbor.

That the Navy and Army were caught off guard in Hawaii
by the Japanese air attack has been explained and explained
away by a posse of apologists. But I was impressed by one
explanation volunteered to me by the late Maj.-Gen. Sherman
Miles, who was in charge of Army Intelligence (G-2) at the
time. He told me this:

. . . A few days before Pearl Harbor an attempt was made to
sabotage Army warplanes in Texas, on their way to Hawaii. G-2
was immediately instructed to warn General Short, commanding
on the island, to institute close vigilance against sabotage of the Air
Corps units under his command and to confirm the message. Not
receiving this confirmation, Miles was directed to send a similar
signal to Short, stressing even more strongly the warning he had
been instructed to deliver immediately after the incident in Texas.
. . . But Short, unknown to Miles, had sent the confirmation
on receipt of the first signal. And the reasons Miles—and hence his
superiors—did not know this were that Short's reply had been
erroneously delivered to G-4 (Logistics) and somehow lost in
transit to G-2. With the result that Short, getting a second warning after confirming the first, concentrated on defense from ground
sabotage. Whether the Navy, hearing of this particular stress by

Washington, was moved to do likewise, Miles did not profess to know.

. . . But in any event, the air watch in Hawaii on December 7, 1941, was in every direction but that from which the Japanese warplanes came. And the mislaying in the War Department of Short's second reply may be a partial explanation.

The canvas of wartime activity is too vast for more than a marginal sketch or two in this record of what one reporter saw and heard of it. But these are set down in the hope that they will provide some footnotes to the colossal record.

Among the high-level United States policymakers, military and civilian, who were my news sources in the war years were Secretaries of State Cordell Hull and Henry L. Stimson, Gen. George C. Marshall, Adm. Ernest King, Under or Assistant Secretaries James V. Forrestal, Robert A. Lovett, and John J. McCloy, industrial mobilization directors Donald Nelson, Ferdinand Eberstadt, Edward R. Stettinius, and William S. Knudsen, and (constantly) Bernard M. Baruch. Though Baruch's part in policymaking resembled a proximity fuse—in that it worked by delayed action—eventually many of his proposals for a more effective conduct of the war were adopted. But in a disconsolate judgment that he repeatedly expressed to me, "the adoption was so little or so late or both" that hundreds of thousands of American casualties could be attributed to the hesitations.

A conversation with Hull on December 11, 1941, four days after Pearl Harbor, indicated the administrative disorganization so typical of Roosevelt that it once led a political boss, Edward F. Flynn, his devoted admirer, to say: "The Boss either appoints four men to do the job of one or one man to do the job of four." And it may be, Flynn added, that often none of the four knew what the other three were doing or the one knew the scope of his authority. Only in this context is it astonishing that, as Hull told me, he knew nothing of the details of our losses at Pearl Harbor until I gave them to him from a list I had received privately from Honolulu.

In the memorandum I made of this conversation with Hull

the following may also help to convey the covert procedures and confused atmosphere in the Administration at the time:

. . . Hull said that toward the end of his discussions of the critical nature of American-Japanese relations with the Japanese envoys, Ambassador [Kichisaburo] Nomura and Special Envoy [Saburo] Kurusu, he had "warned everyone to expect a Japanese assault anywhere in the Pacific." Though he had mentioned only the Philippines and the Canal Zone specifically, he could not understand why Pearl Harbor never seems to have entered the minds of his hearers as another obvious target.

. . . It was "infamous," Hull said, for a fellow member of the Cabinet, Secretary of the Interior Harold L. Ickes, "to inspire newspapermen to write that Ickes had seen the Japanese threat from the beginning, had urged total embargoes and other forceful acts, but was opposed by [Hull], who had hoped to appease the unappeaseable." [These statements had been published that morning in a column to which Ickes was suspected, with excellent reason, of feeding "information."] Hull said that the President, the Navy, the Army, the British and he knew all along what our Japanese policy was, "but Ickes had not been taken into our confidence."

I asked Hull if the Soviet Union "was to become our active ally, make a separate peace with Germany and/or Japan, collapse or what?" "I wish I knew," was his answer (though the USSR had provided a clue in the prewar 1939 pact with Nazi Germany, the archenemy of Communism, that in every instance Soviet policy would be governed by the one test of whether it served the Kremlin's aggressive world imperialism). The related failure of Roosevelt to realize until shortly before his death that this factor would also govern the USSR's postwar policy has already tragically generated the Cold War and the phony "wars of liberation," whose cost to the United States is climaxed, for the time being, in Vietnam.

In unburdening himself of his private feelings on a later occasion, December 29, 1941, Hull entered into a broad review of the internal differences on the part of the Administration and the Allies toward the prospect of war. The following is from my notes:

. . . At the beginning of 1940 three opposing government groups were urging three opposing policies toward Japan. One wanted to attack them at once, saying we could smash Japan to bits. Another wanted to "freeze" everything, on the argument that Japan would never go to war with the United States. A third urged that there should be "limited freezing," insisting that the Japanese would never go to war with any nation.

. . . When Secretary Ickes announced the dispatch of two oil tankers to Vladivostock to aid the Russians, the war party in Japan made full use of the announcement to stimulate popular sentiment against the United States. The militants shut off all illuminating oil and gasoline, putting houses in blackness, and causing charcoal to be used as fuel for ordinary transportation. "This is what the United States has done to you," they said, "while arming Russia. The plan is to starve us out."

. . . Those who were urging an attack on Japan did not know, as Hull did, the proportion of our Navy that had been sent and was to be sent into the Atlantic to aid the British [and to the West Coast]. Even if that strength had been kept in the Pacific, it could not "alone" have attacked Japan. What was left could hardly have defended the Philippines. That is why Hull could not adopt the "firm" policy urged on him before the Japanese had made their dispositions in Indo-China and prepared their ground in Malaya and Thailand.

. . . The Army, the Navy, the British, and the Australians, throughout the conversations with the Japanese that began in May, kept urging Hull to avoid a break. They said they wanted time above everything else. He had proceeded in conformity with these representations.

. . . Early in November, Special Envoy Kurusu made the "bob-tailed" offer that we cease giving aid to China, accept the invasion of Indo-China, and give Japan all the oil it required for its military operations. Hull called Kurusu back a few days later and asked him if he had anything new to propose. Kurusu said "not a thing." Hull then told his Cabinet associates that the prospect was so precarious that "if an American soldier in Hawaii knocked down a Japanese," it might be used as the pretext to start the war.

. . . Two situations had made it necessary for the Administration to veto the plan of invading the off-Canadian islands St. Pierre-Miquelon [then governed by Vichy France] when the Free French first proposed it and after the coup occurred. One, the pledge made by the United States at the Havana Conference in

1940 against intervention and seizure of territory in the Western Hemisphere belonging to countries with which we are at peace, and the promise that Latin America would be associated in any defense move we made. Two, our Vichy policy, "which has kept Hitler for months from taking over the French fleet," sustained [Premier Henri Philippe] Pétain and brought [Commander of the Vichy armed forces Maxime] Weygand over to our side.

. . . To consent to, or turn out backs on, the St. Pierre coup would be to install [Vichyite Admiral Jean François] Darlan, give Hitler the excuse he wanted, and impel Admiral Robert at Martinique to attack the Free French on St. Pierre. Then they in turn might attack Martinique, Guadaloupe, and French Guiana. This would upset the delicate balance in Latin America and "produce Christ knows what kind of a mess." There was nothing to do but denounce the coup. "Churchill started off on a tangent with me about St. Pierre," said the Secretary. "But I brought him up short." The President, he said, entirely supported his policy.

One of the most dramatic episodes of the internal Administration divisions over foreign policy was the personal breach between Hull and his brilliant, experienced Under Secretary, Sumner Welles. It was basically created by Roosevelt's growing habit of secretly consulting Welles on policy moves that the President constrained him to keep to himself. Like many covert dealings of less import in Washington, this bypassing of Hull by Roosevelt became known to the Secretary. At dinner on December 21, 1943, Hull gave his version to me in the presence of only one other person, Ambassador A. J. D. Biddle, Jr. It follows:

. . . For more than two years Hull "knew" that his Under Secretary, Sumner Welles, "had joined with Vice-President Wallace . . . and their New Deal group" in an attempt to undermine the Secretary's control of policy and eventually to supplant him. Welles was encouraged to believe that he would then be made Secretary and that the President was agreeable to the plan.

. . . Welles then set out to cultivate certain publishers, columnists, and radio broadcasters, some of whom were led to believe that the choice of them to serve on secret Department committees, made by the Secretary himself, were made by Welles, and that he was the man to approach for "favors." This has influenced some of them since, producing articles highly favorable to Welles and most exaggerative of his contribution. Welles, for example, would save up information coming to the Department and release it when the Secretary left town, or make major speeches in which this information was revealed, often having been kept from the Secretary.

. . . In line with the Wallace-Welles plan [Wallace's design was to make himself Roosevelt's successor] the President was induced to sign the 1942 Executive Order that transferred control of economic foreign policy from the State Department to the BEW [Board of Economic Warfare]. This was done in Hull's absence, and the President was told that "the State Department had been consulted and approved."

. . . When Hull came back, he told the President this was an "infamous lie." The President was astonished. He rebuked Wallace . . . and canceled the order by sweeping amendment. He then informed the Cabinet how he had been led to sign the order. Wallace, "stammering like an eighteen-year-old schoolboy caught in a lie," said: "We didn't consult the State Department because we knew it would disapprove." Later consequences were the abolition of BEW and the separation of Wallace from economic foreign policy.

. . . Hull told the President that if he was not vigilant, the Wallace-Welles combination would "ruin him as Woodrow Wilson was ruined" by idealistic and reckless promises that could not be fulfilled and that the American people would not redeem. The President said he agreed. In this James F. Byrnes, then director of War Mobilization with powers that caused him to become known as "Assistant President," was most helpful. He backed to the utmost the Secretary's position as to Wallace, Welles, and others. He particularly stressed the political danger of encouraging the Wallace group and thus helped to avert the necessity of a resignation by Hull.

. . . The actual occasion of Welles's separation from his high post was the penetration into the Capitol of whispers against the Under Secretary of a scandalous nature. In referring to this, Hull said that only when he decided the whispers would "explode in Congress with great damage to the State Department" did he ask the President to request Welles's resignation. Had Welles, continued Hull, come to him for counsel when the whispering began to circulate, he would have given him an extended foreign assignment, at the end of which "the storm would have blown away." This, he said, he had told Welles at their parting, whereupon

Welles "extended his hand, I grasped it, and no further word was spoken." [They never met again.]

. . . In this same dinner conversation Hull discussed the inter-Allied controversies. At Teheran, he said, Stalin was interested only in the date and preparations for the second front. That is why he spoke roughly on several occasions to Churchill. The British backed and filled on this issue at [the previous conference in] Moscow. Hull had the advantage of being able to say, "My government expects to cross the Channel in May or before." It was a job to "keep Eden from going sour." Eden was vexed with the Russians. When he or his military advisers would say, "There are a hundred and twenty [or whatever it was] German divisions on the west coast of Europe," the Russians would reply, "Suppose there are a hundred and thirty or a hundred and forty? Does a second front depend on the number of German divisions? Does the decision to start it or not depend on statistics?"

. . . Churchill, said Hull, also was balking at Teheran. A statement by General [Henry] "Hap" Arnold, Chief of the Air Corps, a few days after Teheran, that the Germans were almost defeated by air power was "terrible," Hull thought. He didn't know whether or not the President had encouraged the statement to help out Churchill with Stalin.

The President of the United States is his own Secretary of State to the extent he wishes to be. This is implicit in the responsibility assigned to him by the Constitution for the formulation and conduct of foreign affairs. The consequences of the measure in which he seeks the "advice and consent of the Senate" prior to fixing and executing policy are entirely political, with the Senate and among the voters. The consequences of limiting the role of the Secretary of State, if the President chooses, to a mere supervisor of the conduct of his foreign policy adversely affect the international relations of the United States and internal Administration morale, especially in the State Department.

Roosevelt sought to assure the Senate's contentment that it was his silent Constitutional partner by choosing Hull, a member of that body, to be Secretary of State. Because of this strategy, the President ventured only covertly to demote Hull's

function to that of a front man when fixing on foreign policies
he knew the Secretary would argue against if informed. But
whenever this practice became known to Hull, as in the Welles
affair, the relations between the President and his Secretary of
State cooled well below the climate of intimacy and trust in
which ideally they should exist.

How much these relations had cooled was measured for me
in conversations with Hull and Mrs. Hull shortly before and
after he had retired as Secretary of State. In the first of these
conversations, September 29, 1944, Hull remarked that he
could not understand why the President "remained aloof from
him and always had someone between them in matters of foreign policy." The President, said Hull, "was basing his hope
for re-election on a foreign-policy record which I personally
made—often after talking the President out of 'some folly.'"
Nevertheless, he had never been Roosevelt's complete agent.
And he went on to say:

. . . He [Hull] did not know in advance that [Treasury Secre-
tary] Morgenthau was going to the Quebec Conference, or that he
went there to press his fanatical plan to reduce postwar Germany
to an agrarian society. And "until someone in Quebec gave [Hull]
the facts that proved it," he did not know that Morgenthau's
mission had been encouraged by the President. "It was beyond
[Hull] to fathom" why the President had dealt with him thus or
had permitted Morgenthau to do the "damage" he had done to
constructive victory in the war.

(I had learned of Morgenthau's secret errand to Quebec at
the time, and in this fashion: One day at the hour known to the
South as bull-bat time, I was summoned to partake of liquid
refreshment with an official just below the Presidential echelon.
"Do you know where Henry Morgenthau is?" he inquired. I
didn't. He suggested that I would do well to find out. As it
developed, Henry was at the Quebec Conference, pressing his
mad scheme to transform postwar Germany into a wholly agricultural nation. I also learned that his mission had received
Presidential sanction and he had left for Quebec without notice
to either the Secretary of State or the Secretary of War. That
one really stirred up the animals.)

. . . Regardless of the outcome of the 1944 election, Hull would voluntarily retire, "though he regretted leaving [his] work of the peace and with Congress."

The grave effects of the Morgenthau episode and its implications on Hull's morale extended to his health, as I learned from Mrs. Hull in a telephone conversation on October 21, 1944. The Secretary had just gone for a check-up to the Naval Hospital at Bethesda. She said that for the last month his appetite had "fallen away" and he was unable to sleep. Also, though he had a persistent cold, he insisted on telephoning his office constantly from his bed, and on reading and signing papers, until she took the situation in hand and "made him promise to go to the hospital" and submit to strict medical discipline.

. . . "This Morgenthau business was the final blow," said Mrs. Hull. To Hull, Morgenthau's was an "inconceivable intrusion in a desperate and delicate affair," and Morgenthau's lobbying with the British for his plan at Quebec, with Roosevelt's knowledge and encouragement, "might undo everything" the Secretary had accomplished, including the scheduled organization of the United Nations at Dumbarton Oaks and the cooperation with the Republicans and Congress in the field of foreign policy.
. . . The Secretary, his wife commented, "could not understand how the President could conduct matters of such grave import, and foreign affairs in particular, with such irresponsibility and deviousness."

The following notes of a visit I made to Hull in hospital, May 26, 1945, after his retirement from office and Roosevelt's death, may serve as a summing-up of this unfortunate cleavage, existing even during a time of war, between a President and his Secretary of State:

. . . Hull is dissatisfied with certain activities of our delegation at San Francisco [to organize the United Nations], particularly that relating to Argentina. He said that by the time [Secretary of State] Stettinius got there he had, it is true, little choice, but that we "lost our leadership," especially of Latin America, first at Rio ("when

Sumner Welles let the Argentines frighten him"), then at Mexico City, when Stettinius yielded to Latin American tactics he should have circumvented. The result, said Hull, was that we supported "and even led" a movement to admit [to the group that was organizing the United Nations] the "Fascist government of Argentina which had aided the Germans throughout, is still aiding them, and has not repented." He feels that all this discouraged hope of the democratic elements in Argentina to throw out the government, and also lost the effects of his policy in Latin America. He thinks the action dangerously alienated Soviet Russia, and unnecessarily.

. . . I noted, however, that he defended our hands-off policy [on issues growing out of Soviet postwar aggression in Europe] by asking "what was the alternative [meaning war or very bad American-Russian relations]?" yet declined to accept the same excuse from Stettinius on the Argentine decision at San Francisco. It is obvious that [Hull] does not think Stettinius up to the job, blames Roosevelt and Hopkins rather than Stettinius for the appointment —and thus his successor's plight—but doubtless has conveyed his impression to the President [Truman]. This, I think, contributes greatly to the insecurity of Stettinius as Secretary of State.

. . . Hull gave me the chronological details of his resignation. He said that before he went to the hospital last October he told Roosevelt he could not carry on and must retire. Roosevelt was "horrified"—it was during a campaign in which important support of Roosevelt [by *The New York Times*, for example] was partly based on the stated belief that Hull would continue as Secretary in the postwar period, and Roosevelt evidently thought that the resignation at that time might beat him. Hull agreed not to leave officially until the campaign was ended. Then he carried out his plan, though Roosevelt still tried several times to dissuade him.

. . . He said he had not suggested [James F.] Byrnes in any way as his successor. "I knew," he said, "I would have had no voice in it anyhow, and no suggestion from me was wanted or would be effective—probably to the contrary." He said Roosevelt called on him the day before leaving for Warm Springs, "and he was not functioning well—either mentally or physically."

. . . In general, Hull was as critical of his successor as most men would be who were obliged to quit in the same circumstances and at such a time, and who had so many personal policies, likes, and dislikes.

. . . He said that Nelson Rockefeller and Avra Warren had "deceived" the President about the real conditions in Argentina, after the Warren mission, and it was on this "false representation" that Truman had agreed to the admission of Argentina to the United Nations' organization group. Hull conceded that this did not make that government a member of the United Nations, but he said the effect was the same, despite the "technicality." He said that Argentina had not "really" met the specifications required of participants in organizing the United Nations and this made the action "worse."

While candid or mass news conferences held by the American military leaders were not conspicuous by their numbers during the war, Gen. George C. Marshall, the Army Chief of Staff, and Adm. Ernest King, his counterpart in the Navy, often talked freely on current and prospective operations with a small group of reporters. Of the two King was the more communicative.

King was by nature a loner. Of his iron discipline, including that he imposed on himself, even four-star Admirals stood in awe. As for Navy ratings, I was made aware how thoroughly King was feared and respected in the ranks by an experience with a taxicab driver. We were tooling along normally toward an intersection when the driver suddenly put on the brakes and ducked under the wheel. The only person in sight was a tall, erect naval officer approaching the intersection; on a second look I recognized him as King. Not until the Admiral was out of our orbit did the driver proceed to my destination.

"What made you slap on the brakes and hide?" I asked.

"Did you see *him?*" the driver asked back. "Well, I served under him during his last sea duty before I was invalided out; he knows me well. If he had seen me driving a cab, he would have had me back in the Navy this afternoon."

But in the almost weekly sessions at which, for a considerable period during the war, King met with about a half-dozen reporters at the suburban house of one of their number, there was no suggestion of the bucko Admiral the taxicab driver portrayed. Once convinced there would be no "leaks," he talked and answered questions on the progress of the war with the utmost freedom and candor. A set of notes I made of a session with King on October 16, 1944, ten months before the War ended, is indicative of these aspects of them all:

. . . King had opposed British juncture with us in the Pacific because they have no sea fleet, are untrained for carrier work, and will be most difficult to coordinate in a battle pattern. But after the President promised this, the best King could do was to arrange, after they joined, to give their task forces a job and let them do it independently.

. . . The Russians often oppose decisions of the Anglo-American Combined Chiefs of Staff because they don't trust the British. Accordingly, we have followed the custom of reporting the CCS decisions separately to Moscow, to the Russian General Staff there. The Russians dislike the chief of the British military mission to Moscow, which adds to the trouble, and the British won't change him. "Doubtless Churchill is working out such things with Stalin now."

. . . The defeat of Japan will be most difficult because the Japanese Army is undefeated and will have to be conquered on land somewhere—in China, Manchuria, or the home islands. [King was so firm on this point that I assume he regarded the atomic bomb, which he must have known was in the experimental stage, as a highly uncertain project.] Formosa can't be taken by any force we are ready to muster for the purpose yet. We put out "some bait" for the Japanese fleet which he hopes they will swallow, but probably won't. By the end of the week there may be great news, however, and his listeners assumed, correctly as it proved, that this meant the Philippines proper will be invaded. . . .

. . . Chiang Kai-shek, by distributing our supplies among all his divisions instead of concentrating on a few and by [maintaining] his guard at the Communist border [of the Chinese Communist enclave], has let the Japanese get where they are [in the heart of China]. General [Joseph ("Vinegar Joe"] Stillwell did what he could to change matters but succeeded only partly. The situation is very bad, but the [Nationalist] Chinese are at last persuaded that air alone can't dislodge the Japanese in China.

. . . King fully expects the Russians to come in with us in their own time. The Japanese can't exist with Russia's Maritime Provinces in other hands, and the Russians must defend them. Why the Japanese didn't take these provinces when they could he will never understand.

. . . He explained the composition of our fleets; we have

twelve. The odd-numbered ones and their forces are in the Atlantic and contiguous waters; the even-numbered are in the Pacific. We have fifteen carriers and will have more. Enlistments in the Navy are satisfactory and it will need no fresh expansions. Fleet officers, who first wanted armor and guns at the expense of speed, then wanted to reduce armor and now guns to increase speed so they can catch the Japanese.

. . . The Admiral said that "assault [combat] shipping" is now the paramount item in the Navy program but that manpower failures are delaying it seriously. He said he did not know whether the War Manpower Commission was enforcing its rule against men transferring from vital jobs to others, but the results did not indicate that it was. He quoted Vice-Admiral E. S. [Jerry] Land as having told him regretfully that he could not deliver craft as promised because of manpower shortages that no agency in the government had corrected.

Although General Marshall seemed much less relaxed in talking confidentially with even small reportorial groups, he had been extremely informative during a two-hour session on the afternoon of this same day, October 16, 1944. The Battle of the Bulge was to take place two months later. He showed maps that gave the locations of all the Allied armies and their components in France, Holland, and Belgium. He explained that the difficult terrain and longer arm of supply had slowed up the Russian advances at the Vistula and against East Prussia, but said he was nevertheless "disappointed" at their showing. However, said Marshall, he thought that the Russians were trying to keep the promise they made at the Roosevelt-Churchill-Stalin conference at Teheran—when the Allied invasions of France from the Normandy beaches and from the Marseilles area were decided on. But by way of contrast, and with a rare show of pride in any accomplishment by anyone, he characterized the "breakthrough at Saint-Lo," into Normandy from Brittany, under the command of Gen. Joseph ("Lightning Joe") Collins as "one of the greatest military feats of all time."

On a few occasions I did see General Marshall alone, or with a single aide, in my professional capacity. In 1939, in concert with Louis Johnson, then Assistant Secretary of the Army, Marshall supplied me with data (for an article in *The Times*

Sunday magazine) supporting their inter-Administration pressure for the prompt creation of a standing United States Army of at least 2 million—a daring figure because its very mention cast an alarm over the Presidential politics of the time.

In vivid memory of those cold steel-blue eyes and distant manner, I still feel the glow of my discovery, in 1947, that Marshall's purpose in asking me to meet with him alone at the Pentagon was to ask for counsel.

The great current political topic was whether the United States should support the partition of Palestine and recognize the state of Israel, and the Republican Presidential candidate, Thomas E. Dewey, was racing President Truman to advocate both actions before they were announced as United States policy. Secretary of Defense Forrestal opposed both projects on grounds of military security—that they threatened a shutoff of the vast Arabian oil resources on which the Navy greatly depended.

General Marshall told me he had been asked "by very high authority" (I assumed this was the President) to express the public judgment, as a military man, that no such foreseeable threat to national security was involved. Whatever his judgment might be, he said, did I think he should enter the controversy in any way? To my comment that, of course, he realized someone was trying to use him to make political capital and that this was unfair to him and prejudicial of his military function, he gave a brief nod and replied, "I had concluded as much." It was obvious from his manner that I had given him the counsel he wanted to hear. And he followed it.

But he took the same view of his obligation to keep forever aloof from public controversy when the shoe was on the other foot—mine—several years afterward. Urging him to clear up several still unresolved mysteries that had become interparty disputes—for example, his activities on the night before and the morning of Pearl Harbor—I submitted four questions, the answers not to be released for publication until any future date he chose, including a date after which both of us in all likelihood would be dead.

The General politely but very coldly declined. Yet he was

capable of a restrained kind of geniality, which he displayed on purely social occasions, including several visits to my farm in Virginia. And he completely cast off this restraint, I am told, at the very private weekly luncheons of The Alibi, a club composed of an especially hand-picked group to whom "off the record" is taken as a commitment without any time limit.

But he chose most sparingly those who stood to him in the literal relationship of "friends"—among whom I venture only to enumerate the late Senator Harry Byrd of Virginia, Benjamin M. McKelway, the distinguished Washington journalist, and Gen. Wade Hampton Haislip, an old comrade-in-arms. To Haislip he presented a photograph inscribed "With warm regards from his friend, George C. Marshall." A unique item, insofar as Haislip is aware. And my inquiries of others with apparent eligibility to receive a similar greeting have produced none.

But though Marshall's unusual manner was that of a man who had forced his personal emotions below the surface and bade them stay there, this was not the case with his emotions arising out of professional activities. These burst out in intra-governmental war councils and—more rarely—in wartime briefings of the press as well. A notable instance of the latter occurred on August 25, 1943.

The representative of *The Times*'s Washington Bureau was Turner Catledge, and in a report to me of the proceedings are these passages, disproving the public impression of Marshall, which he encouraged, as a very cold cutomer indeed:

. . . Concerning expected Congressional protests of his plan to re-retire several hundred officers, mostly colonels and lieutenant-colonels who had been temporarily recalled for war service but now are in the way of the advancement of more aggressive and more able younger men: "I know there is political dynamite in what we are doing, but that's our policy and, by God, we're going to stick to it!"

. . . The immediate future prospect of the military situation: "From now on we're going to take more chances—goddammit, we've got to get along with this war. . . . We've got to dare to get bloody noses occasionally, [and] I want you . . . to know this so that when the going seems to get tough, and we're set back on our rumps here and there, you'll know what's behind it all and keep things in their proper perspective."

. . . The problem of explaining our strategy—delayed new fronts, etc., to the Kremlin: "Its forces have nothing to think about but roads, railroads, mountains, and rivers. Hell, we have everything else to think about—air, sea, trackless mountains—keep everything in mind and try to line up our forces to strike and hold. . . ."

If Marshall had been visited with a vision of the military problem of the United States in Vietnam, he could not have stated it more precisely.

Of the turbulences into which my reporting led me during the twelve years of Roosevelt's Presidency, two were the most violent. Yet in each instance I was a second-hand dealer in the publication that brought down on my head the full force of the storm of denials from executive officers and Democratic Party leadership quarters.

One day, turning as I always did to Frank R. Kent's political column in *The Baltimore Sun*, I read the flat statement that Harry L. Hopkins, in a conversation at a New York racetrack with personal friends who were criticizing the spending policy of the New Deal, had retorted, "We will spend and spend, tax and tax, and elect and elect." I was impressed with the aptness of this capsule of the technique of the regime in power. But I made no reference to it until it was repeated in a column by Joseph Alsop. Then I asked Kent for his sources; he named them, and on my inquiry they supplied me with details, which, though imparted in private, impressed me as undoubtedly authentic. Accordingly, I republished Hopkins' apothegm in a Sunday article in *The New York Times*.

That Sunday I lunched at the Harold Talbotts' in Virginia in a small company that included Hopkins. Not only did he make no mention of the article, he gave no indication of any diminishment in our friendly relationship. And several nights later, at a dinner given by Richard C. Patterson, then an Assistant Secretary of Commerce, Secretary of the Interior Ickes, who often feuded publicly with Hopkins, said to me gleefully, "I see you have Harry by the short hairs."

But soon it developed that the appearance of the quotation in *The New York Times* had acquired for it a general circulation among Hopkins's ill-wishers in Congress (there were plenty) that complicated his prospect of being confirmed as Secretary of Commerce, the office to which Roosevelt had nominated him. Whereupon Hopkins—brushing aside the fact that he had made no protest of two prior publications of the remark—issued a flat denial that he had ever made it, together with some uncomplimentary comments on my professional behavior.

And who should come to Hopkins' defense and my professional derogation, with full acceptance of the denial, but the gentleman who had expressed to me his delight over my article —Secretary Harold Ickes himself! What had happened, as Ickes' intervention made very plain, was that the publication in *The Times* of the remark about "taxing, spending, and electing" was climactic, seriously embarrassing the President in the pursuit of pending New Deal measures, and also imperiling Hopkins' confirmation as Secretary of Commerce.

Under the unusually strong pressure that is generated at the seat of the highest power, Kent's informants and mine took to the tall timbers; one on the counsel of Baruch and Swope that the memorandum he had composed "would ruin Hopkins"; the other even omitted all mention of the incident in his memoirs. And since Kent, Alsop, and I (who were summoned before the Senate committee considering the Hopkins nomination) were bound by given word not to reveal their identities, and Hopkins vowed the incident had never occurred, he was duly confirmed.

The second of these two violent disturbances over a quotation in a report published under my name occurred during the Democratic National Convention of 1944. In this case, though I got the news at second hand, my account was the first to be published. It consisted of the report of a meeting in Roosevelt's private car in the Chicago yards—at which the President, Democratic National Chairman Robert Hannegan, and Mayor Kelly of Chicago were among the principals—for the purpose of consolidating the choice of the President's running mate in the fourth-term election. The account quoted Roosevelt as making the following caveat in his instructions to the leaders to agree on a Vice-Presidential nominee: "Clear everything with Sidney"—"Sidney" being organized labor's principal spokesman, Sidney Hillman.

My source was Turner Catledge of *The Times*'s convention staff. He obtained the story and the quotation from an informant who had it first hand and whose eminent public position, closeness to the event, and personal character left no reasonable doubt of its authenticity.

But since Catledge's intimacy with him was well known, and this would pretty thoroughly have identified him as the source of the story under Catledge's byline, it was arranged that it appear under mine. This time the publication was promptly followed by a deluge of denials from the principals, and authoritative confirmation did not come until the issuance of James F. Byrne's reminiscences, *All In One Lifetime.**

Some who issued denials justified them to their consciences by resort to a technicality. I had phrased the quotation "Clear everything," etc., instead of "Clear it," etc., but the context indisputably limited the direction to the Vice-Presidential choice. However, the word Roosevelt used was "it." And though I made the correction in using the quotation thereafter, the Administration spokesmen stuck to their original denial for the duration of the Presidential campaign.

I have never found a satisfactory explanation for the continuous professional public assurances of Franklin D. Roosevelt's physical condition, unsupported by the definite and wholly objective process previously employed, either in the 1932 campaign or in the period just before his death. Since I am not qualified to pass judgment on a medical proposition and Roosevelt's doctors were respected in their profession for skill and personal integrity, I set down this note about Roosevelt's career as one of the many mysteries that baffle all but cocksure contemporaries:

The last time I saw Roosevelt was at the White House

* New York: Harper, 1958.

Correspondents' annual dinner in early 1945. In this period, despite the evidence of physical deterioration that was provided by the news photographs of the conferees at Yalta, the White House doctors were still giving optimistic public diagnoses of his condition. So I was shocked at the President's appearance in the flesh. If ever impending death was written on a human countenance, it seemed to me I saw it that night.

I was at some distance from the President during the dinner, but to reach the ramp whereby he could move onto the exit in his wheelchair, he had to pass me en route. My face as he passed must have so clearly reflected my distress at the change in his own that he noticed it. Anyhow, he looked up at me as he was wheeled by and said gaily, "Cheer up, Arthur. Things have seldom been as bad as you said they were."

Several weeks thereafter he was dead at Warm Springs.

12

TRUMAN

MY ACQUAINTANCE with Harry S. Truman was slight until, as he expressed it, "all the stars and the planets fell upon him" with the sudden death of Roosevelt. I recall that, admiring as I did his objectivity at the total expense of partisanship in heading the Senate committee on the conduct of the Second World War, I invited a few newspapermen to lunch with him at the Metropolitan Club—at the request of a colleague who was a friend of his—and the excellent impression he made there. I had been particularly impressed with Truman's quality as a statesman in a certain exchange on the Senate floor with Arthur H. Vandenberg of Michigan.

Chairman Truman had reported to the Senate a delay of eighteen months in the formulation and enforcement of several steps vital to the successful conduct of the war. Whereupon Vandenberg interrupted to inquire "at whose doorstep" the blame could be laid. "The White House," calmly replied Truman, thereby forever—at least in my mind—dispelling a prevailing impression that even when the stake was the national interest, he would act as the unswerving Democratic partisan he was reputed to be.

But the occasions on which Truman acted one way or the other were conspicuous enough to fortify a public judgment that his character curiously combined pettiness with greatness.

It cannot be persuasively argued that when he stated that the departure of Attorney General Francis Biddle from the Cabinet was on Biddle's initiative, he had merely forgotten having requested Biddle's resignation. Or that when he allowed Secretary of Defense Louis A. Johnson to take the blame for the critically inadequate military defense budget of $13.2 billion in fiscal year 1950, he lived up to his famous desk placard of final Presidential responsibility: THE BUCK STOPS HERE.

In the same category was his sudden dismissal of Attorney General J. Howard McGrath. McGrath, whose partisan brand as Chairman of the Democratic National Committee had been as highly visible to the President as to anyone else when he was appointed Attorney General, merely acted in character when he fired Newbold Morris, Truman's own investigator in the probe into Administration corruption, for misguided but honest zeal that had angered Congress as an invasion of privacy and embarrassed the Democratic Party. But because this action lent crushing weight to the Republican charge that the Administration's intent was to investigate itself, the President ruthlessly sacrificed his henchman for misguided zeal in the other direction.

His personality is that of a very charming man whose determination sticks out all over him. Nearly invariably he showed complete courage in making momentous decisions and an iron backbone that kept him from ever going back on such a decision once made. In these respects alone he would, in my judgment, rate as a "strong President." And in these instances of paramount policy-making he seldom sought to shift to others the initiative for the policy or the blame for adverse consequences.

Truman was the one President who, though I wrote as critically about him as I have about any other, never held it against me personally. We became friends, on his motion, and he never reproached me for any criticism or changed his friendly attitude toward me.

In any relaxed conversation with President Truman his wide reading in general and in American history was usually reflected in some degree. But what was almost certain to emerge on such occasions was Truman the military buff—the joint product of his in-depth perusal of the chronicles of decisive battles and of his combat experience as World War I commander of a Missouri National Guard battery on the Western Front.

One day his central topic was Creasy's classic account of the battle of Arbela, the engagement in Mesopotamia (331 B.C.) in which Alexander the Great defeated Darius and destroyed the Persian Empire. I remarked that after the breakthrough of the United States forces into Normandy from Brittany, General Marshall had described it to me as "one of the greatest feats of American arms" and asked the President if he was familiar with it in military detail. If not, I said, "there is a young General in the Pentagon who can tell you all of them, since he led the successful assault on Cherbourg of which the breakthrough was a direct sequel. He is J. Lawton Collins, known after Cherbourg as 'Lightning Joe.' " Truman made a note of his name.

When I returned to my office, I telephoned to Collins. "I don't know how soon," I said, "but I am reasonably sure you will get a call from the White House to brief the President on the Cherbourg-Saint-Lô-Caen advance. So have your maps and your pointer ready." Later that day Collins telephoned me to say that he had been given half an hour's notice after my alert, but had done the best he could in the circumstances.

When the circumstances of his accession are considered, including the fact that he had not been kept informed of the matters on which Roosevelt had founded his vital policies, it is remarkable how well Truman managed to take over his predecessor's duties and to become President in his own right in the 1948 election. In 1945 President Roosevelt's doctors were still assuring the world that the President was in reasonably good health; thus everyone in the world was totally unprepared for his death. Perhaps Truman may at times, in Roosevelt's company, have felt that death was an increasing possibility. But apparently, and curiously, the timing, if not the actual event, was as much a shock to Truman as to people in general.

The meeting at San Francisco to complete the organization of the United Nations, and the summit meeting at Potsdam, both in 1945, were matters of such primary concern to the new President that his need of an intensive briefing of current and future relations between the United States and the Soviet Union had to be postponed. So it was not until the summer of 1946 that Truman assigned an aide to supply him with a fully comprehensive report. And it was not until September 24, 1946, that the memorandum was laid on the President's desk.

If Truman had been equipped with this Memorandum in May and June of 1945—manifestly impossible because of the suddenness of his succession—the Cold War, in the degree of intensity to which it grew, might have been averted. For Prime Minister Churchill in those months sent the President the sound counsel that is epitomized in his telegram of June 4, "which," as Churchill wrote in 1953, "few would now dispute":

I AM SURE YOU UNDERSTAND THE REASON WHY I AM ANXIOUS FOR AN EARLIER DATE [for the Allied Tripartite Conference set for July 15, 1945, in Berlin] SAY THE 3RD OR 4TH [of July]. I VIEW WITH PROFOUND MISGIVINGS THE RETREAT OF THE AMERICAN ARMY TO OUR LINE OF OCCUPATION IN THE CENTRAL SECTOR, THUS BRINGING SOVIET POWER INTO THE HEART OF WESTERN EUROPE AND THE DESCENT OF AN IRON CURTAIN BETWEEN US AND EVERYTHING TO THE EASTWARD. I HOPED THAT THIS RETREAT, IF IT HAS TO BE MADE, WOULD BE ACCOMPANIED BY THE SETTLEMENT OF MANY GREAT THINGS WHICH WOULD BE THE TRUE FOUNDATION OF WORLD PEACE. NOTHING REALLY IMPORTANT HAS BEEN SETTLED YET, AND YOU AND I WILL HAVE TO BEAR GREAT RESPONSIBILITY FOR THE FUTURE. I STILL HOPE THEREFORE THAT THE DATE WILL BE ADVANCED.

Truman rejected this advice, committed as he felt he was to President Roosevelt's acceptance of the July 15 date, and to

FDR's conclusion that full and peaceful cooperation with the Soviet Union could be counted on after the end of the war. The American material resources and the vastly more precious American blood being expended in Vietnam are only one of the consequences of the rejection of Churchill's proposal in June, 1945.

The aide who prepared the September, 1946, memorandum was Clark M. Clifford, of whom more later in this narrative. And the memorandum, which reached a total of nearly a hundred thousand words,* was a fundamentally important American state paper for a number of reasons. Not only did it supply the New President with every past detail of the wartime relationship with the U.S.S.R., it charted the postwar prospect with startling prescience in which the shape and thrust of Truman's subsequent great programs—the Greek-Turk aid legislation, the Marshall Plan, the North Atlantic Alliance (including NATO), and what later became known as the "Truman Doctrine"—were outlined. The first summary provided to the public appears in the following pages.

But before that, a word about its author, Clark Clifford, is appropriate. He was summoned to the White House temporarily, from duty with the Navy, to act as the White House Naval Attaché during the absence at the Potsdam summit meeting of the incumbent in that post, James K. Vardaman, Jr. Finding that in the circumstances this duty required only a small amount of his time, Clifford, by profession a lawyer in St. Louis, was spending the remainder in assisting the President's Special Counsel, Judge Samuel H. Rosenman; and so useful did he prove in this capacity that on the return of the President and Vardaman from Potsdam, Truman appointed Clifford as Rosenman's successor when the latter resigned to resume his private law practice. And it was in this capacity that Truman assigned Clifford to prepare the memorandum of September 24, 1946.

It is divided into an introduction and six chapters, the titles of which give a rough idea of the comprehensiveness of the study: Soviet Foreign Policy; Soviet-American Agreements,

* The complete text will be found in Appendix A.

1942–1946; Violations of Soviet Agreements with the United States; Conflicting Views on Reparations; Soviet Activities Affecting American Security; and United States Policy toward the Soviet Union. Because of the length and scope of the memorandum it is necessary to confine the citations here to a very few. But in my opinion they establish the importance of the document [*circa* 1946] as review and forecast of the new President's problem in shaping foreign policy on the basis of American-Soviet postwar relations:

Our fear of Germany and Japan is gone, but our suspicion of the Soviet Union, and suspicion is the first step to fear, is growing. Suspicious misunderstanding of the Soviet Union must be replaced by an accurate knowledge of the motives and methods of the Soviet government. Only through such knowledge will we be able to appraise and forecast the military and political moves of the Kremlin; without that knowledge we shall be at the mercy of rumors and half-truths. Sudden moves, or unexpected or misunderstood moves, by the Soviet Union might, if we do not understand the methods of the Kremlin, lead us into a showdown of force for which we would probably be unprepared, or might lead us into blind or hasty diplomatic retreat. Only through an accurate understanding of the characteristics of the one nation that can endanger the United States will our government be able to make and carry out policies that will re-establish order in Europe and Asia and protect this nation at all times.

The concept of danger from the outside is deeply rooted in the Russian people's haunting sense of insecurity inherited from their past. It is maintained by their present leaders as a justification for the oppressive nature of the Soviet police state. The thesis, that the capitalist world is conspiring to attack the Soviet Union, is not based on any objective analysis of the situation beyond Russia's borders. It has little to do, indeed, with conditions outside the Soviet Union, and it has arisen mainly from basic inner-Russian necessities, which existed before the Second World War and which exist today.

The key to an understanding of current Soviet foreign policy, in summary, is the realization that Soviet leaders adhere to the Marxian theory of ultimate destruction of capitalist states by communist states, while at the same time they

strive to postpone the inevitable conflict in order to strengthen
and prepare the Soviet Union for its clash with the Western
democracies.

The Soviet Union's main concern regarding the other nations of Western Europe is to prevent the formation of a
Western bloc. It will also, of course, encourage the growth of
local Communist parties.

The Near East is an area of great strategic interest to the
Soviet Union because of the shift of Soviet industry to southeastern Russia, within range of air attack from much of the
Near East, and because of the resources of the area. The
Soviet Union is interested in obtaining the withdrawal of
British troops from Greece and the establishment of a
"friendly" government there. It hopes to make Turkey a
puppet state that could serve as a springboard for the domination of the eastern Mediterranean. It is trying by diplomatic
means to establish itself in the Dodecanese and Tripolitania,
and it already has a foothold in the Mediterranean through its
close alliances with Albania and Yugoslavia.

Soviet policy with respect to the United Nations, as with
individual nations, is designed to increase the position and
prestige of the U.S.S.R. at the expense of other states. It now
appears that the Soviet Union joined the United Nations as a
matter of expedience and not because of any devotion to
abstract principles of peace. The United Nations, to Soviet
leaders, is another international arena in which they can
propagandize and compete for a dominant position. The Soviet Union will continue to make every effort to impose its
will on the organization so that United Nations decisions will,
insofar as possible, implement Soviet policy. Soviet tactics
will include unrestricted use of the veto power, use of member
satellite states to support the Soviet viewpoint, and pressure
for admission of other satellite states in order to increase the
Soviet "bloc."

The Soviet Union is evidently reluctant to withdraw from
the United Nations so long as it can carry with it only a small
fraction of the other members, for this would leave the majority of the other nations conveniently organized against it.
However, if the Soviet leaders decide that membership in the
United Nations is working too much to their disadvantage,
and that their hand is being called on too many issues, they
may decide to withdraw anyway. If they make this decision,

they can be expected to use the entire Soviet propaganda machine and all the agencies of Soviet diplomacy to discredit the United Nations. . . .

Although the Soviet Union at the present moment is precluded from military aggression beyond the land mass of Eurasia, the acquisition of a strategic air force, naval forces and *atomic bombs in quantity* [author's italics] would give the U.S.S.R. the capability of striking anywhere on the globe. Ability to wage aggressive warfare in any area of the world is the ultimate goal of Soviet military policy.

In addition to increasing her own military strength to a point where an attack on the United States would be possible, the Soviet Union is jeopardizing the security of the United States by her efforts to weaken the military position and to destroy the prestige of the United States in Europe, Asia, and South America. Red Army troops and Red Air Force planes, maintained in combat readiness, outnumber American units in Germany, Austria, and Korea in overwhelming strength, thus placing our forces literally at the mercy of the Soviet government.

The U.S.S.R. has a widespread intelligence net in China covering all phases of American activity, but the Soviet propaganda program presents an even greater danger. This campaign is designed to discredit American forces in China, to convince all political groups in China that American forces should be evacuated at once and to arouse suspicion as to American postwar aims in the Far East. The Soviets, by supplying captured Japanese military material to the Communists, not only endanger the United States Marines in North China but also, by prolonging the Chinese civil strife, make more difficult, if not impossible, the attainment of the American aim of a unified and stable Chinese government.

The Soviet espionage ring in this country has found it easy to load baggage aboard Soviet vessels without Customs inspection. A shortage of personnel makes it impossible for the United States Customs, without special instructions, to maintain an adequate watch on Soviet vessels for the purpose of determining who goes aboard and what luggage is placed aboard prior to sailing.

One of the objectives of the American Communist Party is the subversion of the armed forces of the United States. Important activities in this connection were the recent soldier demonstrations relating to demobilization and the recent anti-caste agitation. There is continuous Communist propaganda within the United States Army and from without to promote left-wing sentiment among soldiers. Strong and continuous efforts are being made to infiltrate the educational service of the Army and to color the material used in indoctrination and education of troops. A definite campaign, in the making at present, is being sponsored by the Communist Party to indoctrinate soldiers to refuse to act in the event the United States Army is called on to suppress domestic disturbances, to take over essential industries, or to operate public utilities. The Soviet government will never be easy to "get along with." The American people must accustom themselves to this thought, not as a cause for despair, but as a fact to be faced objectively and courageously. If we find it impossible to enlist Soviet cooperation in the solution of world problems, we should be prepared to join with the British and other Western countries in an attempt to build up a world of our own which will pursue its own objectives and will recognize the Soviet orbit as a distinct entity with which conflict is not predestined but with which we cannot pursue common aims.

Unless the United States is willing to sacrifice its future security for the sake of "accord" with the U.S.S.R. now, this government must, as a first step toward world stabilization, seek to prevent additional Soviet aggression. The greater the area controlled by the Soviet Union, the greater the military requirements of this country will be. Our present military plans are based on the assumption that for the next few years at least, Western Europe, the Middle East, China, and Japan will remain outside the Soviet sphere. If the Soviet Union acquires control of one or more of these areas, the military forces required to hold in check those of the U.S.S.R. and prevent still further acquisitions will be substantially enlarged. That will also be true if any of the naval and air bases in the Atlantic and Pacific, upon which our present plans rest, are given up. This government should be prepared, while scrupulously avoiding any act that would be an excuse for the Soviets to begin a war, to resist vigorously and successfully any efforts of the U.S.S.R. to expand into areas vital to American security.

The language of military power is the only language the disciples of power politics understand. The United States must use that language in order that Soviet leaders will realize that our government is determined to uphold the interests of its citizens and the rights of small nations. [A principle since asserted in the vast military expansion of the "Truman Doctrine."] Compromise and concessions are considered, by the Soviets, to be evidences of weakness and they are encouraged by our "retreats" to make new and greater demands.

Whether it would actually be in this country's interest to employ atomic and biological weapons against the Soviet Union in the event of hostilities is a question that would require careful consideration in the light of the circumstances prevailing at the time. The decision would probably be influenced by a number of factors, such as the Soviet Unions' capacity to employ similar weapons, which cannot now be estimated. But the important point is that the United States *must be prepared to wage atomic and biological warfare if necessary* [author's italics]. The mere fact of preparedness may be the only powerful deterrent to Soviet aggressive action and in this sense the only sure guaranty of peace.

The United States, with a military potential composed primarily of highly effective technical weapons, *should entertain no proposal* [author's italics] for disarmament or limitation of armament as long as the possibility of Soviet aggression exists. Any discussion on the limitation of armaments should be pursued slowly and carefully with the knowledge constantly in mind that proposals on outlawing atomic warfare and long-range offensive weapons would greatly limit United States strength, while only moderately affecting the Soviet Union. The Soviet Union relies primarily on a large infantry and artillery force and the result of such arms limitation would be to deprive the United States of its most effective weapons without impairing the Soviet Union's ability to wage a quick war of aggression in Western Europe, the Middle East, or the Far East.

In addition to maintaining our own strength, the United States should support and assist all democratic countries that are in any way menaced or endangered by the U.S.S.R. Providing military support in case of attack is *a last resort* [author's emphasis]; a more effective barrier to communism is strong economic support. Trade agreements, loans, and technical missions strengthen our ties with friendly nations and are effective demonstrations that capitalism is at least the equal of communism. The United States can do much to insure that economic opportunities, personal freedom, and social equality are made possible in countries outside the Soviet sphere by generous financial assistance. Our policy on reparations should be directed toward strengthening the areas we are endeavoring to keep outside the Soviet sphere. Our efforts to break down trade barriers, open up rivers and international waterways, and bring about economic unification of countries now divided by occupation armies, are also directed toward the re-establishment of vigorous and healthy non-communist economies. [This represents the genesis of the "Truman Doctrine," as designed by its namesake, which has been progressively militarized in the Kennedy-Johnson Administrations.]

With respect to the United Nations, we are faced with the fact that the U.S.S.R. uses the United Nations as a means of achieving its own ends. We should support the United Nations and all other organizations contributing to international understanding, but if the Soviet Union should threaten to resign at any time because it fails to have its own way, the United States should not oppose Soviet departure. It would be better to continue the United Nations as an association of democratic states than to sacrifice our principles to Soviet threats.

Since our difficulties with the Soviet Union are due primarily to the doctrines and actions of a small ruling clique and not the Soviet people, the United States should strive energetically to bring about a better understanding of the United States among influential Soviets and to counteract the anti-American propaganda the Kremlin feeds to the Soviet people.

In conclusion, as long as the Soviet government adheres to its present policy, the United States should maintain military forces powerful enough to restrain the Soviet Union and to confine Soviet influence to its present area. All nations not now within the Soviet sphere should be given generous economic assistance and political support in their opposition to Soviet penetration. Economic aid may also be given to the Soviet government and private trade with the U.S.S.R. permitted, provided the results are beneficial to our interests and do not simply strengthen the Soviet program. We should continue to work for cultural and intellectual understanding between the United States and the Soviet Union, but that does not mean that under the guise of an exchange program, Communist subversion and infiltration in the United States will be tolerated. In order to carry out an effective policy toward the Soviet Union, the United States government should coordinate its own activities, inform and instruct the American people about the Soviet Union, and enlist their support based upon knowledge and confidence. These actions by the United States are necessary before we shall ever be able to achieve understanding and accord with the Soviet government on any terms other than its own.

Even though Soviet leaders profess to believe that the conflict between capitalism and communism is irreconcilable and must eventually be resolved by the triumph of the latter, it is our hope that they will change their minds and work out with us a fair and equitable settlement when they realize that we are too strong to be beaten and too determined to be frightened.

These are statements of the foreign-policy principles, with particular bearing on the U.S.S.R., that Truman took as his guide. In his letter of transmittal Clifford reported that they were the result of consultations with "the Secretary of State, the Secretary of War, the Attorney General, the Secretary of the Navy, Fleet Admiral Leahy [who had been Roosevelt's Chief military adviser], the Joint Chiefs of Staff, Edwin W. Pauley [Ambassador in charge of negotiating postwar reparations], the Director of Central Intelligence, and other persons who have special knowledge in this field."

The first major international event of the Truman Administration was the organization of the United Nations at San Francisco. The new President was carrying out the policy of the Roosevelt Administration, as well as furthering a dream of the American people, in proceeding with the formation of the United Nations. Once again they thought and hoped that an association of nations would be an effective means of restoring a durable world order, and Truman believed this himself.

This belief came under its first shadow, though the true believers ignored it, as the delegates gathered at San Francisco. The Kremlin reneged on its Yalta pledge to modify its cruel tyranny in the communization of Poland, thus mocking the whole concept of the U.N. while the delegates were writing the Charter. And from the start of the proceedings the United States delegation, and especially its advisers from the State Department, divided into two groups with respect to the competence of Edward R. Stettinius, the holdover Secretary of State from Roosevelt's Cabinet.

It was known that, while the U.N. was being formed, President Truman was in the process of deciding which members of Roosevelt's Cabinet he wanted to retain, and for what period (in about three months he had replaced six). And it also was known that he was getting impressive counsel to supplant Stettinius—counsel that had already impeded the Secretary's usefulness before the word was circulated that the President had commissioned an emissary to check on his performance at San Francisco.

Stettinius' good points were nevertheless conceded. By adopting the passive role of referee of disputes within the United States delegation, he gave much greater scope to the role of its members, assigning to them direct negotiations with the representatives of other nations, among whom those of the U.S.S.R. were making themselves especially difficult to deal with. Consequently, Senator Arthur H. Vandenberg, Harold E. Stassen, and John Foster Dulles (Republicans) and Hamilton Fish Armstrong and Leo Pasvolsky (career diplomats) had such latitude of speech in the delegation's internal discussions and controversies that the United States delegation was preserved as a unit instead of the disputatious and shifting group it might otherwise have been. Rivalries in the delegation were held to a minimum, because policies were talked out in private before being made public.

But Stettinius was required *ex officio* to take the lead at critical stages of the proceedings. And there his inadequate knowledge of and experience in foreign affairs showed plain, often to the embarrassment of his colleagues and the displeasure of the President, to whom these deficiencies were promptly relayed.

Conscious of this inadequacy, the Secretary reacted by imposing a tight information policy on American news reporters. Their protests were finally recognized when Stettinius set up a small agency on what I believe was my suggestion. At least it was I who proposed that Thomas K. Finletter and Adlai E. Stevenson be put in charge of what became known as "the Leak Office."

Its job was to keep the American press unofficially but accurately and fully informed of the whole range of the news at San Francisco. With the assistance of Edward G. Miller of the State Department, Finletter and Stevenson admirably discharged a function that, officially catalogued as "secret," was well known to everyone on the scene.

But the effect of Stettinius' shortcomings was to force the United States to evolve policy—such as preserving the Monroe Doctrine in the U.N. Charter—under the pressures of the Conference, particularly the pressures engendered by the *"nyet"* position of Molotov, whose rudeness in maintaining this position had shocked Stettinius when he first encountered it in person. And the Soviet attitude at San Francisco, even though Truman at Potsdam "liked old Joe" Stalin and said as much, proved to be the oncoming shadow of the ground-traffic blockade of Berlin and other aspects of the Cold War that were to shatter Roosevelt's rosy dream of postwar cooperation with Moscow and to burden Truman, his successors, and all mankind.

Moreover, though Stettinius finally heeded Vandenberg's urging to "start being Secretary of State" at San Francisco and in relations with the President, and salvaged a superficially promising U.N. from the Soviet's destructive operations, he paid with his head for the lack of experience and capacity he had revealed in the field of foreign affairs. Truman found the man he had wanted from the first in James F. Byrnes, his Party Leader when both were Senators, former Supreme Court Justice, and former "Assistant President" under Roosevelt.

After the formation of the U.N. postwar domestic problems inevitably intruded, and the Congressional elections of 1946 produced one of the few occasions on which Truman retreated under political pressure. The Republicans had made an issue of the rationing of meat that had been imposed by the war. Public opinion was set against its continuance after the end of hostilities, but the President stood by it firmly until Democratic

candidates for Congress thoroughly bombarded him with the
estimate that if meat rationing continued (Senator Robert A.
Taft had attacked it as no longer justified), the Republicans
would surely regain control of Congress—Truman's first. He
revoked the meat rationing under this pressure, but too late to
save the Democratic majority in Congress. It was this lesson of
the political cost of open retreat, I am sure, that accounted for
the bold and unyielding quality of his 1948 campaign.

In the same category of yielding under pressure, I would
place Truman's greatest error as demobilizing too soon the
American military forces of the Second World War, an error
he conceded in a conversation with me on April 8, 1948. But
these are exceptions in the record of a very determined President, once he made up his mind.

The demobilization was, in a sense, an act of deference to a
public opinion that had been beguiled by Roosevelt's blunder of
counting on a cooperative U.S.S.R. postwar foreign policy.
Only a few of Truman's advisers in 1945—among them Secretary of the Navy James Forrestal and Ambassador W. Averell
Harriman—urged him not to perpetuate, in the demobilization
and other policies, this gross and costly error of FDR's.

But Truman, who felt a commitment to abide by Roosevelt's
judgments, was lured by Stalin's demeanor at Potsdam as
FDR had been at Yalta. Among the direful consequences
were the Cold War and, indirectly, the tragedy of Forrestal. In
his last cogent moments, the nation's first Secretary of Defense
flagellated his own record for not having resigned in protest
against the demobilization he believed, and time has proved, to
have been a disastrous mistake of national policy.

The evidence of internal government corruption, together
with the infiltration of Communists and crypto-Communists
within the official structure, plagued Truman (despite such
sacrificial offerings as Attorney General McGrath) from the
time they began to be exposed until the end of his Presidency.
And they plagued the American people because the infiltration
of subversives was real and costly in terms of advancing the
U.S.S.R.'s atomic-weapons potential. Unfortunately, wild ex-
aggeration of the degree of this subversion by the Republican
Senator from Wisconsin was the foundation of the nationally

demoralizing "McCarthyism" that took its name from the Senator's attack on what really were Augean stables, but with a dirty broom.

General Dwight D. Eisenhower and other Republican spokesmen vigorously attacked corruption and subversion in the 1952 campaign. And though Truman was not the Democratic Presidential nominee, Adlai E. Stevenson, who was, could not shake off his load and was further burdened by the unpopularity of the United Nations' control of the Korean War that led to the military stalemate in that part of Asia.

But true to the American character, the revelation of official acceptances of vicuña coats, deep freezes, and so on from persons with a material interest in the decisions of these officials also became the object of humorous stories and comments. Typical is the jest with which James Vardaman regaled small private companies.

As a naval officer on duty in the Pacific, said Vardaman, he was viewing pessimistically one day his prospect of soon returning to the pursuits of peace when a cable arrived from the President. It directed Vardaman to report to the White House as Truman's naval aide. Vardaman, he recalled, made the journey back in record time, and was received by a beaming President. According to Vardaman this was the sequel:

"Let's have a drink on your new job."

"Mr. President, I don't drink."

(Facial evidence of disappointment.) "Well, then, you join me and some of the boys I want to introduce you to tonight: we're having a little poker game."

"Mr. President, I don't play cards."

(Greater facial evidence of disappointment, and end of colloquy.)

"A few months later," as Vardaman told the tale, "I was relieved as naval aide and appointed to a fourteen-year job as a governor of the Federal Reserve Board. . . . And this is the only time that clean living ever got anybody a promotion in the Truman Administration."

To the postwar generation, except for those whose personal choice or college curriculum has acquainted them with its history, the Marshall (European Recovery) Plan, a major accomplishment of the Truman Administration, is known only in the broadest of generalities. Yet though one of its extrusions—the military arm of the North Atlantic Treaty Organization—got a share of the billions devoted, in the last phase of the program, to protecting the economic recovery of Western Europe the program had made possible, the Marshall Plan was the central gem in the cluster of great and fruitful decisions made by President Truman.

Both in concept and in execution the Plan merits this estimate. And it provides an instance of cooperation among those in the State Department, who conceived it and developed it from the nucleus in the Clifford memorandum, the 80th Congress, which financed and improved it, and the Executive, which set it in operation.

The operating machinery was the creation of the State Department's policy planning group, largely of the Chairman, George F. Kennan, with indispensable details supplied by Under Secretary Robert A. Lovett, Assistant Secretary Dean G. Acheson, and others. It was these who presented the Plan masterfully and persuasively to Secretary of State Marshall. And to Clifford, in his eventual capacity as special legal counsel to the Chief Executive, belongs the enormous credit of expounding the Plan as masterfully and persuasively to President Truman, whence came the decision to submit it to Congress. Finally, to the 80th Congress, and in particular to Arthur H. Vandenberg, Chairman of the Foreign Relations Committee, the credit is due for improving the framework, freeing operations by entrusting the Plan to an agency independent of the bureaucratic processes of the State Department and headed by a citizen drafted from private industry, Paul G. Hoffman.

When the Administration proposed that the Plan be operated by the Department, and Marshall summoned his enormous prestige to achieve this design by dramatically telling Congress there could not be "two Secretaries of State"—referring to his office and that of the administrator of E.R.P.—it was Vandenberg who used his unique power as the Senate's bipartisan leader in foreign affairs to give notice that there would be independent management, and under Paul Hoffman, or Congress would not provide the means of establishment and administration.

American journalism, especially since the advent of the specialized reporter, has often created the balanced, informed public with respect to complicated undertakings by government that the self-interest of bureaucratic and administration politics preclude government from creating. A particularly shining example has been the reporting in *The New York Times* by Felix Belair, Jr., of foreign-aid programs that began with the Marshall Plan. On the basis of this personal assessment I asked Belair to prepare the brief history and analysis that is here appended:

> The event that crystalized the Marshall Plan . . . was a sudden pile-up in 1947 of requests for monetary assistance from the non-Communist nations of postwar Europe. To Washington they sent their top diplomats, flanked by economic experts, to persuade the government of the pressing need for fulfilling these requests.
>
> Truman then made three fundamental decisions: (1) To provide this postwar financial assistance; (2) not to deal separately with each of the claimant nations (the U.S.S.R. declined to seek participation) but to deal with them as a unit, and only after they had pooled their requests through the OEEC (Organization for European Economic Cooperation) that was later established in Paris, and then make the loans and grants through bilateral treaties between the United States and each of the claimants; (3) to administer the program through a United States agency independent of the State Department.
>
> The major consequence of the Marshall Plan, second only to the restoration of a viable European economy, was to force the economic unity on the Continent that has since been projected in the Common Market. And when this recovery and unity was attained, it had been done in three years instead of the allowed four, and at a United States outlay of $12.6 billion instead of the $16.8 originally estimated and approved.

In the government quarter the clearest and most persuasive explanation of the Plan and its administrative principle that I

heard at the time was made by Under Secretary of State Robert
A. Lovett. To him primarily is due credit for the brilliant
device for the use of foreign currencies impounded in the operation of the program. This was to make bilateral treaties with
the sixteen client nations.

At a news conference on October 25, 1948, Lovett gave a
notable synopsis that is essential to the postwar generation's
full understanding of the Marshall Plan:

> By the end of the program we may have to our credit in
> London 50 millions of pounds sterling which have been used
> by the three United States trustees [of the program] to buy
> such stocks as Roan Antelope, Tanganyika, and South Afri-
> can gold mines. Then if and when these trustees sell the
> stocks to American citizens, there will be no loss of dollars to
> the British, and we can use the proceeds to buy raw materials
> held by the companies whose stocks we hold and which we
> may need badly.

The British law obstructing the plan, he pointed out, could be
set aside in the bilateral treaty with that nation. And he went
on to say:

> . . . All nations including our own are conditioned by
> history to the transition from war to peace. But this time we
> did not go from war to peace. Instead, we witnessed a transi-
> tion from war to invisible aggression, a new kind of inter-
> national situation in the handling of which we seem to be
> curiously inept. Plainly, too, the economic pattern of this
> period has not been according to our traditional thinking.
> . . . This summer we had a situation in which our ex-
> penditures were keeping alive from 240 million to 260
> million people abroad. For the most part they are good peo-
> ple, industrious and intelligent. In fact, they seem possessed
> of much more than average intelligence, considering the aver-
> age for the world as a whole.
> . . . Our choice, then, was and is between becoming a
> little island of prosperity and democracy, or fulfilling the
> second corollary of our foreign policy and supporting an at-
> mosphere in which an international exchange of goods and

services is possible and in which our own future would be most secure.

. . . If the Marshall Plan is to be regarded as a blueprint of this country's ability to supply European requirements, then certain basic assumptions must be granted. They are: that labor costs must remain about the same, that supplies will remain about the same as they have been, that labor relations will continue reasonably quiet and without serious work stoppages, and that fiscal affairs will remain stable and in order. But I for one do not believe that these assumptions can be carried beyond the first year.

. . . I don't see how Europe can ever repay us for the soft consumption stuff like food, fuel, fibers, and fertilizer. But the major portion of the amounts provided for Marshall Plan aid should be in loans under definite conditions.

. . . Also we have to draw a line between relief items and what are a combination of relief and recovery. We all know that people can't work unless they eat. On the other hand, where people are fed and not required to work, the result is a hotbed of unrest, which is the very thing we are trying to combat with this plan.

. . . We cannot do this job if everything going into the plan has to be bought in this country. This would keep prices out of line here and complicate things immeasurably. On the other hand, if we buy too much in Canada, she will come into this market and spend dollars for products that we need at home or which we should send to Europe. Canada presents a special problem and no one has yet come up with the answer to it.

. . . The program must be elastic. We can't feed the whole world. As long as there is a black market in Europe, the normal market will not work. Thus, the supplying markets must be brought in the program as much as possible.

. . . With respect to administration of the program, I don't think the State Department [as Marshall later and unsuccessfully urged on Congress] should have it. I think it should be an agency combining the characteristics of the War Production Board and Lend-Lease, so that we can have an injection of the industrial and management executives through establishing foreign missions and drawing an overall policy through the State Department. Because the whole program depends for its success on the observance of the first corollaries of policy and the bilateral agreements with the sixteen nations.

The clarity and foresight of this synopsis is typical of this major administrator in war and peace who, in my reportorial judgment, had no superior in able, wise, and devoted public service during two Administrations. That Lovett accepted only one—Secretary of Defense—of four Cabinet posts tendered by Presidents (Kennedy offered him a choice among State, Treasury, and Defense) may account in considerable part for some of the destructive differences between the United States and its North Atlantic allies that have arisen since the successful completion of the Marshall Plan.

The aspiration of this chapter, as of all the others except for remembrances of my childhood and my youth, is biographical—of the history-makers with whom my calling and its location made me more or less intimate. This purpose is best served by recording certain views and meditations these personages expressed to me from time to time that I consider the legitimate stuff of the history they made. And among these views and meditations, Truman's were especially pertinent to a true and fair measure of his Presidency.

The larger and much more valuable media of biographical conveyance are the broad historical reviews of Roosevelt's tenure such as those made by Arthur M. Schlesinger, Jr., and Raymond Moley, Cabell Phillips' notably thorough and objective work *The Truman Presidency*,* and Schlesinger's and Theodore H. Sorensen's accounts of the Administration of John F. Kennedy. But I hope that the following notes I have made of Truman's current thinking from time to time may serve at least as footnotes to his personality and his record.

On April 8, 1948, for example, the President surveyed for me a wide range of subjects. On V-E Day, he recalled, he had felt sure he would be able to make durable arrangements for peace and hence had made up his mind to retire in January, 1949, when he had served out the remainder of Roosevelt's

* New York: The Macmillan Company, 1946.

fourth term. "But I was wrong on that," he reflected. "I have
started measures for peace which I must see through. I am not
a quitter. The worst mistake we made was to demobilize [in the
immediate postwar period], and I helped make it. But there
was nobody urging anything else at that time" [a faulty re-
membrance, at least with respect to Forrestal and Harriman].

. . . As for the Democratic leaders who were opposing his
renomination, he remarked that they were "acting very foolishly:
they cannot get away from me." And even if they nominated some
one else, "he would have to run on my record, which would put the
party hopelessly on the defensive after having rejected the maker
of that record."

. . . He explained that his reason for limiting the new air-com-
bat groups below the point desired by Air Secretary [Stuart] Symington and the Air Force generals was, "we are on the verge of an
aviation discovery that will make obsolete everything now being
manufactured." [Evidently, new big bombers.] His plan, as he
described it, was also to maintain flexibility in aviation production
so that it could be stepped up when desired, and planning altered,
"as we did during the Second World War."

. . . The Republicans, it seemed to the President, were having
hard going in criticizing his foreign policies because they had no
substitute to offer for the European Recovery Plan (ERP) or for
the new measures of preparedness. For instance, the "only suggestions [Thomas E.] Dewey was able to make" were that the Voice
of America should be entrusted to more competent hands, and that
a Republican President would not make the mistakes his partisan
critics imputed to Truman. "There are plenty of domestic issues
they [the Republicans] could go after, but they are not doing it."
And he saw trouble in store for a party that tried to match and
improve his civil rights program [which, when submitted to Congress, had generated the independent Democratic States' Right of
1948 and, pressed into the Democratic Convention platform of that
year, had produced the "walkout" of several Southern delega-
tions].

. . . He had chosen Paul G. Hoffman to administer the Marshall Plan for reasons now made apparent by the popularity of the
choice. He had told Hoffman that declination was "impossible in
the circumstances," and Hoffman, after getting a medical check-
up, had agreed.

. . '. The President had telephoned an offer to Lewis W. Douglas, Ambassador to Great Britain, to be Roving Ambassador to the ERP, but Douglas had not only expressed a preference to retain his post, but had made his point with Truman by prophesying that if he took the new job, the fifteen other nations in ERP would suspect and imagine a partiality toward Great Britain, "which is going to get the lion's share anyhow."

. . . Had Truman detected any change [by the April 8, 1948 interview] in his makeup since he became President? He could think of none, he said, except that he felt a growing sense of being "walled-in"; and that it was necessary for him ever to remember that "two persons are sitting at this desk—Harry Truman and the President of the United States. And I have to be sure to remember on all occasions that the President is there, too."

. . . Turning to his press secretary, Charles G. Ross, a lifelong friend and old Missouri schoolmate, Truman said he noticed that Ross did not talk to him any more "with the same mouthful of brass tacks." Such was the fate of Presidents.

. . . Was he not troubled when he got conflicting counsel of great decisions from advisers equally able, informed, loyal, and sincere? No, said the President, he came to his decisions by the best rationalization within his powers and then didn't "worry about them. There is always a new one waiting to be made."

Truman's 1948 campaign—and the circumstances whereby he left with the Democratic National Convention at Philadelphia the choices of nominating him or dooming the party to inevitable defeat at the November poll—were, as previously noted, a twin masterpeice of practical political strategy. The principal obstacle to his nomination was the strong party sentiment for substituting Eisenhower, whose lonely eminence as the national hero, it was contended, would overcome the hazard of rejecting an incumbent President.

The following is an account I made at the time of the Eisenhower-Truman negotiations which was confirmed as "substantially correct" by its main source, Kenneth B. Royall, Truman's Secretary of the Army. In so confirming it to Cabell Phillips, for incorporation in Phillips' book *The Truman Presidency*, Royall made the exception that is noted below:

. . . In 1947, when Eisenhower's name began to be pressed by important Democrats for 1948 nomination, Royall, then Secretary of the Army, went to Truman. He said he thought it proper to advise the President that he could not work against Eisenhower if Ike was receptive or even under serious consideration; he would vote for Truman as a matter of loyalty; but perhaps in the stated circumstances the President might prefer to have Royall's resignation. [This is the detail Royall repudiated to Phillips.] The President said . . . that Royall should go to Ike and say that if Eisenhower would be a candidate for the top nomination, he, Truman, would help him get it and go on the ticket for Vice-President if Ike so desired. On being told this, Ike first expressed his incredulity, but then, when convinced that Truman meant what he said, told Royall he wanted to have nothing to do with politics and would appreciate advice about how to have that finally accepted by the politicians. This Royall reported back to the President.

Later in 1948, during the week before the Democratic Convention, one of the usual bull sessions of key Administration figures was held on the South Portico of the White House, the topic being whether Ike's name would go before the Convention as Claude Pepper, James Roosevelt, and a number of other Democrats were saying it should and would. Truman asked them all what they thought would happen in this event, and everyone but Royall assured the President he could make short shrift of the attempt. The President, observing that Royall had been silent, asked for his opinion. Royall answered that there was a belief that Ike would be nominated by acclamation if his name were presented. This angered some of the group, particularly Secretary of the Interior Oscar Chapman. A couple of drinks were served and the party broke up quietly. At the White House door, when Royall was leaving, an usher informed him that the President wanted to see him upstairs. He found Truman in the Oval Study with John Snyder, Secretary of the Treasury.

"I wanted to tell you," said Truman, "that I agree with you." He then asked how the presentation of Ike's name could be prevented. Royall, remarking that the President and Ike had the same objective, said he would try to see how this could be accomplished. In a telephone conference with Ike, Royall worked out the statement that Eisenhower sent to Pepper and others that put an end to the effort to present his name. Royall assured Eisenhower that he need not trouble to give out the telegram himself, that "five minutes after Pepper receives it, it will be public property."

On the Republican side in 1948 a number of leaders opposed the renomination of Dewey and sought Vandenberg's assistance in promoting the nomination of the Michigan Senator. Prominent among these Republicans was Harold E. Stassen (who in 1956 initiated and then abandoned a hopeless effort to have Governor Christian Herter of Massachusetts substituted for Richard M. Nixon as President Eisenhower's second-term running mate).

On a night in June, 1948, at a small dinner in my Georgetown garden, Vandenberg explained the reasons that led him to discourage the effort in his behalf. The dinner, which commemorated a joint wedding anniversary of the Vandenbergs and the Krocks, had been a practice for some years. Present also were the new British Ambassador Sir Oliver (now Lord) Franks, who must have been confused by the political technicalities of the conversation; John J. McCloy, then President of the World Bank; John Walker, Curator of the National Gallery of Art; and James Reston of my staff.

The Senate sitting late, Vandenberg did not arrive until nearly 10 P.M. He was in an expansive mood and talked freely about his prospects to be nominated for President at the Republican National Convention the following week.

Vandenberg insisted that, first, he was the symbol of the Republican Party disunity over foreign policy, and had deliberately emphasized this in his attack on the House cut in appropriations for the Marshall Plan, with the result that "at least two hundred members of the House—mostly Republican—hate my guts"; second, the Party should nominate someone who could "unify it," not dramatize its differences; third, therefore, he should not be nominated and would not, he thought, be nominated; fourth, he had circulated this view continuously to delegates who called on him in droves, most recently to a group from New Jersey who, after hearing Vandenberg's argument, however, went away saying, "He's wonderful"; fifth, and a member of Congress could not vote to draft citizens, as he had, and then reject a draft of himself.

He added the familiar argument that he would be much more service to the Party and the country if he remained as Chairman of the Committee on Foreign Relations. He professed confidence that he not be nominated and asked how he could assure that absolutely. I reminded him of what Gen. William Tecumseh Sherman had said in somewhat similar circumstances in 1884: "If nominated, I will not run; if elected, I will not qualify." The Senator smiled. Then, when I observed that General Eisenhower had complained that no citizen should utter such an "abrupt" rejection, he indicated that he agreed with Eisenhower. McCloy remarked that General Marshall had once asked him how to remove himself wholly from political speculation, and he—McCloy—had also quoted Sherman; that Marshall eventually said virtually the same thing. The Senator commented that he shared Eisenhower's stated belief that a professional soldier should not take high political office.

Senator Vandenberg expressed the opinion, during this conversation, that Governor Dewey of New York would not accept the Republican nomination for Vice-President if the Convention chose Vandenberg as its Presidential nominee. McCloy and Reston differed with this interpretation, and pointed out that Dewey could not, at this time, admit he would accept the Vice-Presidential nomination without hurting his chances for the Presidency. Vandenberg agreed with this and commented that he "could take Dewey up on the mountain" and show him the possibilities of the Vice-Presidency. This was a reference to the Senator's support of a proposal to make the Vice-Presidency a strong executive office, and to his known attitude that he would not agree to serve more than one term as President.

The dinner ended with a strong impression that Vandenberg feared he would be drafted, a prospect that Reston and I, at least, did not envisage.

It required three ballots for the Dewey forces to shake off the bid of Senator Robert A. Taft for the Presidential nomination. In the course of this maneuvering, according to a later account in the Downingtown, Pennsylvania, *Archive* by its editor, now

Ambassador, Robert McIlvaine (who was associated in the convention management of the effort in behalf of Vandenberg), Taft agreed to throw his strength to Vandenberg, but the deal was nullified when Governor Earl Warren of California refused to go along. When I asked Stassen after the convention (on July 2) about this report, however, he strongly disputed the story. At no time, he said, would Taft consider Stassen's proposal to help nominate Vandenberg: "Taft, who overrated his own strength, felt he was himself entitled to a finish run for the nomination."

Soon after he inherited the Presidency, Truman found his Cabinet divided over United States policy toward the Soviet Union, with at least two dramatic public exposures of the rift.

Henry A. Wallace, the Secretary of Commerce, was an early believer in what is now the popular policy of building bridges to the East. He was opposed to containment, which, after Stalin invoked the Cold War, had become the official policy of the United States with respect to the Communist nations. And Wallace's attitude evoked the incident that forced the reluctant Truman to dismiss him.

On September 10, 1946, Wallace brought to the President for approval a speech he was to make in New York; subsequent developments demonstrated that either the President had not read the speech through or had forgotten about it. For when the speech was delivered, it was so clearly a challenge to his own foreign policy, particularly as conducted by Secretary of State Byrnes, who was conferring in Paris at the time, that Byrnes in a teletyped message to Truman said quite justly, in effect, that either Wallace or he must leave the Cabinet; that Wallace was urging a foreign policy, as Byrnes understood it, contrary to the President's own; and that for Byrnes at least this was an untenable situation.

Though, typically, he blamed himself more than Wallace for the Cabinet crisis, the President felt obliged to agree with Byrnes. He asked for and obtained Wallace's resignation on

September 20. And the event culminated in Wallace's independent candidacy for the Presidency in 1948.

Normally the defection of a Cabinet member (Secretary of Commerce Wallace), plus the nomination of the Independent Democratic (States' Rights) ticket composed of two Southern Governors (Strom Thurmond of South Carolina and Fielding Wright of Mississippi), would have defeated Truman. Wallace's position attracted several Democratic affiliates of the "liberal" persuasion, and the Independent Party ticket disaffected Southern Democrats. But the Communists took the offered opportunity to infiltrate the management of Wallace's campaign. Only four Southern states, with a total of thirty-nine electors, gave their electors to the Democratic bolters. And once Truman had Eisenhower's assurance that he would not enter a contest for the Democratic Presidential nomination, the President was not only certain of renomination but was thereby liberated to make the bruising type of campaign at which he was highly proficient. He won the farm states' votes that elected him by successfully blaming the Republicans in Congress for a shortage of farm storage facilities, whereas the blame actually lay at the door of his own Secretary of Agriculture. He struck at Dewey's jugular which had been foolishly exposed by his attempts to out-promise the Democratic liberals. And shrewdly appealing to the inbred Southern preference for the nominee of a regular Democratic ticket, Truman was able to hold to a minimum the support of the Independent Democratic ticket. This minimum, canceled out by surprising victories in the Midwest and California, won Truman the election in his own right.

Years after the Byrnes-Wallace foreign-policy-speech controversy Truman expressed the confident belief that he had "the finest, most integrated Cabinet in history"; that the "throat-cutting in the Executive Branch has ended"; and that "State, Treasury, Defense, and Commerce" were a happy band of brothers, harmonious on all important points of policy and

action. This was the President's characteristic that was catego-
rized and criticized as "cocky." And certainly several Cabinet
members, in talking privately and separately, did not give the
impression that a "happy band of brothers" sat around the big
table in the President's office.

But when Truman so described them, he had not only
weathered the Wallace-Byrnes explosion, he had also appointed twenty-four persons to his Cabinet; Harry Hopkins had
been dead for years, as more recently was Defense Secretary
Forrestal, and smaller vestigial remnants of the Roosevelt regime had been lopped off the Administration. But all these
changes left wounds and sowed political turbulences that endured throughout Truman's last years in the White House.

The lingering troubles that beset the Truman Cabinet began
with its session of September 21, 1945. The subject was what
policy the Administration should follow in making its atomic
secret available to other nations. Forrestal, who was taking
notes, recorded in his diary that Wallace was "completely,
everlastingly, and wholeheartedly in favor of giving it to the
Russians . . . [arguing that] failure to give them the knowledge would make an embittered and sour people." When the
bowdlerized diary appeared in print, Wallace promptly assailed this entry as "a lie."

The account was challenged by others. I undertook in October, 1951, to determine the strength of its foundation by interviewing several of the principals. The then Assistant Secretary
of War, Robert P. Patterson, had taken no notes and could not
remember whether Wallace had expanded on the proposition
advanced by Patterson's chief, Secretary of War Henry L.
Stimson, whom Patterson was about to succeed.

This proposition was that the United States submit to the
U.S.S.R., with the assent of Great Britain and Canada, that an
end be put to the manufacture of the atomic bomb and the
research for improving it; probably impound the bombs in the
possession of the Nuclear Powers; and arrange to share with
Russia the technical atomic information for humanitarian and
commercial purposes, if the U.S.S.R. would agree to outlaw
the bomb as a weapon and make no further effort to manufacture it.

The Chief Justice of the United States, Fred M. Vinson, who had attended the 1945 meeting as Secretary of the Treasury, gently cited his position as a bar to giving me any account of the event, adding, however, that if he found any notes, he would turn them over. (No notes were forthcoming.) Associate Justice Tom Clark, who sat in the session as Attorney General, merely said he had "supported Vinson." John W. Snyder, by now Secretary of the Treasury, offered a generalized opinion. "Hell," he said, "you know as well as I do that Wallace was all for giving the Russians everything we had, including all the scientific stuff we developed before and during the war. As nearly as I can recall he urged that line consistently from the time he was Secretary of Commerce."

My final approach was to Wallace himself, by telephone. He said that Truman had started the Cabinet discussion by subscribing to Stimson's view and that "instantly Tom Clark and [Secretary of Labor Lewis] Schwellenbach began supporting it vehemently. I didn't go so far," said Wallace. But if anybody supposed the United States could keep the atomic secret, that, he said, was foolish: other nations would have it in three to five years. He, Wallace said, had proposed offering to share certain limited kinds of information with all nations, including the Russians, providing we had "full access" to everything the Russians had. But, he added, he definitely opposed sharing with Russia or any other nation the "know-how" of detonating atomic energy in the form of a weapon.

I asked Wallace how he could account for the Forrestal diary entry that he had characterized as "a lie." He said he believed that the mental and emotional troubles that preceded the Forrestal breakdown (in 1949) had begun as early as the Cabinet meeting of September 21, 1945.

I had come to know Forrestal intimately in the period (1923–1932) in which my permanent working and living base was in New York City. We were social companions, sharing the group that consisted of members of what is anachronistically referred to as "society" and the habitués of Swope's and

Neysa McMein's salons in the city and on the North Shore of Long Island.

I was drawn to Forrestal by the charm of his personality, his independent and intellectual quality, his zeal (though a Wall Street investment banker) to bring long-overdue reforms to the marketplace, and the fierce competitive spirit with which he contended on the golf link and tennis court and in the amateur boxing ring. And when he chose, he could invest any social gathering with a rare degree of wit and gaiety.

After he entered government in Washington, which had become my year-round working base, we maintained our friendship despite the inherent conflict between his professional obligation and mine. When Roosevelt summoned him for the first time, he spent with me the evening before his appointment at the White House. In the course of that evening he asked what I thought the President wanted of him, and for a suggestion as to how he could persuade Roosevelt that he was not the man for the job of Presidential Assistant that, I ventured, he was wanted for.

"Just tell him I am your closest friend in Washington," I said, "and that will put an end to the summons." However contrary to his protestations, Forrestal was intrigued by the prospect of an important public service worthy of his abilities; and next day he duly signed on—without, of course, mentioning my suggestion to Roosevelt.

The White House job, after an interval in which Forrestal returned to his banking firm, developed into his appointment as Under Secretary of the Navy, to be followed by his succession of Frank Knox as Secretary and eventually to his incumbency as the first Secretary of Defense. On the witness of this relationship I disagreed with Henry Wallace that Forrestal's emotional and mental troubles dated back as far as 1945.

But from the time of his appointment as Secretary of Defense in 1947, my wife had begun to detect inner disturbances in Forrestal that I had not. He visited us regularly, and often discussed with me on the telephone the intra-departmental difficulties that he said he was encountering, notably in his relations with Air Force Secretary Symington. But not until the succession of radio broadcasts by Drew Pearson of which

Forrestal was the target did I get an impression of irrationality and indecisiveness that was so completely at variance with the man I had known so well. After each of these Sunday broadcasts Forrestal would telephone me to discuss, but never decide, what to do about them.

Then came a broadcast that upset him more than any—a report that when Mrs. Forrestal was being held up in front of their Beekman Place home in New York City, her husband "hid" in his quarters. It happened by chance that I was in a position to refute the charge, having spent that evening in Forrestal's company and having slept in his guest room that fronted on the East River, a location where we could not—and did not—know of the holdup until the following morning. It was typical of Mrs. Forrestal that she did not awaken her husband to inform him of what, after all, was a *fait accompli.*

To Forrestal's fervently expressed relief, I volunteered to acquaint Pearson with the facts, offering the opinion that he would undoubtedly withdraw the charge. But though Pearson, on receipt of a written and detailed account, wired me "THANKS. WILL DO," the retraction was never forthcoming. From that time forward I did observe a deterioration of spirit in Forrestal, though, in fairness, it should be noted that the broadcast was only one of the causes.

An example concerns a telephone call from Forrestal one Sunday morning, the subject being a *New York Times* report of a speech made in Los Angeles by Symington. This report, by Gladwin Hill, a correspondent with a well-earned professional reputation for accuracy and integrity, quoted some remarks by Symington that were manifestly and definitely a criticism of Forrestal, his chief. And the purpose of Forrestal's telephone call—like some that had gone before—was to ask whether he was not now bound to ask President Truman to request Symington's resignation.

But whatever the explanation may have been, the offending passage did not appear in the speech as delivered, according to a telephone conversation I had that Sunday morning with John A. McCone (later Chairman of the Atomic Energy Commission and eventually Director of the Central Intelligence Agency), who had been present and had heard what Symington actually said. When I passed this on to Forrestal, he was obviously relieved that once again he could evade the issue with Symington. And this attitude was so untypical of the man that I was not surprised at a sequel that came soon.

Symington, with whom I was also friendly, but not in the intimate terms of my relationship with Forrestal, asked me to lunch with him at the Pentagon. He supplied me with chapter and verse to demonstrate that he had never merited Forrestal's doubts of his loyalty that were constantly being engendered by the troublemakers who abound in political Washington. I told Symington that I would publish the material if Forrestal agreed that it was accurate. From Symington's office I went downstairs to the Secretary's, and Forrestal listened to what I proposed to write. "Do you take any exception to this, and would you like to have it published?" I asked him. He replied that he would be pleased. Which, accordingly, I did, under the heading "The 'Insubordination' of Secretary Symington."

Since Forrestal for some time had been expressing the opposite judgment—once to Truman, who impatiently told him he would accept a recommendation to dismiss Symington if Forrestal ever got around to making it—I felt for the first time that there was some basis for being concerned about my old and beloved friend.

I did not even anticipate tragedy when a visibly shaken Forrestal told me of the cold reception he got from President Truman at Key West, in January, 1949. The following is from notes I made at the time of the Truman-Forrestal situation in general:

. . . The Secretary had lost favor with the President for two reasons in particular. The first was his opposition, in the middle of the 1948 campaign, to the partition of Palestine that Truman had endorsed. This opposition was on military grounds—that the creation of the State of Israel would threaten the supply of Middle East oil to the West, especially to the United States Navy. And with rare foresight he considered it a dangerous political concept, provocative of an eventual Third World War, to create a state surrounded by enemies and give it a guarantee of protection that some day, he predicted, the United States would be called upon to redeem, would not do for practical reasons of national security, and hence would make its pledged word ring hollow in the world. Although Forrestal confined these objections to private speech and intra-governmental discussions, his persistence irritated the President.

. . . The second, and more basic, reason for Forrestal's loss of Presidential favor grew out of his sound and patriotic desire to assure a smooth and uninterrupted transition of government power if Dewey should win the 1948 Presidential election, as was widely expected. Accordingly, the Secretary proposed—and to some degree executed—a plan whereby a representative of Dewey would be given a pre-election education in the procedures, though not in the information, operations, and policies, of the Defense Department and the Bureau of the Budget.

. . . By this time Forrestal's abstention from the 1948 campaign [he believed it would be improper for a Secretary of Defense to play a partisan political role], and his balking at the Palestine policy, had made him powerful enemies in the Administration, especially Brig. Gen. Harry Vaughan, the President's military aide at the White House. They interpreted his idea of assuring a smooth continuity in government, if the Republicans won, as his wish for and belief in this outcome of the election. And they persuaded Truman that was so.

. . . In consequence, Forrestal was barred the Presidential door for some weeks after Truman's election, despite repeated efforts to gain an audience. Finally, in January, he was told that the President would receive him for luncheon at Key West, where Truman was vacationing. But when Forrestal appeared, he found also present the Mayor of Key West, who remained throughout the meal, preventing any discussion with the President of the important matters Forrestal had come to lay before Truman. And as soon as luncheon was over, the President retired for his customary siesta, offering no further audience to his Secretary of Defense.

. . . It was in the deepest dejection of spirit that Forrestal told me of this episode, but I felt that, despite its clear forecast that Truman intended to replace him, Forrestal still clung to the hope that he would be allowed to remain. And with this feeling came a realization that he no longer was the realist whom I had always found equally unaffected by the prospect of triumph or disaster.

Not long after his barren visit to Key West, Forrestal was informed by Truman of his desire to replace him as Secretary of Defense with Louis A. Johnson. Johnson had raised a large campaign fund for Truman in the campaign of 1948, and among his qualifications for the post was the fact that, as Assistant Secretary of War under Roosevelt, Johnson was largely responsible for whatever Army preparedness there was at the outbreak of the Second World War in 1939.

Forrestal's reception of the news of his displacement was to tell the President that not only did he want to return to private life, but that he preferred Johnson as his successor. This, however, was the response of the sportsman that Forrestal was: it was irrelevant to the impression of friends who detected a steady decline in his mental state and his morale from that time forward. A very close associate in business and government, whom I shall refer to as "Z," gave me the following account of Forrestal's condition just prior to his stay at Hobe Sound and his subsequent removal to the Naval Hospital at Bethesda, Maryland.

It had long been Z's habit to lunch with Forrestal when in Washington, and on March 29, 1949, he phoned Forrestal's office to say he would be over as usual. An aide informed him that Forrestal was sorry, he could not lunch with him but would like Z to phone him afterward. This he did, and when Forrestal came on the wire, his voice was so strange that it disturbed Z greatly.

"Where are you?" he asked.

"I'm at home."

"I'll be right out."

"For your own sake I advise you not to."

"I'm on my way," said Z, closing the conversation.

When he reached the house on Prospect Avenue, the door was opened by Remy, the Filipino butler, whose usual yellow complexion was a gray-white. When Z asked what was wrong, the butler said that his boss seemed to be very sick. Mrs. Forrestal was in Hobe Sound, and the house was dark, with all the blinds drawn. At this point Forrestal shuffled down the stairs. The skin of his neck and face was hanging loosely and his loss of weight was noticeable.

Forrestal told Z not to say anything because "they are watching this house and they have wired it." Z was unable to discover who Forrestal meant by "they" (at one point he indicated that "they" were Senators who planned to investigate him). Then Forrestal pointed to a corner of the street where two bums were standing. Z said they did not look to him like shadows, but Forrestal insisted they were.

Just then the doorbell rang and a "dilapidated-looking man" was asking to see the former Secretary. He told Z, who answered the bell, that he had been an Alternate from North Carolina at the Democratic National Convention and wanted to be an assistant postmaster in his town. When the man left the house, Forrestal watched him through the blind and saw him stop to speak to the two bums on the corner. "You see, he is one of them" said Forrestal excitedly.

It was soon apparent, however, that the third man was only asking directions, because a trolley car came along, the others pointed to it, and he got aboard. Forrestal insisted, however, that the house was wired, that he had suspected this when he saw three strange men in the garage the previous morning for that purpose.

"Why didn't you ask them what they were doing?" Z inquired.

"I could not seem to decide what to do," said Forrestal.

Z then told Forrestal he would have to leave the house promptly; that he was going to send him to Hobe Sound by plane and bring a doctor there as soon as he could. Forrestal resisted for an hour or so, but finally agreed. Z phoned to Robert A. Lovett and Artemus L. Gates at Hobe Sound and told them to meet the plane on which he put Forrestal, who had boarded it quietly. Z then flew to New York and inquired of Dr. Howard A. Rusk the name of "the best psychiatrist in the country." The result was that Z and Dr. William C. Menninger flew to Hobe Sound on Friday morning.

The Navy, however, having heard something of Forrestal's condition, had sent their top alienist to Hobe Sound. This complication was dissipated by the fact that the Navy doctor recognized Dr. Menninger's eminence in the field and gave way to him.

When Z approached Forrestal in Hobe Sound, the latter insisted that they talk in an open place because, he said, the house where he was staying was watched and wired by the same mysterious "they." In the conversation Forrestal was amenable to the arrangements made; Dr. Menninger was produced; and an agreement was reached that Forrestal should be taken to Bethesda. After dinner Forrestal went to bed and slept soundly, and Z and Forrestal's former aide, Rear Adm. John Gingrich, watched him through the night. He slept so soundly, with the aid of a sedative, that he did not hear a siren blow at about six o'clock in the morning. After noting that this had not awakened Forrestal, Z went down to the beach for a swim. He thinks that whoever was reporting to Drew Pearson saw Z come out of the house at that point, and that this gave rise to Pearson's statement that Forrestal had rushed out of the house when the siren blew, thinking the Russians had attacked the United States.

That day Forrestal went willingly with Z and the two doctors by plane to Washington and rode peacefully in a car to Bethesda. He was not violent at any time. But he did have delusions and he had lost his health and his power to make decisions.

Z added that during the first conversation at the house on Prospect Avenue, Forrestal said he had not "slept a night through for months" and that his intestinal functions had not been normal for more than six weeks. Also, said Z, he was unsmiling at all times—both in Washington and Hobe Sound —and attempts to evoke his ordinarily acute sense of humor were vain.

Indicative of Forrestal's condition in the Naval Hospital was a conversation with Rear Adm. Sidney Souers, Secretary of the National Security Council, whom Forrestal had asked to bring a detector of hidden dictaphones and the like, which he believed had been concealed in his suite. When Souers, after a close search, reported he could find none, Forrestal commented: "They knew you were coming and took them out. Now they'll put them back again."

In his mental agony Forrestal saw Zionist spies and assassins lurking in doorways near his residence bent on revenge for his attitude toward the Palestine partition. And after he returned, unrecovered, from Hobe Sound, Florida, and entered the Naval

Hospital, he never left it until he jumped to his death from a tower window.

Both President Truman and former Secretary of State James F. Byrnes have written copiously of the circumstances that led to their official separation. They differ in fundamental particulars, notably Truman's contention that he rebuked Byrnes in a degree that left the Secretary no choice but to resign, and Byrnes's insistence that no such rebuke was ever spoken and that he left the Cabinet on his own motion because of an estrangement, personally and over policy, that had arisen between them.

But there is sufficient evidence for one conclusion: Byrnes was glad to leave and Truman was overjoyed at the opportunity to install as Secretary the man he probably admired more than any other, George C. Marshall. With this the facts of the wide-open disputatious record can be left to history.

But there is no such record in the case of Truman's brusque dismissal of Attorney General McGrath. So it may be of material value to students of the Truman Administration to relate the circumstances as told to me by McGrath, on February 26, 1952, after his removal from the Cabinet.

T. Lamar Caudle, the Assistant Attorney General in charge of the Tax Division, had got himself deeply involved in the charges of official misfeasance that induced the President to remove him and eventually sent him to prison. Before Caudle's removal, McGrath recalled he had noticed a number of news stories that he considered "sniping," with himself as the target; decided these had been inspired by Presidential intimates with Truman's knowledge and approval; that therefore the President was displeased with him. Accordingly, McGrath sought out "a personal friend," Clark M. Clifford, then legal counsel to the President, with a message for Truman. The message was that if McGrath's presence in the government was in any way unwelcome, the Attorney General would cheerfully resign; and that he was using Clifford as a relay instead of delivering the message in person because the President might want to "say things to a third person" he might not want to say to McGrath.

Clifford delivered the message, and brought back the response: the President knew nothing of the origin of the "sniping" stories; he resented them and recognized them as part of the technique of attacking the President through his top aides and friends; and he wanted McGrath to stay on as long as he, Truman, did.

The President then went to Key West. After the Caudle scandal was ascending to its unhappy climax, McGrath was telephoned by Charles Murphy, who had succeeded Clifford on the White House staff, to say that the President was disturbed and thought Caudle should leave the government. Would McGrath ask him to resign? McGrath would. Murphy expressed his satisfaction; but when McGrath telephoned to read the required letter, Murphy informed McGrath that there had been "another huddle" and it was decided the President himself should dismiss Caudle.

McGrath twice asked to speak to Truman. The first time he was informed that the President was having a siesta; the second, that he was out walking. McGrath decided Truman was avoiding him and dropped his request after asking when Caudle's dismissal would be made public. "At Joe Short's [the White House press secretary] four o'clock news conference today," he was told.

The Attorney General nursed his wounds in quiet, realizing that political expediency was being served and depending on the reassuring message from Truman that Clifford had relayed. But on the evening of January 2 Clifford went to see McGrath. He said he regretted to convey to the Attorney General that the President had decided it would be best to transfer McGrath to another post—Ambassador to Spain. McGrath then telephoned to Truman and this time was put through.

The Attorney General said he would, of course, resign and take the Madrid post, if that was what the President wanted. But first, he suggested, he would like an interview so that the public aspect of the transfer could be presented "on an amicable basis." The President directed McGrath to come to see him at Blair House at 8 P.M. the following day and to bring Clifford along.

On Thursday morning, January 3, McGrath, having been informed overnight that Truman had offered the post of Attorney General to a former Federal Judge, got together the FBI and other files on the individual concerned and awaited his Blair House interview. The same day Truman, as was his practice in certain circumstances, encouraged the belief that McGrath was on his way out by refusing to repudiate a suggestion to this effect made in the form of a question at a White House news conference.

At Blair House, McGrath repeated his willingness to resign, but said he had changed his mind about taking the post in Spain: he wanted his separation to be a "clean-cut affair." He counseled the President against appointing the ex-judge (who had already accepted by telephone), classifying him as something less than a true Trumanite—an estimate the President agreed was supported by a newsletter (which he produced), quoting the ex-judge as having attacked one of the Truman's government reorganization plans as a nullification of the very Hoover Commission recommendation it professed to carry out.

The President then suggested that the matter of McGrath's resignation be dropped "for the time being" until it could be worked out "happily." And next morning Truman telephoned McGrath to inquire if he planned to attend that day's Cabinet meeting, getting an affirmative answer. At this meeting the President announced that McGrath would stay on "as long as this Administration lasts" and praised him highly.

As late as January 10 the President told his news conference that there was to be an investigator of "corruption" who would be a special assistant to the Attorney General and not an independent official. Newbold Morris, a political figure in New York City, was publicly invested with that status. But, as it proved, he was not the man for an investigation of official corruption by the insiders. He branched out very much on his own, his activities culminating in an intimate questionnaire to be filled out by government personnel, including members of Congress. Though hailed by critics of the moral climate of the Administration, this raised a handsome intra-party political row; McGrath, disavowing the questionnaire to a Senate committee, dismissed Morris; and very soon after the President

learned of this, he summarily dismissed McGrath by telephone.

This is the record, according to McGrath. It was confirmed
to me by the late Philip B. Perlman, who resigned promptly as
Solicitor General when Truman failed to reward his unbroken
record of Supreme Court victories in civil rights cases by
appointing him Attorney General in McGrath's place.

Just after the outbreak of the Korean War, Truman analyzed the prospect in a number of conversations that revealed a
grasp of the subject that put to shame the cavilers who had
continued to sneer at him as "just a haberdasher." It included
these observations:

. . . We have decided to retake Korea, even if we are forced off
the beaches and back to Japan. But, if any fire breaks out elsewhere and it is to our advantage to fight there, we will abandon
Korea. There is no military agreement to resist aggression everywhere. Certainly neither Generals Omar Bradley, "Lightning Joe"
Collins, and [Douglas] MacArthur, nor Senator Vandenberg nor
Admiral Sherman [Chief of Naval Operations] want to fight the
Russians in their own backyard. We want any showdown to come
in Western Europe "where we can use the bomb."

. . . But it happens that the weakest of the Communist satellites [North Korea] is licking hell out of us, which is very bad from
the propaganda point of view of our position with the rest of the
world and with the United Nations.

. . . Our chief concern, or at least one of them, is the "Trojan
horse Commies" in the United States. There is great fear of
sabotage. We have no machinery adequate to police or check our
strategic air bases, where we have the big bombers that would
carry the bomb; and many of the "fifty thousand Communists in
the U.S.A." in contact with Russian agents are bent on sabotage,
which would prevent many of our planes from leaving the ground.

Some of the considerations on which the foreign policies of
the Truman Administration were evolved appear in my 1950
and 1951 interviews and in previous conversations with the

President. In *evolving* foreign policy, he depended more heavily on his Secretaries of State—Byrnes, Marshall, and particularly Acheson—than Roosevelt had, and to about the same degree (with respect to Acheson) that Eisenhower depended on John Foster Dulles. But like all our decisive Presidents, he accepted the burden of final responsibility for major policies that requires making a choice among several laid before him.

Thus, even when giving his approval to the bombing of Hiroshima and Nagasaki toward the end of the Second World War, he rejected the proposal of some advisers, whose judgment he valued highly, that the Japanese government be warned shortly in advance of the bombing. This, it has thereafter been contended, would have spared the lives and lifetime injuries the bombing inflicted on civilians, while accomplishing its objective of knocking Japan out of the war and avoiding the land battle between the Japanese and American armies that the United States military held was otherwise unavoidable and would cost the nation many tens of thousands of casualties.

My notes of the conversation on May 24, 1951, with the President dealing with his foreign policies—both diplomatic and military—include the following account of his views:

. . . At no time did Truman believe the Soviets would go to war with the United States. By 1951 they still were "not in a position to initiate it," and this would increasingly be true. World peace in his time depended on "making some arrangement with the Russians," which, when the United States attained his objective of "full military parity" with the U.S.S.R., would be feasible and durable.

. . . Stalin was having trouble with the satellites, "and also at home." Truman did not specify. He admiringly quoted Edwin W. Pauley, one of his quondam officials, who, he said, really got behind the Iron Curtain in Europe and Korea some time ago and concluded that the Russians don't know how to create the industrial machine they would require for World War Three.

. . . One of these requirements is oil, and the President believes the Russians are hundreds of thousands of barrels short of the daily million they would need. To get the oil of Iran into Russian centers, he said, would call for a U.S.S.R. pipeline to the Caspian that would take years to build. And to make this supply certain, the Russians would be obliged to occupy Iran, which would mean war. Thus, he thinks, in moving to fit themselves for war by obtaining the essential oil supply, they would have to provoke war itself—an untenable program.

. . . The British, he said, dealt ineptly and disastrously with the Iran oil matter. We told them how to avoid it but they did not follow our counsel. The head of the Anglo-Persian company (from his photographs) looks like a typical nineteenth-century Colonial exploiter. The contrast with the oil policies our people have followed in the Middle East is striking.

. . . But these foreign oil countries have a good case against some groups of foreign capital. The President said he thought Mexico's nationalization of oil was "right," even thought so at the time; but it was regarded as "treason" to say so. If, however, the Iranians carry out their plans as stated, Venezuela and other countries on whose supply we depend will follow suit. That is the great danger in the Iranian controversy with the British.

. . . The President shared the impression that General Eisenhower veers from optimism to pessimism toward his assignment as Supreme Commander of NATO. Never, said Truman, had he thought of NATO as anything but a gamble, a deterrent to war provoked by Russia, not a "blueprint" that would take form in detail. He was told and believes that the only people "over there" with a will to resist by fighting are the British, the Scandinavians, the Greeks, and the Turks. He hopes this spirit will be created, but his hope is very slight with respect to the Western Germans. He acknowledged the danger that the European economy may be bankrupt by the rearmament program and that the United States could be also. But he does not think this will happen.

. . . There is one "blueprint," however, that will become a fact in detail—Point Four (technical assistance to undeveloped nations). As on previous occasions, the President walked over to his big globe and pointed to vast areas in South America and Africa, where he said Point Four would prove its greatest value. He agreed with Joseph P. Kennedy and Eisenhower that nationalism, not a wish for "communism," was the reason for the tumult in the various countries. Communists shrewdly stimulated these movements in their own interest. But "communism" was not the cause, and this ideology is waning in attraction throughout the world.

. . . When I told him our people in Germany had informed me that they could not give vital information to the French because of the number of Communists in the French Army command, "You can't tell the French anything in confidence," said Truman. In World War One he often had first heard of American battle plans from French troops.

. . . The war in Korea would end like the Berlin airlift, and for the same reason. When the Russians got enough and were made certain of our resolution, they lifted the Berlin blockade. When the Far East aggressors come to the same conclusion, and it will be soon, it will be the same story. [This position is President Johnson's with respect to Vietnam.]

Each time Truman reviewed his program for world peace he stressed Point Four. His aim was to "save the lives of seven or eight million people." On one occasion I said, "Fortunately for this program you are not bound by the new two-term amendment." The President had just enjoyed a field day with the press on the topic of his running for a second elective term, so this remark increased his good humor. "When they passed that limitation on the Presidency," he said, "Congress should have had enough guts and honesty to limit their own tenure, too."

Historians may find parallels between Truman's rationale for his "Doctrine" and Point Four, and some of the thinking that materialized in the active military intervention of the United States in Vietnam. This developed into a major war from the nucleus of President Kennedy's decision to increase the number of U.S. military "advisers" in South Vietnam from fewer than eight hundred to sixteen thousand, and to send them by air to the combat zones. But before parallels are drawn, it should be taken into major account that by joining the battle in Korea under the flag of the United Nations, Truman made the war a *collective* action, even though Americans furnished 95 per cent of the U.N. force and its equipment.

This policy, it is true, was ultimately to force the ending of hostilities in a stalemate. Once, in talking about Korea with the President, I got the impression that he at least had dallied with General MacArthur's proposal to invade North Korea and bomb the Chinese mainland, after the Chinese Communist "volunteers" appeared in battle at the Yalu. But even if, as a war veteran and man of action, Truman was momentarily attracted by the idea he did not lay the proposal before our U.N. partners, who, in any event, would have rejected it, aghast. And the U.N. aegis, although under it the United States bore nearly all the burden of the Korean war, also made this officially, in Truman's words, "a police action" to uphold the U.N. Charter and its protective role over South Korea, instead of a defense of the national security of the United States as the war in Vietnam has finally been justified by the Johnson Administration in the last of a half-dozen other and abandoned explanations.

From time to time, in this reportorial narrative, I have mentioned some public activity by, and conversations about it with, Bernard M. Baruch. He was such an outstanding figure among Presidential advisers over more than three decades that the references will recur before this narrative is concluded. But with apologies to the reader for digressing from the order of the calendar, this seems as good a point as any to halt for a survey of this extraordinary, public-spirited, foresighted man.

With respect to his incredible, intuitive foresight, he enjoyed quoting an observation I once made: "Either your counsel to the powers that be has been lousy or they haven't taken it." For on numerous occasions he urged action to forestall an approaching economic crisis he saw plain, only to behold this action become official policy after it was too late for its basic wisdom to be demonstrated. Thus, the economic controls he pleaded for early in the Second World War and in the postwar period were deferred until their partial adoption, and premature abandonment, by the Administration provided no true test to their merit when proposed.

Franklin D. Roosevelt grew bored with Baruch when he persisted in urging policies that, though sound at the time, and eventually proved to have been, ran contrary to the Administration's political concerns. An example of the contrast between Truman's bigness in big things and pettiness in petty things was his break with Baruch over the latter's refusal to help make up the Democratic Party deficit after the campaign of 1948. Truman's subsequent letter, asserting, as evidences of Baruch's "ingratitude," that the Party had honored Baruch conspicuously, and that he (Truman) had appointed Baruch's brother Herman as an Ambassador, is one of the least admirable entries in that President's record.

As far back as 1924 I made the following appraisals of Baruch's patriotic contributions, which—though often moved by congenital vanity, I agree—he always hoped would produce the recognition and praise of his contemporaries:

. . . By 1911 Baruch was one of the first men in Wall Street. His personal equation completed, he applied his fine mind to both abstract and practical economics. When Woodrow Wilson began to illumine the political scene, Baruch turned to his aid in the belief that Wilson's ideals, pursued through Democratic Party principles, would help to establish that economic balance in the earnings of all classes of workers that is Wilson's goal. . . .

During the months immediately preceding the World War, Baruch's counsel, when sought by Wilson, proved always so wise, disinterested, and penetrating that he was asked to mobilize the industries of the nation for and during the war, in behalf of the government. This service, rendered by Baruch as chairman of the War Industries Board, after disposing of any holdings that conceivably could even suggest a conflict of interest, was a brilliant, flawless performance. He was to the armies of workers in America what Pershing was to the United States armies of soldiers in France. . . .

Postwar problems brought agricultural depression, and Baruch turned all his energies to bear on the farmers' condition. The result was the spread of the cooperative marketing movement, which he was the first person of national importance and influence to initiate, and which brought about higher agricultural prices (from below subsistence levels in cotton, tobacco, etc.) and the political independence of farm workers. . . . If there is any worldwide problem loose that has economics and human well-being mixed up with it, the free service of one of the best living solvers of such problems can readily be procured. . . .

The League of Nations, the American farmer, the memory of Woodrow Wilson, the plight of a friend, a gallant piece of horseflesh [I left out a "lovely lady"], a good grouse season in Scotland, the world economic situation—any or all of these are as a trumpet to Baruch, anywhere, any time.

He was an old man—although still erectly tall, slender, and magnificent in looks and bearing—when he came to Washington in March, 1957, to see his brother sworn in as Ambassador. But the unimpaired vigor of his mind and the lessons of his experience in international negotiation were evident in his account to me of a conversation with Secretary of State Acheson on the Truman aid proposal to Greece and Turkey that developed into the "Truman Doctrine" and its wide distortion. According to Baruch the conversation went like this: Acheson had called Baruch into his office and began by asking if it was true, as Acheson had heard, that the new policy "disturbed" Baruch. The answer was that Baruch was disturbed because he was confused.

"What is the policy?" he asked. "Why are the British quitting Greece?"

Acheson: "They are out of dollars."

Baruch: "Don't say that at the Capitol; it is nonsense. They've got three billion dollars left, their wool clip, etc. How many troops, by the way, have they in the Near East?"

Acheson: "They have eight thousand in Greece and a hundred thousand in Palestine."

Baruch: "Then the whole thing is about oil. How could they hold one hundred thousand in Palestine if it is all about dollars? . . . What do we intend to do if we stand alone—if we intend to do anything?" he asked the Secretary, and got "nothing like a satisfactory or informed reply."

Baruch's comment on this was that "he thinks the British got rattled by their coal crisis, that there is nobody in their government with courage, and that when they came to us with the March 31st deadline for withdrawal from Greece, we should have said: 'Don't get excited, why the cold feet? You are not going down the drain. Remember how you stood alone in the war.' " And, he commented, he would have told them to cool off and think it over as we couldn't possibly make a policy so rapidly and ask Congress to move so fast.

Baruch added that when Marshall sent him a wire from China on Baruch's atomic energy statement last fall ("Our choice is between the quick and the dead"), he replied that when Marshall became Secretary of State he should definitely not "hurry" things. That advice Marshall certainly did not take in this instance, observed Baruch.

On the night of January 23 Baruch was advising Truman there should be no tax reduction for anybody, was asking the President why foreign credits to pay the expenses of the Marshall Plan are "sacrosanct," and was getting no answer. He also was telling Truman that the British were resisting the franc devaluation in order to protect an "overvalued pound" and to stall off a decision what to do about their 3.5 billion in frozen sterling. He said the British resistance was a smokescreen; and that, through British policy, the U.S. now has Greece, Turkey, Germany, Palestine, China, Korea, and Japan "on our hands." The British "have all the benefits and all the Mideast oil."

When Truman praised Ambassador Lewis W. Douglas highly and said he had great and useful influence with British Foreign Minister Aneurin Bevan, so did Hopkins have with Stalin, replied Baruch, and where did that get us?

For Presidents after Wilson, Baruch often became an inconvenient visitor to the White House in periods when political considerations dominated the thinking there. The reasons are apparent in the preceding paragraphs. But until Baruch died he continued to supply his counsels to Presidents, lesser executives, and members of Congress on the less numerous occasions when they were sought, and volunteered them when they weren't. And though his monument is more mournful than most, because the adoption of these counsels by several Presidents would have spared a number of agonies the American people have endured since the Depression, nevertheless this monument looms large and impressive in the catacombs of the Might-Have-Been.

Throughout the seven years of Truman's incumbency—but once again after he left the White House—I found myself involved in only one of those controversies over my report of a Presidential act or word that were so numerous in the Roosevelt Administration.

This controversy as to fact with Truman was whether he had, as I reported in *The New York Times* on November 7, 1951, sounded out General Eisenhower, then NATO Supreme

Commander, on his attitude toward accepting the Democratic Presidential nomination in 1952 for which Truman offered his support, repeating a similar offer he had made to Eisenhower in 1948.

When this dispatch was published, Truman denied it, with the added barb that the article was one he would have expected from a gossip columnist but never from me. The denial was widely accepted in the press when Eisenhower in Paris refused specific confirmation (in his subsequent memoirs and private conversations, however, he obliquely established the fact). And my columnist colleagues with a few exceptions—including Alexander ("Casey") Jones of the Gannet newspapers and Kyle Palmer, Political Editor of the *Los Angeles Times*—denounced me as a fabricator.

I had described my informant as a "Democrat in an eminent public position" who had the story of the feeler direct from the President himself.

With the consent of that informant I append, save for non-essential details, and in condensed form, the account I wrote, on November 8, 1951, and that has remained in my private files until that consent was not only obtained but volunteered:

About 9:30 P.M., November 6, 1951 . . . I was called to the telephone by Associate Supreme Court Justice William O. Douglas. He said he had some information to give me that would inevitably become public property soon, and was, he thought, of great political interest and importance. We arranged to meet the following morning at 11 o'clock in the office of Dr. Morton Finn, on the seventh floor of 1825 I (Eye) Street, where the Justice had an appointment for some dental work he expected to be finished by that time.

At the appointed hour I was in Dr. Finn's office and told the Justice, who was in the chair, that I was awaiting him. He came into the anteroom in about ten minutes and we walked into the hall. There he gave me the account of Truman's conversation with Eisenhower which I wrote for today's *New York Times* and which was published in that issue.

When Justice Douglas told me the story, he said I could use it if I wanted because "it's bound to come out soon, anyhow, and I have so few opportunities to tell you anything." I promised to protect him as my source completely, have done so, and will continue to do so.

Because of the attack made on *The New York Times* and me by *The Herald Tribune*, for publishing the story as we did, and because of other doubts, denials, and suggestions that I fell for a "plant," I herewith set down the details, to remain indefinitely in my private file:

On Monday, November 5, the same day the President and Eisenhower met privately, Truman received the Supreme Court at Blair House. That was in the afternoon. The reception scattered into little groups and at one point Justice Douglas, Chief Justice Fred M. Vinson and (Douglas thinks) Justice Minton were alone in a corner with the President.

Truman said he had had a big day; that he had an interesting talk with Eisenhower; that he told Eisenhower his offer of 1948 held good for 1952; that Eisenhower said that would present a great problem to him, his differences with the Democratic (Truman) Party over the Wagner Act and labor policy alone being typical.

Justice Douglas said he gathered from the President that at this response the matter was dropped.

Justice Douglas attested and also corrected these notes with the following:

He struck out "and (Douglas thinks)" in the next-to-the-last paragraph of the memorandum and inserted "Justice Burton, Justice Clark, the Solicitor General [Philip B. Perlman] and. . . ."

After "typical" in the last paragraph he inserted "as he [Eisenhower] did not agree with the labor policy of the Democratic Party, since it was not severe enough on labor, etc."

In an appended note Justice Douglas explained that he had "changed" the memorandum "in interest of accuracy, and initialed the changes." In the same interest he put "Wm. O. Douglas" under my own signature at the end of the memorandum.

Truman's tendency to rely on what often proved to be a faulty memory was solely responsible for the second of these disputes (but of only temporary duration) over something I had written. Like FDR before him (in 1937), Truman (in

February, 1950) had given me an exclusive authorized interview—still a rarity in those times but which under Kennedy
and Johnson was to become a commonplace. In this interview I
quoted the President as viewing 3 to 5 million unemployed as
a tolerable condition.

After he left the White House, he denied the attribution
as well as the authorized interview itself, telling a Senate committee the latter had never taken place. This forced me to
publish the background of the interview—how he had proposed it at a social evening at the 1925 F Street Club, how he
had approved the submitted prepublication text, etc. Whereupon, typically honest and forthright, Truman withdrew his
denial as publicly as he had made it, confirmed what he had
denied, and wrote me in his own hand a letter that was generous to the point of magnanimity.

The background of the authorized interview is unusual in
the history of such publications, not only because of the actual
facts, but because it was characteristic of one of the most
misunderstood and underrated Presidents in our history. Truman was the guest of honor at a dinner given at the club by
Senator and Mrs. Brian McMahon of Connecticut to which my
wife and I were invited. After dinner, during the period when
the sexes separated according to Washington custom, I was
talking in a corner with the Chief Justice of the United States,
Fred M. Vinson. Indicating the President, who was with a
small group in another part of the room, I remarked that there
were several questions I would like to put to him, that the
answers could shed much light on his national stewardship and
several complex public issues.

"Why don't you ask him," said Vinson, looking straight at
Truman, and in a carrying tone. Overhearing this, Truman
walked over and said to me, "Ask me whatever it is, and I'll
give you a straight answer." When I suggested, in thanking
him, that a private session, with plenty of time, would provide
a more satisfactory setting, the President directed me to make
the engagement through his press secretary, Charles G. Ross.
The interview, his approval, and the publication followed within
a few days.

Some months afterward, on May 24, 1951, when Truman's

previous espousal of the Greek-Turkish aid legislation and the Marshall Plan, and his smashing of the Berlin blockade by the U.S.S.R., had begun to acquaint the American people and the world with the President's bold vision and decisiveness, he proposed another interview in this fashion.

It was a Sunday afternoon. When I returned from walking Snickers, my Alsatian—a noble animal, the great-grandson of the first of his family to enrich my own—my wife informed me that the President had telephoned from his temporary residence at Blair House (Margaret Truman's piano had poked a hole in a White House floor and the Executive Mansion was undergoing reconstruction) and wanted me to call him back as soon as I returned. When I reached him, Truman, who does not like dogs but for years was a champion pedestrian, began by commenting that the walk was good for both "the pup" and me. Then he remarked that he had some views on public issues I might be interested in, suggested I come to Blair House to hear them, and added that while such a meeting was usually arranged by his press secretary, his initiation of this one was to be strictly between us.

The outcome was a two-column presentation of these views. But by agreement I wrote them in the form of "wholly authoritative information," so that while the source would be obvious to the reader experienced in this Washington journalistic technique it would not be specified.

This left the President free to turn off inquiries from the press about the subject matter in any way he chose. And the way he chose was to say that he could not be expected to comment on unattributed dispatches. But since he refused to disavow the views ascribed to him, he left his interrogators in no doubt as to my source.

Truman's elected term, especially the final two years of it, was spent in laying the political foundation for what, under Lyndon B. Johnson, became the legislative program of the Great Society; in searching for a Democratic Presidential nominee who could be elected as his successor; and in trying simultaneously to fight and negotiate the Korean war.

Congress generally refused to legislate his limited blueprint of a welfare state, leaving Truman only whatever may be historical credit for having submitted it. Adlai E. Stevenson, whom Truman diligently promoted to become the reluctant, drafted Democratic Presidential nominee in 1952, fell afoul of the fatally bad luck of encountering the No. 1 national hero, Eisenhower, along the path to Election Day. And when Truman left the White House, the Korean war was still a military stalemate—under negotiation but with mounting U.S. casualties—partly because he had initiated it as a "police action" under limitations prescribed by the United Nations, partly because just before favorable conditions arose for a cease-fire and armistice during Truman's tenure, the attitude of the Administration shifted on important issues during the negotiations with the Communists.

These concerned (1) the postwar line of demarcation between South and North Korea; (2) the repatriation of prisoners taken by both sides; and (3) the arrangement by both sides of a cease-fire.

According to an account given me by two diplomats who, under Acheson's supervision, believed they had produced a favorable atmosphere for an armistice in 1951, these shifts assured the continued existence of the Korean War as a major issue throughout the 1952 political campaign in the United States.

That enabled Eisenhower to clinch his victory over Adlai Stevenson by announcing to a war-weary American people that after the election "I shall go to Korea." And the fruit of this visit was the eventual North-South Korean armistice, which, as Phillips admirably phrased it, "was a poor substitute for victory but a tolerable substitute for war."

While the record is confused with respect to the shifts of position by Truman during the armistice negotiations, two at least are documented. First: On June 7, 1951, Secretary of State Acheson announced specifically that the United States would agree to a "reliable armistice" line at the 38th Parallel in Korea. Not long thereafter Truman approved the recommendation of Gen. Matthew Ridgway, the new Supreme Commander of the United Nations Forces, that the line should be the one that existed *de facto* at the signing of the armistice. Second: The negotiations at Panmunjom were at least moving ahead when Truman directed that there must be no compromise in the matter of the exchange of prisoners of war, that each must be left free to determine whether he wished to be repatriated. On this issue the negotiations stalled for the remainder of Truman's term, and though the principle he stood on so firmly was admirable, it was eventually settled on something less than a 100-per-cent humanitarian basis.

So, on January 20, 1953, after that awkward ride from the White House to the Capitol with a successor burning with resentment over Truman's personalized campaign attacks, the outgoing President boarded the train for home with satisfaction for his accomplishments and no regrets for his failures.

He is not one to brood, having in his judgment done the best he could with the Presidential problems that confronted him. And neither then nor since has he disclosed even a fractional degree of the "Potomac fever" that plagues those in Washington whose exercise of official power has come to an end.

In 1956 he sought, at the Democratic National Convention, to prevent the renomination of Stevenson, who, Truman's experience had persuaded him, could not successfully stay the grueling course. But like Jefferson, who had laid down his burdens with rejoicing at the prospect of going home to Monticello, Truman went home to Independence, Missouri, in the same unusual state of mind—unusual among those who were Presidents of the United States and constitutionally eligible to serve another elected term.

13

EISENHOWER

IT IS still fashionable, in the dominantly leftist press here and abroad, and especially among my journalistic colleagues in Washington, to assess President Eisenhower's Administration as one of the least notable in American history. But I view it as one of the most notable, and to be in this kind of minority is not, after all, an unusual or dismaying personal experience. In international affairs the Eisenhower Administration maintained the nation at peace and in unity. This fortunate attainment—rare in the twentieth century—was reached in several ways:

> by "brinkmanship," as in the instance of landing troops in Lebanon to preserve the Mediterranean from the threat of Russian domination—having sought and obtained advance approval of the landing by Congress;
>
> by the show of naval force that discouraged the Chinese Communists from trying to take over Formosa;
>
> by the President's rejection of the counsels of major officials, including Vice-President Richard M. Nixon, to try to rescue the French from defeat in Indo-China with

active military aid, at the clear risk of involving the United States in a ground war in Southeast Asia;

by limiting our support of the United Nations' war in the Congo to the delivery of material of war at Leopoldville, and by declining to ferry it in U.S. Air Force planes to the combat zone;

by such practical aid to the underdeveloped nations as food and atomic energy for peace.

A blemish on this record, in both the contemporary and hindsight judgment of some experts in foreign affairs, was the frustration by the United States of the 1956 Israeli military expedition against Egypt that Great Britain and France were preparing to join when the Israelis were warned off by Washington's resort to the United Nations Charter. It is conceivable that these allies, probably the Israelis alone, could have kept the Suez Canal international and free for all shipping, overthrown Gamal Abdel Nasser's regime in Egypt, and at least postponed for a while the threat of general conflict generated in 1967 by the provocations and by the fact of the six-day war in the Middle East. It is also probable that during this postponement the defeat of the Arab states could have been exploited to effect a durable peace.

But the 1956 intervention of the United States, as in all the other international crises of the Eisenhower years, was in nominal application of the United Nations Charter. And many who have criticized the intervention then and since have been among the loudest of those who cite the Charter in dissenting from or approving the foreign policy of any nation.

A more firmly imprinted stain on the excellent Eisenhower record, on the testimony of later developments, was the State Department's encouragement of the revolutionary movement in Cuba under Fidel Castro. Here the "moralism" expressed at Suez took the form of disapproval of the dictatorship of President Fulgencio Batista. To that consideration was wholly subordinated his pro-American, anti-Communist policy that kept Cuba a secure United States base in the Caribbean. The Administration weakened Batista with an embargo on military supply and financial assistance to the Cuban economy; accepted Castro on trust as an anti-Communist patriot, disregarding the evidence to the contrary submitted by the later Ambassador Arthur Gardner; and laid the deep foundation of a militantly Communist, bitterly anti-American state ninety miles from the American mainland—a neighbor of the type President Kennedy later vowed would never be permitted in the vicinity.

Except for the proposed American troop involvement in Indo-China that Eisenhower rejected, these policies were successfully conceived and urged on the President by his Secretaries of State, principally John Foster Dulles. But the record of an Administration, good or bad, depends in part on the wisdom of Presidential choices for the Cabinet. Eisenhower not only selected Dulles and, on Dulles's suggestion, his colorless but experienced successor, Christian A. Herter; also their chief in the White House supported them in domestic, political, and international weather, fair or foul.

Despite the economic recession toward the end of Eisenhower's second term, American society as a whole in that period was spared the seizure of the deep malaise that has afflicted the two succeeding Administrations. Although the Eisenhower regime spent more on domestic and foreign undertakings than had been spent in any previous period of peace, the 1967 current level of inflation of consumer-goods prices and services was an advancing shadow, so distant as to be barely visible except through the telescopes of non-partisan classic economists. The Democrats claimed that the cost-of-living rise under Eisenhower was 7 per cent as contrasted with 4 per cent under Truman. But this calculation depended on which set of statistics was employed. And another set, used by Administration economists, controverted the Democratic figure.

The industry-government spending combination, which Eisenhower so prophetically warned the nation against in his final State-of-the-Union report to Congress, was checked in its pace (but reaccelerated under his successors) by the President's realization of its developing character. The city streets at night were still generally safe for citizens, including lone women, to traverse in their normal pursuits.

Politicians in Congress (and other ardent champions of the

Supreme Court decision that forbade compulsory racial segregation in the public schools) were already engaged in irresponsible, vote-seeking, riot-breeding assurances to the Negro minority that a fully amalgamated American society was on the verge of attainment. But only when these assurances were fully demonstrated to be cruel hoaxes of the Negro population (in 1966–1967) did the surge of violent Negro civil disobedience appear. Non-violent, as were the marchers under the leadership of Martin Luther King, Jr., they were invariably and inevitably provocations of violence by criminal, marauding Negro juveniles urged on by demagogic agitators of their race —some of them outspoken anarchists.

The lower Federal courts—guided by an increasing number of Supreme Court decisions, for which, as in the desegregation of schools case, neither clear constitutional nor statutory warrant existed—began to usurp more and more constitutionally separated power in the area of Legislative and Executive action. But the scope of supporting legislation proposed in the 1950s was limited by the Congressional blockade, led by Senate Majority Leader Lyndon B. Johnson, of radical compulsory racial integration measures that would have infringed the "civil rights" of the American people as a whole. Since then these measures have been incorporated in the laws and by judicial decree. And the Department of Justice under Presidents Kennedy and Johnson has spinelessly established the fact of being a Negro as a grant of immunity for most notorious flagrant violators of both the civil and criminal laws.

In the Civil Rights Bill of 1957, for example, Johnson used the power and influence of his post to jettison the sections that prescribed desegregation of privately owned facilities for public accommodations and supererogation of the electoral law-enforcement and judicial processes of the states by Federal power. But, ironically, it was Johnson as President who applied the political force with which all the Federal compulsions, and more, that he had blocked in 1957 were either enacted by Congress or newly "discovered" in the Constitution by the Supreme Court.

The growing power of labor unions, acquired through the Wagner Act and kindred measures in President Franklin D.

Roosevelt's time, to impede or totally shut down the process of the national economy was at least halted in Eisenhower's Administration by the Landrum-Griffin Act and by the rulings of the President's appointees to Federal agencies that restored the placement of the public interest above that of the unions in major industrial disputes.

This halt, incidentally, was maintained on one occasion, and at the last moment, only by an eleventh-hour intervention of Secretary of Commerce Sinclair Weeks. President Eisenhower had trustingly bought a legislative package from his Secretary of Labor, James J. Mitchell, on the representation that this package would have tightened the restraints of the Taft-Hartley Act on organized labor's abuses of the overriding economic and political power it was granted by the Wagner Act. In reality, it would have had the opposite effect. And Eisenhower was about to send the package to Congress, with his imprimatur, when Weeks convinced him that it was loaded with new labor union powers.

But under Eisenhower's successors the abuses of the general interest by labor leaders, in the use of their special powers that were entrenched in the Wagner Act, have made the unions supreme over the economy. The right of collective bargaining has been employed, under these unilateral powers, to force annual wage increases without respect either to productivity or profits. The right to strike has been distorted into the right to come out victorious in any labor dispute. And when one powerful union has imposed an excessive wage contract—often through coercion by the White House—on one industry, or a large unit thereof, this contract has become the norm for other settlements.

One glaring deviation in the Eisenhower record was, in particular, the Federal budget. Its steady increase established him as another of the great spenders against whom he inveighed. But he never lost sight of the goals on which, with congenital simplicity, he identified even before he entered active politics:

> a search for incentives "to get our minds fixed on real accomplishments, not a shorter work week, more un-

productive leisure," and ever rising Federal subsides to groups and individuals;

a solvent government;

leaving it to, and inspiring, private enterprise to do much more in the social-economic field than government, by Executive fiat and acts of Congress, could ever do.

On this policy, opposing a proposal of a Federal appropriation of $350 million for health research, Eisenhower once remarked that the cure of cancer would "probably be found by some little guy working in an attic without a Federal grant" in a non-regimented society.

Nevertheless, the rising budgets of the Eisenhower Administration were sowing the seeds of the consumer-price inflation that later sprouted like Jack's beanstalk in the astronomical increases of the welfare-state budgets sent to Congress by President Johnson to establish "The Great Society." Yet there still was enough responsibility in the fiscal and monetary policies of Eisenhower and his advisers, and in Lyndon Johnson's coordinate Senate activities, to hold in fallow ground the seeds of the galloping inflation it had sown.

Eisenhower, as the Bible expresses it, had "the poor always with him" throughout his eight years in the White House. (Kennedy wildly exaggerated this in the 1960 campaign when he declared that "seven million Americans go to bed hungry.") Yet if there were no grandiose and vastly expensive government agencies created in Eisenhower's Administration to bring the poor (both deserving and shiftless) to a comfortable subsistence level, there was also no drain of billions of dollars from the national exchequer (as there is now) into the runoffs of incompetence, political exploitation, and waste that have only slightly ameliorated the poverty in the nation.

If therefore it be treason to look nostalgically to the Eisenhower years, or inhumane to oppose the libertarian concept that the Federal government's mission is that of an over-all, benevolent, and generous despotism, in which Federal spending is the solvent of all social problems, I plead guilty to one or both charges.

Physical vigor, a ruddy and pleasing countenance, a per-

sonal warmth of manner, high intelligence, professional competence, and a most infectious grin—these are my outlines of a
portrait of Eisenhower on early acquaintance. Of that countenance, and especially that grin, Secretary of Defense Forrestal
was to remark, when Eisenhower was the postwar Army Chief
of Staff, "Ike, with that puss you can't miss being President."

It was in this postwar period that I first met him, in circumstances that enabled me to form a personal appraisal. The
occasion was one of those luncheons of the merrymakers who
style themselves the Circus Saints and Sinners. Placed next to
Eisenhower at one of the tables, I found him a most agreeable
companion. He laughed unaffectedly at the brilliant political
satires of Walter Kiernan, the group's chairman and jester-in-
residence, especially at those which "shafted" him—a favorite
term in John F. Kennedy's vocabulary.

I recall finding it remarkable that war—in which he commanded 11 million of the Allied armed forces and was obliged
by that duty to send thousands of young men to their deaths—
had not darkened his mind to the simple enjoyments of common humanity. I remember thinking also that if, incredibly, I
myself had been obliged to make his military decisions, I would
forever have been haunted by the wraiths of those who died in
executing them.

But I also found remarkable, when we got to talking, a
modesty and generosity toward the war achievements of others
that history and experience had not taught me generally to
associate with great and successful personages.

Sitting near us was General of the Army Omar N. Bradley,
who had been Eisenhower's field marshal, and this led him to
observe that none of that rank had been Bradley's military
superior. The burden of his comment was that if any General
deserved direct credit for winning the war against the Nazis, it
was "Brad." And he told me of incidents during the assault of
the First Army on Arnhem and Aachen in which Bradley had
to make the on-the-spot decisions and did so unerringly.

Unaccustomed as I was to such magnanimity among both
military and civilian popular leaders in sharing their glory with
those who helped them attain it, I came away with a personal
judgment of Eisenhower's innate character that, in times of

official error and achievement alike, I have found no reason to abridge.

There is a mass of documents, locked up at Camp Ritchie, Maryland, that will provide future historians with a sound test of the validity of the denigrating judgments of Eisenhower's Presidential capacity that have been publicly and incessantly made—and not only by Democratic partisans and the left wing of political philosophers.

Among these papers is a full account of the proceedings of the small National Security Council in crises that arose during the Eisenhower years. Also among these papers is a full set of the minutes of the even smaller official group that grappled with the threat to the national security posed by Fidel Castro and his Cuba.

Gordon Gray, a high official of both the Truman and Eisenhower Administrations who was intimately involved in these discussions, characterized the documents for me as follows:

> Whenever they become available to the public, they will demonstrate that, his critics to the contrary, Eisenhower made all the vital decisions, firmly and fully enforced them; that his reliance on the staff system stopped at the deciding line; that his grasp of complex issues was profound; and that his expositions of his own views were both forceful and clear. The mythical Eisenhower, who left decision-making to subordinates, whose mind was "lazy" and/or not very bright, cannot be found in these records of the most important business he conducted for the nation.

The same evaluation was given me by others in a position to know the facts and on whom I had learned by experience to rely for the truth as they saw it, whether in confidence or for some measure of attribution. Their reasoning was:

The Democratic campaign talk of a "debacle" in international relations (1960) was nonsense, mostly of partisan origin. It was proved to be nonsense by the contrast between (the then) current state of the world and what it became after Kennedy's accession. Under Eisenhower's leadership the United States had ended the Korean military stalemate and the war; had developed strong allies from weak in France and

West Germany; had halted Khrushchev's "ultimatums in their tracks"; had preserved Lebanon for the West; and had protected Formosa from the Chinese Communists. The latter was especially notable, since Dean Acheson, while President Truman's Secretary of State, "had omitted South Korea and Formosa" from the essential Pacific perimeter he drew of the zone of our national security; half a billion Chinese had been "lost" to the non-Communist world during the Truman Administration; and the military power of the United States had been "reduced" by that Administration from 1946 forward.

As Chief of Staff of the Army, Eisenhower urged a 1949–1950 military budget much larger than Truman had accepted. But when Eisenhower heard from Secretary of Defense Louis A. Johnson that his orders from the White House were to cut the budget from $15.1 to $12.2 billion, the Chief of Staff "quit trying."

A meeting with Eisenhower in December, 1947, marked the beginning of the period in which I came to know him quite well. Mr. and Mrs. John Gross of Bethlehem, Pennsylvania, gave a dinner at the 1925 F Street Club. The Club occupied Mrs. Gross's former house (when she was Mrs. James Curtis); and on the night of December 5 she pre-empted it to introduce some new Pennsylvania Congressional Republicans and State leaders to important members of the Party in Washington and to their neighbor-to-be at Gettysburg, General Eisenhower, the Army Chief of Staff.

After dinner and the customary temporary separation of the sexes I joined a group that included Gross, Senators Robert Taft, Arthur Vandenberg, Martin of Pennsylvania, Bridges of New Hampshire, and Austin of Vermont; plus Governor James Duff of Pennsylvania and the professional colleague I esteemed, and still do, above any other—the late Frank R. Kent of the *Baltimore Sun*. We sat around a table and there followed a typical Washington "bull session," the main topic being the postwar inflation that was plaguing and discrediting the Truman Administration.

Eisenhower took the floor and everyone listened with intense interest to the victorious Allied commander in the Second World War. He vigorously deplored the rise of inflation in a "great country" that had acquitted itself so nobly in battle. He spoke of the Americans he had commanded and of the future he said was due them when they came home. Everyone, he said, must make personal sacrifices if inflation was to be halted. His answer to a request from Taft for more specific counsel startled the politicians. What he said was this:

The only group in a position to make sacrifices, and make them quickly and effectively, is industry. Labor is "political, and so is politics, which I don't know anything about and don't want to." Congenital in these latter groups are delay, compromise, and inaction on a spiky issue like inflation. So why should not someone—for instance, Benjamin Fairless, President of the United States Steel Corporation—announce that for a year his company would not raise prices, taking the risk of foregoing profits, saying, "you can put us in the red if you want to, and you can ruin us," and urge other industries to emulate? Then, said Eisenhower, a wonderful example would be set for labor, the politicians, and the general public that would strike effectively at the spiral of inflation.

The Senators were not impressed. And except for Martin, they began to needle the General, sometimes humorously. For instance, when replying to Eisenhower's exclamation "How did I get the floor?" Vandenberg said, "You took it." And, when Ike, pounding the table, exclaimed, "If I had the power——," Vandenberg slyly murmured, "You may."

But Taft's needling was wholly serious. "Oh, it's not that simple," he said; the farmers would not go along with the sacrifice idea, and inflation could not be effectively attacked without their cooperation. Bridges wisely commented that only by Presidential leadership could inflation be effectively restrained, and with this the Republican Senators agreed. The conversation also made it clear that the Pennsylvania businessman and politicians present, except Governor Duff, were hostile to Eisenhower's basic suggestion, and thoroughly approved the heckling to which he was being subjected.

On the day following the dinner one of the guests—a Senator was strongly indicated—leaked the incident in the misleading form that Eisenhower had advocated the foregoing of all profits by industry for five years. But Kent and I, in response to queries from the Associated Press and other news media, were in a position to deny this version, and did so.

The organized process of inducing Eisenhower to announce his availability as the Republican Presidential nominee in 1952 began on December 4, 1951. The principal moving spirit was Senator Henry Cabot Lodge of Massachusetts, though at the time Lodge did not positively know that the hitherto scrupulously non-partisan Eisenhower was inclined to become an affiliated Republican.

In the December meeting a three-man board of strategy was established to promote Eisenhower as the Republican candidate for President. But it was not until February, 1952, that Gen. Lucius Clay, George Edward Allen (the business executive and humorist), and Sid Richardson (the Texas oil magnate) visited the NATO Supreme Commander in Paris and got his agreement that he would run for President if nominated by the Republican Convention. (At this time Eisenhower appeared to assume he would be nominated by acclamation.)

But prior to the organized pressure on Eisenhower, his mail to the same purpose was growing. This often took the form of both urgency and reproach for discouraging "sincere friends" who wanted him nominated for President in the national interest. One such letter, dated November 4, 1951, to Eisenhower from W. L. White, Editor of the Emporia (Kansas) *Gazette*, reflected this feeling very well:

AS A REPUBLICAN WHO HAS ATTENDED EVERY NATIONAL CONVENTION SINCE 1916, AS EDITOR OF A PAPER WHICH RECENTLY COMMITTED ITSELF TO YOU AS REPUBLICAN CANDIDATE FOR PRESIDENT, AND AS ONE WHO ALSO ENJOYS A CLOSE FRIENDSHIP WITH MANY REPUBLICAN DELEGATES WHO HOPE TO SUPPORT YOU, MAY I VENTURE TO TELL YOU THAT RECENT STATEMENTS HAVE DISCOURAGED SOME OF YOUR BEST FRIENDS, INCLUDING MANY IMPORTANT MEN IN THE PARTY, WHO HAVE AT GREAT RISK TO THEIR INFLUENCE AND OFFICES, HOPED TO MAKE YOU THE NOMINEE OF OUR 1952 CONVENTION. . . .

GENERAL EISENHOWER, I THINK I REPRESENT THE SENTIMENT OF HUNDREDS OF DELEGATES WHO HOLD IT TO BE A DEEPLY SERIOUS AND RESPONSIBLE DUTY TO CHOOSE A CANDI-

DATE FOR PRESIDENT OF THE UNITED STATES. THEY MAY NOT BE POLITICIANS ON A HIGH LEVEL AND MANY OF US WHO SUPPORT YOU ARE NOT POLITICIANS AT ALL. BUT I THINK I REFLECT THE SENTIMENT OF THE REPUBLICANS IN MY BRACKET WHEN I SAY WE HOLD THAT AN OFFER OF SUPPORT FOR THE REPUBLICAN NOMINATION FOR PRESIDENT IS SOMETHING WHICH SHOULD BE MET WITH CANDOR AND RESPECT BY ANY CITIZEN. FURTHERMORE, I DO NOT THINK THERE COULD BE A CALL TO ANY HIGHER DUTY.

I HAVE BEEN LED TO CONCLUDE BY THESE SAME LEADERS OF MY PARTY THAT YOU WOULD ACCEPT SUCH A CALL, AND THAT I SHOULD SO INFORM MY FRIENDS WHO WILL BE THE REPUBLICAN DELEGATES FROM THIS REGION. BUT EVERY STATEMENT YOU MAKE CHALLENGES THIS CONCLUSION AND MAKES ME DOUBTFUL THAT, IF I DO AS THESE LEADERS SAY, THE DELEGATES WILL FIND YOU AVAILABLE WHEN AND IF THE TIME COMES. I DO NOT THINK THIS COURSE OF YOURS, IF LONGER PURSUED, IS JUSTIFIABLE BY ANY REASONABLE CONCEPT OF YOUR IMMEDIATE DUTY BECAUSE:

WITH THE FORMAL ANNOUNCEMENT OF SENATOR TAFT AS A CANDIDATE, A NEW SITUATION HAS BEEN CREATED. THIS SITUATION, IN PROFESSIONAL POLITICAL TERMS IS, "YOU CAN'T BEAT SOMEBODY WITH NOBODY."

I FAVOR YOUR NOMINATION ABOVE ALL OTHERS IF YOU WILL ACCEPT. BUT IF YOU WILL NOT, WITH WHAT CAN ANYONE CHALLENGE THE CLAIMS OF SENATOR TAFT? HE IS HONEST, ABLE AND CANDID. HE DESERVES THE HIGHEST CONSIDERATION OF REPUBLICANS LIKE MYSELF. HE HAS FRANKLY INFORMED REPUBLICAN DELEGATES THAT HE WISHES THEM TO CONSIDER HIS QUALIFICATION AS A CANDIDATE, THUS ACKNOWLEDGING THAT RESPECT FOR THEIR FUNCTION AS DELEGATES WHICH THEY FEEL THEMSELVES.

IN VIEW OF THIS I THINK YOU SHOULD NO LONGER WRAP YOUR ATTITUDE IN MYSTERY. IF YOUR REPUBLICAN FRIENDS ARE WILLING TO GIVE DELEGATES THE ASSURANCE THAT, SHOULD THEY ORGANIZE A MAJORITY FOR THEIR CHOICE, YOU WILL ACCEPT THIS CALL, I THINK THIS SHOULD BE MADE CLEAR. . . .

Five months later, in March, 1952, Taft's supporters calculated that he already could count on the support of six hundred of the six hundred and three convention delegates that constituted a majority. In the face of such a claim it was necessary that Eisenhower become an active candidate or repudiate the movement in his favor. Accordingly, after a considerable amount of pulling and hauling, he resigned from his NATO post and came home in June to assist in the promotion of his candidacy. The argument that persuaded him was that Taft was an isolationist in international policy, an attitude the General believed boded disaster for the United States if Taft became President.

The opening of the 1952 Republican National Convention at Chicago supplied good and sufficient evidence that it would require a mighty effort, including the kind of practical politics that was so distasteful to Eisenhower personally, to overtake Taft. This strategy took the form of challenging the credentials of a number of Taft delegates elected in several states, particularly in Texas, on an issue of honesty in the electoral process.

The Taft forces dominated the Republican National Committee, which gave the first seal of validity to the credentials of most of the contested Taft delegates, to be followed with a like decision by the convention committee that passed on such controversies, and the issue went to the floor. But so completely did Eisenhower embody the issue of integrity that the Taft managers, apprehensive of its triumph on the floor, made their fatal errors.

These were, first, a proposal by the Senator to the General that they divide the Texas delegates; and, second, the recommendation of the Taft-controlled National Committee that sixty-eight of the contested delegates be permitted to vote on the minority resolution to unseat them. These gave Lodge and the other Eisenhower managers the full opportunity to pitch the contest on the outcry that honesty and "morality" were at stake. On the test vote at the Convention the claimant and crucial delegates for Eisenhower were seated by a majority of seventy-six. And this action, as Lodge in particular had anticipated, presaged the General's nomination over Taft by approximately the same majority, and on the first ballot (which the Eisenhower managers realized he must carry in order to avoid the risk of losing out on a later one).

Before this result could be attained, however, two obstacles to the choice of Eisenhower had to be removed. One was Governor Earl Warren, who wanted to maintain—at least for a couple of ballots—his "favorite son" delegation from California, and thereby his prospect of eventually getting the Presidential nomination for himself. The other obstacle was Harold E. Stassen, who had the same design for his "favorite son" delegation from Minnesota. The idea was to stop Eisenhower from a first-ballot nomination, on the judgment—shared by the Eisenhower managers—that this could open the way for a nominee other than Taft, whose name Warren or Stassen could readily have supplied if called upon.

Despite the pro-Eisenhower activities of Richard M. Nixon in the California delegation which earned him Warren's permanent hostility, its seventy delegates stood solidly for the Governor on the first ballot.

There was a different story, however, with the twenty-eight-member Minnesota delegation. Under the leadership of Minnesota's National Committeewoman Mrs. Peavey Heffelfinger and over Stassen's tearful pleadings to stay with him until released, the nineteen delegates who had voted for Stassen on the original first-ballot roll-call switched to Eisenhower before the official count was announced. And it was these nineteen delegates who provided the General with the majority required to nominate him. After his majority was officially certified, the California delegation spokesman joined others in proposing that Eisenhower's nomination be made unanimous. And it was.

Hence it was a surprise, even to some members of Eisenhower's convention and campaign management, when early in the new Administration the President appointed Earl Warren Chief Justice of the United States—a choice for which he later indicated strong misgivings. And these same managers shared the general inability among Republican Party workers to understand why Eisenhower showered offices and other dignities on Stassen, and admitted him to terms of friendship, trust, and instant access.

It may well be true, as I was informed at the time, that Eisenhower's convention managers promised Warren—in exchange for the indispensable support of the California delegation for the minority motion to require contested delegates to abstain from voting on the validity of their own credentials—to push him for Chief Justice if and when. However, if Warren and Stassen had succeeded in blocking his nomination on the first ballot in 1952, Eisenhower might well have been displaced on a subsequent roll-call, and any convention deal made by his managers would have had no future at all.

After Eisenhower (as President-elect and in execution of his campaign promise) "went to Korea," the armistice that eventually followed with the Communists of the North in that country was far from a perfect instrument from the standpoint of either party or even from that of the Chinese Communists, who loomed in the background. That an armistice could be concluded at all is traced by some authorities to credence given to an intelligence report in Moscow and Peking that Eisenhower would invoke the tactic of "hot pursuit" of the enemy to any land or air base, wherever it might exist, if the Korean War continued much longer. Moreover, the intelligence report was allegedly credited by the Communists because of Eisenhower's full employment of the strategy of attack during the Second World War, and because of appraisals made to the Kremlin by its agents in Western Europe during his tenure as the Supreme Commander of NATO.

These appraisals were that he would be prepared, if necessary, to assure the effectiveness of his small NATO force as a deterrent to positive Russian military aggression in Western Europe "by any necessary and practical means," with the complete support of President Truman. And a shift of the nuclear strategy from Europe to the Pacific, after Eisenhower became President, also helped to persuade Moscow and Peking that they must conclude a cease-fire and armistice in Korea.

He was speaking on the line of this record in 1967, when, asked to comment on the limited military policy of the United States in Vietnam, he advocated using "any necessary force" to gain a victory; and answering a question, said he would not in certain circumstances exclude the employment of nuclear weapons. Also when, in a televised interview on November 24, 1967, he advocated the tactic of "hot pursuit" (even into China) in the Vietnam war.

As often before, when his forthrightness had slipped through in extemporaneous speech, Eisenhower modified the positiveness of his statement about a resort to nuclear weapons. Since President Johnson, playing on Eisenhower's reverence for the Presidential office, sought incessantly and successfully to associate the General with the Administration's policy in Vietnam, it is conceivable that this modification was a consequence of White House pressure.

Certainly, only that pressure can explain Eisenhower's activity to induce other prominent citizens to sign (as he did) the "Declaration" in 1967 of the hastily formed Citizens' Committee for Peace with Freedom in Vietnam. For this document, in addition to several passages that contradicted each other, was at variance with a number of public statements Eisenhower had made on the same general subject—particularly that he would employ nuclear force if all other military devices failed to crush the enemy. The attempted distinction between "the President" and "the Presidency" was merely a feeble exercise in dialectics. And the Declaration was also at variance with the plans by which Eisenhower alone had made the tiny NATO military arm an effective deterrent to Moscow.

It was inconsistencies like these on Eisenhower's part that often have baffled his supporters, and, while in office, exposed him to sneers in Democratic and libertarian circles. But in many conversations with him, and in inquiries among the foremost officials in his Administration, I found the President firm and clear with respect to the principles by which his private and public life have been guided.

Near the end of his Presidency, I remarked to Eisenhower that his political philosophy was very much like that of Woodrow Wilson, and that in my judgment he was not a Republican but "a Wilson Democrat." To that he replied, "Or a T.R. Republican." But this political ancestry was difficult to trace in view of Theodore Roosevelt's efforts to invade the Congressional function, his advocacy of the recall of acts of Congress and judicial decisions, and his extreme interpretations of the reach of the antitrust laws.

And the "T.R. Republican" comparison fitted even more loosely a political self-portrait Eisenhower once exhibited to a visitor.

Generally, as the President then described himself, he was a believer in moderation; on this principle he had counseled Vice-President Nixon not to allow himself to be pushed into extreme positions of civil rights, expansion of the Federal function and the like. And he expressed the hope that the 1960 Republican platform would reflect this viewpoint, which certainly did not rest on the "liberal" concept that all problems can be solved by more Federal spending and by less local self-government and by putting more and more governmental restraints on individual initiative.

Though Eisenhower delegated an unusual degree of foreign policy formulation and conduct to John Foster Dulles, his Secretary of State, the President nevertheless was constantly concerned—often preoccupied—with foreign affairs.

The Far East occupied a large segment of Eisenhower's concerns over foreign policy from the beginning of his first term. In May, 1955, he was concentrating on Chinese Communist belligerence toward the offshore islands held by Chiang Kai-shek. As previously noted, toward the end of the Truman Administration, Dean Acheson had publicly drawn a perimeter of national security that excluded both Korea and Formosa. And though I hold the belief I then held—that the perimeter was sound from military, diplomatic, and geopolitical standpoints—the prompt Communist attack on North Korea and Truman's invocation of a collective defense through the United Nations had, by the time Eisenhower became President, permanently extended the line to include both Formosa and Korea. Thus in 1955 (according to notes of conversations I have kept) Eisenhower was thinking in these terms:

. . . The United States must hold Formosa; otherwise Southeast Asia and the Philippines would be laid open to the aggression of world Communism, and Japan greatly endangered. The British had never specifically said they would join a military action in defense of Formosa, only that "the free world" would be on the side of the United States. But Eisenhower had not asked Chiang Kai-shek to give up Quemoy and Matsu without a fight and did not expect to. However, he was troubled by the emphasis Chiang placed on these offshore islands, so that the whole Nationalist cause now appeared to turn on their retention or loss.

He thought this emphasis obscured an important military fact: if the Chinese Communists planned to take Formosa by force, an amphibious landing would be necessary, and a previous landing on the offshore islands would double their effort and its costs, making no military sense. But so far as the United States was concerned, if the Chinese Communists should attack South Korea, Chiang would have a good opportunity to attack the mainland; and the United States, which was building up his air force, would encourage him to do that—in Dulles' famous words, "unleash him."

However, Chiang's overwhelming emphasis on holding the offshore islands evoked a lot of letters to the White House from American private citizens. Some urged the President "to kick the Reds in the teeth." Others merely expressed confidence that Eisenhower could and would solve the whole Far East problem. But the subject of them all was Formosa. And when Eisenhower's bursitis awakened him at the usual hour of 4:30 A.M., Formosa popped into his head instantly. But like Truman, dismissing a question raised by Adlai Stevenson, "Is this decision not too grave to leave with one man?" Eisenhower accepted and acted on the fact that only the President can make the decisions, grave or otherwise, in certain vital categories under the United States's system of government.

The President was faced with particularly painful decisions in the fall of 1956, during Egypt's struggle to take over the Suez Canal, contrary to the wishes of France, Great Britain, and Israel. One of the aspects of the Allied crisis over Suez that especially disturbed Eisenhower was its impending effect on the unity of the Atlantic community; that, even before the Marshall Plan, had been among his greatest goals. As Supreme Allied Commander in the Second World War and later of NATO, and also during his tenure as Chief of Staff of the

United States Army, he had worked for this unity in roles more conspicuous than those of any other man. Consequently, the blackout of intimate communications between London and Washington that followed Anthony Eden's conclusion Dulles had reneged in supporting the combination of the "users" of Suez, thereby preceding the Israeli attack on the Canal, was of enormous concern to Eisenhower. He had specifically warned Eden, in the course of a correspondence still held in the archives, that the United States government would disapprove of any armed attack.

In a conversation with a visitor just after the Suez crisis, President Eisenhower deplored the new obstacles to what he termed his "paramount policy" to promote the unity of Western Europe and the Atlantic community; and he made a comment the shrewdness of which refutes the caricature by his American critics of a President whose perceptions were shallow and dim. The attainment of Western European unity, he said, was "especially difficult because they love their hates so much."

And incidentally, in speaking to this visitor of France, with a humorous turn that many Americans did not grant him until the appearance in 1967 of his book *At Ease: Stories I Tell My Friends*,* Eisenhower once remarked, "You know, over there I belong to the *intelligentsia*. I am a member of the French Academy, and I have often sat around with Siegfried, Mauriac, Sartre, and those fellows."

General Eisenhower, unlike Roosevelt and Churchill, had managed during the war to get along pretty well with General Charles De Gaulle. But as President he was finding De Gaulle the statesman a more difficult partner. For illustration of the French leader's thorny personality he recalled this incident:

During Eisenhower's tenure in command at SHAPE, he was informed that De Gaulle, then the leader of the political opposition in France, wanted to see him. Since it was the custom of every prime minister who came to Paris to visit Eisenhower, he suggested that De Gaulle do the same, particularly because the Supreme Commander must not appear to be taking a position in French politics. But De Gaulle insisted that as a former

* New York: Doubleday.

President of France, he should be the host, not the visitor.

The impasse was broken by Marshal Alphonse Juin. Availing himself of the fact that Eisenhower and De Gaulle were among the handful of great personages belonging to the Order of (French) Liberation, Juin arranged a dinner of the Order, so that both Generals could meet on common ground and have the conversation sought by De Gaulle. And this they did, for an hour and a half.

As the Eisenhower Administration grew older, there was, of course, a growing lack of policy accord with the government of France; but the President's attitude was that the United States was obliged to "live with it" and the problem it imposed. If, he once said in commenting on this problem, you are afloat on dangerous seas and one in the boat isn't pulling his oar, you gain nothing by tossing him and his oar overboard. The task is to demonstrate to him that only by pulling his own oar can he and you get to safe harbor.

Another "Latin" problem of a different nature was forming ninety miles off Florida; and analyzing it, much less dealing with it, proved to be exceedingly complex. Until Castro publicly aligned himself with the world Communism, Eisenhower was uncertain about the prospect of Communist infiltration in the Cuban government. Of those with whom he discussed this subject, a third believed that Communists were in control, another third believed they were not and would not be, and the last third—including our then Ambassador to Havana, Earl Smith—counseled a wait-and-see attitude. Eisenhower concluded to accept the latter for the time being, with great sympathy for the objectives of the anti-Batista revolution and a determination not to alienate the people of an island vital to the security of the United States.

But as the end of his tenure approached, Eisenhower was prepared to call for action by the Organization of American States on any violation of the Rio Treaty by Castro. And "in grave circumstances" he was prepared to act unilaterally, whether or not the OAS endorsed the procedure. For example, if the lives of American citizens were involved, he would order a blockade of Cuba by the Army and Navy, and, as a last resort, intervene. But he felt certain that Castro would stop short of any such provocation (a belief that was controverted by the events that led up to the October, 1963, "missile crisis" faced by the Kennedy Administration).

Soviet Premier Nikita Khrushchev was one of the most troublesome contemporary statesmen with whom Eisenhower had to deal on a personal basis. During their meeting in September, 1959, at Camp David, Maryland, for instance, Khrushchev took as a challenge Eisenhower's casual observation that the ever present telephone made it impossible for him to have a "real vacation."

"Don't think it is different with me," bristled Khrushchev. "Telephones are always near me. I, too, believe in vacations, but when I was having one at the beach recently, I had hardly got into the water when a courier waded out to me with a telephone in his hand." Then, unwittingly disclosing that he had reacted to the President's casual remark about the ever present telephone with Russian sensitivity over the superiority of American technology, Khrushchev added, "We haven't as many telephones as you have. But very soon we will have a lot more."

The fundamental difference between the two worlds over which Khrushchev and Eisenhower presided emerged in another form at a dinner given by the Soviet Ambassador during this same Khrushchev visit. At one point in Khrushchev's speech, illustrating the word by the action, the Premier said all he had to do was to "hold up my little finger" and the Russian people would do anything he asked them to do in their treatment of a distinguished visitor.

Eisenhower put aside his prepared toast and said instead that he would not "hold up his little finger" to regiment the American people in any of their attitudes or views on any public matter. And even if he *could* think of doing such a thing, the President added, the American people would very properly tell him to stick to the job he was elected to perform. He could only request that Khrushchev be treated with the courtesy due so distinguished a visitor—but that, too, was unnecessary, because they needed no such admonition.

Mrs. Robert B. Anderson, wife of the Secretary of the Treasury, turned at that point to her dinner partner, Khrushchev's son-in-law Aleksei Adzhubei, then Editor of *Izvestia*, and inquired how the Kremlin attained such total conformity in the U.S.S.R. This question promoted a long consultation between the *Izvestia* editor, the representative of *Pravda*, a couple of other characters, and Khrushchev's son, Sergei. The latter then supplied the answer. It was that the conformity was achieved through the various media by which the "people's government" communicated with the people. In other words, a thorough mixture of controlled and propagandist journalism and the healthy fear of non-conformity that is inherent in a police state.

It was obvious to her, said Mrs. Anderson later, that the Russian visitors firmly believed that the United States government, if it chose, could exercise the same control over the American people and their communications media.

These are small facets of the problem of the U.S.S.R. and its leaders that engaged Eisenhower throughout his terms, as they had Truman after the crumbling of the false façade of peaceful postwar policy the Soviets had exhibited at Potsdam. Before and after Khrushchev's visit this problem was a recurrent topic in Eisenhower's private conversations as well as in his public statements.

Toward the end of Eisenhower's second Administration, some events of unique interest occurred that bore on the nuclear weapons testing issue.

After Eisenhower and Khrushchev had met at Camp David a communiqué was issued. It expressed Eisenhower's "unshakable resolution" to put the burden of good faith on Soviet Russia whenever its actions gave him the opportunity, while resolutely maintaining at least as promising an inspection system as the *sine qua non* of any protracted agreement on nuclear testing. Although Eisenhower thought the Soviets would "probably cheat a bit" around the North Pole ("where it would be difficult to catch them at it"), his position would permit any nation to make the occasional tests "reasonably" demonstrable as a requirement for evolving an effective inspection system. When Prime Minister Harold Macmillan arrived in Washington in March, 1960, Eisenhower explained his position, and Macmillan's comment was, "This is exactly mine, too. Let's sign right away."

Eisenhower found it gratifying that all the Presidential aspirants in 1960 had endorsed his propositions for ending atomic tests, and also that the "people everywhere" were reacting favorably. And those in his Administration who had been fearful of the potentials of peril in the Camp David agreement with Khrushchev "now realized" that their fears had no "important foundation." These same officials, moreover, had joined him in the belief that when a temporary agreement on inspection had been reached with the Soviet Union, preceding a treaty, it should be announced separately by the three principals (the U.S., U.S.S.R., and the U.K.) instead of jointly. This would emphasize the right of each to take protective steps if it deemed these necessary to its national security.

For several weeks prior to the Camp David conference between Eisenhower and Macmillan in March, 1960—on the proposal submitted by Khrushchev at his September, 1959, conference with Eisenhower to terminate all nuclear weapons tests, including underground explosions—many tense and dramatic exchanges had reflected the internal divisions on the pact within the Administration. According to several of the principals on one side of these exchanges, only by the continuous and intense activity of their group were they able to block the other group's plan for an unguarded agreement with the Soviet Union on a system of inspection, to be announced jointly by the United States, Great Britain, and the U.S.S.R. in advance of an over-all treaty.

The intensity of the dispute can be gathered from the following account given me by some of those involved:

On Thursday, March 24, 1960, there was a meeting attended by the President, Secretary of State Christian Herter, Secretary of the Air Force James H. Douglas, and Gordon Gray, Eisenhower's special assistant on national security matters, and other insiders. At one point, when John A. McCone, Chairman of the Atomic Energy Commission, strongly argued the necessity of maintaining the U.S. "show me" policy on inspection, the danger of a long moratorium on underground testing, the great mistake he envisaged in a tripartite declaration, etc., the President pounded the table and said he intended to follow Herter's counsel in favor of taking these ventures. Later he calmed down, but his rebuke to McCone scared the Pentagon also into silence.

At this same meeting the President directed that any speeches on the subject be approved by Herter's department. McCone, who was flying that afternoon to make such a speech in Los Angeles, left his transcript behind for Herter's inspection. When he got to Los Angeles an AEC aide informed him Herter had flatly vetoed the whole speech.

McCone got Herter on the telephone, but the Secretary would say only that he had sent the speech to the White House and would have no more to do with it. McCone then got in touch with Col. Sherman Goodpaster of the White House staff who told him the speech was "out." Then, inquired McCone, does this mean we have changed our test policy entirely? McCone's reaction must have induced second thoughts at the White House, because soon afterward Goodpaster phoned McCone to say that if he would put in one sentence estimating the Soviet proposal as "hopeful," the remainder would be acceptable. McCone put in the sentence and delivered the speech as written.

In a meeting at the British Embassy prior to March 24, not attended by the President, a pledge of secrecy was imposed on all present. Herter remarked that Chalmers Roberts of the *Washington Post* nevertheless "knew of this meeting, and some of you will get a call." When Roberts' story next day demonstrated a "leak" of these discussions, McCone (who all along had suspected the State Department of leaking with a deliberate anti-McCone slant) reminded Herter of this remark. Herter replied he didn't recall having said anything of the kind.

In their eagerness to win world opinion, some of the Administration policymakers wanted to specify a pledge that in any underground tests which might ever be made, the explosion would be of TNT, not of any nuclear device. This proposal was withdrawn when AEC scientists observed that the method would require a cavern as big as Mammoth Cave, into which two hundred thousand cases of TNT, each of fifty pounds, would have to be carried, with constant risk to all involved. The alternate nuclear device is about the size of a small fireside bench.

This account indicates that Eisenhower changed his mind about the desirability of a tripartite declaration and opted for the separate-statement form. At any rate, that is how this particular issue was resolved.

In looking forward to the Paris summit conference of 1960 (before the shooting down by the Russians of the U-2 espionage plane manned by Francis Gary Powers gave Khrushchev the pretext to break up the conference), Eisenhower was concentrating on the status of Berlin. To him the proposal to withdraw all Allied troops from the city and substitute the protective custody of the United Nations was a "retreat," and he would not countenance that. The act would be exploited by the Kremlin and the East German government as a backdown, and this could engender "disastrous" events. But Allied troop reductions were a different matter entirely.

He could not understand, however, how Acheson could have said that the Berlin situation was not "abnormal" and presented nothing for discussion at the summit conference. (Eisenhower himself had called the situation "abnormal" at a press conference, and stuck to it despite a suggestion from one of the reporters present that he might wish to withdraw the word because it was the unvarying Communist description of the condition of Berlin.)

These exhibits of Eisenhower's turn of mind on some of the serious international issues before him refute—at least in my judgment—the caricature drawn by many of his critics, including that of a President who let his subordinates, particularly Secretary of State Dulles, do all his reading and thinking, and most of his deciding.

One of the most important items in the record of constructive and peacekeeping foreign policy during the Eisenhower Administration was the Antarctica Treaty with several nations, most importantly Soviet Russia. This compact, which reserved the whole continent to non-military and scientific uses, was conspicuously free of the two major criticisms that for years have been cited against the concept and conduct of postwar international affairs by the United States: first, Washington merely reacts to Soviet or Soviet-inspired thrusts of foreign policy instead of initiating them; and second, that the bipartisanship urged on the opposition by those in Executive power is precluded—as Harold E. Stassen put it—by inviting the political minority to share in the "crash-landings" but not in the foreign-policy "takeoffs."

The entire process by which the Antarctica Treaty was negotiated and affirmed in August, 1960, was also unique in setting up a system whereby the agreement with the U.S.S.R. could be effectively policed for violations. As I commented in *The New York Times*, it was conceived and initiated by the Eisenhower Administration; and while negotiating the Treaty for the President with eleven other nations, the eminent lawyer, Herman Phleger of San Francisco, then Legal Adviser to the Secretary of State, constantly consulted the foreign-policy representatives of both parties in the Senate.

The result was that fully informed leaders of the majority, notably Senators Johnson and Fulbright, recruited for the Antarctica Treaty the Democratic support it absolutely required to overcome the opposition of such influential Senators as Russell of Georgia, Anderson of New Mexico, and Byrd of Virginia (whose famous younger brother, Admiral Richard E. Byrd, had widely explored Antarctica and planted on its vast reaches the flag of the United States).

International lawyers and scientists were among the groups in support of the Treaty who joined diplomatic workers. Their viewpoint was clearly represented by Professor Charles E. Martin, President of the American Society of International Law. The agreement, he wrote,

> offers an excellent opportunity for genuine international cooperation between the signatories. Science and the consequences of scientific discovery recognize no boundary lines or national barriers. However, nations will compete in scientific development, in the areas of security and power, either unilaterally or by means of rival blocs or combinations of power and defense. . . . It is only in the non-military functions of governments, and under conditions of peace, that genuine and even universal efforts at scientific advancement may be undertaken.

This, Professor Martin submitted, was assured by the pledges of the Treaty's signatories. Antarctica should be used for peaceful purposes only, with freedom of scientific investigation, exchanges of information and personnel, and prohibition of nuclear tests.

Eisenhower was not the first, nor will he be the last, President whose appointments to the Supreme Court revealed a concept of the role the Court should play in government that clashed directly with his own. But seldom has a President been more responsible than Eisenhower for the sweeping reversal by the Court of his own constitutional philosophy.

This reversal was effected by his appointments of Earl Warren as Chief Justice and of Judge William J. Brennan, of the New Jersey high court, as Associate Justice. As the Supreme Court under Warren's driving leadership entered upon the series of decisions that began with the ban on state statutory compulsions to keep the public schools racially segregated, Eisenhower became more and more disillusioned with his choices that made up the Court's new libertarian majority.

It is true that the public-schools decision was unanimous. But I have reason to believe that this unanimity was due to the acceptance, by Justices disposed to dissent, of a strong tactical argument. This argument was that in such a revolutionary finding—for which no plain Constitutional warrant or statute could be cited—the public interest acutely required unanimity on the record.

When Eisenhower declined to comment on the school decision, one way or another, he was assailed by critics for not expanding this show of unanimity to the White House. This attitude, he said in private, he never "could understand." Any comment by him, he remarked, would inevitably carry the implication of Executive review of Supreme Court decisions: it was contrary to the basic Constitutional concept of the division of Federal powers.

As he saw it, he explained, his job was to enforce the Court's decisions, regardless of his approval or disapproval ("and there have been several I just can't comprehend"); and this function he had carried out faithfully. It was obvious, at least to me (and on good evidence), that Eisenhower believed that the militant integrationists, on and off the bench, were trying to move too fast toward a fully integrated national society at the expense of the rights of the general public; and that Eisenhower thought the Southern whites were entitled to much more moderate procedures during the demolition of their deeply ingrained way of life.

Equally obvious to me, on equally good evidence, was that Eisenhower felt increasing disappointment at Warren's increasing show of finding law for libertarian political doctrine where there was none in the books, and at the support of this practice by his first Democratic appointee to the Court, Justice Brennan. The President told friends that Chief Judge Arthur Vanderbilt of New Jersey, who had an enviable reputation for decisions based on "the law of the case," had assured him that Brennan had the same "ideal judicial concept." And, said the President, he had got the same mistaken impression of Brennan in a conversation prior to the appointment.

Toward the end of his term, in 1960, Eisenhower was finding and expressing gratification in opinions by some Justices, that in his view showed their realization of the damage they had done to the Constitutional system by joining Warren in earlier decisions. He indicated that John M. Harlan and Felix Frankfurter were the "brethren" he had particularly in mind. At the same time Eisenhower highly praised Justices Whittaker and Potter Stewart, and was quoted by one visitor as saying that if Justice Hugo Black would retire, the President could further "improve" the Court.

This latter statement is another illustration of the unexpected courses on which Supreme Court Justices embark. For as the Court under Warren has increasingly substituted the political doctrine of a majority for the judicial process, Black has become the chief voice of protest against this amending of the Constitution by judicial fiat, as well as by the accompanying usurpation of the Legislative and Executive provinces.

In consideration of the fact, previously demonstrated, that Warren's holdout of the California delegation could have prevented Eisenhower's nomination on the first ballot if Minnesota had not broken away from Stassen, Warren's selection by Eisenhower to be Chief Justice of the United States mystified many of those who supported the General's cause at the 1952 convention. The alleged deal previously mentioned on the issue of the contested delegates would surely have been unknown to Eisenhower then or thereafter. So this could not be the whole explanation of a choice which Eisenhower not only lived to regret, but which wrought a violent and fast-paced social and Constitutional revolution.

I have asked several of those who participated in recommending Warren to Eisenhower. Their answers were these:

The feuds and vituperative dissents of the Court that physically broke down Chief Justice Harlan F. Stone, and that his successor, Fred M. Vinson, had not sufficient time to repair, created a vital requirement for leadership. No lawyer in public office had shown more of this quality and had had it more positively confirmed by a large non-partisan voting majority, and for a longer period, than Governor Warren of California. Also, he was a lawyer of wide experience in public office and private practice; no breath of scandal had touched him in either career; and he had been Thomas E. Dewey's Republican running mate in 1948 on a platform that, by contrast with the Democratic, was conservative.

On the basis of these qualifications, Attorney General Herbert Brownell proposed Warren for Chief Justice, and the President agreed. But not before the qualifications of several others, two in particular, had been reviewed and evaluated. The two were Justices Robert H. Jackson and Harold H. Burton.

The idea of promoting Jackson attracted Eisenhower temporarily, on two counts. First, Jackson had one of the most brilliant minds in the history of the Court; he was a Democrat, which appealed to Eisenhower's strong non-partisan bent in filling judicial offices. Second, including his public quarrel with Justice Black, in which Jackson roughly impugned Black's ethical sensitivity, he was the nearest of the liberals to a conservative.

Burton, a Republican, had nevertheless been appointed to the Court by President Truman, who, during his Senate service with Burton, had formed the highest regard for his colleague's integrity, judicial temperament, and learning in the law.

But Jackson had not only initiated a public brawl with Black in which the reputation of the Court was damaged. As Solicitor-General he had been the lead-off witness before Congressional committees in favor of FDR's plan to "pack" the Supreme Court with a pro-New Deal majority. And this record, on review, removed Jackson from consideration—the second instance in his career. (Until the day of his death he believed that Black, during Jackson's absence at the Nuremburg trials, was responsible for Truman's appointment of Vinson instead of himself as Chief Justice.)

Burton was eliminated from consideration by the agreement between Eisenhower and his advisers that the Court stood in great need of a strong leader and forceful administrator. Burton did not meet either requirement, and the President's choice settled on Warren, who was Attorney General Brownell's original candidate.

Although it is speculation that under Jackson the Court would have practiced much more restraint in interpreting and amending the Constitution to suit the majority's view of what Congress and the Executive should have done and had not done (by way of revising public policy to fit the changing times), Jackson's opinions strongly indicate that this would have happened if he had become the Chief Justice instead of Warren. In that event, the Constitutional, political, and social history of the United States in the last two decades would not have recorded the most complete assertion of judicial supremacy over the States and in the Federal system since John Marshall "found" theretofore undiscovered power in the Court to invalidate acts of Congress.

When Franklin Roosevelt was awaiting the Supreme Court's ruling on the constitutionality of Executive repeal of the clause guaranteeing repayment of government currency obligations in gold, he was prepared with a public statement refusing (on the ground of the nation's solvency) to enforce an adverse decision. But the three incumbents of the Presidency while Warren has been Chief Justice—Eisenhower, Kennedy,

and Johnson—have executed the Court's findings without even
the challenge of critical comment.

There is ample evidence that on two of the three occasions
when Eisenhower was seriously hospitalized, his illnesses
created what Sherman Adams, his intensely devoted aide, described on May 23, 1957, to James Reston and W. H. Lawrence of the *Times* Washington Bureau as a "hiatus" in the
Presidency. Had it not been for the alertness and sagacity of
Eisenhower's subordinates—particularly Press Secretary
James C. Hagerty, Adams, Vice-President Nixon, Attorney
General Brownell, and Treasury Secretary George M. Humphrey—a Constitutional crisis could readily have arisen when a
heart attack felled the President at Denver in 1955. And the
same was true, and for the same cause, in the early months of
Eisenhower's second term.

Of his associates in the government, none behaved with a
higher sense and perceptiveness of his responsibility than
Nixon. An example is provided by a telephone call Nixon made
to me at 5:56 P.M. on September 26, 1955. Immediately after
hanging up, I reconstructed the following statement from notes
made while Nixon was talking:

"It is vitally important to the stability of the country that I
minimize whatever my role is to be during the President's inactiv-
ity. The feeling that the President is really in charge must be
maintained to the limit of possibility, and actually we [the Cabinet,
Hagerty, Adams, etc.] are carrying on in the way he planned. It is
very important, too, that I not be subject to the charge that I am
trying to make personal—which is political—capital out of this
distressing situation.

"We want to be sure that no decision is postponed or delayed as
a result of this temporary situation. It is a natural tendency in the
circumstances to let things pile up, but the President never wanted
it that way in these circumstances [obviously they had previously
discussed the circumstances as potential]. He never wanted anything held up. We could do that with routine matters, but an
important consideration is that the President come back to a clean
desk. So we will act on routine also.

"We are checking the legality of every act. The meetings I have called of the Cabinet and the Security Council [some were criticizing Nixon for this and muttering about 'unconstitutional procedure'] are not in that category. I have authority from the President to call and chair such meetings: you will remember I called one meeting of the Council after the President left for Denver.

"We can make a healthy precedent of the continuity of government and will try. It didn't lapse importantly in [James] Garfield's illness: that was summer and the country was at peace. But in Wilson's case the interregnum was tragic. We shall, I hope, be able to say that this and that was done with the President's approval and are making the necessary arrangements.

"My reports from Denver are remarkably encouraging. The President has a powerful constitution, and that heart muscle which was strained was extraordinarily strong to begin with—the result of his exercise and habits of life."

Eventually, on the President's initiative, letters were exchanged between him and Nixon that specifically delegated to the Vice-President the emergency use of such of the "powers and duties" of the Executive as events might require. And before Congress finally got around to giving statutory sanction for the arrangement, President Kennedy had repeated, with Vice-President Johnson, the Eisenhower-Nixon exchange.

But during Eisenhower's illness at the outset of his second term it was still a verbal arrangement for which the Vice-President's version provided the only authority. And this was the state of the matter when Adams discussed it on May 23, 1957.

Adams talked very frankly of the effects of the President's second illness on the conduct of the Executive Branch. He said that during the "hiatus" it was unclear who was in charge or how the Executive department was being conducted. But he felt, said Adams, that Eisenhower was entering a "period of renaissance." He now was interested, Adams said, in the current political problems, "primarily because for the first time in the last few days he [the President] has had to look over the brink into some of the possible consequences of following his past procedure." More than anything else, the imminence of serious trouble (foreign and domestic) had forced Eisenhower to tighten up emergency provisions; and, said Adams, he hoped this new interest would be sustained.

The advent of the third serious illness—the operation for ileitis—supplied sufficient proof that Eisenhower had already done the "tightening up" to which Adams referred.

The general public mood during Eisenhower's Administration (one of confidence that Eisenhower would preserve the Constitutional system in prosperity and at peace) was periodically shaken. Being a soldier by profession, Eisenhower placed great reliance on the staff system. Thus, some decisions that should have been referred to him before being put in operation were made on the lower levels. Some decisions were made against wiser counsel; Eisenhower's stubborn support of his chief White House adviser, Sherman Adams, is typical of these. And they inflicted severe political wounds on the Republican Party.

Adams, revealing a carelessness in his personal relations that was in amazingly sharp contrast to his coldly impersonal native caution, had come under increasing political fire as the scope of his indiscretion was disclosed in Congressional inquiries into the influence-seeking, influence-peddling of Adams' close personal friend and gift-giver, New England textile manufacturer Bernard Goldfine.

The President's characteristic and immediate reaction was to repel demands for Adams' resignation with the simple statement, "I need him." This proving unpersuasive, to Eisenhower's apparent surprise, Adams ultimately removed by resignation the handicap he embodied to the Presidential function and the Republican Party. But a permanent consequence was a chip in the stature of the national father figure, standing high above the lowly political battle, that the American people had created of Eisenhower.

The atmosphere of official corruption and Communist infiltration in government in the Truman Administration had contributed to the broad feeling of a "need for a change" in management in Washington that was one of the reasons for the defeat of the Democratic Presidential nominee in 1952. But what, in the kindliest appraisal, were imprudent relaxations of the high official standards proclaimed by Eisenhower in the 1952 campaign arose in the early years of his Presidency before the incident affecting Sherman Adams. And though Eisenhower sought and obtained the resignations of the few officials involved, the damage inflicted on his Administration was certainly one of the reasons, except for the Congress that was elected with him in 1952, the voters biennially chose Congresses with a Democratic majority in the last six years of his White House incumbency.

A word about the extraordinary character of Sherman Adams is in order at this point. Never, in my judgment and observation, did Adams wittingly place himself or his own interest above that of the President. No Chief Executive has had a more loyal and patriotic, and—with one exception—wise subordinate. The lapse inherent in Adams' careless relations with Goldfine, including the acceptance of gifts from an obvious name-dropper and influence-peddler, probably brought to Eisenhower the most personal distress and official deprivation of any happening in his career, military and civilian.

In my opinion, the one source of Adams' grave error was not the intoxication of his unique power to influence a President. It was the consequence of tremendous arrogance that in turn was the consequence of excessive egotism. Adams, being—and knowing that he was basically—incorruptible, that his devotion to Eisenhower and to his official responsibilities was complete, drifted into what, in his case, was the unforgivably political sin of assuming that both qualities foreclosed any question arising from any act of his.

To excessive egotism I also attribute the careless act of Harold E. Talbott, Secretary of the Air Force, that finally obliged a distressed Eisenhower to call for Talbott's resignation. I base this view on a close, longtime personal association with Talbott, in New York and after he went to Washington. This egotism took the form of a conviction that Talbott knew what was the wise and sensible thing for anyone to do. Hence it never occurred to him that anything he proposed out of benevolence could possibly be linked with self-interest in any circumstances.

In this confidence he used Air Force stationery to urge a number of corporation heads he knew to avail themselves of the services of a firm of efficiency engineers in which Talbott had been a partner before he took office. It seems never to have occurred to him that his activities in behalf of a firm in which he had transferred his reduced partnership share to members of his family could be considered a conflict of interest; or that this conflict was the more flagrant because of his use of Air Force stationery. He was satisfied in his own mind that the corporations he was in effect soliciting stood in dire need of services for whose value he could vouch personally. And such was Talbott's makeup that he thought only of the favor he was doing them.

There were special reasons that the Adams and Talbott incidents—although not the only examples in the Eisenhower Administration of depressed official standards that ranged upward from mere imprudence—were particularly embarrassing and grievous to the President. He had made much in the 1952 campaign of the issue of "corruption" and influence-selling in the Truman Administration. He relied on Adams for the information on which Presidential decisions necessarily are largely based, and the way this information is presented has a pilot role in that function. As for Talbott, not only was he in a position to choose among bidders for huge military contracts: he had, when Eisenhower was President-elect, been the chief recruiting officer of talent to serve in vital Federal posts.

It is conceivable that some day a historian will turn from his main task to produce a biography of Adams: the material could furnish a fascinating study. Or some student, browsing in the documentation of the Eisenhower regime, might take the subject for his doctoral dissertation. But for the purposes of this narrative there is room only for another glance or two into Adams' mind and at his indifference toward the amenities that is unique in anyone who is a professional practitioner of the politician's trade. So indifferent is he that I could never understand how, even among the no-nonsense denizens of New Hampshire, he got himself elected Governor.

Adams almost habitually was curt to the point of rudeness,

and sometimes deliberately rude. An example was his reception, on June 18, 1958, of two callers, compassionately aware of the political storm he had drawn upon his head by his Goldfine indiscretions, who came on legitimate government business. These two were Christian A. Herter, then Under Secretary of State, and Eric Johnston, head of the Association of Motion Picture Producers, who, with the blessing of Eisenhower, was conducting public rallies in behalf of foreign aid.

What they sought to learn from Adams was whether the President wanted these rallies continued. When they entered, Herter, in the kindly way that was natural to him, said to Adams, "I sympathize with what you have had to go through these last few days," and put his arm on Adams' shoulder.

With ice in his eyes, looking straight at Herter, Adams inquired, "Is this the subject you came here to discuss?"

"Sorry, I shouldn't have mentioned it," said the embarrassed Herter.

"I don't want to seem mean or disagreeable," said Adams, proceeding to be both. "But when I want you to discuss my personal affairs with me, I'll let you know."

I believe even then he did not realize that, in the context, the political controversy his indiscretion had created was not just a "personal affair." At any rate, not until the reality was borne in on him that his continuance in office was an increasing embarrassment and possibly damaging to the President to whom his was a single-minded devotion did Adams resign.

He is a man of such reserve, even beyond the tight-lipped New England pattern, that it was always an interesting experience when he spoke frankly on public matters. For when he did, his natural bluntness took the form of most engaging candor. In the same conversation in which Adams conceded the Presidential "hiatus" of 1957 he made these other observations:

. . . He revealed what Eisenhower later made public—that the President had drawn up a list of possible successors and expected to play an active role in the Convention's choice of the 1960 Republican nominee. Eisenhower, he was sure, would watch the potential aspirants objectively, and "sometime in 1959" would make clear to the Party that he would be able to campaign only for a candidate who shared the President's political philosophy. In Adams' own expressed opinion, a rigidly conservative Republican candidate would be a "disaster," and he did not think, he said, that Eisenhower would lend his influence with the electorate in behalf of a fixed "right-winger." In that event, said Adams, "Ike will be farming at Gettysburg."

In this conversation with Adams there appeared the germ of the idea of a First Secretary of the Cabinet that Eisenhower later advanced, and then dropped, as a recommendation for the makeup of future Administrations. In that reorganization, as envisaged by Adams, the Vice-President would not preside over the Senate, but would concentrate on being the second Executive officer, discharging such functions as the President assigned, plus "ceremonial duties." Indeed, mused Adams, there really should be four Vice-Presidents: the first in charge of foreign affairs at the second level, the second for domestic affairs, the third to be liaison between the White House and the Executive departments, and the fourth responsible for personnel and related questions, including supervision of the Bureau of the Budget.

Thus, behind the façade of frost and icicles, an imaginative and constructive mind can be seen at work. As Burns deplored the common lack of seeing "ourselves as others see us," so might Adams, had he served out Eisenhower's tenure and not fallen a victim to his own arrogance, have "from many a danger freed us, and foolish notion."

Among the miseries that from time to time tarnish the splendors of the Presidency, one of the most poignant for Eisenhower was the Senate's rejection of his nomination of Rear Admiral Lewis L. Strauss, U.S.N. (ret.), to be Secretary of Commerce. Something has previously been noted here of Strauss's major role in keeping United States weaponry ahead of the enemy's in the Second World War; also of his vital part, when a member of the Atomic Energy Commission, in assuring the development of the hydrogen bomb against the contrary efforts of eminent dissenters who included J. Robert Oppenheimer.

Because of great services to national security, because of Strauss's long and successful experience in finance and industry, and finally because of his exceptional loyalty to the A.E.C., the President sent his name to the Senate for the Cabinet post. But there already were two liabilities against the nomination: the F.B.I.'s presentation of Oppenheimer's security record (a function his official duty and the President's direction obliged him to perform); and the personal dislike of Strauss by Senator Clinton P. Anderson of New Mexico, chairman of the Congressional committee that supervised the operations of the A.E.C.

Strauss had become involved *ex officio* in the Oppenheimer case. When the matter of continuing the Q (top-security) clearance of the great nuclear physicist—this clearance admits its possessor to all the classified information on national defense —was laid before Eisenhower by Strauss as a matter of routine, it was also routine for the President to require from Strauss, as Chairman of the Atomic Energy Commission, a recommendation pro or con. An intensive study of the record convinced Strauss that because of Oppenheimer's indiscretion in associating with certain persons whose loyalty to the United States was at least dubious, and because of evasive and conflicting answers to questions inherent in this association, the scientist's Q clearance should not be continued.

Accordingly, when asked by the President for a judgment on an FBI report to the same effect, Strauss made that recommendation. In consideration of the storm it was sure to raise in politically libertarian and scientific circles, Eisenhower appointed a board to review the F.B.I.'s judgment. This board was presided over by Gordon Gray, who as a public servant in five major capacities and as a private citizen had earned a shining reputation for personal and mental integrity, objectivity toward any task assigned him, and the courage to stand by his principles.

After exhaustive inquiry, in which Oppenheimer testified at length, the Gray Board upheld Strauss's recommendation. Its finding was that though Oppenheimer never consciously wavered in his loyalty to the United States, the facts in the case proved him to be sufficiently uncandid and unfirm of judgment in his personal associations as to make him a security risk.

This finding created bitter enemies in powerful quarters for

Strauss and Gray, and the former's nomination as Secretary of Commerce made him the target for these enemies. However, they might not have prevailed over the normal Senate disposition to confirm Cabinet appointees of adequate capacity and good moral character had it not been for the determined opposition of Anderson.

As Chairman of the Joint Congressional Committee on Atomic Energy, Anderson formed the opinion that Strauss had on several occasions withheld from the committee vital information to which it was entitled, and distorted his own role in such Executive-Legislative policy disputes as that over the steam-plant-building contract granted to the Dixon-Yates industrial complex. In the course of the Senate hearings on Strauss's confirmation which lasted from March 17 to May 14, 1959, Anderson, on these bases, rested the issue on adverse appraisals of Strauss's character, methods, and personality.

The Senate committee to which the nomination of Strauss was referred voted in favor of Strauss's confirmation by the narrow majority of nine to eight. In the showdown on the Senate floor, June 19, with only three of the ninety-eight Senators not voting, the nomination was rejected, forty-nine to forty-six. And among those registered for rejection were Majority Leader Lyndon B. Johnson, John F. Kennedy, Richard Neuberger, William Langer and Margaret Chase Smith (the latter two being Republicans).

This was the first Senate veto of an Eisenhower Cabinet appointment, and the first of any Cabinet nominee since 1925. Strauss duly resigned his pro tem incumbency as Secretary of Commerce on June 30.

I have reason to believe that Strauss had sound reasons for expecting favorable votes from Johnson, Neuberger, and Kennedy, and that none would have voted to deny the President a Cabinet choice had Anderson not made rejection a personal matter. Johnson had often called on Anderson for support in a pinch and got it. Kennedy was in debt to Anderson for an important assist in his Senate career that furthered his ambition to qualify for the Presidential nomination in 1960.

Since Kennedy also had spoken and written most favorably to Strauss with respect to his chairmanship of the Atomic

Energy Commission—which Anderson bitterly attacked in the confirmation fight—I was especially curious over the change of front by the young Senator from Massachusetts. (Johnson's was readily explainable as repayment to Anderson, on demand, for support of the Party leader on critical occasions.) So I sought enlightenment on Kennedy's shift from his father. The elder Kennedy said that Anderson, reminding his son of the aforementioned service, had represented the situation to be that a vote for Strauss was a vote against Anderson; and that on this representation Senator Kennedy reluctantly yielded his preference to confirm.

Even allowing for the clashes of personalities and for those over the Executive-Legislative provinces that had occurred between Anderson and Strauss, I have never been able to understand the violence of Anderson's reactions. He had always seemed to me to excel in both courtesy and objectivity, and I greatly admired his earnest effort as Truman's Secretary of Agriculture to supplant the wasteful and wholly political national agricultural policy with permanent sounder measures. And in doing so, he had taken political risks that his immediate predecessors had not ventured. But in the excess of his successful effort to prevent Strauss's confirmation I found a vein of implacability I had never suspected.

The public record of General Eisenhower's assessment of Richard M. Nixon as a person and as a public servant is so contradictory in places that it will probably remain a matter of speculation for historians. But in my judgment as a close observer of their relations, whatever Eisenhower's respect for Nixon's character, mentality, and political acumen may have been at the start, it grew steadily with exposure to his ability. This respect has not since declined.

After the General got to know Nixon, and during the Presidential illness worked harmoniously with one who, he was aware, was his potential successor, I believe that Eisenhower formed a high opinion of his Vice-President's qualifications. Certainly he made increasing and extended use of Nixon's talent.

In Jefferson's time the Vice-President, James Madison, was a partner, philosophically and otherwise, of the President, and was deep in his confidence. Following the terms of Jefferson and his successors, Madison and Monroe, the Vice-Presidency lapsed into a watching brief. Sometimes the President and the Vice-President of the United States were hardly on speaking terms, generally the latter was outside the Establishment, which was Truman's situation when he succeeded.

Except for what he had learned as Chairman of the Senate Committee on the Conduct of the War, Truman knew little of the making, conduct, or sources of policy; and he came to the Presidency perhaps as ignorant of these as any predecessor had ever been.

Therefore, when nominated and elected in his own right in 1948, Truman resolved that Vice-President Alben W. Barkley should not be subjected to the same handicap. He began to make more use of the Vice-President than had any President since Jefferson. But Eisenhower expanded even beyond Barkley's the duties and confidences of the President and the Vice-President. Consequently, Nixon was the first Vice-President for a hundred years or more who really was a policymaking participant on the highest level in the Administration. Except for Secretaries Dulles and Humphrey, Nixon became the most important member of Eisenhower's Cabinet.

When the General assumed the Presidency, he inherited grave and acute foreign-policy problems because of Roosevelt's colossal misjudgment of the international course of Soviet Russia after the war, the product being the Cold War. Dulles was the number-one Presidential adviser on foreign policy because of Eisenhower's total reliance on Dulles' expertise in these matters, on his wisdom as an individual, and on his abilities as an international lawyer. But had it not been for this special relationship, I believe Nixon would have been the number-one Presidential counselor in the foreign field—as indeed as he was after Dulles died.

The outcome of the famous incident of the 1952 campaign charges against Nixon and his dramatic rebuttal was the dispersal of Eisenhower's doubts of his running mate's integrity, marked by that emotional meeting in which Eisenhower threw his arms around Nixon and said, "You're my boy." But until then Eisenhower's comments on the charges, and even his silences, had left a strong impression that he believed it would be wise for Nixon to withdraw from the ticket. And periodically their relations continued to mystify the public. This led to an impression that Eisenhower did not greatly admire Nixon and preferred someone else for renomination for Vice-President in 1956. But to some extent that was a consequence of Eisenhower's way of responding to news-conference questions. For instance, on the occasion when a reporter asked him to name some policy in which Nixon's counsel had figured importantly he said, "Give me a week and I'll try to think of one."

This, of course, was duly exploited as a thumbs-down of Nixon's aspirations for the Presidential nomination in 1960. But my conclusion was (and is) that if Eisenhower had been as articulate as Kennedy, for example, he would have said, "Well now, offhand I can't answer an omnibus question like that. There were a number of occasions and if you want me to look up some, I'll give them to you later."

In the long run the General has demonstrated the greatest admiration for Nixon. He very much wanted him to be elected President. Eisenhower wasn't as active in the 1960 campaign as he was expected to be because he wasn't called on. He did what was asked of him, apparently assuming that this was all Nixon wanted him to do. But in the final stage no one was more vehement in his support of Nixon.

With respect to the Presidential nomination in 1968, Eisenhower's attitude, I think (before the disaster that overtook Nixon in the 1962 contest for Governor of California), was that a man who missed the Presidency by a fraction of one per cent deserved another chance. But that event, and others which may arise between this writing and its publication, could persuade the General that the Party can profitably make a fresher choice.

Nixon was very philosophical toward this possibility as he approached its test in the 1968 Presidential primaries. He was aware that destiny might be operating unfavorably. For had he been born before or later than he was by several years, he would not have met Kennedy. And he realized, long before the 1960 campaign, that Kennedy was the most effective opponent who could have run against him.

In a conversation with Nixon afterward I brought up the theory that he was perhaps a victim of the calendar as Clay, Webster, and Adlai Stevenson had been. I suggested that if Stevenson, for example, had met any other Republican nominee than Eisenhower, he would probably have been elected in 1952. The same circumstance doomed Stevenson in 1956. And when in 1960 he encouraged the effort to nominate him for a third time, Stevenson had been totally eclipsed by the rise of Kennedy.

The great extent to which Nixon was assigned by the President to project the Administration's foreign and domestic policies is implicit in several conversations that I and others had with the Vice-President during and after 1954. One of these provided an interesting sidelight on the Administration's activities toward "McCarthyism." In February, 1954, Secretary of the Army Robert L. Stevens called on Nixon as Eisenhower's deputy at the Capitol for counsel preparatory to Stevens' showdown with the Wisconsin Senator before the Senate subcommittee that sat on McCarthy's accusations in the case of Major Peress. Present also were three Senators on the subcommittee. Stevens was told that if he adhered to his disposition to instruct Army officers to decline to obey the subcommittee's subpoenas, the issue would surely come before the Senate and he would be overwhelmingly repudiated.

The group advised him to meet with McCarthy and the Republican members of the subcommittee, saying they were sure he could work out a settlement. They counseled him on what he could give and what he could take. The product was a statement by Stevens prudently backtracking from his rigid attitude and acknowledging that the subcommittee had given him "assurances" of good treatment of the Army witnesses. This statement was read to Eisenhower, who said he would back it up.

Nixon's general conclusions, proved sound by the event, were that Stevens probably couldn't be salvaged. But he was hopeful that McCarthy could be "tamed," relying on five in-stances he cited in which McCarthy had tangled with the Administration and retreated when he was shown that to stand pat would be against his self-interest. Nixon's analysis was that McCarthy had a power complex, and any impressive argument that an action of his would endanger his possession of power would win him over.

Nixon did not accept the "Machiavellian theory" that McCarthy's attacks on the Army were part of a plan to become President. According to this theory, McCarthy, often discredit-ing the Army as much as he could, would blame the conditions on Eisenhower and use this as his springboard to the nomina-tion. "I don't buy this one at all," Nixon told visitors. And he described the President as taking the Stevens-McCarthy epi-sode calmly, and as being prepared, at his next news con-ference, to "restate general principles" in dealing with the controversy in terms critical of McCarthy and defensive of Stevens. Nixon's information was accurate, as soon demon-strated by what Eisenhower said on the subject.

One of the attributes that makes Nixon unusual is his ability to appraise, with almost total objectivity, situations and politi-cal prospects in which he himself is deeply involved. This quality is demonstrated by appraisals he was making of the Eisenhower Administration's domestic and foreign policies at a point in Nixon's second term, when he was the unmistakable heir apparent:

. . . The successful launching of the Sputnik by the U.S.S.R. weakened the American people's reliance on the President's leader-ship in foreign affairs and defense. The only effective answer would be superior scientific space achievements by the United States.

. . . The President had to send troops to Little Rock [to quell the interracial disturbances] when he did. But this will not neces-sarily help, and may hurt, the Party's chances to keep control of the Executive office in 1960. It damaged the prospect in the South and all the border states except Kentucky. And as for the Negro vote in the North, the Republicans "on balance" would not gain more than about 10 per cent in the two subsequent elections.

. . . Whether or not the large Eisenhower budgets lost public

support, they disaffected the Republican organizations in the
states. These workers felt that the Administration had abandoned
the fiscal principles on which the Party had successfully cam-
paigned in 1952 and 1956. The result was organization apathy—a
dangerous political condition.

. . . Republican popularity was eroding in the farm states,
though as yet it was showing against the Party's Congressional
nominees and not so much against the Administration. Since the
farmers were now doing better with respect to income, the reason
for the erosion was probably a matter of "personalities," that of
Ezra T. Benson, the Secretary of Agriculture, in particular.

. . . As for the Democratic charge of a "missile crisis," an
investigation will show that since Eisenhower, in 1954–1955 and
in 1957, acted on two memoranda of urgency that [John] McCone
had vainly presented to the Truman Administration in 1950, the
Armed Services have made a massive effort to outdistance the
U.S.S.R. The U.S.A. is now definitely ahead in missiles with a
fifteen-hundred-mile range, though the Russians may excel in
long-range missiles.

Nevertheless, the Democratic charge of a "missile gap," ar-
ticulated by Senate Majority Leader Lyndon B. Johnson and
his subcommittee, was used effectively against Nixon in 1960.
Not until the Kennedy Administration came to power, and
Defense Secretary Robert McNamara, in apparent innocence
of the political background, told a news conference that the
charge was unfounded currently and also at the time it was
made, was Nixon's 1957 personal analysis verified.

The history of the development of missiles by the United
States began with the Truman Administration. But not until
Eisenhower's attention was drawn to two memoranda submitted to his predecessor's regime on August 10 and 15, 1950, by
(then Air Under Secretary) McCone, and to the inadequate
response to them, did he pull out all the stops to pursue the
endeavor. The scientific genius of Vice-Admiral Hyman Rick-
over, and the constructive genius of Rear Admiral William F.
Raborn, Jr., had given the nation a long headstart in the production of the Polaris missile and the nuclear submarine well

before the end of the Truman Administration. But a chronology of the development of the land-to-land, air-to-air, and air-to-land missiles places the first real drive within Eisenhower's tenure.

This chronology confirms President Truman's statement—in a series of articles that appeared in 1957—that in 1950, "as soon as I saw the long-range missile program lagging," he had called in a top industrial engineer, "put him in full charge of the program, responsible only to the President, and with instructions to knock heads together whenever it was necessary to break through the bottlenecks. . . ." But the main recommendation of the McCone memoranda in 1950 was for a "Manhattan-type missile project [like the one that produced the first atomic bomb] under a chief with absolute authority and responsible only to the President." And though Truman offered this post to K. T. Keller of the Chrysler Corporation, on the scope drawn by McCone, Keller declined the role on several grounds. After investigating the infant state of the missile program, he decided that a "Manhattan-type" project would require a year to institute, and that his best contribution would be made by serving with a small staff as an "appraiser" and coordinator of the program instead of as its administrative czar.

In the former capacity, Keller traveled more than a hundred thousand miles and issued a series of recommendations, all of which were made official orders by the three Secretaries of Defense—Louis A. Johnson, George C. Marshall, and Robert A. Lovett—who served after Forrestal during the Truman Administration. Having worn himself out, Keller declined the new President's, Eisenhower's, offer to stay on, and in the plenary role Truman again had offered him. But he did continue as appraiser and analyst of the program until 1953.

So the gist of the chronology is that Keller, despite Truman's account in the articles referred to, was never "in full charge of the missile program," and was not "dismissed" by Eisenhower.

Toward the end of October, 1957, Eisenhower first saw the full text of McCone's 1950 memoranda. In the meantime the U.S.S.R. had perfected not only the hydrogen bomb but two earth satellites. Concluding, therefore, that it was too late for the Manhattan-type project he had proposed in August, 1950, McCone, at the President's direction, updated his recommendations. These called for:

(1) the appointment of a Deputy Secretary of Defense to give full time to missile development and with full control over every aspect of it;

(2) the assignment to the Defense Department of full responsibility for the integrated progress of the program, instead of keeping this responsibility divided among the three Secretaries of the Armed Services;

(3) —repeating his recommendation of August 15, 1950— the procurement and use of completed missiles to be left to the armed service "requiring the missile in its particular mission."

Intensive work on the project began with this updated McCone memorandum. But as any chronology shows, the delay was long; the diffused authority in the Department of Defense that could not be quickly overcome was partly responsible; Truman, though he had intended to, did not set up the full project as he later remembered it; Eisenhower did not "dismiss" Keller, as Truman charged him with doing; and there was enough blame to cover both Administrations. But there was no "missile lag" when the Democrats in the campaign of 1960 charged its existence, and the responsibility for it, to the Eisenhower Administration.

Toward the end of his second term as Vice-President, I also found Nixon thinking along these lines:

. . . Our foreign policy has been sound when we opposed armed force with law. But when, as with President Nasser of Egypt during the Suez Crisis in 1956, the issue was between armed force and anarchy, the issue has not been so clear. Increased and well-administered foreign aid to Africa and Asia is one answer. Perhaps also we should reduce our support of the armies we pay for in Korea, Thailand, and possibly Vietnam, and divert the money saved to social-economic aid.

In retrospect Nixon, like the postwar Presidents and the spokesmen of the major parties, changed some of these views: he obviously abandoned his militant position that the United States should send armed air assistance to the beleaguered French in Vietnam. But the views cited above, even in the new and often shattering light of today, are those of a thoughtful, well-informed, and constructively intelligent public man. And however much or little his views were translated into the policies of the Eisenhower Administration, their inherent qualities of realism and foresight account for the admiration of his Vice-President that breaks through the cloud of some of Eisenhower's comments on their relations.

One of these clouds hovered for a time over the General's proposal to Nixon (in 1956) that it might better serve his Presidential ambition to transfer to a Cabinet "or equivalent" post. But except for those with a dogged preconception to the contrary, the sincerity (if not the political wisdom) of the proposal was plain in Eisenhower's explanation.

He said he had reminded Nixon that no man who served eight years as Vice-President had ever been elected President. But the matter ended when Nixon, after thinking it over, expressed his preference to be renominated, partly on the ground that his acceptance of a Cabinet post would be generally taken as a demotion, partly on the ground that with the opportunities for conspicuous public service Eisenhower was disposed to give him (neither mentioned the factor of the President's two serious illnesses), he might steadily improve the national estimate of his Presidential qualifications four years afterward.

Eisenhower readily went along with this judgment; and Nixon was renominated. By 1960 the General was expressing the opinion that, though there were "at least a dozen Republicans" fully capable of filling the Presidential office, Nixon was the best qualified.

In the period just prior to the 1960 conventions, visitors who talked politics with Eisenhower found him much interested also in the identity of the Democratic nominee. He was disturbed at the thought that this could be anyone as "immature" as John F. Kennedy. But the visitors detected a considerable change in his appraisal of a certain other potential Democratic nominees.

On a previous occasion (in 1959), when asked how he rated the qualifications of House Speaker Sam Rayburn and Senate Majority Leader Lyndon B. Johnson, he had promptly replied, "Sam would be fine." But in April, 1960, he was quoted as saying privately that Johnson—who had been steering the Senate Democrats to a course of cooperation with the President— was the Democrat best qualified to succeed him, with the surprising addendum that Adlai E. Stevenson was the only other Democrat with acceptable Presidential qualifications.

Even including three illnesses in office, the Administration and Republican Party problem incarnated in McCarthy (until he struck himself out), the Senate's rejection of Strauss, and the imprudences of Adams and Talbott, I think the passing of Dulles was Eisenhower's heaviest burden. Personally and officially, no two were ever closer. And American history supplies few if any parallels of this essential relation of a President with his Secretary of State. It was enhanced and made even more confiding on Eisenhower's part by the fact that no Secretary of State was more assiduous in establishing the President's final authority in foreign affairs: "He used to give me little lectures on that," Eisenhower once recalled.

He became accustomed to evolving acts and policies with Dulles verbally, in full confidence they would be faithfully executed. For in the President's judgment, the man and the hour had one of their rare conjunctions when Dulles took charge of the State Department in a most crucial period of American history.

In this period the Soviet Union, dedicated to the destruction of the American political and social-economic systems, acquired a potential of industrial and military strength exceeded only by our own—and not in all particulars. In this period, because Moscow-Peking interests were still commingled, the Communist and satellite nations made up the largest world complex of population and geography. And the United States had become vulnerable to sudden and devastating nuclear attacks from one quarter, and to the consequences of subversions of anti-Communist governments in several areas of the world where, unlike Vietnam, our national security was clear.

In recent years the job of Secretary of State has grown into an actually impossible one. If the incumbent makes a diplomatic move or issues a statement to counter one by a hostile regime, he invites disunifying criticism by the political opposition at home unless he has procured their advance clearance. But this cannot always be had. There are occasions when, even after this consultation, the President and the Secretary must proceed on their responsibilities to depart from a framework of agreement without time to give notice and risk the leak implicit in renewing the consultation.

The foreign-policy-makers of a totalitarian government have no part of this problem. They can retreat or advance overnight, yet continue to present to the world the full face of national unity. And this situation confronted Dulles more so than any predecessor. Its critical nature, I think, was largely responsible for the flights of phraseology that drew upon Dulles the bulk of the adverse criticism to which he was exposed: "unleashing Chiang Kai-shek," "liberation," "massive retaliation," and going to "the brink of war" to forestall it.

Another Dulles trait was his full persuasion that the Judeo-Christian theology and the American Constitutional system are righteous in God's sight, and, being so, must for this reason prevail over "godless" Marxism. This mistaken conviction that the Communist system was crumbling from within was a main source of his errors in policy, act, and speech, definitely including the abrupt cancellation of United States aid to Nasser in building the Aswan Dam; and then, most inconsistently, the Eisenhower Administration's pressure on Britain, France, and Israel to abandon their military expedition to keep Nasser from nationalizing the Suez Canal.

But in all things, wise or unwise, hailed or denounced, Dulles retained the full faith and confidence of his chief. I believe that when illness and then death removed him from the Administration, the miseries of high office weighed on Eisenhower more heavily than any of its splendors exhilarated him, and continued to do so to the end of his term.

In 1959 Eisenhower almost decided on a drastic Cabinet

reorganization that again could probably be traced to the staff system on which the military establishment is founded. The idea was to propose to Congress legislation to create the new office of First Secretary of the Executive Department—the occupant to rank all the Cabinet, including its premier, the Secretary of State. This officer would have been the President's statutory deputy in total charge of consolidating policy and operation, would have represented the President in primary negotiation with foreign governments, acted as Vice-Chairman of the National Security Council and the National Advisory Council; he also would have had the authority to interfere in the internal affairs of the Executive, though only in matters of extreme emergency, the definition to be left to him.

The resignation and death of Secretary of State Dulles had imposed on Eisenhower the burdens of foreign travel and negotiation, and to this must be largely attributed the genesis of the idea. But that he was thinking of his successors, and not of himself, when his mind turned favorably to this revolutionary change was demonstrated by his plan to ask Congress not to give it effect until his successor took office.

On more detailed examination, Eisenhower dropped the plan and decided on a substitute. This was to make his Assistant for National Security—Gordon Gray at the time—the head of the existing Operations Coordinating Board, which was presided over by the Under Secretary of State. When the Eisenhower Administration ended, Gray was making headway in projecting all Presidential decisions on policy into smooth and consistent operational procedures, down to the smallest executive units—a badly-needed improvement in the functioning of the Executive machinery. But the promising reform was terminated by President Kennedy, who abolished the O.C.B.

Such was Eisenhower's popularity that though he vetoed a number of measures expressing the post-1932 shift of the Democratic political philosophy to that of a leftist welfare state, only one was overridden by the required two-thirds of both branches of Congress. The exception was a pork-barrel raid on the Treasury that even the divided Democrats, and some Republicans, were vocationally unable to refrain from joining. And few of those with demonstrated qualifications to assay future voting probabilities—the managers of Federal, state, urban, and rural party political organization—disputed that if Eisenhower had been eligible under the Twenty-second Amendment to seek a third term in 1960, he would have been overwhelmingly re-elected.

Yet Eisenhower had liabilities that could have made such a forecast inconceivable: an aloof attitude toward the profession of politics that de-energized that arm of the national Republican organization which has the function of getting the regular Party members to the polls; the impressions he created at news conferences that, relying as he did on the staff system, the President had not done his homework sufficiently to give informed answers to basic news conference questions; an oral syntax that frequently made the meaning of his statements an impenetrable mystery; the official denial of the real mission of the U-2 planes over Russia that Moscow shatteringly exposed; and finally, a succession of serious illnesses that in the case of any other citizen would have persuaded the people that his vitality had become inadequate to shoulder the burdens of the Presidency.

In private conversation, however, Eisenhower spoke with full clarity and full grasp of the problems of the Presidency. His syntax was orderly and unconfused, his sentences parsed. In a talk with the President on July 7, 1960, I ventured to suggest that he provide himself with a bedside tape recorder (he had said he often wakened in the night and then "oh, boy!" as he mulled over his problems), so that his public addresses, at least, would sound more like the easy way he expressed himself in conversation, dangling participles and all. But the President dismissed the general subject, including his often bewildering news conference syntax, with this: "What if I do leave out verbs, hitch singular nouns to plural verbs, and all that? They know what I mean, and that's what's important." And on the record of Eisenhower's abiding influence on public opinion, he was right.

In my judgment, Dwight D. Eisenhower was the President the nation wanted and needed the most for the eight years of his tenure—a conservative, but a progressive conservative; a candid, honest spokesman of the interest of the people of the nation and the free world that no credibility gap (not even the blundering deception of the true mission of the U-2) did or could separate from them; often confused in his choice of words, but never intentionally misleading; not as sensitive at all times to social needs and economic malproportions as Presidential leadership in this age requires, but a man of deep compassion nonetheless.

In the present parlous state of the nation there must be a host of Americans who, reversing the favorite joke of the liberal groups in the 1950s, do more than "wonder what the country would be like if Eisenhower were President": they wish he were.

Nostalgia for "the good old days" is a perilous luxury. And if luxury alone were the source of that wish, it would be merely a silly exercise in futility. Because the burdens that seem a heavier pack on the back of mankind than ever before are simply the old ones in new forms and degrees, with the exception of the development of nuclear weaponry.

But it is neither futile nor silly to seek to revert to the more practical and effective approaches to these problems that were in use before the current socialist-liberal philosophy and the new economics weakened this nation and others in the non-Communist world. For the twentieth-century liberals have made a titanic failure of their own approaches, among the most grievous being the breakdown of law enforcement and the rise of mob rule in the United States.

These liberals pursued the theories that ever increasing and loose Federal spending can dispel poverty; that Supreme Court decrees and compulsory statutes can end discriminations that are bred in the bone and stimulated by powerful racial differences of which color is but one; that peoples used to being governed by an elite or by dictatorships can be inspired, by occupying armies and bombardment from the air, to love the American democratic system; that this nation can continue to spend beyond income and productivity, and do at once everything that may be desirable without a set of priorities; that government-guaranteed personal security from cradle to grave can be established without weakening the incentives to work and to succeed by which the character of this and other peoples have been forged. And, on the application of these theories, produce utopia.

Such are the fallacies which were generally opposed and combatted in the Eisenhower years, and account primarily for the Republican gains in Congress in 1966. It is not mere nostalgia to long and hope for the replacement in office of those responsible for the conditions which are the product of the present direful melange of doctrinal aberrations and vote-seeking hoaxes.

14

KENNEDY

AS HAS been noted by deeper thinkers and better writers, the Kennedy family is a clan, a tribe, a sovereignty, and a dynasty, tied loosely enough within a package to allow each member a good deal of independent freedom of movement. But never to the point of a fracturing collision, a limitation I have observed in the many years since 1935, when I began to be an intimate of the family under the sponsorship of the patriarch, Joseph Patrick himself.

In recounting this relationship, which grew taut under the strain of differences during the Presidential campaign of 1960, and broke apart forever some months before the colossal tragedy at Dallas on November 22, 1963, I owe my readers a preliminary confession: as the Kennedy boys grew into manhood, although I was early aware of the limitless ambition their father was stimulating in them, I did not foresee that John Fitzgerald Kennedy, the second son, would be the one to attain it, and that the attainment would be claimed by the third son as his rightful heritage.

But fate denies the knowledge of its intentions to the finite creatures who inhabit the earth, and two calamitous strokes of fate serve to explain, if not to excuse, my shortsightedness of the political future of the Kennedys. In their feudal family structure the eldest son, Joseph Patrick, Jr., was designed by the patriarch to be the first Roman Catholic President of the United States, and it was only because of his fatal valor in the Second World War that the quest descended to the second son. And if the next stroke of fate had not occurred in circumstances that made him and his name a legend throughout the world, the claim of the third son on the inheritance would not have been fortified by the popular sentiment that automatically envelops one who was the heir to a legend until the tragic circumstances of *his* death made him a legend, too.

But at least I did perceive potentials of high achievement, though in what field I did not precisely discern, in the young John Fitzgerald Kennedy, in the maturing of his mind and the development of his personality.

I was made aware of these potentials in the wide-ranging discussions of large affairs that were invoked by the senior at the family dinner table; in the impressive supporting data and clear prose of the Harvard thesis that John F. Kennedy brought to me for an appraisal of its durable value; and in the personal grace and charm this youth effortlessly diffused in any company. However, I did not begin to envisage the Presidency that these qualities greatly aided in obtaining until John Kennedy's victories in the early state primaries in 1960.

Probably even then I would not have conceived the possibility of their triumphant culmination at the subsequent Democratic National Convention and the November election if I had not already learned from personal experience to credit information collected by his father. When JFK's pre-convention campaign proceeded, and the outcome of a state primary was certified as doubtful by the press and the political professionals, Joseph P. Kennedy prepared me for the victory that followed with confidential accounts of the pressures being exerted on leaders of the state's Democratic organization.

In each instance, the primary result bore out his prediction. And as the Los Angeles convention ran its course, the key state delegations that arrived divided or uncommitted affirmed his prophecy that in the crucial stage they would provide the necessary number of votes for his son.

The fraction of one per cent of the popular vote by which John F. Kennedy defeated Richard M. Nixon can be attributed to the outcome in any one of several states or election districts. But no stronger claim can be made than for the returns on Chicago's South Side. And since this was the contribution of the organization headed by Mayor Richard Daley, on whom the elder Kennedy exerted special influence, it can be argued that the father was a foremost factor in the election victory of the son.

I had encountered Joseph P. Kennedy, Sr., several times in the entourage that accompanied Governor Franklin D. Roosevelt of New York on his campaign for the Democratic Presidential nomination in 1932. At the Chicago convention, where this ambition was realized, I was sufficiently in touch with Kennedy's activities on behalf of Roosevelt's nomination to know of his successful intervention by telephone with William Randolph Hearst, Sr., that clinched Roosevelt's victory on the fourth ballot. "If you don't take Roosevelt," Kennedy warned Hearst, "you'll get Newton D. Baker"—perhaps the nominee least acceptable to the press lord at San Simeon.

In Chicago, and in the subsequent pre-election campaign, I had seen enough of Joe Kennedy to be impressed with the fact that for vigor, intelligence, forcefulness, political sagacity, and charm, this tall, red-haired, red-faced, blue-eyed man was outstanding in the circle dedicated to the proposition that Roosevelt should become President of the United States.

On one of these occasions, in Roosevelt's hotel suite, during a pre-convention stopover in Chicago, I had admired the skill with which he engaged in light banter with the Governor without overstepping the limits of the deference appropriate in the circumstances. But not until 1934, when President Roosevelt appointed Kennedy to the new Securities and Exchange Commission (of which he became the first chairman), did I become really acquainted with him. This was at a meeting in Kennedy's office, on his initiative, that two of his New York friends commended to me as an opportunity to take the measure of the man who, as a news source and later as an intimate companion, was to be of great significance in my professional and personal life.

These two friends were Bernard M. Baruch and Herbert Bayard Swope. Both the President and Kennedy were the targets of criticism for the appointment to ride herd on Wall Street of a daring and often ruthless stock-market operator, whose demonstrated genius as a "bear" had made him many millions at the expense of other speculators and the gullible victims-at-large of market manipulation. Baruch and Swope had urged me to make a first-hand estimate of the validity of the widely published fears that in his job of policing the market, Kennedy would subordinate the public service to his own monetary interests.

Our brutally frank conversation convinced me wholly to the contrary. I wrote an article for *The New York Times*, commending the choice of Kennedy for the post, that, he assured me, had helped materially to give him the public confidence he lacked and greatly needed for a full opportunity to refute the criticisms by his official performance. As chairman of the SEC, Joe Kennedy proceeded to justify every word in that article.

To the Commission he also brought the most talented and public-spirited men he could induce to serve with him, among them Yale Law School Professor William O. Douglas, Harvard Law School Professor James M. Landis, and a host of younger men who were to win popular approval and official promotion by their technical skills and their zeal to protect the average investor in stocks and bonds.

After a year or so as Chairman of the SEC, Kennedy had established the agency as a devoted and most efficient guardian of the responsibility the President and Congress had invested in it. He retired again to private life as a financial consultant and corporate reorganizer, and in this capacity he straightened out the complicated troubles of Pathé, the Hearst properties, and others. And during this period our personal relationship extended to the Kennedy family as a whole.

He was as scrupulous as I in excluding material considerations from this relationship, comprehending my insistence on this with a delicacy that would have surprised his detractors—many of them animated by envy of his accomplishments. So it was that, solely as a friend and admirer, I helped him in an editorial capacity with the production of his book *I'm For Roosevelt*, which was (successfully) designed to convince the business community in the Presidential campaign of 1936 that Roosevelt, as at least was true of the First New Deal, aspired to be the savior instead of the wrecker of capitalism and the free-enterprise system of the United States.

This was a typical example of the relationship existing between Joe Kennedy and me when he returned to government as Chairman of the Maritime Commission in 1937; in this capacity he restored the American merchant marine to the capability that was to prove so vital a factor of national security in the period when Hitler was steadily embroiling Europe to the point of a disastrous war in which the United States eventually became involved. And this relationship endured during his brilliant discharge of his new duties as Ambassador to Great Britain and until the inevitable strains between a political commentator and a politician severed my comity, first with his sons John and Robert, and finally with Joe Kennedy himself.

But in the years preceding, my life was greatly enriched by my close associations with the Kennedys—in Washington, at Joe's country house, Marwood, nearby, at Palm Beach, and at Hyannis Port. The households were gay and mentally stimulating, the more so as the boys grew into manhood. Among my recollections, several in particular can serve as illustrations:

One day, while Kennedy, Sr., was Chairman of the Maritime Commission and I was in his office on a professional errand, the White House telephone rang. I rose to leave, but Kennedy signaled to me to remain. Whereupon a conversation began, with the President very obviously on the other end. As I recall it, the subject was a very controversial order by Kennedy to a United States skipper in South America to discipline some mutinous seamen by putting them in irons. And something like the following was Kennedy's part of the conversation:

"Yes, Mr. President . . . Yes, sir, I know you're getting complaints. . . . Yes, Mr. President, but I'd do it again; we can't allow things like this and get the job done. . . . No, sir, I don't go with that idea of a compromise. . . . [And then, forgetting the punctilious "sirs" and "Mr. Presidents"] Listen, boy. If we do that we'll land in the —— ——." [At which mention of the ignoble but functional edifice to which Kennedy was wont to refer, came a delighted roar, the voice clear and unmistakable, from the other end of the wire.]

One night I was dining alone with Kennedy at Marwood when the President's eldest son, and in that period his father's secretary, appeared. The pair retired to another room for a half hour or so, after which James Roosevelt departed and Kennedy returned to the table. It was a time when the liberals, having heard a report that the President intended to appoint Kennedy to London, were putting heavy preventive pressure on Roosevelt. And Kennedy's report to me of his conversation with James Roosevelt implied that the President was yielding somewhat to the pressure. Kennedy was angry. "You know what Jimmy proposed? That instead of going to London, I become Secretary of Commerce! Well, I'm not going to. FDR promised me London, and I told Jimmy to tell his father that's the job, and the only one, I'll accept."

Kennedy was as good as his word, and the event sustained him. But meanwhile I was obliged to sit on a big news story, having learned of it in this confidential manner. Kennedy agreed to my proposition, however, that if and when I could get a release from the White House, I could publish the fact of the selection of the first Roman Catholic to represent the United States at the Court of St. James's.

The incumbent Ambassador, Robert Worth Bingham, my earlier employer in Louisville, was ill in the Johns Hopkins University Hospital in Baltimore, and as a matter of decorum I waited about a week before approaching James Roosevelt for the release. He assured me it was "all set" for Kennedy and, in answer to my further question in consideration of Bingham's condition, told me to "go ahead and print the story," which I did.

What followed was an experience with the Roosevelt family with which in time I was to become very familiar. At a news conference the President in effect accused me of halting Bingham's recovery by the publication (he died shortly afterward), and vowed that no one in the White House had released the information to me. Possibly, of course, Jimmy had neglected to tell his father that he had authorized the release.

After assuming his post, Joe Kennedy began a series of letters to me about his impressions, experiences, and views of the international situation. According to him, the first letter he wrote as "Ambassador to Great Britain" was to me. Dated March 8, 1938, it began: "Your persistent urging me to come here, and your holding my hand during those uncertain days, will always remain in my mind and heart." From the outset he was deeply disturbed about the British lack of military preparedness for a war toward which he felt the nation's jingoes were urging her, and deeply determined that the United States should keep out of the conflict if it came.

It was also clear in this correspondence that the Ambassador feared the President and his Administration were engaging in activities, making speeches, and moving toward policies that were provocative of producing the very result he opposed, and felt that the President had given him the strongest of assurances to the contrary.

On the verge of his relinquishment of his post in the fall of 1940, I had a letter from Kennedy from which I gathered an implication that he had resolved, as a private citizen, to do nothing to aid in the re-election of the President that would associate Kennedy with the drift of the United States into involvement in the war in Europe and Asia.

Insofar as I could determine, Kennedy was never impressed with the Presidential qualifications of the Republican nominee, Wendell L. Willkie; rather, he hoped to sit out the campaign except for a speech of warning against United States involvement. There was an impression in the political community, which I did not share, that he would specifically oppose the President's re-election. And he returned from London to an atmosphere of great apprehension of this among the Democrats and hope of it among the Republicans.

From what are often in my profession attributed to "authoritative sources," and in this instance most assuredly were, I compiled an account of the events related to this situation from the time, in October, 1940, when Kennedy returned from London on leave, to December 1, when he publicly announced his resignation as Ambassador to Great Britain. With only a few abridgments, dictated by considerations of personal responsibility for putting this compilation on the public record, it follows as written on the latter date:

. . . On October 16 Kennedy sent a cablegram to the President insisting that he be allowed to come home; other Ambassadors had been given the permission who had not been so long at their posts or been through his trying experiences in a German target area of the war. He had heard that he was not to be allowed to return until after the election.

. . . That same day Kennedy telephoned to Under Secretary Sumner Welles and said that if he did not get a favorable reply to his cablegram, he was coming home anyhow; that he had been ignored for three months—including withholding from him information of the impending destroyer-bases deal—by the Administration, which had sent envoys to London [Col. William J. Donovan, some admirals, and some generals] without informing him in advance or without ordering these envoys to deal with or through him; that he had written a full account of the facts to Edward Moore, his secretary in New York, with instructions to release the story to the press if the Ambassador were not back in New York by a certain date. A few hours after this conversation the cabled permission to return was received.

. . . When Kennedy reached Lisbon, he found a letter from the President asking him to make no public statement of any kind until he had talked with Roosevelt and to say nothing about resigning. A similar letter awaited him at Bermuda and in New York. At New York he was instructed to come to the White House at once.

. . . He was met at the airport by Mrs. [Rose] Kennedy, who urged him to the same effect. "The President sent you, a Roman Catholic, as Ambassador to London, which probably no other President would have done," she said. "He sent you as his representative to the Pope's coronation. You would write yourself down an ingrate in the view of many people if you resign now." The President had asked Mrs. Kennedy to accompany the Ambassador to Washington, and she decided to do so.

. . . When the Kennedys reached the White House—it was October 27—they were told the President would see them in a few minutes. While waiting they were joined by Senator and Mrs. James F. Byrnes, and later by Miss LeHand [the President's private secretary], "proving," commented Kennedy, "that Roosevelt didn't want to have it out with me alone." The party talked about many things, and then Byrnes said, "I've got a great idea, Joe. Why don't you make a radio speech on the lines of what you have said here tonight and urge the President's re-election?" Kennedy said it was not in his heart to do that until he "got off his chest" the things that were disturbing him, and proceeded to do so.

. . . He told the President, "whose face turned white and Byrnes was aghast," that he had been treated "terribly." He said that whenever the President had got in a jam, or a member of his family got in a jam, it was Kennedy to whom he turned. He said he had been humiliated in London and left to cool his heels while Presidential messengers conducted their business independently; and that he would not return.

. . . The President said he had known nothing about these matters; the fault lay with the State Department. . . . He pleaded with the Ambassador to make the speech. "All right, I will," said Kennedy to the President. "But I will pay for it myself, show it to nobody in advance and say what I wish." It was so agreed. [After making the speech Kennedy got this telegram: "I HAVE JUST LISTENED TO A GREAT SPEECH. THANK YOU. FDR."]

. . . The day after election, November 6, Kennedy tendered his resignation to the President, who said he couldn't accept it until he found someone to send in Kennedy's place. They discussed the situation of the British and the President agreed with Kennedy: that we must stay out of the war; otherwise, if the Germans continued to batter the British ports with their present effectiveness, the United States would be left in the position of being unable to help at all, and would be practically defenseless if the Axis struck in this hemisphere.

"You will either go down as the greatest President in history or the greatest horse's ass," said Kennedy.

"There is a third alternative," said the President. "I may go down as the President of an unimportant country at the end of my term."

. . . On December 1 Kennedy returned to the United States to insist that his resignation be accepted and an announcement be authorized. The President agreed, if Kennedy would retain his title as Ambassador until someone else could be found. Commenting on the deal by which the United States traded old-age destroyers for certain bases in Bermuda, etc., Kennedy said the deal was "the worst ever," that we have no contract for the bases, and that when "all the facts are known," they will "shock the American people."

But when he spoke, on a night in October, 1940, it was to urge the re-election of the President, though on the ground that this was the nation's best assurance that it would not become a participant in the war. This served the purpose of the White House meeting: to keep Kennedy on the reservation. It could only have surprised those who were not aware of the overwhelming pressures to which Kennedy had been exposed. For the speech was out of keeping, not only with the wholly opposite view he had been expressing privately (to me, among others), but with Kennedy's earned reputation as one of the most forthright men in public life.

This trait was never more visible than in an interview he had with three newspapermen in Boston some time previously, when he was returning to London after a visit to the United States. Asked about the prospect he envisaged of the outcome of the war in Europe, he answered—on what he justly conceived to be an understanding that his remarks were strictly off the record—that the British had no clear idea what they were fighting for, that their concept of democracy was based on a fixed class structure alien to our own, and that they could not possibly win the war.

When these remarks, most improperly, were published in a Boston paper by one of the interviewers, the consequences followed thick and fast. Joseph Pulitzer, Jr., Publisher of the *St. Louis Post-Dispatch*, whose Editor was one of the interviewers, wrote Kennedy a letter deploring the publication and denouncing it as a breach of faith. The British rose in indignation that developed into an anger against and a dislike for the United States Ambassador that remains unabated. And President Roosevelt was very seriously embarrassed. No one at that time could have foreseen that a son of Kennedy's would become the most popular of all American Presidents with the British people.

But in the years that followed, Joe Kennedy never forsook his judgment that United States combat involvement would lead to what became the Cold War with the Communist world. I believe that though he conceded the Japanese attack on Pearl Harbor made this involvement inevitable, he felt United States economic policies toward Japan had been provocative of the event which shattered his hopes this nation could stay out.

But the ensuing Cold War fortified for him the reasoning that accounted for his rigid noninvolvement position in 1939 and 1940. This is evident in an interview I had with him in 1947, at his instance and designed for publication. This occurred during one of the many visits I made to the Kennedy family in Palm Beach.

In this interview Kennedy argued that if any independent country freely turned to Communism as a governing system, a trial would convince that country of its error, and the United States could sensibly adopt a laissez-faire policy on the confident assumption that the nation concerned would in time revert to democracy and capitalism.

In the meantime, he said, the United States should keep its military establishment at full capability of meeting any challenge, and deny all aid whatever to the Communist-turned nation while awaiting the inevitable day when the reversion would occur. This interview, in my opinion, identified the difference between Kennedy and his sons John and Robert on American foreign policy that materialized as a fact when the first became President and the second his most ardent and faithful disciple and political manager.

But despite this difference, which ultimately expanded to the concept of the welfare state that President Kennedy made his own, the family remained united before the world. During the 1960 campaign, for example, while Joe Kennedy was expressing to me agreement with my own reservations about his son's domestic programs, he was using every influence at his command to win an election by which these programs would be advanced in conformity with the 1960 Democratic platform pledges. The overshadowing purpose was that the Kennedys produce a President of the United States, realizing the ambition the father had instilled in his sons. "For the Kennedys," he had once remarked to me, in disapproval of the decision of John to try for the Vice-Presidential nomination in 1956, "it's the [outhouse] or the castle—nothing in between."

But it was not only in the pursuit of this ambition that Joe Kennedy set for his sons the example of public service. He felt it to be the obligation of the successful, and impressed this on all four as they grew up. And when his own dream faded of being the first Kennedy to occupy the "castle," and the mantle that devolved on Joe, Jr., became the shroud of this gifted and valorous youth, he passed the dream on to the eldest of his remaining sons.

Events and issues were the constant discussion in the household of which for years I was a part. But always, as I think back on it, with the animation paramount that a Kennedy should acquire the political power to influence and direct them. Though the general sense of obligation to contribute lavishly to charitable enterprises was strong in the family, and has taken form in hundreds of millions of dollars spent for the physically and mentally retarded or otherwise afflicted, the compassionate spirit was toward the underprivileged community as a whole, without a concentration on the civil inequality of Negroes that became a political base for the reforms pressed by President Kennedy and his two Senator brothers.

But Joe, Sr., was angrily conscious of another injustice—the social and business discrimination against the descendants of the Irish immigrants that had impelled him to remove the family from Boston to the New York City area. There his daughters could make the proper social debuts denied them by the Back Bay Brahmins.

As it absurdly developed, these same Brahmins fell over themselves to solicit social association with the Ambassador to the Court of St. James's and his family. And the size of the majorities with which John F. and Edward M. Kennedy were elected to the United States Senate by the voters of Massachusetts attest to the same eagerness in the same group to align themselves with the Kennedys in the area of politics.

My relationship with the Kennedy boys was a gradual process. During their father's tours of duty in Washington they were at school or college, or—in the case of the youngest, "Teddy"—in kindergarten. The first time I had any specific relation with the progeny was when Joe Kennedy came to me in Washington in the middle 1930s to inquire whether I could suggest a place where Joe, Jr., and Jack could spend a summer in useful labor to prepare for the athletic activities they planned when they returned to Harvard.

Kennedy, Sr., told me that his second son, Jack, was a frail boy while Joe was in glowing health. I arranged to send them to a ranch called the "Jay Six," owned by a friend, John G. F. Speiden, near Benson, Arizona, where they passed a very good summer (they built an adobe house with only the help of a Mexican laborer), and came back strong and well. Joe qualified for the football team and Jack for the swimming team. Thereafter I began to see more of these boys, and in 1940 I became very closely associated with them for quite different reasons.

As for Joe, Jr., my most significant experience with him was at the Democratic National Convention of 1940, the third-term convention. He had been instructed as a Massachusetts delegate for James A. Farley for President, and the effort of the Administration was to have Roosevelt renominated by *acclamation*. This meant that not even one vote would be cast on the first ballot against him.

The pressure to switch to Roosevelt at the outset of the balloting was powerfully applied to young Kennedy. He was told among other things that his father's political future was at stake, and that if he stayed by his Farley instructions, in view of what inevitably was impending (the third-term nomination), he would be doing his father an injury. That troubled this excellent young man and he came to me as his father's friend to discuss the situation in a conversation that went like this:

"You're instructed for Farley, aren't you?"

"Yes."

"Have you been released? I'm sure Farley would agree to do that."

"No. And I haven't asked him to."

"What do you think your father would want you to do?"

"Well, that's what I came to ask you."

"He would want you to do the honorable thing and that's what you want to do too, isn't it?"

"Yes."

"If you didn't, you wouldn't even ask me about it. You would have sought your release and cast your vote for Roosevelt. . . . Don't worry about the old man. You will neither make nor break him. He'll do either by himself."

Young Joe cast his vote for Farley on the first ballot. Most of the Massachusetts delegation had forsaken their pledge to Farley under the pressure to vote for Roosevelt, but Joe Kennedy, Jr., was one of a very small group that kept faith with its instructions—thereby defeating the effort to have F.D.R. chosen by "acclamation"—joining only in the usual motion to make the President's renomination "unanimous."

There were the usual exceptions, however, to this devotion of the boys to their father and their obedience to his rules. One of the most amusing recollections I have of the latter occurred when I was crossing with Joe, Jr., Jack and their father on the *Normandie* to England while Joe, Sr., was still Ambassador. The ship's company was gay, and there was a beautiful actress aboard to whom young Joe was very attentive. This annoyed his father, because he thought that the boy might perhaps be a little too impulsive and the girl be making a play for a youth of his prominence and wealth. Jack was also staying up late at night, with a girl I think his father didn't know about. So he imposed a curfew on the young men; they would have to be in their quarters in his suite by midnight or thereabouts.

They made the first deadline. But the suite had a service door, distant from the bedrooms. So when thereafter I saw them as my fellow-conspirators, enjoying themselves in the ship's salons in the small hours of the night, I assumed they must have used this facility to elude the curfew.

But their father was not a disciplinarian in any Calvinistic manner. He gave them their heads. He wanted them to have views. He would sometimes say he thought they didn't have much common sense, sometimes that they were talking like "radicals." But there never was any likelihood that the Kennedy boys would be "spoiled." They were instilled with excellent principles, by which they abided. They were reared in a splendid family tradition, as far as manners and their attitude toward their mother and father and one another were concerned.

Fighting, of course, is a common fraternal exercise of the human as well as of the animal progeny, and the two elder boys engaged in it frequently. Bobby was too small to get into the act but, in my opinion, this was lucky for Joe and Jack. I think, given a little more weight and experience, this fiercely competitive adolescent could have made a good showing against either.

This judgment of Robert F. Kennedy in his teens has since, I think, been fortified by his public career. That actually began in the 1950s, when he was enrolled at the University of Virginia Law School, where he appropriately sought and won the presidency of the students' Legal Forum. Spurred on by his father, as in the case of the other Kennedy sons, Bob used to the full the family prestige in booking well-known persons, including Kennedy, Sr., to address the forum. And when he had taken his degree, he was ready for the governmental activity that led to his election as a Senator from New York before he was eligible to vote in the state, and, as the family's designated heir-apparent to the White House, to his open candidacy for the Democratic Presidential nomination in 1968.

I recall several discussions with Kennedy, Sr., initiated by him, as to when and how Bob could be introduced into government, and our agreement that the Congressional staff route was the most desirable. The friendly and, I should say, generally sympathetic attitude of the father toward the objective of Senator McCarthy of Wisconsin—an objective McCarthy missed attaining by pursuing it in muddled, brutal, and irresponsible fashion—led to Bob's appointment as a staff assistant to McCarthy's committee. I remember Bob then as passionately committed to McCarthy's effort to put an end to the supplying by broadly allied governments of strategic materials to Communist China.

The family link with McCarthy was the more visible in other particulars. When Adlai Stevenson was about to speak in Massachusetts in behalf of his Presidential candidacy in 1952, the elder Kennedy warned that an attack on McCarthy would place in jeopardy his elder son's chances to be elected United States Senator; the attack was not made. When the censure of McCarthy was submitted to the Senate by the select committee, John F. Kennedy, though illness accounted for his physical absence from the chamber, failed to be recorded either "yes" or "no." And on at least a couple of occasions the father of the Kennedy clan brought McCarthy to my house in Georgetown as a valued personal friend.

But by the time public opinion had made it very plain that McCarthy's room was highly preferable to his company, Bob had shifted to the Congressional staff job that brought him the opportunity for political fame and fortune. Senator John L. McClellan of Arkansas, acting on influential recommendations and a favorable personal estimate, appointed Bob counsel to the Senate rackets subcommittee. In that capacity he rode into the public view in the bright armor of a nemesis of the gangsters who were infesting the ranks of industry, labor, and the general social order.

The inquiry was both effective and popular, and the young attorney, who previously had successfully clashed with another young attorney—Roy Cohn, counsel to Bob's old boss, McCarthy—decided to write a book about it. He came to me for a foreword, as his elder brother had come to me for various forms of assistance with the book, *Why England Slept*, that he wrote in 1940. Bob informed me that I was also his father's choice, and I duly obliged.

I made only one reservation—that the author excise a highly adverse reference to Edward Bennett Williams, who had been Bob's principal legal adversary during the McClellan inquiry and who was already rising toward the top of his profession as a criminal lawyer. This condition was accepted by Bob, though reluctantly. After both book and foreword were ready for the printer, the elder Kennedy telephoned me. He asked me to modify a passage in which I critically contrasted the zeal Bob had shown in arraigning non-union gangsters with the lack of this zeal where union violence and economic blackmail were concerned. I agreed to soften this paragraph, on the representation that as written it might prejudice readers against the important account of a national scourge that followed.

When the book appeared, neither dust jacket nor table of contents noted the fact that there was a foreword, and by me. To find it, the reader had to stumble across it accidentally. But by this time I had observed Bob Kennedy's makeup long and closely enough to recognize that this denigration of my contribution was in character. He was too far committed to eliminate the foreword (and perhaps his father, if they discussed the matter, vetoed that). But I had made a condition to which Bob felt he must submit—the Edward Bennett Williams reference. And the imposing of conditions, never popular with a Kennedy and consented to only when the alternative is less desirable, is a bitterer draught for Bob than for any other member of the clan.

He repeatedly disclosed this trait as he rose to the fore-front of national politics, beginning with his brilliant management of his elder brother's pre-convention Presidential campaign.

The "ruthlessness" that often and justly was said to be characteristic of Bob in political and personal relationships does not emerge from my correspondence file that contains many, many warm letters of appreciation of small services sought and rendered by me from time to time. For instance, in 1948, in sponsoring Bob's application to enter the University of Virginia Law School I wrote: "All the children of the former Ambassador are unusually fine citizens, each seemingly with a special set of superior qualities, and Robert is no exception. . . ." And in supporting his nomination in 1955 for admission to the Metropolitan Club of Washington: ". . . in some respects [RFK] is the number one member of that remarkable tribe . . . distinguished for both scholarship and athletic ability, in the military service for courage . . . of unsurpassed integrity, . . ." etc. (After he became Attorney General he resigned from the Club because it adhered to the policy it followed when he sought membership. This policy, which was of common knowledge when Kennedy joined the Club, was that Negro guests of members, as well as Negro members, were inadmissable. George Lodge, son of Henry Cabot Lodge, onetime U.S. Ambassador to Saigon, precipitated the issue by challenging the rule and then resigning when it was restated to him. Lodge's resignation was instantly employed by the Attorney General as the basis of his own.)

When I wrote these complimentary estimates, I did not foresee the driving Presidential ambition that would greatly alter my appraisal. Between 1948 and 1955 I would have wagered that when Bob Kennedy encountered what he deemed to be the greatest "moral issue" of his time (his description of the war in Vietnam in 1968), none would be able to say of him, as Lady Macbeth of her lord, that he "let 'I dare not' wait upon 'I would,' like the poor cat i' the adage."

Yet, by waiting for clear statistical evidence (in March, 1968) that President Johnson's political vulnerability was deep and real, Bob Kennedy did precisely that. He denied to the candidacy of Senator Eugene McCarthy of Minnesota in the New Hampshire primary that open and active support to which Kennedy was committed by his identical criticisms of President Johnson's conduct of the war in Vietnam.

And both the timing of his candidacy to supplant President Johnson as the nominee of the Democratic National Convention of 1968, and his decision to contest with McCarthy in carefully chosen state primaries, were so baldly expedient as to diminish his claim that a "moral issue," and not the attainment of a driving personal ambition, had impelled him to advance his Presidential target date by four years.

This full turn to expediency was clearly revealed in the period immediately following Bob Kennedy's announcement that he would contest the nomination from the "moral" vantage point that Eugene McCarthy had fought for and won alone.

Robert Francis Kennedy was the most intense of the male members of his remarkable family. In this he more nearly resembled his father than any of his brothers—he had the same capacity for likes and dislikes, for love and hate, for compassion toward the denied and the oppressed but with a simultaneous concentration on serving personal ambition.

Like others who are driven by a thirst for power, he unquestionably sought it in the conviction that among his rivals he was best qualified to make an effective attack on the injustices and kindred evils that afflict the United States and human society as a whole. Into this pattern perfectly fits the desire to become President. Hence, the bitterness with which so many sought to stop him on the way can be accounted for only by the provocations he especially engendered: the obvious passion of his pursuit; the widespread feeling that the Kennedys had come to think of the Presidency as a family fief; and the advantage over competitors inherent in huge financial resources that obviate the need of contracting the obligations that go with campaign contributions.

Yet, despite such pious copybook platitudes as "the office should seek the man, not the man the office," the American people themselves know and are responsible for the fact that this is humbug. The entrepreneurs of television programs, the business community that funds their ever-rising costs in the hope of more profits for the advertised commodities, the long political campaigns that candidates can finance only by soliciting donations—these are among the circumstances that subordinate fitness for the office, including the Presidency, to the means test.

Whether the charge that he was "buying" a primary would by itself have deterred the Democratic National Convention of 1968 from nominating Bob Kennedy will not now be known. But if so, this hypocrisy would have matched the humbug of the copybook platitude. For bought American elections are made regular procedure by the expenditures required to promote a candidate's publicity, organize his forces, and drag a horde of apathetic voters to the polls.

The wherewithal used by an Administration in power is composed by government contracts, politically designed allocation of subsidies, and patronage (government jobs). The currency used by organized labor is both money and bloc voting. The devices by which the business community manages to evade the legal restrictions on contributions from corporations, and their totals as well, include the creation of "committees" that are under no legal requirement to report the amounts of money they receive, or from whom, or how and for what expended.

Since these matters were well known to critics of Bob Kennedy's pre-convention campaign, including editorial writers, it it not astonishing that he deeply resented this particular attack. Moreover, for all his justified reputation as a gut fighter, he was, I think, and as his intimate friends have said, a diffident man, sometimes a shy one. But this trait was expressed only in private intercourse. There is great arrogance implicit in laying claim to the Presidency, and I do not think Bob Kennedy had any difficulty in summoning it.

Inevitably, the deep damnation of his taking-off, the high drama of the fact that he was assassinated in his most golden moment of political victory, have swiftly made a place for him in the forum of the past where men are dehumanized as legends. Yet when slow-paced history meets a public ready for an objective appraisal of Bob Kennedy, I believe he will emerge from the mists of the legend, not only as, in his private life, the "good and decent man" of his brother's eulogy in St. Patrick's Cathedral, but as an inspirer of the best sentiments that are latent in the American people.

He will not be the flawless man of the legend. On several occasions, when under fire, he too submissively accepted politics as the art of the possible. He could and did sound the bugle of retreat for personal political considerations—retreat from his suggestion that American blood donations be shared with the Viet Cong, who were engaging in some of the most abominable acts of war; retreat from the courage and good sense of his vision that peace in Vietnam could be attained only by a coalition government that encompassed all groups of the populace, including the Communist or neo-Communist Viet Cong. And when he required the evidence of the New Hampshire Democratic Primary that President Johnson's renomination and official record, particularly with respect to the war in Vietnam, could be challenged from within the Democratic Party (and as it turned out successfully), Bob Kennedy blurred his image as a politician who would risk an excellent chance eventually to be President on an issue he had proclaimed as the fundamental obstacle to the social progress of the American people—the war in Vietnam.

But there was a supreme irony in the tragedy by which he was cut down in the flower of his promise. For the intensity that pervaded his being was unconnected with the motive, whatever it may prove to have been, for his assassination. If this motive was his position that the United States was committed to preserve Israel as a nation, his statement was made with more moderation than that of other important political persons who said the same thing.

And it was no outraged Southern WASP, no red-necked Ku Kluxer, no demented Bircher, who shot him down. As in the mindless murder of his brother, the President, the assassin appears to have been striking blindly at the *excellence* rather than the passion with which Robert Kennedy advocated a cause or expounded a political philosophy.

A case can be made that violence has attended the history of this continent from the beginning; also that violence is apt to be contagious. But even the most painful stretching of the thin cord of this reasoning does not reach the fact that both assassins were the most untypical Americans imaginable. And for proof that violence is a broadly human manifestation, one need only reread Macaulay's account of the brutal, lawless state of the British social order as recently as the period when the American colonies were settled—the time of the accession of James II.

For the duration of his normal life expectancy, a long span of years, the nation and the world will have many occasions, I think, to miss the voice and dynamic activism of Bob Kennedy —his wit with its strong element of self-depreciation; his qualities of leadership; the courage that impelled him, a liberal of the liberals, to risk the opposition of so many of the leaders of such special-interest groups or organized labor and industry; and, by denouncing—without qualification—the violent disregard of law and order, whatever its claimed justifications, that had been manifest among the very segment of the population where his political following was almost unanimous, to risk disaffection in that quarter, too.

The death of Joe, Jr., was the first break in this circle of nine children, nearly all extraordinary in some way: handsome, intelligent, with a father and mother to whom they were devoted and who were devoted to them. It was one of the most severe shocks to the father that I've ever seen registered on a human being.

I share the opinion of some that Joe had been influenced to undertake his fatal mission—after having completed all his scheduled flights and well knowing the hazard—to disprove a slander, common among the British at that time of their resentment against the Ambassador's Boston interview, that the Kennedys were "yellow." The charge was based on the fact that Kennedy, realizing that if the United States Ambassador became a casualty of the Nazi blitz of London it would increase the prospect of American involvement in the war, spent each night in a house he had rented outside London, at Ascot. This was reported to President Roosevelt by Harry Hopkins as the basis for the British aspersion on the courage of the Kennedys.

But even if the Ambassador had been aware of the speculation that his son and namesake knowingly risked death to prove otherwise, the knowledge could only have deepened a sorrow that has never been assuaged. He is, I'm sure religious: at least we used to go to Sunday Mass together whenever and wherever I was visiting him. But his wife attended Mass every night and nearly every morning. At any rate, she bore up better than he did in the sense that he was truly stricken, whereas the philosophy of her religion clearly helped her. Joe Kennedy was so deeply distressed and hurt by the death of this boy, this eldest son, that when a number of us got together and wrote chapters in a little book called *As We Remember Joe*, each contributing some personal reminiscence, Kennedy looked at it, opened the cover, closed the cover, and, I am told, has never been able to read a line in that book.

As for Jack Kennedy's ordeal-by-war in the Pacific, his father's suffering was tempered by the hope that expires only with the certainty of death. Though Jack was missing for a considerable period, and nothing was known of his fate, his father kept the evil tidings to himself and endured the suspense with remarkable stoicism. But inside, he must have felt that fate was dealing more blows than even absolute, blind reliance on faith can rationalize.

Not until he found that Jack was alive, and had been rescued, did he reveal how the suspense had preyed on his courageous spirit. It was in this period, and for several subsequent years, that Jack Kennedy had successive troubles with his back. Yet only once did I see his father show emotion mindful of that evoked by the death of his eldest son. He came to my office one day—Jack was in the hospital in New York—and told me Jack was dying. (It was one of the two occasions when the young Senator had been administered the last rites of the church.) Then he wept, for the first and last time, in my presence.

It was, I think, after the conclusion that Jack was dying was dissipated by his partial recovery, that Ambassador Kennedy began definitely to plan for Jack the political career he had designed for Joe, Jr. Until then, I think, he shared a belief, which was mine, that Jack was suited to a career in journalism, in literature, or in teaching. I had formed this opinion in conversations on such vocations with the future President, and upon reading the Harvard senior thesis he submitted to me for editing and for consideration of the possibility of making something more permanent of the product.

It was remarkable, not so much for the freshness and precision of the supporting data (since the facilities for this were readily available in the elder Kennedy's files) as for the fine perception of the fundamental problems of a peace-loving democracy threatened with dictatorial regimes bent on subversive annexation or war. We spent some time in my library in Georgetown, editing and polishing; I proposed publication of the expanded thesis in book form under the title *Why England Slept;* and found its author an agent in New York City who made the arrangement. (Recently, and with amusement, I noted, in looking over my correspondence with the agent, that I had referred to Jack Kennedy as "this boy.")

His father sensibly decided that the name of Henry R. Luce as writer of a foreword would lure more readers than mine. But while, of course, agreeing to the soundness of this choice, Jack Kennedy generously acknowledged my assistance by this inscription on the first copy he received of *Why England Slept:* "To Mr. Krock, Who Baptized, Christened and was Best Man for this book—with my sincere thanks." (I never became "Arthur" until he had been in the White House for months.)

In the few years that followed before John F. Kennedy decided to substitute a political career for the sporadic journalism in which he had engaged, he showed great promise. Assigned by the Hearst newspapers to cover the British elections of 1945, he was the only source of my expectation that Churchill would be turned out of office. This he strongly indicated in his dispatches, and more definitely in a private letter to me.

In recognition of his reportorial prescience, he was assigned to report the organization meeting of the United Nations at San Francisco in the same year, and there I saw much of him in the off-hours devoted to social activities. But I shall always regret that I was not one of those in his bedroom at the Palace Hotel one evening, where according to a friend—John Andrews King, and in King's words—this delightful incident occurred:

"Jack, dressed for a black-tie evening, with the exception of his pumps and dinner coat, was lying on the bed, propped up by three pillows, a highball in one hand and the telephone receiver in the other. To the operator he said, 'I want to speak to the Managing Editor of the *Chicago Herald-Examiner.*' (After a long pause) 'Not in? Well, put somebody on to take a message' (Another pause) 'Good. Will you see that the boss gets this message as soon as you can reach him? Thank you. Here's the message: "Kennedy will not be filing tonight." ' "

I think this was the same evening I saw him cutting in on Anthony Eden, the British Foreign Secretary, who was dancing with the beautiful lady who became the Viscountess Harcourt—and getting promptly cut in on again by Eden himself.

The next year, 1946, Jack Kennedy had entered active politics, under his father's urging, as a successful candidate for the seat of James M. Curley in the House of Representatives. Thenceforward, though his gift for mirth and graceful diversion, like his charm, did not diminish, he was finally embarked on the arduous course that took him to the White House fourteen years later, and three years thereafter to the underpass in Dallas where his life came to a brutal, senseless, supremely tragic end.

For days and weeks after the ghastly event was confirmed, my mind constantly reverted from the agonizing details and consequences of the death of the young President to the formative years before the blows of destiny fell upon the Kennedy family. Among these happy and fascinating recollections the following came vividly into my consciousness:

—Of the occasional visits to Hyannis Port or Palm Beach of the grandfather, the former Mayor of Boston for whom the President was named whose favorite topic was the anti-Irishism of the Back Bay. My impression of Honey Fitz was of a political Irishman of the standard type, very talkative, almost garrulous. If you asked him to, or more often when you didn't,

he would sing "Sweet Adeline," the barbershop ballad that was
an indissoluble part of his political career;

—Of the elder boys, still at Harvard, respectful of their
father and influenced by his views, yet whose political philosophy, it was clear, was to be to the left of his own. Bobby was
very young; also family discipline imposed his principal role as
a bystander. Teddy was a baby. But the girls would be heard
from, particularly Kathleen, later the Marchioness of Harting-
ton, a very brilliant and beautiful being. She would challenge
the patriarch more directly than her brothers ventured to do
because she was also the pet, everybody was mad about her,
and her wit and sense of humor captivated all who knew her;

—Of Cardinal Spellman, a frequent house guest, then a
Bishop in the Boston area. With him I formed a lasting friend-
ship. I was mixing a drink before luncheon one day and the
Bishop said to me in his Yankee accent, "What is that drink,
Arthur?"

"It's called an old fashioned."

Said he, "Will you make me one?" I did, he drank it, and
pronounced it "very good." That night before dinner I asked
him if he wanted another. "No," he replied firmly. "Moreover,
when I leave here, I'm going into Retreat. If I saw more of
you and got to drinking these old fashioneds, I'd be lucky to
wind up a parish priest."

On another occasion at Palm Beach, I was telling him about
a girl I was fond of during my years in Louisville, now living
nearby in Del Ray. He had asked me to go deep-sea fishing
with him, but when I told him I had to go to Del Ray instead,
he decided to go along, saying, "I think you may find her a
little older."

This proved prophetic. As we left the lady, whom the Bishop
had charmed almost into forgotten piety, he remarked, "She
doesn't look quite like she used to, does she?"

"No, she doesn't."

"I gathered as much," said the Bishop, "because you blinked
when you saw her."

So I told him the following story about Oliver Wendell
Holmes and the "beautiful Confederate": Holmes, a captain in
a Massachusetts regiment, was wounded at the Battle of Ball's

Bluff on the Potomac River and was taken into the military hospital at Hagerstown, Maryland. There he was nursed by a girl of that area who belonged to a Confederate family. All his life thereafter Holmes would occasionally refer to the great beauty of this Confederate girl and express the hope that he might see her again. Long after he was eighty the Justice got a letter saying, "I've seen your name in the paper. I wonder if you are the same Oliver Wendell Holmes I nursed after the Battle of Ball's Bluff in the Hagerstown hospital." He showed it to Mrs. Holmes. "Now, we've heard so much about this beautiful Confederate, Wendell," she said, "why don't you write and tell her you're coming out to see her? But be prepared to find her somewhat changed." One day he made the romantic journey. After that reunion the Justice never mentioned the "beautiful Confederate" again.

Cardinal Spellman, as he became, often had business in Washington. On one of these occasions I was walking from the Metropolitan Club through Lafayette Square when I saw a priest sitting on a bench reading his breviary. It was Spellman. After our usual exchange about old fashioneds and old flames, I asked what his errand was.

"I'm waiting for a fellow that's over there seeing *him*," he said, pointing to the White House where Roosevelt then dwelt. "You know we have to read this thing an hour and a half a day, and I'm just using the time."

"Your Eminence, am I the only person who has recognized you?"

"Yes, but not the only who has spoken to me. Every bum that sees this collar tries to make a touch. I don't mind it here because in Washington they're satisfied with a dime. But in New York you've got to give them at least two bits."

Another time when the Cardinal and I were both guests at Palm Beach, Joe Kennedy got a special dispensation from the prelate for the use of the living room as the locus of a Requiem Mass His Eminence would perform "for the repose of my mother's soul." I suggested to Kennedy that he also invite the Governor of Michigan, Frank Murphy, a devout Catholic, who was staying at a hotel nearby.

At eight o'clock the next morning we all were present, the

servants standing behind the sofa where Kennedy, Murphy, and I were sitting. The Cardinal had prepared a little altar on a taboret, putting his various religious articles upon it. As he began to intone the Requiem Mass, I followed Kennedy in the ritual until it was obvious that he was making procedural errors. So I followed Murphy, who proved letter-perfect.

When the Mass ended, with Kennedy, in his emotional Irish way, overwhelmed by the memory of his mother, I said, "Look here, you're not a very proficient Catholic. You made me make several mistakes and so I turned to Murphy."

In a choking voice Kennedy replied, "That character (though he used a much more pungent word) ought to have been a priest."

Just as he said this the Cardinal, who had forgotten something, came back to pick it up. We froze. The Cardinal pretended not to have heard the comment of the chief mourner.

—Of Mrs. Rose Fitzgerald Kennedy, serene, calm, beautiful, a cultivated woman keeping the peace when necessary (which wasn't very often); exercising a kind of soothing influence on the many arguments and debates that went on in that extraordinary family. She was very much in charge of and intimate with her children. Of course, their father was away a great deal—in California on movie business, in New York on financial business, in government when his family was not in Washington. Hence she carried the burden of rearing the children. They owe much of what they were and are to their mother.

—Of Bobby, who became heir apparent to the political dynasty, bullied by his elder brothers but still managing to keep a kind of savage individuality. At whatever sport it was, this boy of fifteen was always trying to beat one of the older boys to overcome the age handicap.

—Of Jack, recovering at Palm Beach from another spinal operation—this one after he had been elected to the Senate. He had a suite just off the living room, where he lay on a board, his head propped up on pillows. There was a small slanted lectern on which was placed a pad of ruled yellow foolscap, and on this he was incessantly writing. Once I asked him what the product was. "A book," he said. This is the now-famous set of political biographies that was published under the title *Profiles in Courage*.

He pondered deeply on which public men to include in these profiles. He consulted me, among others, and I strongly urged the inclusion of Robert A. Taft. I cited Taft's lone courage, as a politician, in opposing the *ex-post-facto* guilt thesis of the Nuremberg trials, and for defying organized labor's blackmailing tactics to encompass Taft's defeat for re-election as reprisal for the Taft-Hartley Act. Kennedy accepted my nomination, but with considerable reluctance.

During his contest for the 1960 Presidential nomination of the Democrats, he remarked, "One of the things I wish you had never persuaded me to do was to put Taft in the *Profiles*."

"That," I answered, with a conviction I still maintain, "was probably the best thing I ever got you to do."

For more than a decade in the prewar, wartime, and postwar period my wife and I had a farm, Limestone, on the west bank of the Shenandoah River, four miles east of Berryville, Virginia. I recall in particular one visit from John F. Kennedy before he departed for the service with the Navy in the Pacific from which he emerged a hero—and with the spinal injury that plagued him for the rest of his life.

He was accompanied by his good friend and Navy companion-in-arms George Mead, Jr., of Dayton, Ohio (destined to die on the beach at Iwo Jima), and the pair were under orders of early embarkation. Their spirits were high and infectious enough to cozen me into taking part in a touch football game, with pickup teams including a couple of other guests and our two farmhands. But the victory claimed by my side was hotly contested by Kennedy—a dispute he maintained during his Presidency—on the ground that a touchdown I claimed to be a legitimate quarterback sneak was illegal procedure.

When the young ensign drove out the gate with Mead, to report in Washington for sea duty, I could conceive the sequel of war hero, United States Representative, and Senator from Massachusetts. But not that we had drunk a stirrup cup with a future President—only with one of the most shining youths I ever had encountered.

I knew him well enough, however, to realize that Kennedy was highly intelligent as well as gifted with a special grace of mind and manner; deeply interested in information of all kinds; perhaps a historian or a teacher of political science in the making. In conversation, then and thereafter, he disclosed a keen sense of the correlation of men and events and of their causes.

Kennedy was an enthusiast for the "mental" games we often played at my house in Washington. And his capacity for coming out first in "Twenty Questions," "Shedding Light," and similar tests of a player's knowledge, reasoning, or pure intuition, was impressively demonstrated on each occasion.

When he came to take his seat in Congress, in 1947, my long relationship with the family accounts for the fact that I was asked for counsel on some of his personal as well as political problems. One, arising from the circumstance that Kennedy was on a very strict diet, was how to maintain it at the Capitol as well as at the Georgetown house he had rented, where his mother had imported a cook from home—Margaret by name—who had adored Kennedy from infancy. This was solved by transferring from my household to his George Thomas, a fat, good-natured Negro of high competence as a domestic. Every day George brought to the Capitol the special lunch prescribed by the young Congressman's diet. This association ripened with the years, and George eventually went to the White House as the President's valet. The only complaint Kennedy ever made to me about George was, "Why *can't* he learn to tie a white tie!"

In the House, and before Kennedy replaced Henry Cabot Lodge, Jr., in the Senate, he obliged me by what I think was his last venture in reportorial journalism. President Eisenhower had called a meeting in which Representative Kennedy was included, and I asked him if he would make notes of what went on. He furnished me with a comprehensive, clear set of handwritten notes of the proceedings. (This document, after Kennedy's election as President, I presented to Mrs. Henry Suydam, Jr., the then Mrs. George Wheeler, wife of his roommate at the Choate School, a beautiful lady from New Orleans who was among his most fervent admirers and personal friends.)

The move to the Senate was inevitable in the pursuit of the ambition that Kennedy's father conceived before the future President had. Service in the House denied him the scope he required to impress his talent for public service on the American people. He quickly perceived the House to be a way station on the upward road to which he had firmly set his feet. Ironically, Kennedy's opportunity to mount required him to contest, as he did successfully, the seat of the Massachusetts politician, Henry Cabot Lodge, Jr., who, from his Harvard days, had been his ideal as a public servant.

With their sense of mission and special claim to the seats of the mighty, I don't think he or the other Kennedys felt anything akin to anguish over displacing his college hero. Yet Lodge, as the Republican candidate, had been substantially aided by Joe Kennedy, Sr., several years earlier in his contest with the Democratic senatorial nominee, Representative Joseph E. Casey, Jr.

Once in the Senate, Jack Kennedy began studiously, industriously, and intelligently to cultivate in the national field the "public image" that had attracted the voters of Massachusetts. He specialized, and with enormous burning of the midnight oil, on issues of education, labor, and foreign policy.

He was a young Senate freshman when he made a speech on the plight of the French in Indo-China that is notable for two reasons in particular: it demonstrated deep and constructive thinking on the international level, and it irrevocably opposed commitment of United States armed forces to a combat role in a ground war on the Asian mainland.

One of history's cruelest ironies, and one of the irreparable blunders of the Senate expounder of this sound military principle after he became President, was his making the very commitment he had abjured—and this led inevitably to its expansion by his successor.

There follows a memorandum I wrote of a White House luncheon conversation with President Kennedy on the problem of Vietnam, on October 17, 1961. The talk ranged over a broad field of issues, but this is the passage in the memorandum pertinent to Vietnam:

The President had just come from a meeting on the problem in that country. He said the Pentagon generally approved a recommendation by the Chiefs of Staff to send forty thousand troops there. [They were designated "military advisers" to the South Vietnam armed forces in that period.] The President said he was not favorable to the suggestion at this time and therefore was sending General Maxwell D. Taylor to investigate and report what should be done. [He began the "escalation" by sending an installment of ten thousand.] It was a hell of a note, he said, that he had to try to handle the Berlin situation with the Communists encouraging foreign aggressors all over the place. The President said he was thinking of writing Khrushchev, urging him to call off these aggressors in Vietnam, Laos, etc., and asking Khrushchev how he thought he could negotiate with Kennedy if their positions were reversed. The President still believes, he said, in what he told the Senate several years ago—that United States troops should not be involved [in combat] on the Asian mainland, especially in a country with the difficult terrain of Laos and inhabited by people who don't care how the East-West dispute as to freedom and self-determination was resolved. Moreover, said the President, the United States can't interfere in civil disturbances created by guerrillas, and it was hard to prove that this wasn't largely the situation in Vietnam.

I asked him what he thought of the "falling domino" theory— that is, if Laos and Vietnam go Communist, the rest of Southeast Asia will fall to them in orderly succession. The President expressed doubts that this theory has much point any more because, he remarked, the Chinese Communists are bound to get nuclear weapons in time, and from that moment on they will dominate Southeast Asia.

Not long afterward he accepted the clear risk of United States combat involvement implicit in the Taylor-Rostow recommendation. He sent a greatly enlarged force of United States military advisers (raising the number from less than eight hundred to sixteen thousand) to be ferried (in Pentagon helicopters) to join the South Vietnamese troops on the combat front. And by encouraging the downfall of the Diem regime, Kennedy inevitably made the conflict a dominantly United

States war, but one hampered by built-in hazards of inciting Soviet Russian and Communist Chinese interventions that were clearly to be discerned in advance.

While John F. Kennedy was first availing himself of a Senate seat to strengthen his grasp on public issues as well as to become visible on the national scene, I do not believe he gave much thought to the Democratic Vice-Presidential nomination in 1956 as a stepping stone to the Presidency. This was an on-the-scene development in the National Convention period at Chicago, and it proved a temptation to the young politician that, despite knowledge of his father's coolness toward the idea, he found irresistible.

The center of the movement developed in the delegations from the Southern states with several primary victories of Senator Estes Kefauver of Tennessee over Adlai E. Stevenson. Kefauver was intensely unpopular among his Southern Democratic colleagues for personal attributes they disliked as well as for his "liberal" political philosophy. And when the prospect of Stevenson's renomination became overwhelming at Chicago, and Kefauver materialized as the most formidable aspirant for second place on the ticket, the Southern Senators fixed on their very popular Northern Democratic colleague, Kennedy, as the man most likely to reverse the prospect.

As the record shows, they almost succeeded on the roll call, after Stevenson had announced he would leave the choice of his running mate to the convention. It was only when Speaker Sam Rayburn, in the chair, "failed to see" a delegate who was trying to get recognition for a switch in the Kefauver versus Kennedy tabulation that Kefauver's majority was affirmed. Soon afterward I talked with Kennedy at the Drake Hotel, where we both were lodged, to congratulate him on his remarkable showing. I found him highly elated over the support he, a Roman Catholic, had received from delegations from the South, where it was assumed his religion was an insuperable handicap to his chances of winning national office. "I'll be singing 'Dixie' the rest of my life," he said.

And it was, in fact, this aspect of the contest with Kefauver that, I believe, fixed his determination to aspire to the Presidential nomination four years thereafter. This aspect, as well as the closeness of the count in 1956, rang a loud warning bell to Lyndon B. Johnson. At the same Chicago convention the Senate Majority leader had sent emissaries to Stevenson, with the message that he was available for second place, and the offer had been politely declined by the renominated Democratic candidate for President.

For the next four years a growing rivalry between Johnson and Kennedy for first place at the 1960 convention was clear to all well-placed observers. The pattern of support for Kennedy had changed from 1956, notably in the South. There, perceiving in 1960 the first good chance since the War Between the States to nominate a Southern Democrat for President, the Party political leaders in that section of the country began to unite behind the Senate Majority Leader, Johnson. He was very popular with his Southern colleagues in both branches. The record he was making as Leader was that of a right-lane middle-of-the-road political philosopher in the matter of domestic issues, particularly "civil rights" and economic affairs; of a militant architect of an armed defense structure that would maintain the United States as the world's foremost power.

The fact that Senator Harry F. Byrd of Virginia, the most conservative and influential Democrat in Congress, was in charge of the Johnson-for-President movement in the South attests to the firmness of what proved to be one of the most mistaken concepts in the history of American politics—that Johnson would campaign on the line of his Senate record and pursue it as national policy if elected to the Presidency.

The stop-Kennedy trend of the activities of Johnson and Stevenson, the undeclared aspirants for the Presidential nomination, and Hubert H. Humphrey and Kennedy, the declared aspirants, mounted steadily. On May 26, 1960, I wrote to myself the following memorandum reflecting this situation:

Some examples of the personal tensions, which rivalry for the Presidency of the United States creates, appear in the following experiences I have just had:

1. On Tuesday, May 24, I telephoned Senator John F. Kennedy for more exact information on his statement in Oregon that it might have saved the Summit Conference if the President, prior to

or at the Paris meeting of the Big Four, had expressed "regret" as a form of apology for the U-2 espionage mission. Adlai E. Stevenson's Chicago speech, attacking the government record in this episode, came into the conversation, and I remarked that Stevenson was running hard for the Democratic nomination. Kennedy, who last week had said Stevenson merited deep consideration as Secretary of State in the Cabinet of a Democratic President, exclaimed: "And how!" It was the tone in which Kennedy said this that lent it significance. This tone clearly reflected Kennedy's irritation that Stevenson is encouraging support for his nomination among Democrats Kennedy felt would otherwise be for him, and, especially in California, were impeding his prospect.

2. Today I called on Lyndon Johnson, and he complained about Kennedy. He listed a number of things he had done as Majority Leader to "build up" Kennedy and said that in return "Kennedy's people" were constantly "circulating lies" about his attitude as Leader toward the Labor Relations Act of 1959 and other bills in which Kennedy has a special interest. "I have scrupulously refrained," said Johnson, "from saying or doing anything, covertly or otherwise, in derogation of any of the candidates. I have said always that any of them would make a great President. I told Kennedy about this sniping from his camp the other day and afterward he sent me a copy of a memo to his staff forbidding this activity.

"But today a reporter, who is practically a Kennedy hired hand, asked me a needling question based on an untruth about my scheduling of the minimum-wage bill, and my staff informed me he got this version from the Kennedy people. I am going to have to tell Kennedy that if this underhand sniping keeps up, I will take steps to protect myself."

A moment later, after praising Kennedy's abilities, Johnson got on the telephone to a farmers' spokesman in St. Paul named Thatcher. "I'm in your corner, too," said Johnson in evident response to a similar statement by Thatcher. "You and I have got a lot in common, and I don't think you and your people have any with Boston."

Thus the Democratic Band of Brothers.

The bitterness thereby revealed moved onward to a series of predictable events and one incredible happening.

As Kennedy triumphed over Humphrey in key primaries the wisdom of Johnson's strategy in keeping out of the primaries became more and more dubious, and Stevenson began to show unmistakable signs that despite his claim of final immunity, he had never recovered from the bite of the Presidential bug.

The predictable events were:

> the charge, voiced in the form of heavy implication by Humphrey's reference to the "little black bag" in the West Virginia primary, that the Kennedy millions were buying the nomination.
> the scathing attack by Johnson on the elder Kennedy's record as Ambassador to Great Britain, not too subtly implying complacency on the part of the Ambassador at the prospect that Hitler would win the war. [This occurred in a joint debate with Kennedy, before the Texas and Massachusetts delegations, during the 1960 convention.]
> the recantation of Stevenson from his statement that if Kennedy carried the Oregon primary, he merited the Presidential nomination. [When Kennedy, returning from Oregon, visited Stevenson at Libertyville, Illinois, and reminded him of this statement, Stevenson failed to repeat it either to Kennedy or publicly—an incident Kennedy related to me with an expression of deep and justified indignation.]

The unpredictable happening was Kennedy's tender, and Johnson's acceptance, of the Vice-Presidential nomination at the 1960 convention. The following account of this episode is a memorandum I wrote on September 22, 1960:

I have finally pieced together, in what I hope is a symmetrical pattern, the events leading up to the nomination of Lyndon B. Johnson for Vice-President at the Democratic National Convention of 1960. My sources are some of the participants in these events.

On Wednesday night, July 13, Senator John F. Kennedy, encountering Senator Stuart Symington of Missouri in a hotel corridor, said to him privately, "You are my first *available* choice for Vice-President." [It was later explained that Kennedy at this time did not think Johnson was "available."] Symington and his group went to bed convinced his nomination was assured.

At about 8 A.M. Thursday, Thomas G. Corcoran [FDR's famous Brain Trust operator] telephoned Edward H. Foley [Under

Secretary of the Treasury]. They agreed that Kennedy would surely be defeated unless Johnson was chosen as his running mate, this being their estimate of the popular reaction. Corcoran said he had conveyed this opinion to Johnson, who replied that he couldn't even think about taking second place unless Speaker Sam Rayburn recommended it. Corcoran and Foley then met at the Biltmore, and Corcoran went in to urge Rayburn to make this recommendation to Johnson. Meanwhile, Governor Almond of Virginia had been a passenger on the elevator that took them up to Rayburn's floor, and when they stated their proposition, he said it was the only way to keep Virginia in the Democratic column.

While Corcoran was talking to Rayburn, Representative Hale Boggs of Louisiana joined Foley outside the Rayburn suite. Foley told him what was going on and Boggs immediately said its consummation would assure Louisiana to the Democratic electoral column. Corcoran then came out of the suite and said he had been unsuccessful in urging Rayburn to tell Johnson he approved of the effort. Since Boggs is a close friend of the Speaker, Foley asked Boggs to join him in another try.

At first Rayburn was adamant against the idea. "I saw another Texan, Jack Garner agree to run twice with Roosevelt, of whose political philosophy he disapproved intensely, and go back to Texas embittered for life." Boggs then gave Rayburn his estimate of what Louisiana would do if Johnson were nominated for Vice-President. "What about Virginia?" asked Rayburn. By reason of the fortuitous meeting with Almond, the two were able to quote the Governor of Virginia directly. Finally, Rayburn said that if Kennedy would make the request of Johnson, and then confirm it to him, the Speaker would go along.

Corcoran was waiting in the corridor. When the pair told him they had got Rayburn's agreement, and on what representations, Corcoran said, "You persuaded him but with the wrong reasons." Apparently this meant that, in Corcoran's view, not the Southern, but certain Northern, states [perhaps the midlands] represented the important stake involved—an [adverse] reaction to the issue over Kennedy's [and Corcoran's] religion.

In about the same period Governor Lawrence of Pennsylvania was urging the same course on Kennedy, saying he spoke also for Mayor Daley of Chicago and Carmine di Sapio of New York [the leader of Tammany Hall]. Obviously, some telephoning among Kennedy, Johnson, and Rayburn had also occurred.

Kennedy then went to see Johnson and made his request, on the ground that it was Johnson's duty to make this contribution to the interests of the country which Democratic victory best could serve. Johnson agreed very quickly, to Kennedy's surprise. Kennedy then called on Rayburn, who was getting angry over what he conceived to be the reason for the delay—indecision by Kennedy—whereafter Kennedy returned to his own suite to announce his unpopular decision to his union labor and "equal rights" allies. They protested so bitterly that he twice sent his brother Robert to Johnson to make sure Johnson was willing to join Kennedy in a fight for second place if necessary. This was an act of extreme fraternal devotion by Bob, whose distaste for the choice of Johnson was intensified by Johnson's attack on [Joseph Kennedy] before the Texas and Massachusetts delegates. Johnson and Rayburn at first construed this as a hint that Kennedy wanted to withdraw his promise, and when I checked with the Johnson group they were breathing threats about what Johnson would do to Kennedy in the post-convention session of Congress and elsewhere. In this way I gathered, to my surprise, that Johnson was eager for the Vice-Presidential nomination despite his attacks on Kennedy and his clear distaste for the platform.

But Kennedy in person then informed Johnson that he would fight to get Johnson nominated, and happiness was restored all around except among the labor union leaders, certain roving liberals and the NAACP. However, when Kennedy went on television and firmly announced his decision, the outcries subsided to murmurs that quickly died away.

Not until the fall of 1965 did my sources give me permission to summarize this document for publication, which I did in *The New York Times*, without any controversial sequence. The President, I was informed by Foley, commented that it was "a good story" and took no exception that I ever heard of.

Although Lyndon Johnson was a scrupulously dutiful and loyal Vice-President to John F. Kennedy in public, I saw numerous indications that this relationship was a façade behind which lay a mutual distrust and dislike which extended to the intimates and families of both. A friend of the Kennedy family recalls that, after Bob and Ethel were informed that the wounded President had died, among their identical reactions was an expression of anxiety and dismay that the fate of the nation was now in the hands "of such a man as Lyndon Johnson."

During the pre-convention campaign in 1960 I saw Senator Kennedy frequently and talked with him by telephone more often, though not so regularly as with his father. I recall only one direct complaint from the candidate on any commentary of mine.

A rumor had spread in the Senate Democratic cloakroom, after Hubert H. Humphrey had been effectively disposed of in the Presidential primaries, that the Senator from Minnesota was Kennedy's leading choice for the Vice-Presidential nomination. This was reported to me by Senator Harry F. Byrd of Virginia, very influential with his Southern colleagues, who said the prospect was causing "consternation," even among those regional party politicians who were prepared to give cordial support to JFK if he was nominated at Los Angeles. I published this reaction as a fact, which it was.

Kennedy reached me on the phone from somewhere on his campaign tour and remonstrated vigorously on two grounds: first, that the report was without foundation and never would have any; second, that I should have checked with him before publication and discovered this total lack of substance. "With Governor Patterson of Alabama [a rigid segregationist] already hanging around my neck like a millstone," he said, "this story will complicate my difficulties very seriously."

The lecture on journalistic procedure did not impress me, because I had written the "consternation" commentary against a deadline. And efforts to reach the airborne Kennedy had been unavailing in the time I had for the purpose. But I told JFK that I would at once write a refutation of the report on the basis of his assurance, and this I did. Typical of situations that must constantly arise between newspapermen and politicians, Kennedy's complaint was much more prompt than his acknowledgment of the reparation.

But he acknowledged it after his nomination in a gracious letter from Hyannis Port, dated July 20, 1960, in summary as follows: He had greatly appreciated the second article, and should have said so earlier. But, like doctors and politicians, one of the inherent burdens of the newspaper "trade" was hearing complaints from their correspondents; but never hearing from them when things were going well. And, erasing the previous lecture on journalism, he commented that I had been a friend of the Kennedys as long as he could remember, while maintaining my responsibilities as an objective reporter.

Only two other incidents that I recall during the period between JFK's nomination and election foreshadowed the eventual severance of that long friendship with "the Kennedys":

First, on October 19, 1960, Joseph P. Kennedy telephoned me to discuss a letter in which I had interpreted some of his son's campaign pledges as certain to produce a dangerously inflationary economy and as favoring "total racial integration" in the United States. He assured me I was mistaken on both points, and then urged me to "stop writing those fuzzy columns that you have been writing and try to see such favorable sides of Jack as you are able to see in your other personal friends." I have no reason to believe that Joe Kennedy had since changed either of these judgments, any more than I have changed mine on the same subjects.

Second, late in October, 1960, *The New York Times* editorially announced support of the Democratic national ticket. It was definite, but not enthusiastic, and in the final couple of paragraphs certain doubts about Kennedy were expressed. I was not consulted about the editorial position, or shown the text in advance of publication, it being as well known to the *Times*'s management as to the newspaper's readers that I was deeply disturbed by the Los Angeles platform and some of JFK's campaign extensions of the pledges.

The candidate was naturally gratified by the general fact of a *Times* endorsement. But that same morning, riding in a political parade in New York City with James A. Farley, he expressed disappointment over the concluding paragraphs, saying, "that was the hand of Krock." Of all his dissatisfactions with my newspaper product, this one at least had not the slightest foundation in fact. But it revealed a hostile tendency, from which he recurrently relaxed for a while after his inauguration, but which was firmly embedded in his mind at the time of his death.

There have been times in American history when a new President took office under dark skies heavy-laden with problems demanding instant and radical measures. This was the situation that confronted Lincoln on March 4, 1861. But when the new President is the very incarnation of a sweeping optimism that he will be equal to the emergencies, gaiety infuses the national mood on Inauguration Day and for a subsequent period, varying in length. This was the mood of the country when Franklin D. Roosevelt was inaugurated in 1933, and Eisenhower twenty years thereafter.

But the special grace of John F. Kennedy—his youth, his air of confidence, and the quality of his prose after the oath-taking on January 20, 1961—induced this mood that could not be dimmed even by one of the most severe blizzards Washington's temperate climate is capable of generating. This mood was noticeably prevalent at a dinner given for the new President by Mr. and Mrs. George Wheeler.

It was a peculiar sensation to look across the dinner table to which I was assigned at a youth and young man I had known so well now transformed into the President of the United States. But in an exchange between us the old relationship, which inevitably must enter a new phase when the door of the White House closes on one of those who shared it, briefly resumed its former footing.

The President asked what I "thought" of his Inaugural Address. I answered that it was the first whose qualities, including the excellence of the prose, seemed to me to match Woodrow Wilson's.

"Are you going to write that in the paper?" boyishly inquired Kennedy.

"I already have," I said.

His question recalled the times when, as a Senator, he had suggested good-naturedly that the praise I had made to him privately of a speech might have more usefully lent itself to public comment of the same nature, "instead of your giving all that space to the doings and sayings of Lyndon Johnson."

Throughout the Wheelers' dinner the President was wholly relaxed, very obviously enjoying the informality that was about to become the rarest of his privileges in a large company. This enjoyment was manifest in the difficulty Foley, the Inaugural Committee Chairman, experienced in getting the President to start his plighted round of the Inaugural balls. At least three times before he succeeded Foley besought the President to leave.

The death of John F. Kennedy, after less than three years in office, deprived his contemporaries as well as history of the full record required for a balanced judgment of Presidential capabilities. But, speaking for myself, I shall always believe these things:

> Kennedy would have been re-elected in 1964 with the emphatic popular endorsement denied him in 1960, thus eliminating one of the prime sources of his failure to make much headway with his domestic problems in Congress; these programs would have been adjusted to a much more modified welfare state, with less of the element of Federal compulsion with which his successor and the Supreme Court majority have sought to change human nature and simultaneously finance a domestic utopia and a major war; since, according, to my observation, the profit Kennedy gained from his mistakes was larger than their debit, the world tensions—including the U.S. involvement in Vietnam—for which Kennedy has the initial responsibility, that are susceptible of relaxation by a more realistic United States foreign policy would be in more manageable form today if Kennedy were President. At the time of his death, at least, he had not allowed himself to become as deeply entrapped as his successor is in a public record of unrealistic international and domestic programs and pronouncements;
> by the conclusion of a second term, Kennedy would have established himself in history as a "strong" President, if not a "great" one.

Some political professionals maintain the thesis that if Kennedy had put the restraints he could have on the soaring promises of the Los Angeles platform, and thereby been freer to appeal to middle-of-the-road voters, he would have been elected in 1960 by an emphatic majority, thereby removing one of his weaknesses in dealing with Congress and the people. In this judgment, the Los Angeles platform, and his more extravagant campaign expressions of alignment with it, would otherwise have brought about his defeat by Richard M. Nixon *if* there had been no televised debate between the nominees.

This, of course, is speculation beyond the point where political reporters and scientists can sensibly venture. But I share the view that when Nixon agreed to the TV debates with Kennedy, on the terms both accepted, he took an unnecessary gamble that cost him hundreds of thousands of votes in an election that was decided by a popular plurality of 118, 574 in a total of 68,838,219 votes cast.

If the design of this book were the comprehensive, in-depth evaluation by a professional historian of the men and events with which it deals, here would be the place for such an assessment of John F. Kennedy and his times. But, to the contrary, the design of the book is to sketch the profiles of these men and these events as they were available to one reporter within the obvious limits of so narrow a purview.

Consequently, what follows are accounts of conversations with President Kennedy, covering a wide range of the domestic and foreign issues which confronted him. These necessarily have the defects of one person's versions of the views expressed to him by another, written without the support of notes made on the spot (which I have always found to be a distraction and restraint on the person interviewed). But I composed the notes immediately, or shortly after, while the conversations were clear in my memory, such as it is.

The first occurred on May 5, 1961, just four months after the celebrated news conference in which Secretary of Defense McNamara, without conceding that he had done so, demolished the charge of a "missile gap" in the national defenses that had been a major 1960 Democratic campaign indictment of the Eisenhower Administration:

I spent an hour-plus with President Kennedy last evening from 6:50 to 8:00. The topics of our discussion and what was said follow:

On the resumption of nuclear testing, confined to underground, he said he was going to send our people back to Geneva for a last try at a treaty possible for the United States to accept. He isn't worried about the small "neutron" bomb, which the Soviets are "supposed to have in the attic," and to have perfected during the long moratorium we observed by total inaction of testing. There are so many nuclear weapons now, said the President, that he can't feel another one will be as significant in defense or attack as others seem to believe. Also, he is moved, perhaps uselessly, to prolong efforts at Geneva by an intense desire to do everything possible to assure that Communist China won't have a bomb.

But if the new effort fails, and possibly while it is just in the process of failing, he is considering representations to Premier Khrushchev in the matter. The idea is to put squarely before Khrushchev his government's responsibility for obstruction of a reasonable treaty and to appeal directly to the Premier for action. But there is also a need to make certain that Khrushchev doesn't misunderstand [our policy toward] Cuba, Laos, etc., to indicate that the United States is in a yielding mood on such matters as Berlin. I asked if these representations to Khrushchev would be made in person or in writing and perhaps during the President's visit to De Gaulle. He said he hadn't decided on those points.

I asked him if it is sound to base so much of our foreign policy on how it will be received by the Afro-Asian bloc in the United Nations General Assembly. [He had said previously that to resume nuclear testing would risk the consequence of violently unfavorable "world opinion."] His answer to my question was that there was unsoundness, of course, in the acceptance of majority Assembly votes as "world opinion." But any revision of policy based on that would have to be very gradually and tactfully made.

I offered the example of our support of the Angola resolution as an extreme and, I thought, irresponsible deference to this policy-base because of the sweeping text of that resolution. When I told him that the text committed the United States to the immediate, unconditional independence of all the African peoples, he expressed doubt that any such language was included in the resolution. Then he telephoned Assistant Secretary of State [Harlan] Cleveland and was informed I was [theoretically] correct. But the President expressed the view that since the reference was "oblique," it didn't commit us as I think it did.

He has put the preparation of an assistance program for South Vietnam in the hands of Deputy Secretary of Defense [Roswell] Gilpatric. This will include military aid in all forms considered necessary by us, in consultation with the South Vietnam government. The President supposes a lot of people will complain about the Communist representation that will probably occur in a "neutralist" government in Laos, if that should become attainable. But we have no better alternative there. As for Southeast Asia in general, the President said General MacArthur had prophesied to him that eventually it would go Communist by popular choice. But, said the President, whether or not that is true, our policy must be to avoid a positive formal withdrawal and help protect the area as long as the governments and peoples want this. He said also that General MacArthur had remarked to him: "Our chickens are all coming home to roost, and you are in the chicken house."

I asked him if he wouldn't agree that there is a weakness in statements by him that we, who have ringed Russia around with military bases, could not accept a pro-Communist base in the Western Hemisphere—Cuba in particular. He said yes, and he intended in any such reference hereafter to try to make clear the point that our purpose is to protect the independence and self-determination of nations, whereas the Soviets, by their own repeated proclamations, are committed to force international communism on the world.

The President severely criticized the Joint Chiefs of Staff in the Cuban affair [Bay of Pigs]. He said Secretary McNamara had brought the Joint Chiefs into conference, strongly urging action on the plan that failed, and they had assured him that the chances of success were "as great as in Guatemala." The President said he had "lost confidence" in the Chiefs of Staff. When I asked him if I could publish that on my own responsibility, he agreed. And I did so, knowing it would not be denied by the White House, if challenged.

With respect to the revival of the C.I.A. Advisory Committee, to be headed by Dr. [James R.] Killian, I asked the President if he knew about the group "with real teeth" that President Eisenhower had set up [including] Gordon Gray, the President's national security assistant, the number-two men in State and Defense, and Allen Dulles. I observed—and he seemed to agree—that with his own man heading a group making detailed and regular supervision of CIA pending projects, the President could get much more protection than from an advisory committee with no official powers. He told me that the revival of the Killian group had been arranged "before Cuba. We just decided that to announce it now, as new, would be a good idea."

On subsequent occasions foreign-policy affairs continued to be the subject of my conversations with President Kennedy. What is appended also concerns these:

October 11, 1961. The President came in about 1:20; the butler brought in a very good lunch on two tables, and the President started off with a Bloody Mary. Among the subjects he discussed and what he said were the following:

The [international] status quo, which so many of his critics expound, is no policy at all. The situation there is as undesirable for the United States and the West as it is for the Russians in a good many particulars. It is Mr. Kennedy's "inheritance," "a dangerous mess," and his critics, especially the Republicans, should come up with concrete suggestions to clear up the mess instead of yelling "appeasement" whenever he tries to find out if any compromise is possible—using "compromise" in the dictionary sense of a "settlement reached by mutual concessions."

The President spoke impatiently of the obstacles to this effort constantly being set up by the West German and French governments, and he mentioned with specific exasperation some sour comments made in Washington by West German Ambassador Grewe on the reports of the President's talks with Gromyko. "And we are still paying," he said, "for the wartime slights Roosevelt imposed on General De Gaulle." He said that Adenauer, De Gaulle, and Chiang Kai-shek seemed to want to operate as makers of United States policy and not as allies.

The President expressed a good opinion of the reporting of Max Frankel and Tom Wicker of our staff. I told him I thought he was very wise in having responded to Frankel's request for some details on his conversations with Gromyko, and urged him to get the habit. He said he rather thought he would.

The President discussed the various *modi vivendi* of working out an easement of the Berlin situation that have been publicly discussed, particularly complimenting Senator [Claiborne] Pell of Rhode Island on his speech in that quarter. He also urged me to continue to publicize that and similar speeches, and recalled that I had performed that service originally for Senator Pell. The President said he made a mistake in sending David Bruce to London, where our easy relations with the British required no use of Bruce's great talents. "I should have sent him back to Bonn," said the President. "The career man there is all right, but it is a job for a diplomat like Bruce, who is experienced in politics and executive government as well."

November 8, 1961. President Kennedy telephoned me at 3:30 today, as he told Orvil Dryfoos [the Publisher of *The New York Times*] last night that he would. I had asked Mr. Dryfoos to tell the President that I would like some direct information, if possible, on whether he thought his conversations with Prime Minister Nehru were giving the Indians a clearer understanding of the destructive effects on American good will toward India of Krishna Menon's constant anti-American positions in the United Nations— positions that were maintained by Krishna Menon's subordinates during his absence.

The President told me that he had taken up this subject with both the Prime Minister's daughter [Mrs. Indira Gandhi] and Nehru himself, actually more vigorously with the lady than with her father because of the very close friendship prevailing between the daughter and Krishna Menon. The President said he thought he had made some progress; that he got the impression that both the Nehrus were surprised and disturbed by what they read about Krishna Menon in the American press since arriving here. "But," he said, "you never can tell how deeply an impression may have sunk in or, if so, how long it will last. Not only is there the factor of the old friendship, but Nehru relies on Krishna Menon to keep the support of the Congress Party leftists for the regime, and I understand he is considered invaluable in that particular thus far."

The most important test, said the President, is whether India can be kept non-Communist. And we should remember that India has . . . momentous problems represented by the contiguity of Communist China, . . . and Pakistan. The President said that Nehru's United Nations policy was animated by a wish to assure the help of Russia in staving off China. The President expressed doubt that this was a realistic expectation, however.

He remarked that the Indian Ambassador here, another Nehru, dislikes Krishna Menon, "which is helpful." And in the same discussion of personalities, he said that Prime Minister Nehru doesn't like Adlai Stevenson, but had observed to the President that he *did* like Henry Cabot Lodge.

There were two other issues over foreign policy on which I had written critically with respect to the concepts, acts, and attitudes of the Kennedy Administration. These encompassed

the United Nations' war against Moise Tshombe of Katanga
Province in the Congo civil conflict which succeeded only be-
cause of the financial logistical and combat support of the
United States; and the Administrations' abandonment of
Dutch New Guinea to the military blackmail of President Su-
karno of Indonesia, a flagrant violation of the United Nations
Charter.

At the President's insistence, one of his principal foreign-policy aides, McGeorge Bundy, sought me out to expound the
factors that had persuaded the Administration it must force
the surrender to Sukarno to prevent a "confrontation with the
Communist powers" that could lead to a Third World War.
Among these, he said, was secret information that the Netherlands government actually welcomed the opportunity afforded
to be relieved of the burden of defending New Guinea.

This surprised me, because Netherlands Foreign Minister
Luns had been publicly critical of what he identified as "United
States pressure—denying refueling to the Dutch air force on
American soil, etc.—that left surrender to Sukarno's military
blackmail the only alternative of the government at The
Hague. Also, the Dutch Ambassador to Washington had pri-
vately expressed gratification of and agreement with my com-
ments critical of this pressure.

But though I continue to regard the Administration's acts in
this instance as a blot on its foreign policy, as well as a cynical
repudiation of the U.N. Charter that its rhetoric incessantly
extolled, the President's emissary [Bundy] may have had solid
basis for the "secret information" he claimed to have about the
undercover Dutch position.

As for the Administration's indispensable part in the over-
throw of Tshombe, the only pro-Western leader in the Congo,
and for U.N. military suppression of what I still consider to
have been a "civil war" (in which the Charter forbids U.N.
intervention), President Kennedy noted my critical comment
only indirectly. But he did this effectively by ridiculing it.

At a Gridiron Club dinner, where it is customary for the
President to wind up the evening with a light speech, he said he
had a proposal to make to me. If I would entertain Tshombe at
the Metropolitan Club in Washington, he would give Tshombe

the visa to come to the United States whose denial by the Administration I had commented on unfavorably. The audience was delighted by the sly jibe, being well aware that the reference was to my membership in a club that excludes Negroes as members or guests.

Domestic affairs, including politics and press relations, were frequent subjects that arose in my conversations with President Kennedy. The following are from memoranda I made while these conversations were fresh in my memory:

May 5, 1961. I asked the President what he had in mind to propose to the representatives of the press with whom he is about to discuss the problem of guarding national security while maintaining the rights of free publication of the news. He asked me how I thought the press would react to a proposal that a small group within itself be set up in Washington to which anyone could apply for guidance on whether or not to publish a story that might seem to him possibly to pose an issue of national security. "We could get quick Q clearance for the members of this group," he said.

My answer was that first he would have to discover whether the press agreed with his conclusion that the United States is in a period of "clear and present danger" tantamount to that existing in a shooting war; that, lacking this agreement, I did not think the prospect was very good that the press as a whole could be unified on such a committee or formally cooperate with it. We left the subject there. But the President did express the view that, if *The New York Times* would not print [certain] "stories by David Halberstam [from Southeast Asia], most other news editors wouldn't either: "They follow your selection of what is fit to print in matters of national security."

I first thought the only . . . dispatch [from Halberstam] he had in mind was that published on May 2, reporting the plan to send U.N. observers to Laos. But he may have meant also the . . . dispatch dated April 14, revealing that we had prodded Moscow to act on the British request for a Laos cease-fire, and a Sunday piece giving the precise amount of our aid to South Vietnam. The President, incidentally, does not appear to approve of a Congressional watchdog committee over the C.I.A.

October 11, 1961. The President's close reading of the newspapers was again indicated when he seized on a sentence in James

Reston's piece of that day to the effect that men of Speaker Rayburn's generation didn't have their speeches ghost-written for
them. The President said that the charge made . . . that he hadn't
written *Profiles in Courage* was hard to shake off, but didn't I
remember seeing him writing the book at Palm Beach? I replied
that I certainly had, that I recalled seeing him lying flat on his back
on a board with a yellow pad on which he was writing the book,
and that I read enough of those pages at the time to know that the
product was his own.

Another subject was the difficulties he sees in the news-conference system—the long questions, the questions with a "policy
purpose," etc. "I have the habit," he said, "of turning to the right,
and then, every time, I am confronted by those women [naming
two]." [But I noticed at his news conference later that he almost
succeeded in entirely overlooking these females who were often on
their feet.]

. . . He supposed he had better keep a "million miles away"
from the House Speaker selection that would be required by
Speaker Rayburn's illness. . . . He argued with me about my
views that he had unnecessarily involved his prestige in House
matters, such as the Rules Committee fight, and had used extreme
personal pressures when he shouldn't have and refrained from
doing so when he should have. But the President did not dispute
my estimate that some of his reverses in the House were attributable to resentment he had unnecessarily incurred in the House Rules
fight [over packing the Committee to acquire a pro-Administration
majority]. Representative [Carl] Albert of Oklahoma, the President said, would be his choice for majority leader in the House
[this soon followed], but what he needs is someone who can swing
Southern votes to the Administration from opposition to it. Perhaps
that should be a Southerner—Rains of Alabama or [Hale] Boggs
of Louisiana, he wasn't sure which. It was interesting that he did
not mention [Richard Bolling] of Missouri who has gone along
with the Administration's "liberal" programs and is widely supposed to be his preference. . . . *The New York Times* editorials on
his leadership in Congress he finds "wholly unrealistic." Can't
they see the limitations of any Presidency, and his in particular, in
trying to force Congress to go along in controversial matters?

I remarked . . . that his three important victories in this heavily
Democratic Congress had been made possible by Republican defec-
tions from their Party's leadership. He agreed with an air of great
amusement, and said he had anticipated that situation because of

the nature and purpose of the bills involved and the issue in the fight to transfer [to a pro-Administration majority] the powers of the House Rules Committee.

The President remarked on the opposition of Democratic "liberals" and a number of scientists to his choice of John A. McCone as Director of the Central Intelligence Agency, but he said he wasn't paying much attention to "those groups." I confirmed his impression that I thought McCone was a first-rate appointment that would prove itself in action. The President said he had first offered the job to Arthur H. Dean, but that he was well satisfied with McCone.

He added that he would have liked to have had Eugene Black as his Secretary of the Treasury, but discovered he was unavailable. Douglas Dillon, whom he hadn't known very well at the time, had been first suggested to him by Philip Graham, Publisher of the Washington Post, and Joseph Alsop, the columnist. The President said he was very happy with Dillon, that they had had no disagreements on fiscal policy and he didn't expect them to have any.

The President asked whether I thought he should ignore the attacks on his record by Republican National Chairman Miller or leave them to be handled by Democratic National Chairman Bailey. I said I thought he should let them fight the "battle of the mimeograph," a phrase he must have liked because he repeated it at his news conference a couple of hours afterward.

During the Presidency of John F. Kennedy, two events concerned with international affairs alternately brought him the heaviest loss and the greatest gain in public opinion. These were (1) the episode of the disastrous failure of the invasion by the small anti-Castro force at the Bay of Pigs in Cuba; and (2) the conditional retreat of the Kremlin in what is known as the Cuban missile crisis.

The President's refusal to permit the Air Force to cover the Bay of Pigs landing, after his Administration had organized and trained the anti-Castro contingent for the invasion and assented to the attempt, has been spread on the public record in great detail. Only the enforced silence of the Chiefs of Staff over the issue of whether they had approved the expedition as a feasible military proposition, on the definite and fully authoritative understanding that there would be United States air cover when needed, has left this basic issue unresolved.

But though many accounts of the second matter, the missile crisis, have been published (especially the one written by Charles L. Bartlett and Stewart Alsop from official sources President Kennedy made available to them), I append my own account of one facet of the crisis in the hope that it will cast some new light on certain details of the intra-Administration meetings that ended with President Kennedy's speech of October 22, 1962. In this speech he stated his conclusions with respect to the Soviet's missile armament of the Castro government and the measures he had taken to dismantle it.

My own account deals principally with the role played during the crisis by Director John A. McCone of the C.I.A. I wrote it on November 10, 1962, and, like all the others at that time and for several years thereafter, it makes no reference to the participation claimed by Thiraud de Vosjoly, a high official of the French intelligence system. This claim appeared in his memoirs, published in April, 1968.

According to de Vosjoly, who was cooperating with the C.I.A. at the same time he was directing French intelligence from the deGaulle Embassy in Washington, he scouted for McCone the reports of U.S.S.R. installation and supply of missiles in Cuba (to which he had diplomatic access); and came back with alleged eye-witness evidence for McCone that Cuba was being equipped with offensive missiles, and not the surface-to-air projectiles (SAMs) whose presence was beginning to be credited in C.I.A. reports. Meanwhile, in the Senate, Kenneth B. Keating of New York was making, equally unheeded by the Administration, the same allegations of Soviet missile activities on the island.

De Vosjoly's story, if factually established, would make certain sequences even more inexplicable: the long delay, after his reputed report to McCone, before the Kennedy Administration acted to blockade the delivery of the missiles by Soviet ships; and McCone's adherence to his plan to go abroad for his honeymoon on August 30.

My November 10, 1962, chronology follows:

August 10. After examining secret intelligence reports he had received, McCone dictated a memorandum for President Kennedy, expressing the belief that installations for the launching of offensive missiles were being constructed on the island. His subordinates who prepared the "national estimates" papers of the Agency recommended that he omit a statement of this belief until it was completely documented. He ordered that it remain in the paper.

August 17. On the basis of additional material McCone stated his case, at a high-level meeting. Secretaries Rusk and McNamara expressed the view that the buildup was purely defensive, adhering to the prevailing Administration theory that the Kremlin would never take the risk of installing offensive weaponry, missiles in particular, beyond the range of SAM—surface-to-air.

August 22 and 23. McCone pressed his deduction at one of these meetings that President Kennedy attended. A few days later, after he left for Seattle for his wedding, he intensified his alert in code telegrams and on the scrambled telephone. On August 30 he sailed with his bride for a honeymoon on the Riviera.

September 6. Lunching in Paris with Deputy Secretary of Defense [Roswell] Gilpatric, McCone continued to stress what he had concluded were the facts about USSR missile weaponry in Cuba.

September 7, 10, 13, 16, and 19. On the basis of CIA and other intelligence reports forwarded to him from Washington, McCone recommnded that "national estimates" staff of the Agency make a firm statement of opinion that the SAM-sites discovered in Cuba were being developed for emplacements of surface-to-surface missiles with a twelve-hundred-mile range and more, and that these missile parts and IL-28s were already being assembled on the island by the Russian "technicians." He also told his staff to reiterate his recommendation, which McNamara had successfully opposed some weeks earlier, that low-level observation flights over Cuba be made to help verification of what the regular U-2 flights were photographing.

Lieutenant General Carter, McCone's deputy, omitted from the CIA memoranda for the President in this period the statements McCone recommended that the agency include. Carter's explanation is that, as chargé d'affaires, and in possession of *all* the intelligence reports textually, which at that point McCone was not, it was his responsibility to decide whether or not to include these statements.

October 14–19. In the interim McCone had returned and pressed his views and conclusions at high-level meetings summoned by the President, and meanwhile the Strategic Air Command, over CIA protests, had taken over the U-2s. The President

directed that the low-level reconnaissance flights be undertaken in
scope to verify what photographs of U-2 flights had shown on
October 14. Hurricane Ella's interference with U-2 observations
was now a thing of the past; the pictures taken by the low-flying
pilots October 16–19 approximately proved conclusively the
soundness of McCone's deduction that first was the source of his
warnings and then of his firm estimate.

In a discussion of the Cuban problem this week the President
remarked to McCone, "You were right all along."

"But for the wrong reasons," said Secretary of Defense McNamara with a nod of assent from Secretary of State Rusk.

Nevertheless, the Soviet missile-bearing ships ultimately
turned back from their destination at Cuban ports when confronted by the United States Navy's "quarantine" President
Kennedy ordered. In filmed conversations with Nikita Khrushchev, televised by the National Broadcasting Company in the
summer of 1967, the former Premier asserted that the
U.S.S.R. had gained the point for which the missile armament
of Cuba was undertaken—President Kennedy's assurance
against a United States invasion of Cuba by which the one
Communist regime in the Western Hemisphere (and only
ninety miles from the American mainland) was designed to be
overthrown. He could have added that the President's retreat
from his demand for on-the-spot inspection of the missile installations has foreclosed knowledge of just what Soviet armament
Castro actually possesses.

But the President entered his fatal year of 1963 in the glow
of an achievement that seemed basic to the American people,
and strengthened the waning fear of the free world that the
United States would falter in the clutch of a common danger
from aggressive world Communism.

The tragedy of the rifle shots at Dallas on November 22,
1963, was doubly so. For in the continuing glow that infused
his Presidency it will never be known whether, when the Soviet
Union retreated from its greatest open challenge to the security
of the United States, John F. Kennedy would or would not
have risen to the heights of history that he plainly was ascending.

15

JOHNSON

"SHE WEPT to wear a crown," wrote Tennyson, though he was not among the handful of those present in Kensington Palace at 5 A.M., June 20, 1837, when the Archbishop of Canterbury and the Lord Chamberlain informed Princess Victoria, clad in a dressing-gown, of the death of her uncle, King William IV, a few hours before. Hence we owe to a poet that the tears of the young Queen-Empress have become an item of accepted legend if not of history.

But on the night of March 31, 1968, a tear fell in the sight of millions of television viewers throughout the world and thus became an authentic item of history.

Victoria "wept to wear a crown" in 1837. But the tear that coursed down the rugged face of Lyndon Baines Johnson in 1968 was shed in precisely opposite circumstances. He was announcing that, at the end of his current tenure as President of the United States, he would voluntarily relinquish a far greater power than Victoria ever possessed constitutionally, or expanded in practice, as the monarch of Great Britain, Ireland, and India, and "of the dominions beyond the Seas."

He pledged—and the next day he described his pledge as "irrevocable"—that he would neither "seek nor accept" renomination by his Party. Victoria's was a tear of accession, Johnson's of abdication, and the emotion of the occasion of March 31 was poignant enough to account for it. For this proud, strong, and stubborn man was conceding that only his voluntary cession of the Presidency at the end of his current term could reunite a country bitterly and deeply rent by dissatisfaction with his leadership in domestic and foreign policy, and lift the office of the Presidency from the boiling slough into which it had plunged during his incumbency of the White House.

Yet, as a professional politician, Johnson surely anticipated that, as soon as the implicit greatness of his action came under critical analysis, he would be widely suspected of concealing, in the cloak of uniquely high-minded patriotism, a new strategy for his own succession. For in practical effect his move could not have been better designed to confuse some of his critics, disarm others, and thrust both the Republican and Democratic parties and the Presidential aspirants among them into a deep, black quandary, violently resolved for an Administration spokesman—Vice-President Humphrey—by the murder of its chief challenger, Senator Kennedy.

Having founded their candidacies on attacking Johnson as an individual, and also on his conduct of the Presidency at home and abroad, they—particularly the Democratic challengers—were suddenly bereft of their principal target. And, since Johnson had often proclaimed that his political mentor was Franklin D. Roosevelt, his announcement brought vividly and inevitably to mind the maneuvering of Roosevelt in 1939–40 for a third term. Vowing he was ready and anxious to terminate his Presidential tenure at the end of a second term, Roosevelt all the while was deviously and successfully operating to eliminate all potential Democratic successors.

Before the momentous event of March 31, 1968, the Lyndon Johnson whom the people saw and heard was an angry political animal, full of vindictiveness for all of his critics, particularly those who attacked his conduct of the Vietnam war—intent on repairing his failing fortunes by actions that would bring about his re-election. But the President Johnson the people saw and heard on the night of March 31 was a statesman who had irrevocably decided to sacrifice personal and electoral ambition in an effort to try to unite and lead a divided country in its most dangerously troubled time.

Previously he had revealed himself to be compassionate and vengeful; considerate and unfeeling; lofty of aims, but incomparably egotistical in the conviction prevalent among Presidents that the ends which serve them and their potential interests equally serve the country. His pretenses of benignity, especially on television, seemed positively childish, for he is fundamentally a hard man. Childish, too, his obsessive resolve to be always the first in publicizing in person, on television, regardless of import, a decision already made and a step already taken.

When destiny has interfered with the scheduling of even some minor activity he has in train, I believe that Johnson, reacting like Macbeth confronted with a major stroke of fate (She should have died hereafter!"), has been disposed to think first of its effect on his personal fortunes. But, as the events of March 31 affirmed, an aura of greatness, generated by his soaring aims and the awesome powers of his office, surrounded him as he moved from the petty and unadmirable acts to the large and selfless, from public identification as the most crafty of politicians to the general acceptance as the anointed missionary of a noble vocation for which he gladly offered himself as the first sacrifice.

In attempting this transformation Lyndon Johnson is not only "the many men" * who have always contended with their several selves and the contemporary world within the single physiological entity of the President of the United States. He is also the principal embodiment of the greatest anomaly which exists between the ideals and the practices of a public man. For in practice he is expanding a Federal bureaucracy in which the individual and monetary stability are fast disappearing. Yet Johnson's most strongly professed objectives are to create a world community that above all fosters individualism, in egalitarian balance with a prospering society.

* The source of this quotation is the wise and authoritative book, "The President Is Many Men," written by the senior White House Correspondent Merriman Smith, of the U.P.I.

All Presidents, even when taking their ease, are functionally unable to separate themselves wholly from the office. Accordingly, they cannot if they would escape the downright toil and drudgery which invests their function. But there have not been many as congenitally unable to make even the briefest of separations from the office. Hence the nation has deeply and authentically imprinted on its retina the sight of a Chief Executive with a daily working span of inhuman length and intensity. In the same category is the ceaseless drumming of the wings of Air Force One as it carries the President, and the labors of his office, around the circumference of the earth in an unending road-show.

Partly because of this incessant ubiquity, Johnson, as much as any President in our history, has closely identified himself and his office with the disasters, foreign and domestic, economic and social, into which the United States has become more and more deeply involved in his time. This relativity is to a considerable degree the consequence of his innate trait of craftiness. But it also is the product of an evasive or soaring loquacity which induces him to utter and write paragraphs when sentences would cover the point or event, and to allow his promises to run far beyond the clear limits of attainment. Another source of this close identification with all acts, policies and thorny situations is a passion to control every function of government, though subordinates are always available in profusion to take the gaff, or, without diminishing him, the credit.

These practices undoubtedly contributed to the shrinking popular approval of his courses that was being registered steadity when he addressed the people on March 31. But in one dramatic final paragraph he reversed these falling percentages, an effect that conceivably could endure until or unless events bring persuasion that he was engaging in a political maneuver to hold for four more years the very office he foreswore.

Politicians, like lovers, should not be held forever accountable for words spoken and vows taken in the heat of some immediate prompting. But there are words and vows that, if later disregarded or recanted, indicate lack of constancy in basic principle. And President Johnson's limitation on the pursuit of the war in Vietnam is fundamentally inconsistent with the measures Senator Johnson urged in Korea in a speech on July 12, 1950.

The usual defense of a politician when confronted with glaring inconsistency is that the extracts employed have been "taken out of context." In quoting as follows from his 1950 speech, I am content to leave it to the readers of the entire text whether this charge fairly applies:

> We cannot temporize. We cannot win this war by relying upon platitudes about "ultimate victory." Ultimate victory cannot be achieved unless we concentrate on immediate victory. . . . [Contrast this with his 1964 campaign pledges not to "escalate" the war in Vietnam.]
>
> So long as we continue to rely upon words—not upon action—to win this struggle in South Korea, we are as guilty of a crime against freedom as the executioners who fire the bullets in the faces of our sons. [Not until 1965 did President Johnson go much beyond words in Vietnam. And well into 1968 he was still holding off-bounds several sources and routes of North Vietnamese military supply vital to the infliction of heavy casualties on the United States forces.]
>
> The considered opinions of our Joint Chiefs of Staff—the opinions of our highest military advisers—have been straitjacketed in a maze of bookkeeping and accounting procedures. [This was the nub of the charge against Secretary of Defense McNamara by the military that Johnson overruled for many months on end.]
>
> I urge that we [the Truman Administration] immediately order into Federal service all National Guard units and all reserves who are presently on a drill-pay status. This will bring into the armed services . . . 832,028 men. . . . As necessity dictates, order all unpaid Reservists into active service. This would add 1,700,000 Reservists to our strength. . . . Enact the necessary emergency legislation to provide [Presidential] powers necessary for full mobilization of our industrial capacity. [Years after President Kennedy edged this nation into the Southeast Asian quagmire by adding to

United States troops and military advisory personnel in South
Vietnam, and sending them to the combat zone, only a few
reserves were called to the colors.]

It is my opinion that the North Korean forces . . . are
being furnished equipment by Russia itself. The American
people should realize the problem which confronts us. . . .

There is no way out short of total victory. . . . Shall South
Korea be remembered as a slaughter-house of democracy—or
as a graveyard for aggression? . . . Words are useless; criticism is wasteful; delay is unthinkable. [In Vietnam, President
Johnson's policy, except for steadily increasing United States
armed forces and gradually enlarging the target area, has
been a negation of all these admonitions to the Truman Administration. The only tenable justification for this full-circle
shift is that, when he spoke in the Senate, Communist China
had not even begun to develop nuclear weaponry. But even
this does not answer the point that it was foolhardy to become
involved, and ever increasingly, in a war where the factors
that have imposed military restraint were in plain view from
the outset.]

In defense of Johnson's conduct of the war, the argument
has been made that (1) he "inherited" it from Kennedy; (2)
his leadership and the world influence of the United States
would have crumbled if, on his accession, he had even put his
lips to the mouthpiece of the bugle that sounds truce; and (3)
the stepped-up pace of enemy aggression forced him greatly to
expand the United States presence in Vietnam and bomb the
North. But this defense is vulnerable in every respect. (1) It
was Johnson himself, as Vice President, after an official survey
of the Vietnam situation in 1961, who reported to President
Kennedy that the national security was directly and vitally
involved; if appropriate force were not applied, all Southeast
Asia would be lost to the free world (the "domino theory"),
and the United States might well find itself based defensively
on "San Francisco." (2) By actively seeking negotiation soon
after his accession Johnson would have established his moral
leadership, and that of the United States in the free world, by
affirming in action the understanding on which he was overwhelmingly elected—that he would strongly restrict United
States participation in the war. (3) By bombing the North,

with the Air Force barred from destroying the enemy's vital installations and sources of supply, he made the bombing ineffective to achieve the crippling of the enemy that was its stated purpose and only justification.

My first acquaintance with Lyndon Johnson was in the late nineteen thirties, shortly after he had been elected to Congress. This was at dinner, in the house of Supreme Court Justice William O. Douglas (then Chairman of the Securities and Exchange Commission).

Johnson had already had service in Washington as secretary to Representative Richard Kleberg, one of the owners of the vast King Ranch, and the atmosphere in which Johnson worked, as well as the political philosophy of his employer, was constructively conservative. Hence when I met the future President I associated him with this environment. He had been a minor official in the New Deal bureaucracy in Texas. But even in the youth rehabilitation project he served, the New Deal operated, in my judgment at the time, within the framework of the capitalist system, with the preservation of that system its fundamental objective and achievement. Also, nothing Johnson said that evening seemed to me to tend toward the Populist political philosophy which now is often attributed to him as a fixed inheritance, or toward the establishment of reckless deficit spending of the Welfare State which as President he has done more than any predecessor to advance.

I chiefly recall him as a long string bean of a young man, an eloquent young man, progressive but moderately so, giving deference to differing opinion, eager to get ahead in politics. And on the basis of this appraisal and his exploits as a Democratic Senate leader in the art of the possible—an art that deserted him when put to the test of national leadership—my relations with him grew politically close and personally friendly. Throughout this period, which lasted until after he was nominated for and elected to national office, my admiration of his talents was not diminished by any thoughts or actions on his part indicative of the sweeping transformation of the nation that he, in line with the decisions of the Supreme Court, since has pressed.

Johnson, in turn, especially after his choice as Senate Minority and then Majority Leader, constantly expressed his appreciation of articles favorable to his performance that I wrote with what objectivity I may possess as a reporter and commentator. These appreciative expressions took expansive forms, natural to his geographical origin and personality: showers of memoranda in which he set down his thinking on the immediate issues confronting him as Senate leader; signed photographs with most complimentary inscriptions; letters on my birthdays, on red-letter days in the calendar; Christmas gifts of mouth-burning deer sausage from his ranch.

Among his flattering written descriptions were "The Stud Duck of the Washington Press Corps" and "The Statesman of the Press." I mention this phase of our relationship only to demonstrate an important trait in the character of this President. When, at least in my case, praise is punctuated by criticism, the warm embrace is replaced by a vigorous thrust into the deep-freeze.

Looking back, I suppose that the change began when I pointed out, in articles from the 1960 Democratic Convention at Los Angeles, that in accepting Kennedy's tender of the Vice-Presidential nomination, he had committed himself to a super-liberal national platform not only nugatory of his political record, but in total conflict with the conservative Texas Democratic platform on which also he was brazenly standing as a candidate for re-election to the Senate. But when I called on him in the Capitol after the convention, to ask what had persuaded him to run with Kennedy and on the Los Angeles platform, he received me with his usual cordiality. He explained that he had made his decision solely because if he had declined Kennedy's proffer, the Democratic ticket would certainly lose the oncoming national election and Nixon would become the next President of the United States—a possibility that appeared to be, in his mind, something like the bubonic plague!

As the campaign progressed Mrs. Oveta Culp Hobby informed me that Johnson had resolved the conflict between the two platforms he was running on by announcing to a Texas audience that he was committed to "every word" in the docu-

ment drawn up at Los Angeles. This was the honorable position for him to take in the circumstances, and I commented to
that effect, while noting it was inconsistent with his Senate
record. And, though I saw him seldom after his election as Vice
President, and mainly on social occasions, his manner was
cordial until the incident of the dinner of the Alfalfa Club,
January 21, 1963.

The Alfalfa Club is composed of a group of establishment
men ranging from the President to private citizens whom,
irrespective of public attainment, the admissions committee
finds acceptable. Its annual dinners are devoted to merriment,
in which political satire predominates. And the feature of the
evenings is the "Speech of Acceptance" by a member who has
been chosen as "the Alfalfa candidate for President of the
United States."

To compose this speech, blending deft jibes at the current
national Administration with good taste, is one of the toughest
assignments in Washington. And this was the chore handed to
me at the 1963 dinner. It is a particularly difficult assignment
because of its brilliant execution by previous Alfalfa "candidates," notably the late Justice Robert H. Jackson, and I definitely did not come up to the mark. But at one point I described
the imaginary travail of President Kennedy in finding things
for his restless and frustrated Vice-President to do. And this
was an immediate provocation that led Johnson in reply to
discharge at me a volley of sharp personalities.

Surprised and regretful that my feeble jests at him and the
Administration had so obviously aroused the anger of a longtime friend and a frequent object of my admiration, I sent
Johnson what I hoped was a good-humored letter. I wrote that
I had given instructions that upon my demise a tablet be placed
over my remains with the inscription: "Hic jacet Arthur Krock
of Kentucky/Killed in a pistol-duel with Lyndon B. Johnson of
Texas/The deceased drew first." He replied with the good-natured comment that he was "disposed to take my letter as a
capitulation." But as it later developed, a spoof of one of
Johnson's typical handouts of cornpone that appeared in *The
New York Times*, October 18, 1961, was a deeper provocation
of the Vice-President's annoyance with me than the "Alfalfa

Speech of Acceptance," January 20, 1963. While in Pakistan,
on one of the ceremonial visits to which President Kennedy
assigned his restless No. 2, Johnson had invited a camel-driver
he chanced to encounter in a Karachi throng to be his guest in
a visit to the United States, including a stay at the LBJ ranch
in Texas. And Bashir Ahmad, the camel-driver, duly arrived
with his camel and was escorted around by Johnson. Writing
in the vein indicated by the title of this jest—"Tale of The One
Thousandth and Second Night"—and referring to Johnson as
Kennedy's Grand Wazir, the piece reads as follows:

> In the name of Lyndon, the Compassionate, the Beneficent,
> the Well-Publicized, here we indite the moving tale of L.B.J.
> and the poor Camel-Driver of Karachi:
>
> It is related that during the days of Kennedy the King,
> there was a Grand Wazir, a Grandee of abundant opulence
> and amplest livelihood. And it is said that the King, being
> restless one night, sent for his Wazir and vouchsafed unto
> him, "O L. B. J., I am wakeful this night with the burden of
> thinking what new things we could do to arouse in this
> kingdom interest in and approval of our efforts to improve the
> lot of the less fortunate of the peoples of the Middle East and
> at the same time imprint on their minds our image as the
> giver of what is needed and also is good for our side."
>
> It is written that the King said these other things to his
> Grand Wazir: "Alas, my heavy duties hold me here, so that I
> command thee to journey in my name among these peoples
> for the purposes aforesaid," to which the Grand Wazir made
> the reply, "O King, to hear is to obey, and you can count on
> L. B. J. to dramatize the mission thou hast entrusted to me in
> a manner that will imprint my father image ineradicably
> upon a grateful world, and confound the Tartar hordes who
> are seeking to erase it."
>
> And it has reached me that the King said in reply, "See to
> it that in thy loyal diligence thy extraordinarily alert instinct
> for personal projection will be wholly subdued, to the total
> suppression of any aspect of thy mission that could fall within
> the category of what is known as a publicity stunt." To which
> the Grand Wazir responded dutifully, "Of this, O King, be
> wholly assured."
>
> It is written that in due course the Grand Wazir came unto
> the city of Karachi, in Pakistan, and set forth on a tour of the

city in which vast throngs had gathered to welcome him. In strict consonance with the gravity and austerity of his errand, it is further written that the Grand Wazir made this tour of the city in an automobile of length and luxury such as the poor of Karachi had never seen, the more to imbue them with a sense of the humility of his role; that in one of the most crowded of the bazaars the gaze of the Grand Wazir lighted upon a poor man, Bashir Ahmad by name (as it turned out, the chauffeur of a camel), because of the magnificence of Bashir's mustaches. As the tale is told, the Grand Wazir halted his solid-gold conveyance and engaged with this Bashir Ahmad in a conversation that ended with an invitation to visit the Grand Wazir's native land, in especial his personal fief of Texas.

The tellers of the tale relate that, no sooner did information that the camel-driver had accepted the invitation reach the domain of Kennedy the King, than many citizens quoth, "How constructively the Royal mission of the Grand Wazir has been executed. How perfectly the visit of Bashir Ahmad will serve the King's stated purpose, yet leave no ground for linking the Grand Wazir's mission with what is known as a personal publicity stunt."

And thereupon, it is further related, an airplane line in the land of Kennedy the King presented the camel-driver with a flight thereto from Karachi and back again. An airplane manufacturer supplied one of its better transports, with crew and fuel, to fly Bashir Ahmad from New York to Texas, to Kansas City and to Washington. An automobile manufacturer made Bashir Ahmad a gift of a blue truck which it exchanged for a green one, the national color of Pakistan, when he expressed this patriotic desire. And donations for the now-motorized camel-driver of shoes, clothing and rupees to the number of 2,000 flowed into the office of the Grand Wazir in the King's capital city.

But, most wondrous of all, as the story is told, Bashir Ahmad was met as he descended from the transoceanic jet airplane by the Grand Wazir himself, who acted as escort and chaperon thereafter, and also gave him a Texas horse with the brand of L. B. J. . . .

I soon was made aware that the article inflicted a slow burn on the Vice-President, a report first confirmed by the receipt from his office of an article by a Pakistani columnist praising the gesture. And in a note dated March 15, 1962, a plainly annoyed Johnson enclosed "a story on Bashir Ahmad . . . in what I believe to be a reasonably respected newspaper, *The Christian Science Monitor*" with a note saying that he wanted me to know that "our friend, Bashir, is apparently doing well." But under date of April 6, same year, taking exception to a dispatch on the Texas political situation I had written from Corpus Christi, Johnson sent me a letter that began in this amiable fashion: "Two tried and trusted friends shouldn't fall out over either camel-drivers or governors." Hence, until his rancorous reply to the Alfalfa speech, I had no other open indication for several years of personal ill will on the part of the Vice-President.

Nevertheless, a day or so after his accession, he reached me by telephone on what I am sure was a long list—including a number of my colleagues—to say that he stood in need of all the help he could get. This was followed by the usual Christmas tokens; by invitations to my wife and me to state dinners; and by several private interviews, from one of which I came off with a Stetson hat and a signed colored photograph of the President and myself in the friendliest of converse.

But shortly afterward, though my comments on his acts and policies continued to follow a formula in which at least I try to subordinate critical analysis to explication of the facts, the unmistakable signs appeared that Johnson had severed both our personal and professional relations. No more invitations to state dinners. No more tête-à-tête luncheons or interviews. No more signed photographs. No more telephone calls. No more birthday, Thanksgiving, Christmas, or New Year messages.

I have never inquired into the cause. Johnson continued to deal amiably with newspaper critics whose comments on his Presidency remained sharper and more personal than any of mine, and even dated back to his tenure as Senate Leader. My only clue is that when, two years after the silence fell, a mutual friend suggested to the President that he break it, he muttered something about "that camel-driver."

I recount these petty experiences because "style is man," personal traits are essential components of style, and the purpose of these trivia conforms to the purpose of this narrative—

to hold up a mirror to reflect the passing figures of the nation's elect within the range of my limited vision.

The source of Lyndon Johnson's determination to be remembered in history as at least a "good President" if history shall not accord to him the rank of a "great" one is the broadest and most commendable of aspirations. But I think that the enforced competition of the successor President with a legend, the legend of Kennedy, accounts for the extravagance of promises he has made to the people that they soon discovered were impossible of fulfillment.

This Kennedy-Johnson rivalry began when they were competing for the Democratic Presidential nomination in 1960, and it was not long before ill-feeling developed between the camps of the contenders.

Kennedy, after the grand prize was in his possession, needed Johnson too much to indulge in past resentments. On several occasions during their contest for the 1960 Presidential nomination, Kennedy reproached me, but very lightly, for celebrating Johnson's Senate leadership at the expense, as he said, of the younger Democrats who were indispensible to the making of it. But the following history must remain vividly in Johnson's thoughts:

. . . During the Democratic National Convention of 1956 it still is not generally known that Johnson sent two Texan emissaries —John Connally and D. B. Hardeman—to the Presidential nominee, Adlai E. Stevenson, with the message that if Stevenson so desired, he [Johnson] would accept the Vice-Presidential nomination. Stevenson, instead, decided to leave the choice to the convention. Thus Stevenson did not favor another Vice-Presidential aspirant, but by declining Johnson's proffer he gave Kennedy the opportunity to become a national figure by almost capturing the number-two place from Senator Estes Kefauver. And I doubt that anyone who knows Johnson well believes that despite his dislike for Kefauver, it did not gall him when the Texas delegation perforce gave its support to Kennedy on that famous ballot.

. . . One day in the course of Kennedy's 1960 pre-convention drive I was talking with Johnson on various matters. He was indignant over reports which had reached him that some of Kennedy's workers—in West Virginia, I think it was—were spreading stories that he had used his position as Senate Majority Leader to deny Kennedy certain deserved legislative opportunities from which great public credit would flow. Johnson said he had summoned Kennedy to his office and told him that unless there was an end to this allegation, he would expose and denounce it. Kennedy, according to Johnson, disclaimed all knowledge of the activity, promised that if the reports had any foundation there would be no more of it, and thanked Johnson for what he described as many favors the Majority Leader had done for the Senator from Massachusetts. I gathered, however, that there still was little love to lose between the two rivals.

. . . Just before the dramatic occasion in Los Angeles when Johnson and Kennedy matched their claims for the Presidential nomination I was in Johnson's suite at the Biltmore Hotel. Kennedy had requested the Texas delegation to hear him; Johnson had countered with a demand that the Massachusetts delegation also be present to hear them both; and the affair expanded into their joint appearance before the Texas delegation and a token membership of about twenty-five members of the delegation from Massachusetts.

. . . Johnson was tense with what I decided was anxiety over the outcome of a confrontation in which Kennedy already had demonstrated the skills he later employed so successfully in the debates with Nixon. He was abrupt to the point of rudeness with everyone in the room. And when, with his aides, he strode down the corridor to the elevator, in the gait of a trotting horse, he exchanged not a word with his escort. But before we left the suite one very important Johnson aide, Robert G. Baker, said more than a word relating to the debate with Kennedy: "If Kennedy gets the nomination," said Baker, "watch what we'll do to him in the special session."

The plain and startling implication was that the Democratic Senate organization would in various ways, in that body's proceedings, damage the prospects of the Party's Presidential nominee in his capacity as a Senator from Massachusetts. The implication was tenable by reason of the fact that Baker was Johnson's unofficial whip, confidant, legman, and manipulator of Senate action desired by the leader. But whether or not

Baker's remark reflected only his personal bitterness over Kennedy's mounting obscuration of Johnson, the threat of course became moot with Kennedy's choice of Johnson to be his running mate and with Johnson's acceptance.

Yet if the remark can be taken, as I think it can, as an echo of that was in the mind of Baker's boss, it comported with the bitter atmosphere that prevailed in the suite at the time it was made. And certainly bitterness was projected by Johnson into the oncoming confrontation with Kennedy before the delegates in the Biltmore ballroom.

Johnson made critical references to the absentee record of "some Senators" that applied directly to Kennedy. He contrasted absenteeism with his own unfailing presence in the legislative clutches instead of beating the bushes for convention delegates. In the same context he favorably compared his voting record with Kennedy's on measures sought by the farm bloc, the advocates of flood control, etc. But the bitterness fully emerged as Johnson made the following unmistakable allusions to Kennedy's father when United States Ambassador to the Court of St. James's:

> I was never any [Prime Minister Neville] Chamberlain umbrella policy man. I never thought Hitler was right. . . . When [Senator] Joe McCarthy was on the march in this country and someone had to stand up and be counted, I was a voting liberal. . . . I was not contributing comfort to his thinking or contributions to his campaign. [In condemning McCarthy] every Democratic Senator stood up and voted with his leader. That is, *all who were present* [emphasis added].

The debate ended, however, with interchanged compliments and the pledges of the rivals vigorously to support the Convention's Presidential nominee. Within a few hours Johnson had accepted Kennedy's tender to be his running mate. And thereafter, during the campaign and as Vice-President, he faithfully executed the loyalties to Kennedy prescribed by the politician's trade. But there remained a basically arms'-length character in the Kennedy-Johnson personal relationship, for all the warm exchange of public compliments and vows of political fealty. Often since his succession Johnson has told friends that his staff and its work are far superior to those which served Kennedy, and noted that he has achieved the sweeping social-economic legislative programs Kennedy had vainly proposed to Congress.

Neither at this writing nor until a decade hence can there be a balanced measurement of Johnson's successes and failures, exploits and pretensions—of his Presidency as a whole. By the nature of his office and its unsurpassed problems, because of the global plight that finally may be resolved only by a demolishment of civilization, he must move from the scales of the present to those of the distant future before his historical weight and height can be determined.

But it is still possible, by assembling some of the views he has expressed in private against those he has stated publicly, to present an unfinished but definitive profile of Johnson the man and the President. These croquis have been drawn of many Presidents and their contemporaries, most recently of Kennedy by Theodore Sorensen and Arthur Schlesinger, Jr. And Bill M. Moyers, who entered the highest-paid echelon of journalism by the skylight, has begun to release little glimpses of Johnson and some of his comments in private.

Behind the shields of these highly vocal defenders of the ethics of such revelations, there certainly must be honorable room for a presentation of Johnson in shirtsleeves by recording his moods and sayings in the environment of the Presidency.

A visitor on one of these occasions describes how he found Johnson sitting at his desk, seemingly absorbed in a paper before him. The President suddenly looked up, as if startled by an intrusion. Then, welcoming the arrival with a natural grace that does not usually emerge from his public appearances, he ordered a soft drink for two—root beer by preference—and settled down to easy and amiable conversation. Soon afterward he began to list his accomplishments, with Congress, with other statesmen, and the achievements he hoped yet to attain. He dwelt on the spread of education and his unmatched Presidential drive toward this objective. On the need for rapid transit. On the futility and defeat of withdrawal from Vietnam:

it would make scraps of paper our "commitments" elsewhere —in Berlin, the Middle East, South America.

He conceded that a case could be made for withdrawal from Vietnam in recognition of the large body of world opinion that sees the war as an effort by the white man to be the master of the yellow and brown. But though the case could be made, and was being made, he considered it a weak one. He would, he said, continue to follow and enforce present military policy in Southeast Asia, but short of provocation of war with Communist China—an inherent peril he said he was bending the effort of every hour and minute to avoid. One facet of this effort was to ban an attack by American ground troops on North Vietnam.

When engaged in these ruminations, Johnson was sitting beside a table equipped with enough electronic communications devices to resemble a computer. He fiddled with it from time to time, giving the visitor the impression that to the President the machine is a comforting symbol of power. He pressed a button that connected himself with an aide of whom he asked an unimportant question. For example, how much younger than Kennedy's is his staff, which he considers much abler? He stalled off a distaff inquiry as to when he would be ready for dinner. He signed some papers. He plugged in other aides for answers to questions of small detail. He invited some queries from his guest but eluded the hard ones. His visitor left with the impression that he had been in the company of a very anxious man—and a frustrated one because he had not been able to find solutions for the tough problems that beset him.

To another visitor Johnson analyzed the psychology of the obstructions to United States policies by General De Gaulle. He concluded that De Gaulle "will be there when the chips are down" as he was there in the Cuban missile crisis. Johnson said he would like to have a cozy tête-à-tête with the General: he was sure they could adjust a lot of differences. But thus far the maddening protocol of who is to call on whom, and where, remained unresolved.

Johnson was opposed at the time to political retaliations against the recalcitrant Democrats in Congress—mostly Southerners. He noted that Roosevelt tried that in the at-

tempted "purge" of 1938, but said that an important reason
for the failure of the effort was that it was ill-timed. But
Johnson indicated—but did not openly say—the party discipline would and should eventually be successfully imposed
when a general election wiped out the opposition gains in
Congress, as the voters decreed in 1966. The visitor assumed
this envisaged such a mandate in 1968.

Johnson commented that the result of the freedom of
Negroes everywhere to register and vote, which he effectively
pressed as Senate Majority Leader, would have allowed all the
remainder of the Negro problem "to fall in place" if extremism
had not taken over the civil rights movement. Too many politicians, among whom he indicated himself as a shining exception, made too many promises that obviously could not be kept,
and extremism was the ruinous price of Negro disillusionment.

Wasn't he letting himself be overworked? To the visitor
who expressed this concern Johnson said the only effect he had
noticed was that "sometimes I can't think good in the afternoon," but not when he had snatched a nap. And, anyhow, how
could he take things any easier and carry out the obligations of
his office?

In one of these talks Johnson gave a strong impression that
the loneliness which invests the Presidency impels him to impose his own long work schedule indiscriminately on his aides,
including the Cabinet, and summon them for discussions at
unearthly hours. When this impression was conveyed to one of
the principal, but willing, work horses of the Presidential team,
he was told that Johnson's loneliness was particularly noticeable in the absences of his wife.

His courtship of General Eisenhower—by the compliment of
incessant requests for counsel, the dispatch of helicopters to
ferry the General here and there—has been evaluated by many
of Eisenhower's most devoted admirers and former aides as
wholly a crafty and successful tactic to use the General as a
political hostage, thereby forestalling criticism by one of the
most popular citizens in the United States. But when Eisenhower enters Johnson's discussions with visitors, the relationship he has nourished with the President, with whom as Senate
leader he worked in close cooperation, appears to be an expres-

sion of deepest sincerity. The estimate Johnson gives of the General is that he brings the sharpest of minds and ideas to any conference. Every time Johnson talks with Eisenhower, one White House guest was told, the former President brings up critical points and potential consequences that have eluded what Johnson refers to as the "whiz kids" in his Administration and in Kennedy's. History will make a great mistake, Johnson has said, if it accepts the rating of many contemporary critics and denigrates Eisenhower's talents, industry, wisdom, and foresightedness.

Johnson's callers have found him what the TV audience has not—a gifted teller of tales that bear precisely on the immediate point. But among the tales Johnson tells is one that amounts to a revision of an account of the final relations between Franklin Roosevelt and Joseph P. Kennedy, Sr., related earlier in this narrative. My source was one of the principals at the White House meeting that occurred after Kennedy had informed Roosevelt that he was resigning. In this account Roosevelt praised Kennedy's record as Ambassador to the Court of St. James's and grieved over his resignation.

But according to Johnson, he was lunching with Roosevelt when Kennedy, en route to the White House meeting, telephoned his arrival in the United States. He quotes Roosevelt as saying, "Ah, Joe, old friend, it is so good to hear your voice. Please come to the White House tonight for a little family dinner. I'm dying to talk to you." Then Johnson relates that Roosevelt, putting down the telephone, drew his forefinger (razor-fashion) across his throat.

The only defect in this anecdote, told with a disciple's admiration of Roosevelt's talents at the game of spider-and-fly, is that the purpose of the White House dinner was to induce Kennedy not to resign before the election. Moreover, on that day, as previously recounted here, Roosevelt was deeply concerned lest Kennedy also publicly oppose his re-election as the Ambassador now and then had threatened to do in private conversation. And when the "little family dinner" was over, the Ambassador's re-election support was safely in the bag.

If the usual standards of success and failure are applied as a test, then Lyndon Johnson's Presidency has fallen far short of acceptability. The affluence he cites is built on rising inflation and the ephemeral goods and services of a war economy. The resumption of even a minimum peacetime footing will not for years free the nation from the crushing burden of a long and wasteful major war and foreign occupation. The hundreds of billions expended in a secondary peninsula of Southeast Asia, when we dare not press to a military victory, are forever lost in the furnaces of battle—no durable economic strength abides in their expenditure or in the skills thereby furthered or newly created. A war whose magnitude two Presidents made inevitable will stand in history as a perfect example of the disasters wreaked upon a nation by all-powerful chiefs of state who leaped before they looked.

One of the most depressing exhibitions of what politicians will do in a quest for tomorrow's votes instead of day-after-tomorrow's national well-being was the impossible promises they made of a totally egalitarian American society overnight. In consequence masses of Negroes, incited by anarchistic agitators, have expressed their disillusionment in arson, looting, and other forms of criminal violence, slightly and seldom to experience the penalties of the law because of the improvised and false doctrine of the Administration that enforcement of law is placing "property rights" over "human life."

The fires of inflation have been allowed to spread, and actually were fed by government after many had loudly sounded the alarm. And despite several specific promises, Johnson has shrunk from proposing a most essential anti-inflation measure —a legislative curb on the excessive, and excessively used, special legal powers of the labor unions, supplemented by acts of violence.

A lion on the platform, roaring words of denunciation of the shameful lack of protection from criminals of citizens going about their legitimate and peaceful concerns, Johnson at his desk is the lamb who vetoed the better of the two Congressional anti-crime bills when spokesmen of the group principally involved, young Negroes, objected to the inherent targeting. Not incidental, of course, is the fact that the ethnic group containing a large percentage of the criminals brings constant pressure on Congress to legislate Johnson's Great Society programs, and overwhelmingly has voted the Democratic ticket.

As his term draws to an end Johnson actually is presiding over a society sickened by quack cure-alls.

When Johnson was Senate Majority Leader, he supplied me with numerous memoranda of his thinking. But the purpose of one in particular was to illustrate his sense of fiscal responsibility and the lack of it among the self-styled political liberals. This document reads as follows:

1. The basic mistake the present-day "liberals" have made is to equate liberalism with spending the public's money. They have fallen into the trap set for them by the Republican Party.

2. This has become clear on a number of major issues this year. On highways, housing, and depressed areas, the "liberal" bill is invariably the one with the highest price tag and the "conservative" bill is the one with the lowest price tag. As a result, the public has gained the impression— carefully and skillfully nurtured by the Republicans—that a "liberal" is a man who wants to reach into the hip pocket of the American public and extract as much money from the wallet as possible.

3. This approach has detracted from the strength of a number of bills that should have been passed. On the housing bill, for example, the "liberals"—again aided by the Republicans—focused public attention on the money amounts to an extent where the average man in the street never stopped to ask himself what the bill would do. It is probable that almost every American knows that there was a lot of money involved in the housing bill; it is improbable that very many Americans know that only a small amount of this came out of the Treasury. It is a virtual certainty that the average American knows nothing about what the bill would have done for the old folks and for colleges.

4. Somewhere along the line, the realization must be driven home to the "liberals" that spending has no more relationship to liberalism than the salt content of sea water. Spending is purely a practical question. The amount to be spent should be determined solely by the need. Ten dollars is no more "liberal" than five dollars and three billion

dollars is no more "liberal" than one billion dollars. If liberalism as a philosophy is going to come equipped with a price tag, it doesn't have much of a future in this country.

5. Some of the confusion is due to the fact that the word "liberal" has become debased in modern times. A couple of years ago, a heated political contest was staged in a well-known resort city in America. The winner was the man who ran on the "liberal" ticket. His definition of the word "liberal" was a promise to let gamblers, slot machines, and prostitutes operate openly in the city if he was elected mayor. The good citizens apparently liked this type of "liberalism." They elected him. Obviously, this use of the word is ridiculous, but no more so than deciding that the "liberal" position is the one that spends the most money.

6. Somewhere along the line the liberals have got to redefine their terms. They must realize that liberalism, basically, means a genuine solicitude for the needs of people and for individual dignity and freedom. One of the most important "liberal" acts of this century didn't cost the Treasury a red cent. It was the Norris-LaGuardia Act—which outlawed the "Yellow-Dog Contract." By modern-day terms, it would not be considered "liberal" because it didn't cost enough money.

Yet in 1965 and 1966, when the signs pointed to the vital necessity of stemming the flow of inflationary dollars and raising taxes, Johnson continued to practice and expand the very opposite of his preaching. And as this is written, the record of his monetary and fiscal policies is documented as a confused, incompetent, and gigantic failure that threatens the security of savings, the purchasing power of pensions—all the hard-won material rewards of industrious personal achievement.

But, if, under another nominee, the Democratic party that made this sorry record is again successful in 1968, then, once again in the politics of democracies, will be demonstrated the saturnine truth of a comment made sixty-seven years ago by Winston Churchill with reference to another administration. In a letter to Lord Rosebery, young Churchill wrote:

"My own idea is that it does not matter how many mistakes one makes in politics, so long as one keeps on making them. It is like throwing babies to the wolves: once you stop, the pack overtakes the sleigh. This explains why it is that the present [A. J. Balfour] administration prospers."*

* From Randolph S. Churchill, *Winston S. Churchill: Young Statesman, 1901–1914* (Boston: Houghton Mifflin, 1967.)

16

THE GREAT
CHANGE

Woodrow Wilson decided to remain in Washington after his retirement from office. But the tradition established when George Washington returned to Mount Vernon and Jefferson to Monticello has been followed by Wilson's successors who became former Presidents. Harding, Franklin Roosevelt, and John F. Kennedy died in office. But Coolidge, Hoover, Truman, and Eisenhower left the capital city for communities they called "home" as soon as the Presidents who succeeded them had taken the oath.

Theirs is an example, however, that has been widely disregarded by former officials in the lower echelons of the Federal government. After each general election, particularly when there has been a change of party control in the government, there can be encountered—on the streets of Washington, in the luncheon clubs, and in the Capitol—displaced Cabinet ministers, members of Congress, and major or minor civilian and military bureaucrats lingering superfluous on the scene of their quondam power and glory.

Those who have turned plain lobbyist or lawyer-lobbyist—

this term is used without disparagement, for there is legitimacy and public value in the occupation—are able to maintain a relationship to the process of government and thus escape the role of hanger-on that must be more lonely in Washington than in any other seat of political power on earth. But for the latter, who include journalistic purveyors of comment and opinion that once exercised influence over political decisions, the price is a sort of solitary confinement, unless they have the facilities required to keep afloat in the swift current that swirls around the Washington power structure. And these facilities are— money enough for frequent entertaining of the "ins" and a career periodically redeemed from total oblivion by the revival of some celebrated controversy in which they played a conspicuous part.

For everyone else who once counted, the obscuration is remarkably rapid. The instinct of the Washington ins, large and small, social and political, to drop the has-beens is so remarkably sensitive that the process often begins before the actual event. Dinner invitations quickly decline, beginning with those from the Embassies and soon extending to the many hosts and hostesses whose life work is to fill their drawing rooms and tables with headliners.

Perhaps the most disconsolate in the Washington group of the discarded are those who lately wielded vast political power and influence. This was particularly apparent to me one day when I saw approaching on the street a very recent Chairman of a major Senate committee to whom for years Presidents, lesser officials, and "society" had paid assiduous court. He walked slowly, peering into the face of every passer-by with an obvious readiness to be recognized and remembered. None responded.

On another occasion, when I saw him from the Senate Press Gallery, exercising the privilege of a former member to visit the floor, his erstwhile colleagues, many of whom had beseiged him for a place on his prestigious committee, barely observed the amenity of a greeting and a passing word.

The explanation is that there was nothing more of a substantial nature that he could do to advance the ambitions of anyone in Washington. But if at the end of his official tenure he had retired to his home community, he would have remained a leading citizen, showered with attention and newsworthy at times on the national level.

His enforced dropout from the life he had come to savor above any other is a folkway not exclusive to Washington. But there it has reached what I believe must be as perfect a process of automation as cybernetics has ever evolved.

Historians will differ on whether the political philosophy and the economic and military direction of any nation have changed more fundamentally than those of the United States in a comparable period of time—1933–1967. But as an eyewitness of governmental and other public action throughout these years, I formed the opinion that the United States merits the dubious distinction of having discarded its past and its meaning in one of the briefest spans of modern history.

Among these changes are a Federal union almost replaced by a mass Federal democracy controlled by an alliance of politicians and special interest groups; fiscal solvency and confidence in a stable dollar driven from the national and foreign market-place by continuous deficit spending, easy credit, and growing unfavorable balance of payments in the international ledger of the United States; the free-enterprise system shackled by organized labor and a government-managed economy; the Republic transmuted into a welfare state subsidized from Washington; a self-reliant people widely seduced by Federal handouts; spoiled generations—young and old—led to expect the government to provide for all their wants free of any of the requirements of responsible citizenship; a Supreme Court assuming overlordship of the government and all the people to fit the political philosophy of the current majority; and a Congress reflecting the people's apathy toward this assumption and foregoing the use of its Constitutional powers to curb the Court's seizures of jurisdiction in areas for which it has no warrant in the Constitution or the statutes. Yet despite the apparent general acceptance in this country of a judicial autocracy, composed of citizens whose offices were obtained without benefit of suffrage, and whose qualifications the popular branch of Con-

gress—the House of Representative—is barred from appraising, it is also the Federal judiciary that is constantly defied by
the population groups that make a career of violating the law.
Most ironically, the commands of Federal lower-court judges
in the name of the law frequently terminate as mere scraps of
paper.

Winston Churchill, describing the Irish policy of the Tory
Party in a speech at Bradford, March 14, 1914, precisely
forecast the present attitude of certain ethnic groups and organized labor in the United States today:

> They uphold all law except the law they choose to break.
> They are to select from the statute books the laws they will
> obey and the laws they will resist.

With, it can be added, a large degree of toleration of the
law-enforcement arms of government.

Some of the readily discernible results of this spurning of the
basic principles of the American public and private society
have been even graver in portent. The people, with full justification, are more and more disclosing a loss of faith in the
integrity of what government says and does. The rejected disciplines of Federal monetary, taxation, and fiscal policies—piling
spending deficits atop one another in the company of easy
money and credit until the ever-shrinking purchasing power of
the dollar has made its stability suspect at home and abroad—
have created a gap between revenue and expenditure on whose
rim the national economy dangles perilously. For even the
mounting statistics of the Gross National Product are not a
true index of productivity, since a large percentage is accounted for by inflated prices and the ephemeral commodities
of the war being waged.

The growing trend, stimulated by the courts as well, to
equate criminal as well as conscientious civil disobedience with
an absolute Constitutional right, has fostered nihilism and anarchy. Also reflecting this trend, licentiousness, in literature
and personal conduct, has been tolerated by government as a
valid expression of the individual freedom protected by the
Constitution.

In the concept held by self-asserted political liberals of a guaranteed annual income—regardless of the conduct and personal character of its beneficiaries or their will to participate to the full measure of their capacity in the peaceful products of a democratic society—the basic rights have been denied of those who must foot the bills to set the standards by which they are contracted. Typical of this attitude is the total stress of politicians (including those infesting the courts) on the right to a choice of any available privately owned housing that is within the means of the intended purchaser. For in this stress the other and equal basic right of the owner—to dispose of his property as he chooses—is as totally submerged.

Rudyard Kipling's 1919 poem "The Gods of the Market-Place" precisely describes the prospect raised by current political liberalism in the United States:

> . . . we were promised abundance for all/By robbing selected
>   Peter to pay for collective Paul
> But though we had plenty of money there was nothing that
>   money could buy
> And the gods of the Copy-Book Headings said "If you don't
>   work you die."
> Then the gods of the Market tumbled, and their smooth-tongued
>   wizards withdrew
> And the hearts of the meanest were humbled and began to
>   believe it was true
> That all is not gold that glitters, and two and two make four,
> And the Gods of the Copy-Book Headings limped up to explain
>   it once more.

The changes in the area of international policy have been quite as radical, beginning in 1961 with the distortion of the Truman Doctrine that has thrust the nation into the bloody quicksand of a land war on the Asian continent.

When the surrender of Nazi Germany, soon to be followed by the collapse of the Japanese forces, established the United States as the political leader and the military and economic arsenal of the free world, a tragic miscalculation of the postwar prospect by President Franklin D. Roosevelt led directly to the barren harvest of the American military victory. His miscalculation was that, in the rehabilitation of the torn world, the U.S.S.R. would be a dependable partner of the nation that had saved it from the Nazis.

The immediate consequence was the Cold War, long demonstrated to have been the studied design of the Kremlin, which, it was soon apparent, neither the policy of containment nor the no-strings concept of "foreign aid" could halt for very long. Among the other consequences, both direct and indirect, is a United States hated or disrespected by the beneficiaries of its money and power, and without allies—except for a few client nations—who can be depended on to supply the military manpower and equipment to a missionary United States engaged in trying to ram its concept of democracy down the throats of peoples who do not care for it.

The U.S.S.R., which the Nazis might well have conquered without the positive military assistance of the United States in men and matériel, vies with Communist China as this nation's enemy whenever by so being it can deplete our resources of men and treasure. France, twice in this century saved by the United States from becoming a pledged neutral or a German fief, finds no virtue in the assertion of any American interest. Some governments of Latin America, into whose peaceful development this country has poured billions of dollars and to which it has lent its best technical brains, have continued to divert a share of these billions into the pockets of the ruling classes.

A militant Communist state, courting Moscow or Peking according to which is the more suitable to its immediate purpose, grows more and more firmly established within ninety miles of the continental United States, with at least emplacements for the nuclear missiles that the Kennedy Administration backed away from its asserted determination to search for on the spot.

In the United Nations the African and Asian governments, which owe their existence and independence to Washington's policy of putting "anti-colonialism" above the rights of friendly governments and clear interests of national security, mainly serve their own often autocratic systems. They regularly join the U.S.S.R. in making mischief throughout the world and in imposing on the United States the payment of their share of the housekeeping costs of the United Nations. Typical of this debris of American postwar foreign policy was the action of Jordan and Lebanon, both owing their survival to the United States, in supporting President Nasser of Egypt in the 1967 crisis over his blockade of shipping to Israel via the international waterway leading from the Red Sea.

Further contributing to the retreat of the U.N. from both the moral and textual obligations of its creation, the Kennedy Administration actively abetted the military blackmail of President Sukarno of Indonesia against the Dutch in West Irian. With the eager cooperation of U.N. Secretary-General U Thant, the Administration blocked the transport of Dutch military aid to its dependency, on whose shores Sukarno had landed his armed forces, "compelling"—as Foreign Minister Luns of the Netherlands publicly phrased it—the Dutch to sign over West Irian to Indonesia.

Thus the United States government led in assuring the success of Sukarno's clear violation of the U.N. Charter. And when Prime Minister Nehru violated it as clearly by the military seizure of the Portuguese enclaves in India, the United States Ambassador to the U.N., Adlai E. Stevenson, was confined to a verbal protest, on the expedient and inconsistent excuse by Washington that a proposal to censure India would not be carried to the floor of the General Assembly because it had no chance of adoption.

These aspects of United States foreign policy left its government and the U.N. self-confessed as brazen manipulators of the Charter, extolling or violating it according to the identity of the violator.

By the disastrous choice of Vietnam as the battleground on which the national security interest of the U.S. required that the supreme challenge to the advance of militant world communism be made, the Kennedy and Johnson Administrations also imposed the severest of strains on our only strong Pacific ally, Japan. To survive economically, Japan must trade with Communist China. To remain safe from aggression from Communist China, Japan must rely on heavy military protection from

the United States. Nothing could have more greatly complicated these two needs of Japan, and her American alliance,
than an American-mounted war against Asians in Vietnam.

When the Johnson Administration ran out of justifications
for the heavy combat involvement of the United States in the
war in Vietnam, it turned, in the atmosphere of an after-
thought, to the SEATO Treaty. According to the improvisa-
tion of President Johnson and Secretary Rusk, the Treaty fully
and "sacredly" committed the United States to go to war in
face of the North Vietnamese military aggression against the
South, whether or not we were joined by the other signatories
to the same "commitment."

But as the record of the Senate debate on SEATO makes
generally and specifically clear, the Treaty was approved on
the common representation of the spokesman of the Eisenhower Administration and the Senate committee in charge of
the compact that the contemplation of SEATO was a "collective" military action, if undertaken at all; and that it definitely
did not bind the United States to go to war against North
Vietnam.

Yet except for signatories whose sphere of national security
incontrovertibly included Southeast Asia, the other Treaty
partners, notably Pakistan, the United Kingdom, and France,
interpreted the obligation of the Treaty as optional and collective—the clear understanding on which the Senate approved it.

Confronted with this factual refutation of the claim of positive, even if unilateral, "commitment" by the Treaty, the
Administration resorted to another misrepresentation—with respect to the naval incidents in the Gulf of Tonkin. By the use of
clever and misleading rhetoric in drafting the resolution by
which the Senate approved the President's use of "all necessary
force" to retaliate for a North Vietnamese "aggression" against
the Navy, which full and much later reports put severely in
question, the Administration got another item of spurious authority for expanding the military action in Vietnam into a
major United States war.

The fundamental change came about more slowly in the area
of domestic policy. The first New Deal of Franklin D. Roosevelt encompassed vital reforms of ancient social and economic

abuses, but always with the salvage of the capitalist system as its underlying objective. And though the Second New Deal laid the foundations of what has largely become the welfare state, the construction was long halted by the combination of our involvement in the Second World War and the normal reaction of postwar periods—which is to search for paths by which to return to the old and less troubled social-economic order.

After successfully capitalizing on this reaction by electing a Republican Congress in 1946, the leaders of that party sacrificed their opportunity to regain control of the Executive Branch in 1948 by one of the most inept Presidential campaigns on record. But the breathing spell was resumed with the election in 1952 of Eisenhower, which was made possible by the unpopularity of the Korean War and the even more unpopular military stalemate in a nation accustomed to settling for nothing short of victory.

For the succeeding eight years the progress toward the welfare state was held to a snail's pace, first, by the conservative-liberal split in the Democratic Congresses that enabled President Eisenhower to regulate the pace by using his power of veto; and second, by the war-weariness of the American people that assured the support of the measures he employed to keep the nation at peace with all other nations.

By these measures, the wisdom of which, in his retirement, he seems to have forgotten, he set sharp bounds on the military assistance to United Nations interventions in the Congo and our own in Vietnam, the most important result of which was full service to the fundamental maxim against committing American armed forces to the virtually unilateral role of waging a ground war on the Asian continent. And by successfully limiting the application of the Truman Doctrine to the stitch-in-time landing of United States armed forces in Lebanon, Eisenhower held in check the other Arab nations and the U.S.S.R. in their resolve to destroy the new State of Israel.

It was the reversal of this limited application, first by President Kennedy and then by President Johnson, that plunged the United States into the disastrous ground war in Southeast Asia in an area outside a sound perimeter of national security. Only to be soon confronted with the painful choice of applying the same fallacious reasoning to the similar challenge of Nasser in the Gulf of Aqaba, or repudiating the solemn commitment to the defense of Israel's security that both President Truman and the Republican Presidential nominee, Thomas E. Dewey, made when actively championing the partition of Palestine in 1948, and Presidents Eisenhower, Kennedy, and Johnson later reiterated.

In giving full play and military interpretation in Vietnam to the gaudy rhetoric of the Truman Doctrine (that the United States was committed to effective assistance "to any nation or people threatened by external aggression or internal subversion"), President Kennedy at the same time was building on the foundations of the welfare state that were laid in the Roosevelt and Truman Administrations. The American people, beguiled by Federal subsidies for groups and individuals, were assured that the economy was fully able to sustain both policies simultaneously.

But it was not until President Johnson was overwhelmingly elected in 1964, on repeated pledges to the people against an all-American ground war involvement on the Asian continent, that Congress went along with the dual program. The legislative superstructure of the welfare state that Kennedy could not obtain from Congress began to be actively and grandiosely processed. And the consequence is an ever-rising spread between the revenues and costs of government, with each official estimate of both proving as false or at least as fanciful as a fake gold-mine prospectus.

The Congressional elections of 1966 reflected a certain public disillusion with the soundness of this economic proposition and with the policy of limiting the United States offensive in Vietnam on the argument that otherwise it might swell to global proportions. For the unsoundness of the economic proposition was steadily being demonstrated by mounting deficits and taxes. And the argument—that military policy must avoid action that might bring Chinese or Soviet intervention—in justification for limiting the war emphasized the fundamental error of the selection of Vietnam as the area in which the war would be fought.

But the setback to the Administration's power over Congress

that was wrought by the 1966 elections was recognized by practical politicians in both major parties as not necessarily foreshadowing Democratic defeat in the Presidential election of 1968. Because they know, and history gives them knowledge, that if the end of the Vietnam war is not in sight in November, 1968, or if the situation permits an initiation of the recall of American military units there, the disposition of the United States electorate will be to maintain the party in power. And the practical politics reflected by Johnson's 1964 pledges against greater military involvement in Southeast Asia, though he was fully aware from reports to a Cabinet meeting in November, 1963, that the prospect was precisely to the contrary, will not only be at the disposal of his Democratic heir in the campaign of 1968 but will certainly be as unconscionably employed.

In the transformation of the American system toward a mass democracy and a neosocialist welfare state, new interpretations, especially of the Fourteenth Amendment, by the Supreme Court have made the largest and most essential contributions to these objectives. The decisions, often by a close division among the Justices, that are landmarks in the transformation began in 1954. In the so-called "public schools" decision, the Court assumed the function (which the Constitution delegates to the Executive and Legislative branches) of making national public policy whenever, in the judgment of the Court, the public interest requires new policies and the other two Federal branches have not supplied them.

The fact that the Court itself, some years before, had found no Constitutional bar to compulsory racial segregation of public school pupils, provided the "separate" facilities were "equal," troubled the Justices no more than did the total absence of explicit authority in the statutes for the basis on which it overruled its own precedent.

Chief Justice Warren induced a unanimous finding, on wholly sociological doctrines, that "separate" could never be "equal" as a psychological fact: hence compulsory school segregation by the states wrought an inequality among Negro pupils that made them "second-class citizens" and therefore was a state action forbidden by the Fourteenth Amendment.

On the basic rationale of this decision the Court, without explicit statutory or Constitutional sanction, progressed to the formulation of new public policies, among them:

Both State and Federal districts in which legislators are chosen—and now voting districts that select members of local boards—must be reapportioned on the principle of "one man, one vote." But if a popular majority by referendum—as in Colorado and Michigan—registers a preference for shaping election districts for one branch of the state legislature on other than a population basis, the principle of "one man, one vote" does not apply. Because in that case its application would effect the unconstitutional result of a majority depriving a minority of the protection of the principle!

In a state whose legislature has approved a compulsory open-housing law, the voters who elected it cannot repeal the law by making it unconstitutional in a popular referendum, however large the majority may be. The voters of California had done this by ratifying an amendment to the State Constitution forbidding such a law. This, the Court held, violates the Fourteenth Amendment, which enforces "neutrality" on the states in the particular circumstances.

Only another legislature can repeal an act in this category by its predecessor; and in this instance the principle of "one man, one vote" must yield to the principle of "one legislator, one vote." (This bizarre reasoning prevailed by a 5-to-4 Court division.)

In a line of decisions the Court has seriously impeded the police in bringing proved and confessed criminals to punishment, the sequel being a prodigious rise in the national crime rate and in the hazard of moving about on city streets.

In a series of rulings on so-called civil rights, the Court set aside convictions of persons for violating laws that were valid at the time of the infraction; reduced the scope of the laws against trespass of both public and private property; and in approving Civil Rights Acts enacted in the name of anti-discrimination, upheld the discrimination in those measures that is inherent in legalizing segregation in public accommodation facilities with a small number of units and making it illegal in facilities with a greater number.

In this framework the Court majority also equated a parking plaza owned by a supermarket with a public street, to legalize a union "demonstration" in the plaza. That decision impelled Justice Black to comment that he was probably mistaken in believing that any private property rights still existed in the United States.

By taking over unilateral power to fix or alter public policies, by thereby making plain to Congress and the state legislatures what social and political statutes it would approve and what it would invalidate, the Supreme Court, headed by Chief Justice Warren, has become the prime force in the transformation of the American system from a Federal union to a mass democracy, from the careful decentralization of power in the Constitution to concentration in Washington, and from a tripartite Federal government to a government in which the Court is the managing director.

These are among my personal assessments of the consequences of the revolutionary political and social new American revolution. And from these consequences I have contracted a visceral fear. It is that the tenure of the United States as the first power in the world may be one of the briefest in history.

APPENDIX A

THE WHITE HOUSE

WASHINGTON

September —, 1946

My dear Mr. President:

In the course of complying with your directive to prepare a summary of American relations with the Soviet Union, I have consulted the Secretary of State, the Secretary of War, the Attorney General, the Secretary of the Navy, Fleet Admiral Leahy, the Joint Chiefs of Staff, Ambassador Pauley, the Director of Central Intelligence, and other persons who have special knowledge in this field. These gentlemen have prepared careful estimates of current and future Soviet policies, extensive reports on recent Soviet activities affecting the security of the United States, and recommendations concerning American policy with respect to the Soviet Union.

The reports are valuable, not only because of the care and judgment exercised in their preparation, but because of the broad and comprehensive scope of the combined studies. I believe that the simultaneous definition by so many government officials of the problem with which we are confronted is in itself a forward step toward its solution.

There is remarkable agreement among the officials with whom I have talked and whose reports I have studied concerning the need for a review of our relations with the Soviet Union and diligent effort to improve those relations. The gravity with which the problem of Soviet relations is viewed is, in itself, an encouraging sign that every effort will be made to solve it.

Factual statements, studies and opinions have been assembled and summarized and there is submitted herewith the report entitled, "American Relations with the Soviet Union."

Very respectfully,

CLARK M. CLIFFORD
Special Counsel to the President

THE PRESIDENT
THE WHITE HOUSE

[419]

TOP SECRET

AMERICAN RELATIONS WITH THE SOVIET UNION

A REPORT TO THE PRESIDENT BY THE
SPECIAL COUNCIL TO THE PRESIDENT
SEPTEMBER —, 1946

OUTLINE OF THE REPORT

INTRODUCTION

a. Our ability to resolve the present conflict between Soviet and American foreign policies may determine whether there is to be a permanent peace or a third World War.

b. U.S. policy toward the U.S.S.R. will be greatly affected by the extent of our knowledge of Soviet policies and activities. A forecast of Soviet future policy towards this country can be based on the manner in which the U.S.S.R. has maintained her agreements with this country, and on recent Soviet activities which vitally affect the security of the United States.

I: SOVIET FOREIGN POLICY

a. Soviet leaders believe that a conflict is inevitable between the U.S.S.R. and capitalist states, and their duty is to prepare the Soviet Union for this conflict.

b. The aim of current Soviet policy is to prepare for the ultimate conflict by increasing Soviet power as rapidly as possible and by weakening all nations who may be considered hostile.

c. Soviet activities throughout the world, with respect both to individual states and to international organizations, are in support of this policy of increasing the relative power of the Soviet Union at the expense of her potential enemies.

II: SOVIET—AMERICAN AGREEMENTS, 1942–1946

a. By means of written agreements reached at international conferences, the United States Government has sought to lessen the differences between this country and the U.S.S.R. which have resulted from the conflicting foreign policies of the two nations.

b. Since obtaining Soviet adherence to the principles of the Atlantic Charter in the United Nations Declaration, signed by the Soviet Union on January 1, 1942, the United States has attempted to reach understandings with the Soviet Union regarding peace settlements in Europe and the Far East, and regarding an international organization to preserve the peace.

c. Major agreements were made with Generalissimo Stalin by President Roosevelt at Teheran and Yalta and by President Truman at Berlin. Secretaries of State Hull and Byrnes have also conferred with Soviet Foreign Commissar Molotov, and various military and diplomatic representatives of the United States have met in conference with Soviet officials in Washington, Moscow and other European cities.

III: Violations of Soviet Agreements with the United States

a. Soviet-American agreements have been adhered to, "interpreted," or violated as Soviet officials from time to time have considered it to be in the best interests of the Soviet Union in accordance with Soviet policy of increasing their own power at the expense of other nations.

b. A number of specific violations are described in detail. The principle violations concern Germany, Austria, the Balkan countries, Iran, Korea and Lend-Lease agreements.

IV: Conflicting Views on Reparations

a. A major issue now in dispute between the U.S.S.R. and the United States is reparations; the divergent views on this issue illustrate the basic conflict in the policies and aims of the two nations.

b. The major agreements concerning reparations were reached at the Berlin Conference in July 1945 and by the Allied Control Council in March 1946; there have been continuous Soviet violations of these agreements since they were made.

c. Recent statements by Molotov in Paris reveal that the Soviet Union has abandoned the basic policy on reparations to which it had previously given nominal adherence and has embarked on a course of unilateral action.

V: SOVIET ACTIVITIES AFFECTING AMERICAN SECURITY

a. The U.S.S.R. is improving its military position with respect to the United States in such ways, for example, as construction of air bases in northeastern Siberia from which the United States can be attacked, and construction of large numbers of submarines for commerce raiding.

b. The U.S.S.R. is seeking wherever possible to weaken the military position and the influence of the United States abroad, as, for example, in China.

c. The U.S.S.R. is actively directing subversive movements and espionage within the United States.

VI: UNITED STATES POLICY TOWARD THE SOVIET UNION

a. The primary objective of United States policy is to convince Soviet leaders that it is in the Soviet interest to participate in a system of world cooperation.

b. Until Soviet leaders abandon their aggressive policies described in Chapter I, the United States must assume that the U.S.S.R. may at any time embark on a course of expansion effected by open warfare and therefore must maintain sufficient military strength to restrain the Soviet Union.

c. The United States should seek, by cultural, intellectual, and economic interchange, to demonstrate to the Soviet Union that we have no aggressive intentions and that peaceable coexistence of Capitalism and Communism is possible.

INTRODUCTION

The gravest problem facing the United States today is that of American relations with the Soviet Union. The solution of that problem may determine whether or not there will be a third World War. Soviet leaders appear to be conducting their nation on a course of aggrandizement designed to lead to eventual world domination by the U.S.S.R. Their goal, and their policies designed to reach it, are in direct conflict with American ideals, and the United States has not yet been able to persuade Stalin and his associates that world peace and prosperity lie not in the direction in which the Soviet Union is moving but in the opposite direction of international cooperation and friendship.

Representatives of the United States have been conferring, bargaining and making agreements with the Soviet leaders, ever since Cordell Hull flew to Moscow in October 1943, in an effort to lay the foundations for a lasting peace settlement in Europe and the Far East through collective agreements and concerted action. The Secretary of State is now in Paris at another of a long series of conferences in which the United States and the Soviet Union each strives for peace settlements to its liking. And yet peace seems far away and American disillusionment over the achievements of peace conferences increases as the Soviet Government continues to break the agreements which were made at Teheran, Yalta and Berlin, or "interprets" those agreements to suit its own purposes.

Our fear of Germany and Japan is gone, but our suspicion of the Soviet Union—and suspicion is the first step to fear—is growing. Suspicious misunderstanding of the Soviet Union must be replaced by an accurate knowledge of the motives and methods of the Soviet Government. Only through such knowledge will we be able to appraise and forecast the military and political moves of the Kremlin; without that knowledge we shall be at the mercy of rumors and half-truths. Sudden moves, or unexpected or misunderstood moves, by the Soviet Union might, if we do not understand the methods of the Kremlin, lead us into a showdown of force for which we would probably be unprepared, or might lead us into blind or hasty diplomatic retreat. Only through an accurate understanding of the characteristics of the one nation which can endanger the United States will our government be able to make and carry out policies which will reestablish order in Europe and Asia and protect this nation at all times.

[425]

In an effort to summarize the information upon which a sound American policy toward the Soviet Union can be based, the following Chapters will present an analysis of Soviet foreign policy, a description of the agreements made by the U.S.S.R. and the United States during the war, an account of the manner in which the Soviet Union has observed or violated those agreements, and a discussion of current Soviet activities affecting the security of the United States. The concluding Chapter describes our present policy toward the Soviet Union and contains recommendations concerning that policy.

I

SOVIET FOREIGN POLICY

The fundamental tenet of the communist philosophy embraced by Soviet leaders is that the peaceful coexistence of communist and capitalist nations is impossible. The defenders of the communist faith, as the present Soviet rulers regard themselves, assume that conflict between the Soviet Union and the leading capitalist powers of the western world is inevitable and the party leaders believe that it is their duty to prepare the Soviet Union for the inevitable conflict which their doctrine predicts. Their basic policies, domestic and foreign, are designed to strengthen the Soviet Union and to insure its victory in the predicted coming struggle between Communism and Capitalism.

Generalissimo Stalin and his associates are preparing for the clash by many means, all of them designed to increase the power of the Soviet Union. They are assuring its internal stability through the isolation of its citizens from foreign influences and by maintaining strict police controls. They are supporting armed forces stronger than those of any potential combination of foreign powers and they are developing as rapidly as possible a powerful and self-sufficient economy. They are seizing every opportunity to expand the area, directly or indirectly, under Soviet control in order to provide additional protection for the vital areas of the Soviet Union. The Kremlin seeks to prevent the formation of any combination of foreign powers possibly hostile to the Soviet Union by insisting in Soviet participation, with veto power, in any international organization affecting Soviet interest, and by discouraging through intimidation or otherwise the formation of regional blocs or other international associations which do not include the U.S.S.R. Every opportunity to foment antagonisms among foreign powers is exploited, and the unity and strength of other nations is undermined by discrediting their leadership, stirring up domestic discord, and inciting colonial unrest.

The singleness of purpose and the determination with which Soviet policy is pursued can be explained only in terms of its origin. It is based, not upon the interests and aspirations of the Russian people, but upon the prejudices, calculations and ambitions of the inner-directorate of the Communist Party in the Soviet Union. This directorate, the politburo, controls the government, the police and the armed forces with an iron hand. Its nucleus is a group of professional revolutionaries who have survived revolutions, purges and party-feuds for almost thirty years. This small group of able men, headed by Generalissimo Stalin, possesses great practical shrewdness and a remarkable ability for long-range forethought, but it is isolated within the Kremlin, is largely ignorant of the outside world, and is blinded by its adherence to Marxist dogma. Protective isolation, which has enabled Stalin and his associates to survive the attacks of jealous rivals, and allegiance to the doctrine which has been their inspiration, insure that the myopic approach to world affairs of the Politburo is not affected by conventional diplomacy, good-will gestures or acts of appeasement.

It is perhaps the greatest paradox of the present day that the leaders of a nation, now stronger than it has ever been before, should embark on so aggressive a course because their nation is "weak." And yet Stalin and his cohorts proclaim that "monopoly capitalism" threatens the world with war and that Russia must strengthen her defenses against the danger of foreign attacks. The U.S.S.R., according to Kremlin propaganda, is imperilled so long as it remains within a "capitalistic encirclement." This idea is absurd when adopted by so vast a country with such great natural wealth, a population of almost 200 million and no powerful or aggressive neighbors. But the process of injecting this propaganda into the minds of the Soviet people goes on with increasing intensity.

The concept of danger from the outside is deeply rooted in the Russian people's haunting sense of insecurity inherited from their past. It is maintained by their present leaders as a justification for the oppressive nature of the Soviet police state. The thesis, that the capitalist world is conspiring to attack the Soviet Union, is not based on any objective analysis of the situation beyond Russia's borders. It has little to do, indeed, with conditions outside the Soviet Union, and it has arisen mainly from basic inner-Russian necessities which existed before the second World War and which exist today.

Mr. George Kennan, recently Chargé d'Affaires of the U.S. Embassy in Moscow, analyzed for the State Department the reasons why the Soviet Union adopted Marxist Communism as a political faith. Kennan wrote in February 1946:

"At the bottom of the Kremlin's neurotic view of world affairs is a traditional and instinctive Russian sense of insecurity. Originally, this was the insecurity of a peaceful agricultural people trying to live on a vast exposed plain in the neighborhood of fierce nomadic peoples. To this was added, as Russia came into contact with an economically advanced west, the fear of more competent, more powerful, more highly organized societies in that area. But this latter type of insecurity was one which afflicted Russian rulers rather than the Russian people; for Russian rulers have invariably sensed that their rule was relatively archaic in form, fragile and artificial in its psychological foundation, unable to stand comparison or contact with political systems of western countries. For this reason they have always feared foreign penetration, feared direct contact between the western world and their own, feared what would happen if Russians learned the truth about the world without or if foreigners learned the truth about the world within. And they have learned to seek security only in patient but deadly struggle for total destruction of rival power, never in compacts and compromises with it.

"It was no coincidence that Marxism, which had smouldered ineffectively for half a century in Western Europe, caught hold and blazed for the first time in Russia. Only in this land which had never known a friendly neighbor or indeed any tolerant equilibrium of separate powers, either internal or international, could a doctrine thrive which viewed economic conflicts of society as insoluble by peaceful means. After establishment of the Bolshevist regime, Marxist dogma, rendered even more truculent and intolerant by Lenin's interpretation, became a perfect vehicle for the sense of insecurity with which Bolsheviks, even more than previous Russian rulers, were afflicted. In this dogma, with its basic altruism of purpose, they found justification for their instinctive fear of the outside world, for the dictatorship without which they did not know how to rule, for cruelties they did not dare not to inflict, for sacrifices they felt bound to demand. In the name of Marxism they sacrificed every single ethical value in their methods and tactics. Today they cannot dispense with it. It is the fig leaf of their moral and intellectual respectability. Without it they would stand before history, at best, as only the last of that long succession of cruel and wasteful Russian rulers who have relentlessly forced the country on to ever new heights of military power in order to guarantee external security to their internally weak regimes. This is why Soviet

purposes must always be solemnly clothed in trappings of
Marxism, and why no one should underrate the importance of
dogma in Soviet affairs. Thus Soviet leaders are driven by
necessities of their own past and present position to put forward a dogma which regards the outside world as evil, hostile
and menacing. . . . This thesis provides justification for that
increase of military and police power of Russian state, for
that isolation of Russian population from the outside world,
and for that fluid and constant pressure to extend limits of
Russian police power which are together the natural and
instinctive urges of Russian rulers. Basically this is only the
steady advance of uneasy Russian nationalism, a centuries-old
movement in which conceptions of offense and defense are
inextricably confused. But in a new guise of international
Marxism, with its honeyed promises to a desperate and war
torn outside world, it is more dangerous and insidious than
ever before."

Soviet leaders have taken no pains to conceal the main features
of Soviet foreign policy, although many of its subtle manifestations
and those aspects of it most objectionable to other nations have
been obscured or camouflaged. Recent speeches of Stalin and other
Soviet leaders show much less emphasis on Big Three unity and
less reliance on the United Nations as a prop of Soviet security and
guarantee of international peace. In Moscow on February 9, 1946,
in his most revealing statement since the end of the war in Europe,
Stalin made the point that capitalism was the cause of wars, including World War II. Stalin stated that the war "arose in reality as
the inevitable result of the development of the world economic and
political forces on the basis of monopoly capitalism." Stalin in
broad political-economic terms described the Soviet Union's past
and future war planning and neglected virtually every aspect of the
civilian economy. Such public emphasis on an economy adapted to
the waging of war can only have been made for definite political
purposes, both at home and abroad. It points toward a Soviet
future in which a large adequately armed force will be maintained
and strengthened as rapidly as the development of Soviet heavy
industry permits.

The Soviet Government, in developing the theme of "encirclement," maintains continuous propaganda for domestic consumption regarding the dangerously aggressive intentions of American

"atom diplomacy" and British imperialism, designed to arouse in the Soviet people fear and suspicion of all capitalistic nations.

Despite the fact that the Soviet Government believes in the inevitability of a conflict with the capitalist world and prepares for that conflict by building up its own strength and undermining that of other nations, its leaders want to postpone the conflict for many years. The western powers are still too strong, the U.S.S.R. is still too weak. Soviet officials must therefore not provoke, by their policies of expansion and aggression, too strong a reaction by other powers.

The Kremlin acknowledges no limit to the eventual power of the Soviet Union, but it is practical enough to be concerned with the actual position of the U.S.S.R. today. In any matter deemed essential to the security of the Soviet Union, Soviet leaders will prove adamant in their claims and demands. In other matters they will prove grasping and opportunistic, but flexible in proportion to the degree and nature of the resistance encountered.

Recognition of the need to postpone the "inevitable" conflict is in no sense a betrayal of the Communist faith. Marx and Lenin encouraged compromise and collaboration with non-communists for the accomplishment of ultimate communistic purposes. The U.S.S.R. has followed such a course in the past. In 1939 the Kremlin signed a non-aggression pact with Germany and in 1941 a neutrality pact with Japan. Soviet leaders will continue to collaborate whenever it seems expedient, for time is needed to build up Soviet strength and weaken the opposition. Time is on the side of the Soviet Union, since population growth and economic development will, in the Soviet view, bring an increase in its relative strength.

The key to an understanding of current Soviet foreign policy, in summary, is the realization that Soviet leaders adhere to the Marxian theory of ultimate destruction of capitalist states by communist states, while at the same time they strive to postpone the inevitable conflict in order to strengthen and prepare the Soviet Union for its clash with the western democracies.

Soviet activities throughout the world, with respect both to individual states and to international organizations, are in support to the basic Soviet foreign policy. The Soviet Union has consistently opposed Anglo-American efforts to expedite world peace settlements because the longer peace settlements are postponed the longer Red Army troops can "legally" remain in "enemy" countries. Excessively large military forces are being maintained in satellite nations, which the U.S.S.R. is striving to bring under complete control and to make economically dependent upon her. To this end, the Soviets are establishing joint-control enterprises, demanding exorbitant reparations from former enemies, evacuating large quantities of industrial machinery and seizing shipping and industrial properties. To strengthen Soviet economy at the expense of her neighbors, the U.S.S.R. is retaining, either in Russia or in Soviet-occupied areas, large numbers of Germans and Japanese who are being employed in Soviet industry. Beyond the borders now under her control, the Soviet Union is striving to penetrate strategic areas, and everywhere agents of the Soviet government work to weaken the governments of other nations and to achieve their ultimate isolation and destruction.

The Soviet Union regards control of Europe east of the general line from Stettin to Trieste as essential to its present security. It will tolerate no rival influence in that region and it will insist on the maintenance there of "friendly" governments, that is, governments willing to accept Soviet domination. At present, in Yugoslavia, Albania and Czechoslovakia there are governments genuinely "sympathetic" to the Soviet Union. The U.S.S.R. has displayed moderation toward Finland for a variety of reasons connected with the peculiar national character and geographic situation of the Finns. In these countries the Soviet Union seeks to insure its continued predominance by the creation of strong bonds of economic and military collaboration, but it does not have to resort to open coercion.

The elected government of Hungary is willing to be "friendly" but the Soviet Union has apparently remained unconvinced of its reliability in view of the attitude of the Hungarian people. Coercion has therefore been applied in Hungary, as in Poland, Rumania and Bulgaria, to insure effective Soviet political control.

The governments now installed in these four countries are notoriously unrepresentative, but the Soviet Union is determined to maintain them by as much force as necessary inasmuch as no truly representative government would be reliable, from the Soviet point of view. In deference to western views, these countries may be allowed to hold elections and some changes in the composition of these governments permitted, but only after violence, intimidation, purges and fraud have insured the election of a Soviet-approved slate.

Soviet policy in Austria is similar to that in Hungary. Having accepted an elected Austrian government and being unable to reconstruct it at will due to the presence of British, French and American occupation armies, the Soviet Union is seeking by means of deportations and property seizures in its own zone and by demands for similar actions in other zones, to gain economic control of Austria and to lay the foundation for Soviet political control when the other occupation forces are withdrawn.

In Germany, the Soviet Union has recently made herself the "champion" of German unification in opposition to what her propagandists have labelled the "imperialistic" schemes of Great Britain, France and the United States. The Kremlin apparently believes that a German administration strongly centralized in Berlin might eventually be more susceptible than any other to Soviet pressure and also the most convenient means of extending Soviet influence throughout Germany. Moscow recognizes, however, that if Germany were to be unified today, the Communists would not be able to command a majority of the population and might not be able to seize power. Therefore, Moscow opposes the establishment of any central German administration at this time, except on terms which would give Moscow the clear right to repudiate it again at any time if it proved unamenable to Soviet purposes.

The Soviet Government hoped to gain political control of France through the victory of the French Communist Party in French national elections in June, but the defeat of the Soviet protegees led Moscow to sacrifice its fading hope of winning France to the livelier prospect of gaining Germany. The French Communists remain a strong political factor nevertheless, and exercise disproportionate influence through their control of organized labor. That influence will be used to shape French policy in the manner most suitable for Soviet purposes, and to prepare for a renewal of the Soviet attempt to gain control of France by political means.

In Italy the Communist Party is also seeking major influence by political means. For the time being, the Italian Communist Party is embarrassed by the dilemma in which it has been placed by the Trieste issue and its influence was unexpectedly weak in recent elections. Anti-Soviet feeling, aroused by Soviet support of Yugoslav claims to Trieste, has greatly reduced the influence of the Italian Communists, and Soviet efforts to win a dominant role in Italian affairs have received a sharp set-back.

As for Spain, the Soviet Union misses no opportunity to raise the question of Franco as a means of embarrassing and dividing the Western Powers. Any change in Spain might afford a chance for

Communist penetration and the Communist underground in Spain is now being organized and directed by clandestine radio from the U.S.S.R.

The Soviet Union's main concern regarding the other nations of western Europe is to prevent the formation of a Western Bloc. It will also, of course, encourage the growth of local Communist parties.

The Near East is an area of great strategic interest to the Soviet Union because of the shift of Soviet industry to southeastern Russia, within range of air attack from much of the Near East, and because of the resources of the area. The Soviet Union is interested in obtaining the withdrawal of British troops from Greece and the establishment of a "friendly" government there. It hopes to make Turkey a puppet state which could serve as a spring-board for the domination of the eastern Mediterranean. It is trying by diplomatic means to establish itself in the Dodecanese and Tripolitania and it already has a foothold in the Mediterranean through its close alliances with Albania and Yugoslavia.

The U.S.S.R. is attempting to form along its Middle Eastern frontier a protective zone of politically subordinate states incapable of hostile action against it and it is seeking, at the same time, to acquire for its own use in those states ports and waterways, pipe-lines and oil-fields. It wishes to ensure continued indirect control of Azerbaijan and northern Iran, and the withdrawal, or reduction, of British military strength and influence in the Arab states. The U.S.S.R. is playing both sides of the Jewish situation by encouraging and abetting the emigration of Jews from Europe into Palestine, by denouncing British and American Jewish policies, and by inflaming the Arabs against these policies. The long-range Soviet aim is the economic, military and political domination of the entire Middle East.

The basic Soviet objective in China, Korea and Japan is to ensure that these countries remain internally divided and weak until such time as the U.S.S.R. is in a position to exert greater influence there than any other country. The Chinese Communist Party is supported by the U.S.S.R. In Korea the Soviets have shown that they will consent to the unification of the country only if assured of a "friendly" government. Moscow has been extremely critical of the American Administration of Japan which has afforded the U.S.S.R. no opportunity to establish the influence it desires.

The Soviets in the remaining areas of the world will seek to undermine the unity and strength of national states, to foment colonial unrest, to stir up diversionary antagonisms between States, and to disrupt any system of international cooperation from which the U.S.S.R. is excluded. Because of their position in world affairs, the United States and Great Britain will be the primary targets of these Soviet activities. In addition to domestic agitation, the U.S.S.R. will try to distract and weaken the United States and Great Britain by attacking their interests in areas of special concern to them, such as South America, India, Africa and the Pacific.

Soviet policy with respect to the United Nations, as with individual nations, is designed to increase the position and prestige of the U.S.S.R. at the expense of other states. It now appears that the Soviet Union joined the United Nations as a matter of expedience and not because of any devotion to abstract principles of peace. The United Nations, to Soviet leaders, is another international arena in which they can propagandize and compete for a dominant position. The Soviet Union will continue to make every effort to impose its will on the organization so that United Nations decisions will, insofar as possible, implement Soviet policy. Soviet tactics will include unrestricted use of the veto power, use of member satellite states to support the Soviet viewpoint and pressure for admission of other satellite states in order to increase the Soviet "bloc."

The Soviet Union is evidently reluctant to withdraw from the United Nations so long as it can carry with it only a small fraction of the other members, for this would leave the majority of the other nations conveniently organized against it. However, if the Soviet leaders decide that membership in the United Nations is working too much to their disadvantage, and that their hand is being called on too many issues, they may decide to withdraw anyway. If they make this decision, they can be expected to use the entire Soviet propaganda machine and all the agencies of Soviet diplomacy to discredit the United Nations.

The Soviet Government is reluctant to commit itself to membership in other international organizations unless it can foresee opportunities to make use of them. Moscow has not ratified the Bretton Woods agreement establishing the International Monetary Fund and the International Bank for Reconstruction and Development, the United Nations Food and Agricultural Organization, the United Nations Educational Scientific and Cultural Organization,

the International Civil Aviation Organization, the European Coal
Organization or the Emergency Economic Committee for
Europe.

The Soviet Union has, however, been active in various nongov-
ernmental international organizations where it is in a good position
to dominate proceedings. Soviet trade unions occupy a leading
place in the World Federation of Trade Unions, and Soviet representatives took an active role in forming such groups as the International Democratic Federation of Women, the World Federation
of Democratic Youth and the International Cooperative Alliance.

II

SOVIET-AMERICAN AGREEMENTS, 1942–1946

The great differences between American and Soviet foreign policies which are now so apparent were partially concealed during the war by a danger common to both nations—Nazi Germany. Anticipating, however, that differences would arise when hostilities ended, and anxious to secure Soviet participation in a system of collective security, the United States Government sought throughout the war to reach understandings with the Soviet Union regarding peace settlements and an international organization to preserve the peace.

At a series of conferences arranged principally by President Roosevelt, from January 1942 to February 1945, representatives of the United States and the Soviet Union entered into written agreements which, had they been adhered to, would have avoided practically all of the causes of disagreement and mistrust now existing between the two countries.

On New Year's Day 1942 at the White House, the Soviet Ambassador on behalf of the Soviet Union signed the Declaration of the United Nations and thereby subscribed to the principles of the Atlantic Charter, which Prime Minister Churchill and President Roosevelt had formulated in August 1941. By this act, the Soviet Union pledged that it sought no territorial aggrandizement; desired no territorial changes that did not accord with the freely expressed wishes of the people concerned; respected the right of all peoples to choose the form of government under which they will live; and desired to bring about the fullest collaboration between all nations in the economic field with the object of securing improved labor standards, economic advancement and social security.

Faced with the urgent necessity of stopping the German onslaught, the United States and the U.S.S.R. did not undertake discussions on postwar settlements for some time after the signing of the United Nations Declaration. Soviet Foreign Commissar Molotov was President Roosevelt's guest at the White House in June 1942, but their conversations were concerned primarily with speeding up shipments of American supplies to the Soviet Union and the necessity for a "second front" in western Europe in 1942. President Roosevelt, a few months later, urged Generalissimo Stalin to meet with Prime Minister Churchill and him at Casablanca in North Africa in December 1942 or January 1943 but Stalin refused to leave the Soviet Union and President Roosevelt and Churchill would not go to Moscow to see him.

It was not until October 1943 when Secretary of State Cordell Hull and British Foreign Minister Anthony Eden traveled to Moscow that the principal allied powers began a serious and detailed discussion of the peace settlements and it was only at the insistence of Hull, strongly supported by frequent radio messages from President Roosevelt, that a statement on the principles of peace was adopted by the conference at that time. Drafted by the U.S. Department of State, and reluctantly accepted by the U.S.S.R., the Declaration on General Security was signed on October 30, 1943, by Molotov, Eden, Hull and the Chinese Ambassador to the U.S.S.R., on behalf of the Chinese Government.

The Declaration set forth, among other items, that the four signatory nations recognized "the necessity of establishing at the earliest practicable date a general international organization, based on the principle of the sovereign equality of all peace-loving states, and open to membership by all such states, large and small, for the maintenance of international peace and security." They also pledged that "after the termination of hostilities they would not employ their military forces within the territories of other states except for the purposes envisaged in this declaration and after joint consultation."

One month after the Moscow Conference of Foreign Secretaries had ended, President Roosevelt met Stalin for the first time, in company with Churchill, at Teheran. President Roosevelt and Churchill arrived at Teheran fresh from a meeting with Generalissimo Chiang Kai-shek at Cairo where the Sino-Anglo-American war against Japan was discussed. The Soviet Union was not at war with Japan and hence no Soviet representative attended the Cairo Conference, which dealt principally with a plan for coordinated air, sea and ground campaigns in Southeast Asia, China, and the mid-Pacific.

The principal discussions in Teheran centered around a strategy for the 1944 campaign in Europe. Political discussions, which had occupied the Foreign Secretaries in Moscow, were replaced by conferences on the Anglo-American and Soviet campaigns against Germany. Although President Roosevelt did discuss with Stalin in a very general manner his views on an international organization, he was not prepared to go into details and there was no attempt on his part to obtain a written agreement from Stalin on political matters. The major achievement of the Teheran Conference was the military agreement reached by the three heads of government and their military staffs. The British and the Americans agreed that they would launch an invasion of northwestern France in May 1944, and support it with a coordinated invasion in southern France. In return, Stalin stated that the Red Army would launch its spring offensive in conjunction with the western invasions.

The military agreement was, of course, "secret" but two other "agreements" were published at the conclusion of the Teheran Conference. "The Declaration of the Three Powers," dated December 1, 1943, expressed the determination that the three nations would work together "in war and in the peace that will follow." "We shall seek," the Declaration reads, "the cooperation and active participation of all nations, large and small, whose peoples in heart and mind are dedicated, as are our own peoples, to the elimination of tyranny and slavery, oppression and intolerance."

A second Declaration, also dated December 1, 1943 concerned Iran. Extensive promises of economic support after the war comprise most of the document, but the key sentence occurs at the end. "The Governments of the United States, the U.S.S.R., and the United Kingdom," wrote President Roosevelt, Stalin and Churchill, "are at one with the Government of Iran in their desire for the maintenance of the independence, sovereignty and territorial integrity of Iran."

Greatly encouraged by the success of Cordell Hull in Moscow in apparently winning Soviet support for collective security, President Roosevelt rapidly continued making plans in early 1944 for a post-war international organization. At the same time, however, relations with the Soviet Union were growing strained on a number of subjects connected with European politics. A European Advisory Council, composed of representatives of the U.S.S.R., Great Britain and the U.S., ran into apparently insoluble difficulties over Italy's status and the Soviet Union's plans for Poland pleased neither England nor the United States.

In an effort to come to an agreement on these vexing questions and the important ones concerning the post-war occupation and control of Germany, President Roosevelt throughout the summer of 1944 sought another meeting with Stalin. Stalin on one pretext after another refused to consider any of the suggested meeting points. President Roosevelt finally gave up and met Churchill in Quebec in September 1944 for discussions on the Pacific War, Italy, and the post-war control of Germany.

While Churchill and President Roosevelt were in Quebec, delegages from Great Britian and the Soviet Union were in Washington at Dumbarton Oaks, discussing proposals for the establishment of a post-war international organization. Soviet participation in the Dumbarton Oaks discussions stemmed directly from the agreement Molotov had made with Hull and Eden in Moscow in October 1943. In meetings lasting several weeks, the general framework of the United Nations was agreed upon and an outline of the organization and functions of the United Nations was prepared for submission to all prospective members.

There were a number of questions left unanswered by the Dumbarton Oaks meetings due to the inability of the British and American delegates to reach agreements with the Soviets. Worried lest these differences cause a long delay in calling a general conference of nations to draft and ratify the Charter of the United Nations, President Roosevelt in November and December of 1944 renewed his efforts to meet Stalin again. The success of the allied armies in re-conquering Europe brought a host of political problems even more pressing than the plans for the post-war international organization, and Churchill joined President Roosevelt in the attempts to arrange a meeting. North Africa, the Middle East, Alaska, and Scotland were suggested but Stalin refused to leave the Soviet Union.

Finally, in February 1945 the three leaders met at Yalta in the Crimea. Discussions at this conference covered a very broad field of military and political subjects. Stalin agreed that the U.S.S.R. would enter the war against Japan approximately three months after the end of the war against Germany in return for the Kurile Islands and the southern half of Sakhalin Island. It was also agreed that the status quo in Outer-Mongolia would be preserved, that Dairen should be internationalized, the "pre-eminent interests of the Soviet Union in this port being safe-guarded," that Port Arthur should be restored to the U.S.S.R., and that certain railroads in Manchuria should be jointly operated by China and Soviet Russia. The following was also agreed to: "For its part the Soviet Union expresses its readiness to conclude with the National Government of China a pact of friendship and alliance between the U.S.S.R. and China in order to render assistance to China with its armed forces for the purpose of liberating China from the Japanese yoke." This agreement concerning Soviet participation in the war against Japan was secret for obvious reasons.

Most of the political agreements of the three powers however were published at the conclusion of the Conference. These concerned the occupation and control of Germany, reparation by Germany, the convening of a United Nations Conference to establish "a general international organization to maintain peace and security," broadening the basis of the provisional governments in Poland and Yugoslavia, and a "Declaration on Liberated Europe." By this Declaration, President Roosevelt, Churchill and Stalin pledged their "faith in the principles of the Atlantic Charter" and jointly declared "their mutual agreement to concert during the temporary period of instability in liberated Europe the policies of their three governments in assisting the peoples liberated from the domination of Nazi Germany and the peoples of the former Axis satellite states of Europe to solve by democratic means their pressing political and economic problems." The Declaration restated the "right of all peoples to choose the form of government under which they will live," and promised aid to any liberated state or former Axis satellite state in establishing internal peace, forming representative governments and holding free elections.

Agreements at Yalta on voting procedure in the Security Council of the proposed international organization and President Roosevelt's pledge to Stalin to support the U.S.S.R.'s demand that the Ukraine and Byelorussian Soviet Socialist Republics be admitted to full membership removed the last Soviet objection to holding a conference to draft the Charter of the United Nations.

This conference was convened in San Francisco on April 25, 1945. Soviet delegates participated fully in all stages of the discussions and the Charter, when completed, had the full support of the Soviet Union.

What differences of opinion there were in San Francisco between the Soviet and the American delegations, sensational though they may have appeared in newspaper headlines at the time, were insignificant compared to the difficulties which arose almost immediately after the Crimean Conference. Stalin assailed President Roosevelt in bitter and vitriolic tones a few days before President Roosevelt's death in April 1945 for an alleged American attempt to make a separate peace with Germany. At the same time, this government was reacting strongly against Soviet activities in Poland, Yugoslavia, and the rest of the Balkans, believing that the U.S.S.R. was violating the Yalta Declaration on Liberated Europe. The American representatives to a conference on German reparations, held at Moscow in accordance with the Yalta agreement, were able to make no headway against Soviet claims for excessive reparations from Germany.

President Truman sent Harry L. Hopkins to Moscow in May 1945 in an effort to reduce the tension between the United States and the Soviet Union, especially over Poland. Stalin promised some concessions to Hopkins but the principal achievement of the journey was Stalin's agreement to meet President Truman and Churchill in Berlin in July. The sudden and complete collapse of Germany in May made another tripartite conference essential, but the sharpness with which Stalin had replied to President Roosevelt's last messages and President Truman's first ones had given rise to considerable uncertainty as to whether it would ever be possible to meet him again or come to an understanding with him.

At the Berlin Conference President Truman, Prime Ministers Churchill and Attlee and Generalissimo Stalin discussed a wider range of political subjects than had been covered in any of the previous meetings. A Council of the Foreign Ministers of the Soviet Union, Great Britain, the United States, France and China was established to draft treaties of peace with Italy, Rumania, Bulgaria, Hungary and Finland and to propose settlements of European territorial questions. Political and economic principles to govern the treatment of Germany were adopted as were agreements on reparations from Germany, the disposition of the German Navy and merchant marine, and the removal of Germans from Poland, Czechoslovakia and Hungary.

The status of Austria, Hungary, Poland, Czechoslovakia, Bulgaria, Finland, Rumania and Italy was discussed at great length and a number of agreements concerning peace treaties and the reorganization of the governments of most of those countries were also made. Some territorial readjustments were agreed to; President Truman and the British Prime Minister promised to support at a future peace conference Soviet claims to the city of Koenigsberg in East Prussia and the adjoining area. At the insistence of the Soviet delegates, the British and Americans agreed that, pending the final determination of Poland's western frontier at the peace conference, Poland should receive the former German lands lying east of the Oder and Neisse rivers, most of East Prussia, and the former free city of Danzig.

Many agreements were reached at Berlin, but not as many as the American representatives had hoped for. Two of the most controversial subjects concerned waterways. President Truman's insistence that the Danube River be freed from all restrictions on navigation was blocked by Stalin who introduced a counter-proposal that the Montreux Convention governing the Dardanelles be revised. Some of the unsolved questions were omitted from the Conference Communique completely; others, like Tangier and the problem of satellite reparations, were left for discussion through normal diplomatic channels.

In the military staff meetings which ran concurrently with the diplomatic discussions, British, Soviet and American Chiefs of Staff discussed Soviet entry into the Pacific war. Details of the Berlin agreements, political and military, over which there has since been controversy, are given in the following chapter.

The Berlin Conference Communique included a statement that the Foreign Ministers of the United States, Great Britain, the Soviet Union, France and China would meet in London in September.

Secretary of State Byrnes, Foreign Secretary Bevin of Great Britain, and Foreign Commissar Molotov accordingly assembled in London to continue the discussions they had carried on in Berlin. They were joined by French and Chinese delegates. The Council of Foreign Ministers or their deputies have been in almost continuous session since that time preparing peace treaty drafts for Italy, Rumania, Bulgaria, Hungary and Finland.

In addition to the meetings of the Council of Foreign Ministers, Secretary Byrnes and Bevin conferred with Molotov in Moscow in December 1945. Secretary Byrnes proposed the meeting to see if more progress could be made than had been made at London where the Council of Foreign Ministers had reached an impasse. The Soviet delegation had held in London that peace treaties should be made only by the principal powers who had signed the respective armistices, whereas the other delegations had taken the view that all states which took an active part in the war should be allowed to participate in the peace.

At Moscow in December 1945, Secretary Byrnes, Bevin and Molotov reached a compromise agreement providing that the terms of peace should be drawn up by the principal powers which were signers of the respective armistices, and that the terms should then be submitted to a peace conference of all the states who actively waged war against the European members of the Axis.

It was also agreed at Moscow to establish a Far Eastern Commission composed of representatives of the U.S.S.R., Great Britain, China, the United States, France, Netherlands, Australia, New

Zealand, Canada, India and the Philippines. This Commission has the authority to formulate principles to govern the control of Japan and its decisions are incorporated into directives to General Mac-Arthur by the U.S. Government. In addition, it was agreed to establish an Allied Council for Japan of representatives of the U.S.S.R., Great Britain, China and the United States to advise and consult General MacArthur.

Korea was discussed and in an effort to solve the economic and administrative problems created by the division of Korea into Soviet-occupied and American-occupied zones a joint Soviet-American Commission was established. This Commission was instructed to make recommendations for the formation of a Korean provisional government and for a four-power trusteeship to prepare Korea for independence within five years.

A new subject, not previously discussed at any conference with the Soviets, was the control of atomic energy. It was agreed at Moscow that a United Nations Commission should be appointed to inquire into the problems raised by the utilization of atomic energy and to make recommendations to member governments.

The Foreign Ministers' meetings in Paris in April, May, June and July were largely devoted to working out details of the peace treaties now under consideration in Paris and there were no substantive agreements to which the United States and the U.S.S.R. were parties.

A number of agreements and understandings in addition to those which have been briefly recounted in this chapter were entered into by the United States and the Soviet Union during the war years. Those which have a direct bearing on the current relations of the two nations, as well as additional details concerning those which have been described, will be discussed in the following chapter in an analysis of the manner in which the Soviet Union has adhered to these agreements.

III

VIOLATIONS OF SOVIET AGREEMENTS
WITH THE UNITED STATES

The Soviet Government will not admit that it has violated any of its international engagements. On the contrary, it usually argues vehemently, both at home and abroad, that it scrupulously fulfills its international obligations. It is very prone to charge other nations with violations while indignantly denying or completely ignoring charges that it has committed similar acts.

Much of the misunderstanding regarding the agreements to which the United States and the U.S.S.R. are signatories results from the different points of view with which the two countries regard postwar problems. As a result, many of the acts of the Soviet Government appear to the United States Government to be violations of the spirit of an international agreement although it is difficult to adduce direct evidence of literal violations. The Soviets resort in particular to two devices in rebutting charges of violation of agreements when, from the American point of view, the spirit of their commitments is being grossly contravened. First, they utilize interpretations which are entirely at variance with the views of other signatories, exploiting to this end the Soviet definitions of terms such as "democratic," "friendly," "fascist," et cetera, which are basically different from the non-communist understanding of these words. Second, by exerting various forms of pressure, they induce the governments of countries which are occupied by Soviet troops to commit acts which are in themselves violations of agreements to which the Soviet Union is a party. In both cases the Soviets manage to avoid direct charges of violating their agreements although there is no question where the primary responsibility lies.

Notwithstanding the efforts of the Soviet Government to avoid charges of violating the letter of its agreements, it has considered it necessary in pursuit of its objectives to commit some acts of this kind. Most of these violations have concerned matters of vital interest to the United States. Of those, the most serious are listed briefly below:

(1) *Germany.* The Soviets have refused to implement the Potsdam decisions to administer Germany as an economic unit. As a result there is no free interzonal commerce or common import-ex-

port program. Instead of utilizing proceeds from exports to pay for necessary imports to support the German population, the Soviets are crediting exports from their zone to their reparations account, in violation of the spirit of the reparations agreement.

The Soviets have not encouraged "all democratic political parties" in their zone, as provided for in the Berlin Declaration. Only the Communist Party is supported and activities of the democratic parties are hampered in every possible way. Political life in the Soviet zone is not being reconstructed on a democratic basis. Democratic ideas, in our sense of the term, are not being fostered.

The provisions of the Berlin Declaration regarding the elimination of Germany's war potential are also being violated by the Soviets in that the manufacture of war materials, including airplanes, is still continuing in the Soviet zone.

(2) *Austria.* The continued maintenance of unduly large Soviet military forces in Austria has constituted an oppressive burden on the Austrian economy inconsistent with the reestablishment of a free and independent Austria as envisaged in the Moscow Declaration of October 1943 or in the Soviet assurance, at the time of the formation of the Provisional Government, that the Austrians had resisted the Nazis and thus fulfilled the Moscow Declaration conditions.

The Soviet authorities in Austria have refused to regard the question of German assets in Eastern Austria as an appropriate subject for the consideration of the Allied Council. They have consistently attempted in practice to settle the problems connected with this question through bilateral action with the Austrian Government to the exclusion of the Allied Council. They have failed to cooperate with the other occupying powers in working out a constructive program for the development of a sound economic life in Austria as a whole.

(3) *Balkans.* The principle complaint of the United States Government is the failure of the Soviet chairmen of the Allied Control Commissions in Hungary, Rumania and Bulgaria to consult with their American and British colleagues in the enforcement of the armistice agreements with these countries. In effect, this has meant that Soviet influence has been paramount and that the American and British representatives have virtually been excluded from all vital decisions affecting the political and economic life of the countries.

In the view of the United States Government the Soviet Government has failed to carry out the commitment undertaken in the

Yalta agreement to assist the peoples of liberated Europe to form interim governments broadly representative of all categories in the population and pledged to the earliest possible establishment, through free elections, of governments responsible to the will of the people. The non-observance of this commitment has been particularly flagrant in relation to Yugoslavia, Rumania, Bulgaria and Poland. In none of these countries can the present government, each of which was established under Soviet pressure and protection, be said to represent the will of the people.

In the armistice agreements with the ex-satellites the latter undertook to restore the legal rights and interests of the United Nations and their nationals in their respective territories and to return their property in complete good order. Heavy Soviet reparation demands and requisitions and nationalization programs, inaugurated at Soviet instigation, have effectively prevented the defeated countries from complying with these provisions of the armistice agreements.

(4) *Iran.* The refusal of the Soviet occupation forces in northern Iran to permit the Iranian Government to send reinforcements to Tabriz when faced with a secession movement in Azerbaijan was a violation of the Teheran declaration in which the Soviet Government expressed its desire to maintain the independence, sovereignty and territorial integrity of Iran.

(5) *Korea.* During the meetings of the Joint Commission set up under the Moscow Declaration of December 1945 the Soviets consistently refused to agree to consultation with the Commission of democratic parties and social organizations in the southern zone on the grounds that many of these groups had expressed opposition to the Moscow decision on Korea. The Commission adjourned without settling this issue. The Soviets have not replied to American requests to resume meetings of the Commission.

(6) *Lend-Lease.* In violation of the Lend-Lease Agreement the Soviets have turned over Lend-Lease or equivalent material to Poland and probably to other countries of eastern Europe without the consent of the United States. They have thus far failed to honor a request to return certain naval vessels delivered to the Soviet Union under Lend-Lease. They have also failed to begin conversations with the United States looking to the "betterment of worldwide economic relations," "elimination of all forms of discriminatory treatment in international commerce," and "the reduction of tariffs and other trade barriers" as provided for in the Master Lend-Lease Agreement, and have shown no inclination to apply

these principles either in their own commercial relations or in the countries under their control.

The important international agreements to which the United States and the U.S.S.R. are parties, and which the United States considers the Soviet Union has violated in whole or in part, are discussed below in chronological order.

UNITED NATIONS DECLARATION, JANUARY 1, 1942.

The Soviet Union was one of the original signatories of the United Nations Declaration signed at the White House on January 1, 1942 by 26 nations. The Declaration was a broad endorsement of the principles of the Atlantic Charter. Since the Declaration was couched in general terms, it is difficult to say that the Soviet Union has violated it, but it is obvious that the Soviet Union's large-scale acquisition of territory since January 1, 1942 is hardly in keeping with the pledge the U.S.S.R. sought no territorial aggrandizement. The Soviet Union's acquisition of Ruthenia and Bukowina and the drastic readjustment of Poland's eastern frontier cannot be reconciled with the Soviet Union's statement that it desired no territorial changes which were not in accord with the freely expressed wishes of the peoples concerned.

Ruthless suppression of Anti-Soviet political parties in liberated countries of Eastern Europe is a direct violation of the Soviet Union's promise to respect the right of all people to choose the form of government under which they will live. Soviet desire to bring about the fullest possible collaboration between all nations in the economic field, pledged by the U.S.S.R. in its adherence to the United Nations Declaration, is not apparent in recent Soviet behavior in Germany, Austria and Hungary.

PRINCIPLES APPLYING TO MUTUAL AID, JUNE 11, 1942.

On June 11, 1942 the Soviet Ambassador to the United States and Secretary of State Cordell Hull signed "Principles Applying to Mutual Aid in the Prosecution of the War Against Aggression." Article Three of this document stated that the Soviet government would not, without the consent of the President of the United States, transfer title to any defense article which it received under Lend-Lease. It also provided that the Soviet government would not permit the use of any such article by anyone other than an employee of the Soviet government.

Shortly after the liberation of Warsaw, Poland, the Soviet government announced the gift to the Polish Provisional Government of 1,000 trucks, mobile power plants, radio equipment and food stuffs. All of these articles were either Lend-Lease goods or items similar to materials sent to the Soviet Union by the United States under Lend-Lease agreements. No satisfactory explanation of these gifts to the Polish government has ever been made by the Soviet Government. Subsequently, the U.S.S.R. has provided large quantities of military equipment to Polish, Czechoslovak and Yugoslav armies. Although direct evidence is lacking, there is a strong presumption that Lend-Lease material was included in these shipments. In any event, the material given Poland before the end of the war was a clear violation of Article Three of the agreement signed on June 11, 1942.

Article Five of the agreement provides that the Soviet Union will return to the United States at the end of the "emergency" those defense articles transferred under the Lend-Lease agreement, which have not been destroyed or lost and which may be determined by the President to be useful to the United States. An American request for the return of certain Naval vessels furnished the Soviet Union under Lend-Lease has not yet been granted. Soviet refusal to return these Naval vessels is a violation of Article Five of the agreement signed on June 11, 1942.

Article Seven provides that, in the final determination of benefits to be given the United States by the Soviet government in return for Lend-Lease aid, terms and conditions shall be such as to promote mutually advantageous economic relations and the betterment of world-wide economic conditions. This article was intended to eliminate all forms of discriminatory treatment in international commerce and to reduce tariffs and other trade barriers. The Soviet Union thus far has not agreed to discuss these matters with the United States nor has it given any evidence of willingness to adopt these principles either in direct trade with the United States or in countries within the Soviet sphere of influence.

MOSCOW CONFERENCE OF FOREIGN MINISTERS, OCTOBER 1943.

The report of the meeting in Moscow in October 1943 of Secretary of State Hull, Prime Minister Eden, and Foreign Commissar Molotov included a Declaration on Austria. The United States government considers that the continued maintenance of unduly large Soviet military forces in Austria constitutes an oppressive burden on the Austrian economy and is inconsistent with the reestablishment of a free and independent Austria as envisaged in the Declaration on Austria. Recent Soviet seizure of land and industrial properties, together with the removal of factories and the attempted imposition of joint Soviet-Austrian companies, is not in accord with the independence and economic security contemplated for Austria in the Moscow Declaration.

TEHERAN CONFERENCE, NOVEMBER 1943.

The most significant agreement reached at the Teheran Conference of Stalin, Churchill and President Roosevelt in November 1943 concerned military campaigns in Europe in 1944. In return for the Anglo-American pledge to invade France in May 1944, Stalin promised that the Red Army would launch a simultaneous offensive along the entire Eastern Front. Due to a number of military factors, the invasion of Normandy was not launched until June 6, 1944, somewhat later than Stalin was promised at Teheran. However, the Soviet Union kept its side of the bargain and a general offensive on the Eastern Front was begun a few days after the invasion of Normandy.

Although Soviet adherence to the military agreements of Teheran was satisfactory, the U.S.S.R. has violated the Declaration of the Three Powers regarding Iran which was also made in Teheran. On November 29, 1945 the Soviet government admitted in a note to the United States that Soviet forces in Iran had prevented Iranian troops from moving northward after an outbreak in Azerbaijan. This Soviet action constituted at least indirect aid to the Azerbaijan revolutionaries and was therefore a violation of the Teheran Declaration regarding Iran which stated that "the Governments of the United States, the U.S.S.R., and the United Kingdom are at one with the Government of Iran in the desire for the maintenance of the independence, sovereignty and territorial integrity of Iran."

ARMISTICE AGREEMENT WITH RUMANIA, SEPTEMBER 12, 1944.

On September 12, 1944 the United States, the U.S.S.R., and the United Kingdom signed an Armistice Agreement with Rumania. In November 1944 the Russians seized equipment from an American-owned oil plant for shipment to the Soviet Union over the protest of the American Representative on the Allied Control Council and of the American Charge d'Affaires at Moscow, and despite the fact that the Soviet Government had been duly notified in advance of the American character of this property and had been asked to see that it was protected. The Soviets continued such actions even after a joint U.S.-British note of protest was dispatched to Moscow in December 1944. These acts prevented the Rumanian government from fulfilling its obligations to the United States. Under the terms of the Armistice, the Rumanian government was obliged to restore property belonging to citizens of the United Nations in good order and in the condition it had been in before the war.

The Soviet government has presented a reparations list to Rumania incapable of being filled. This is in direct violation of the Armistice agreement which provided that Rumania should pay not more than 300 million dollars to the Soviet Union for losses caused to the U.S.S:R. by military operations.

Although Article Three of the Rumanian Armistice agreement authorized the maintenance of Soviet forces in Rumania, the U.S.S.R. has utilized this article for the continued maintenance of troops after the ending of hostilities. There are at present in Rumania, Soviet armed forces far beyond those needed to maintain order despite the fact that the Allied Control Commission Chairman has repeatedly emphasized that Rumania is now a sovereign state entirely capable of managing her own government and maintaining internal order.

Although not authorized by the Armistice agreement, the Soviet Union in September 1945 took over the entire Rumanian Navy, claiming it as war booty. She recently returned to Rumania a few of the older ships.

ARMISTICE AGREEMENT WITH BULGARIA,
OCTOBER 28, 1944.

On October 28, 1944, an Armistice Agreement with Bulgaria was signed by the United States, the United Kingdom and the Soviet Union. General Crane, United States Representative on the Allied Control Commission, reported on February 4, 1946 that not once in fourteen months had he been able to establish contact with Soviet Marshal Tolbukhin, his colleague and Chairman of the Control Commission. This failure of the Soviet Chairman to consult his American and British colleagues is a basic violation of the Bulgarian Armistice Agreement.

Bulgaria has shipped no food stuffs as reparations to Greece, which was provided for in the Protocol to the Armistice Agreement, and she has made only token restitutions to Greece in carrying out other provisions of the Armistice Agreement. Although the failure in question is Bulgaria's, there is no doubt that it had been sanctioned and encouraged by the Soviet Government.

ARMISTICE AGREEMENT WITH HUNGARY,
JANUARY 20, 1945.

On January 20, 1945, the United States, the United Kingdom, and the Soviet Union signed an Armistice Agreement with Hungary. On March 7, 1945, General Key, U.S. Representative on the Allied Control Council for Hungary, requested copies of all documents issued in the name of the Allied Control Commission. Soviet authorities replied that there were none. After that date, Soviet authorities took various measures, some of which directly affected American property, without informing General Key.

Soviet representatives have systematically failed to inform United States and British representatives concerning Hungarian economic conditions. In December 1945 the American Minister to Hungary raised the question of the plans which the Hungarian government had made to improve economic conditions and requested a prompt reply. The Hungarian government has failed to reply to the American request and Soviet officials of the Allied Control Commission have also refused to reply. The failure of the Soviet authorities to inform other representatives of the economic conditions of Hungary is a violation of provisions of the Armistice Agreement which provide that the representatives of the United Kingdom and the United States shall have the right to receive oral and written information from the Soviet officials of the Allied Control Commission on any matter connected with the fulfillment of the Armistice Agreement.

In January 1946, the Soviet Chairman of the Allied Control Commission put a Soviet representative on the Hungarian National Bank without the knowledge or concurrence of the United States or British representatives. This is a violation of the revised statues of the Allied Control Commission for Hungary regarding consultation among members of the Commission.

On January 20, 1946, Soviet authorities seized a Standard Oil field at Lispe and appointed a Soviet Administrator without consulting the United States Representative on the Allied Control Commission for Hungary. On March 22, 1946, the American Representative sent a note to Soviet Marshal Voroshilov asking for the withdrawal of Soviet personnel. No reply has been received. The Soviet Union by this action has violated two articles of the

Armistice Agreement. It has prevented the Hungarian government from restoring all legal rights and interests of the United Nations as they existed before the war and also from returning their property in good order. It has also violated the agreement which provided that an Allied Control Commission would regulate and supervise the execution of the Armistice terms. The Soviet Representative acted unilaterally, without consultation with British and American representatives.

In April 1946 Soviet authorities requested that the British representatives discontinue publication of their news bulletin in Hungary. The United States government believes that this issue involves a question of principle relative to the scope of Soviet authority under the Armistice terms. The Soviet request appears to the United States to be arbitrary, discriminatory, and without legal warrant. Insistence by Soviet authorities that distribution of a British publication cease is regarded as a derogation of the principle of freedom of the press, and as a denial of the rights of an allied power represented on the Allied Control Council.

There have been many delays in clearance by the Soviets of American official personnel and planes in Hungary. Officials at the American Legation in Budapest have been delayed as much as nineteen days in leaving Budapest. Delay on the part of the Chairman of the Allied Control Commission in granting clearance to American officials is a violation of the statutes of the Allied Control Commission which provide that representatives of the United States have the right to determine the size and composition of their own delegation. The Soviets, by arbitrary restrictions concerning entrance to and exit from Hungary, are denying this right to the American representatives.

On June 28, 1946, the Soviet Deputy Chairman of the Allied Control Commission sent a letter to the Hungarian government on Allied Control Commission stationery demanding the dissolution of various youth groups. This is a direct violation of the statutes of the Allied Control Commission which provide that directives from the Commission on questions of principle will be issued to the Hungarian authorities by the Allied Control Commission only after the British and American representatives have agreed to the directives.

THE CRIMEAN CONFERENCE, FEBRUARY 1945.

The Declaration on Liberated Europe, issued by President Roosevelt, Prime Minister Churchill and Marshal Stalin on February

11, 1945 as a part of the Report on the Crimean Conference, was regarded by President Roosevelt and Churchill at the time as being one of their major achievements of the Conference. In that Declaration, the United States, Great Britain and the U.S.S.R. declared "their mutual agreement to concert during the temporary period of instability in liberated Europe the policies of their three governments in assisting the peoples liberated from the domination of Nazi Germany and the peoples of the former Axis satellite states of Europe to solve by democratic means their separate political and economic problems." It also provided that the three governments would jointly assist the people in any European liberated state or former Axis satellite state in Europe where in their judgment conditions required their assistance in forming interim governments "broadly representative of all democratic elements in the population."

On April 24, 1945, the Soviet Union informed the United States that Dr. Karl Renner had approached the Soviet authorities with an offer to form a provisional Austrian Government. On April 29, 1945, in spite of a request by the United States that no definitive action be taken until the allies had been able to consult each other, Radio Moscow announced that the Renner government had been installed. This unilateral action by the Soviet Union constituted a direct violation of the Yalta Declaration on Liberated Europe.

The Soviet Union's activities with respect to Bulgaria also contravened the Yalta Declaration on Liberated Europe. That provision of the Declaration concerning Allied assistance to former Axis satellite states in solving their pressing political problems by democratic means was violated by the Soviet Union's refusal to consult with the United States, at our request, on Bulgarian democratic parties and elections. On March 29, 1945 the U.S. government instructed our Embassy in Moscow to propose that a tri-partite Allied Commission be established in Bulgaria to insure that all democratic parties in Bulgaria would have full freedom to bring their separate platforms and slates of candidates to the attention of the electorate. The United States made this proposal because of repeated reports of communist pressure in Bulgaria to have elections on the basis of a single election list, which would have given Communists a representation out of all proportion to their actual voting strength. On April 11, 1945 Molotov in reply questioned American motives and stated that the Soviet public would be "dumbfounded" if there were foreign intervention in Bulgarian elections.

The Soviet Union has violated provisions of the Declaration on Liberated Europe by making unilateral trade and economic agreements with Hungary. Although the Yalta agreement provided that the three powers should concert their policies in assisting former Axis states to solve their economic problems, on August 23, 1945 the Soviet Union made a trade and economic collaboration agreement with Hungary. On October 13, 1945 the United States and Great Britain sent notes to the Soviet Union presenting their views regarding this action. On October 30, 1945 the Soviet Union replied that the bilateral agreement it had just made with Hungary did not concern other nations.

In December 1945 the U.S. Representative on the Allied Control Commission for Hungary recommended the establishment of a sub-commission to consider Hungarian industry, finance and economics. The Soviet Union refused to consider the establishment of this sub-commission. The United States sent a note to the Soviet government on March 2, 1946 regarding the grave economic plight of Hungary and calling attention to the burden of reparations and the cost of maintaining an occupation army. Our request that the Soviet government instruct its representatives to plan an economic program for Hungary with American and British representatives was rejected by Soviet Deputy Foreign Minister Vishinsky on April 21, 1946. On July 27, 1946 the Soviet Union repeated its earlier rejection of the American plan for an Allied Sub-commission to aid Hungarian economic rehabilitation. The Soviet position was that this was a matter strictly for the Hungarian government. This Soviet action was another violation of the spirit of the Yalta Declaration.

The Soviet government has also violated the provisions of the Yalta Declaration by its actions in Rumania. On February 27, 1945 Vishinsky demanded that King Michael of Rumania dismiss the Radescu Government. On March 1, 1945 Vishinsky named Groza as the Soviet choice for Premier. Five days later King Michael accepted a Groza government. At no time during this period did the Soviet authorities consult or keep informed the American and British representatives in Rumania.

Prior to the establishment of the present Polish Government, Soviet actions with regard to Poland were marked by a high degree of unilateralism, in violation of the Declaration on Liberated Europe and earlier Big Three understandings on the Polish question. The Soviet Union resorted to numerous technicalities in dealing with the Lublin (later Warsaw) Government and it concluded a Treaty of Friendship and Mutual Assistance with the Polish Provisional Government on April 21, 1945 when Anglo-Soviet-American negotiations on the very question of reorganizing this government had reached an impasse. The U.S.S.R. acted entirely unilaterally in violation of its obligations under the Yalta Declaration.

An agreement relating to prisoners of war and civilians liberated by Allied military forces was also signed at Yalta on February 11, 1945. The record of the Soviet Union in carrying out this agreement for the care and repatriation of American and Soviet citizens has not been satisfactory. In general, liberated American prisoners of war in Soviet-occupied areas of Germany were forced to make their way as best they could across Poland to Soviet territory. During their journey across Poland they were forced to rely for food and necessities on the generosity of the Polish people who themselves had very little. When they entered the U.S.S.R., they were gathered together, put in box-cars, and sent to Odessa. The Soviets refused permission for American aircraft to bring in supplies to liberated U.S. prisoners of war behind Soviet lines or to evacuate the sick and wounded by air. The only United States contact team allowed in Soviet territory was one at Odessa, the traffic point where the Americans were assembled prior to being shipped to the United States. Evacuation of U.S. liberated prisoners of war was accomplished under the most difficult conditions.

With respect to the repatriation of liberated Soviet prisoners of war in U.S. hands, the Soviet interpretation of the Yalta Agreement was that the United States would forcibly repatriate all persons claimed by the Soviet Union to be Soviet citizens. The United States interpretation was that assistance would be given for the repatriation of those who wished to return to the U.S.S.R., while forced repatriation would be limited to those war criminals demanded by the Soviets. The United States has not met many Soviet demands for repatriation of unwilling U.S.S.R. citizens not clearly shown to be war criminals.

The most important military result of the Crimean Conference was the Statement regarding Japan, signed by Roosevelt, Churchill, and Stalin. The pledge that the Soviet Union would enter the war against Japan two or three months after the defeat of Germany was carried out by the Soviet declaration of war against Japan on August 8, 1945. One of the conditions, however, upon which the Soviet Union entered the war against Japan, was the internationalization of the port of Dairen. In contravention of the

Yalta agreement, the U.S.S.R. is now attempting to prevent the internationalization of that port.

DECLARATION REGARDING THE DEFEAT OF GERMANY, JUNE 5, 1945.

On June 5, 1945, the United States, Great Britain and the Soviet Union issued a Declaration regarding the Defeat of Germany. Article 13A specifies that the four Allied Governments occupying Germany will ensure the complete disarmament and demilitarization of Germany. Despite this agreement, the Soviet government has not taken adequate steps to demilitarize industrial plants in the Soviet Zone. On the contrary, some of them are still engaged in producing war materials.

CHARTER OF THE UNITED NATIONS, JUNE 26, 1945.

The Charter of the United Nations was signed in San Francisco on June 26, 1945. Article Two of the Charter reads: "All members shall refrain in their international relations from the threat or use of force against the territorial integrity or political independence of any State, or in any other manner inconsistent with the Purpose of the United Nations."

Iran appealed to the Security Council of the United Nations on March 19, 1946 against the continuing presence of Soviet troops in northern Iran and against interference "in the internal affairs of Iran through the medium of Soviet agents, officials, and armed forces." On May 24, 1946, the Soviet Ambassador to Iran told the Iranian government that the withdrawal of Soviet troops from Iran had been completed on May 9, 1946. However, there have been numerous reports to the United States government since that date that Soviet troops are still in Iran. Soviet failure to withdraw troops from Iran constitutes a violation of the Charter of the United Nations.

AGREEMENT ON CONTROL MACHINERY IN AUSTRIA, JULY 4, 1945.

On July 4, 1945, the United States, Great Britain and the Soviet Union signed an Agreement on Control Machinery in Austria. Article Two of this agreement provides that an Allied Council of the four occupying powers shall exercise joint authority in matters affecting Austria as a whole. The Soviet authorities in

Austria have refused to regard the question of German assets in Austria as an appropriate subject for the consideration of the Allied Council. They have consistently attempted in practice to settle the problems connected with this question through bilateral action with the Austrian government to the exclusion of the Allied Council. They have also failed to cooperate with other occupying powers in working out a constructive program for the development of the sound economic life in Austria as a whole.

EUROPEAN ADVISORY COMMISSION AGREEMENT, JULY 9, 1945.

On July 9, 1945, the European Advisory Commission, composed of representatives of Great Britain, United States, the Soviet Union and France agreed that "armed forces and officials of occupying powers will enjoy free and unimpeded access to airdromes assigned to their respective occupancies and their use." The Soviet Union has repeatedly violated this provision, particularly with respect to the Tulln airport near Vienna. The same difficulty has also been experienced in obtaining clearance for air travel by United States civil and military personnel in Bulgaria, Rumania, Yugoslavia, Hungary, and Austria. In addition, there have been numerous incidents of United States aircraft being intercepted, and in some cases fired on, damaged, and forced to land, by Soviet fighter planes. While these acts violate no specific written agreement in areas where the United States does not have occupation forces, they violate international understanding of aviation courtesy and reciprocity. They are acts of intimidation and in some cases actual assault. Excessive curtailment of legitimate air travel by American personnel has resulted. In all cases U.S. personnel have attempted to comply strictly with Soviet decrees although such decrees have been arbitrary. The entire Soviet attitude toward travel by air by American personnel has been in deliberate violation of the spirit of existing political agreements.

THE POTSDAM DECLARATION, JULY 26, 1945.

On July 26, 1945, President Truman and Prime Minister Attlee issued a proclamation, concurred in by Generalissimo Chiang Kai-shek, defining the terms for Japanese surrender. On August 9, 1945, the U.S.S.R. adhered to the Potsdam Declaration. The Declaration stated, in part, that Japanese military forces, after being completely disarmed, should be permitted to return to their homes. The Soviets have refused, in violation of this provision, to repatriate Japanese prisoners of war who have fallen into the hands of the Red Army. This violation has been repeatedly brought to the attention of the Soviet government in Moscow and the Soviet representatives in Tokyo, together with an expression of American willingness to assist in the repatriation. On August 1, 1946, the United States had repatriated 93% of the Japanese in areas controlled by this country; the British had repatriated 80% of the Japanese in their areas; 98% of the Japanese in China had been repatriated; but no Japanese in the Soviet areas in the Far East have been repatriated.

THE BERLIN CONFERENCE,
JULY 17 TO AUGUST 2, 1945.

On August 2, 1945 Generalissimo Stalin, President Truman, and Prime Minister Attlee signed the Protocol and the Report of the Berlin Conference. In the section of the Berlin agreement dealing with Germany, the Allies agreed on the "eventual reconstruction of German political life on a democratic basis." The question of Soviet fulfillment of this clause depends, of course, on the interpretation of the term "democratic basis." From the American point of view, Soviet tactics in their Zone are not such as to lead to the reconstruction of German political life on a democratic basis. In the Soviet zone of Germany everything is done to hamper the activities of the democratic parties. The Communist Party, on the other hand, is encouraged and given every possible support.

The agreement on Germany also provided for the establishment of "certain essential central German administrative departments" to function under the direction of the Allied Control Council. Soviet obstructionism has prevented agreement to set up such departments.

Paragraph 11 of the agreement on Germany provided that the production of arms, ammunition, all types of aircraft, and sea-going ships should be prohibited in order to eliminate Germany's war potential. Production of metals, chemicals and machinery which are directly related to a war economy were to be rigidly restricted to Germany's peace-time needs. Productive capacity not needed for peace-time production should be removed in accordance with the reparations plan or destroyed. In violation of these provisions, the Soviets in their Zone have allowed the manufacture of weapons of war and airplanes to continue. The Soviets have refused to permit an investigation of actual conditions as requested by Great Britain and the United States.

Paragraph 14 of the agreement on Germany provided for the treatment of Germany as a single economic unit and other paragraphs provided that the payment of reparations should leave enough resources to enable the German people to subsist without external assistance. The Soviet Government has persistently refused to take the necessary steps to implement these agreements. The Soviets, while giving lip-service to the proposals to set up central German economic agencies, have not agreed to take any action along these lines. They have also prevented any equitable distribution of essential commodities among the four zones of occupation. There is no common import-export program. On the contrary, instead of using proceeds from exports from the Soviet Zone for the payment of imports required for the German economy as a whole, the Soviets are taking out German exports as reparations. This, from the American point of view, is a direct violation of the Berlin agreement.

There is nothing in the Berlin agreement which authorizes reparations to be removed from current German production. Molotov's recent attempt in Paris to gain recognition for the Soviet claim for 10 billion dollars of reparations from Germany goes far beyond anything envisaged by the United States and Great Britain at Berlin. Reparations in this amount could only be obtained from current production and could not be fulfilled for decades.

The Soviet interpretation of the reparations clauses concerning German assets in East Austria is another violation of the Berlin agreement from the American point of view. The provisions of the agreement are ambiguous in that the terms "German foreign assets" and "Eastern Austria" are not clearly defined; however, Soviet seizure of property taken under duress by the Germans from the Austrians after the Anschluss undoubtedly constitutes a violation of the spirit of the Moscow Declaration of October 1953.

In a section of the Berlin agreement concerning peace treaties, it was agreed that "representatives of the Allied press will enjoy full freedom to report to the world upon developments in Russia, Bulgaria, Hungary and Finland." Despite this agreement, the Soviets have not allowed freedom of the press for American correspondents in the Soviet Union nor have they allowed it in countries under Soviet domination. In May 1946 a correspondent of the *Christian Science Monitor* was ordered to leave Rumania within five days despite the protest of the United States delegation to the Allied Control Commission. The same correspondent and three others were refused entry into Bulgaria a few weeks later. No explanation was ever given.

Under the terms of the Berlin agreement concerning Germany, unfinished German naval vessels were to be reported to a Tri-Partite Naval Commission. Incomplete vessels were to be destroyed by a specific date. Approximately twenty-seven naval vessels (destroyers, mine-sweepers, and submarines) were under construction in East German shipyards at the time of the Soviet occupation of that area. However, these vessels have not been reported to the Naval Commission by Soviet representatives. Recent American intelligence reports state that construction has been continued on at least four of these vessels. Photographs have been received in Washington taken during March and April 1946 showing new construction at some shipyards in the Soviet zone.

MOSCOW CONFERENCE OF FOREIGN MINISTERS, DECEMBER 1945.

At the Moscow Conference of Foreign Ministers in December 1945, it was agreed that an American-Soviet commission would be called for a conference within two weeks at Seoul, the capital of Korea, to establish coordination in economic and administrative matters in Korea. The Soviet delegates to the conference were late in arriving and, when they did arrive, they refused to consider a number of problems clearly within the scope of the Moscow agreement. These included the improvement of the rail and water transport systems, the removal of the 38 degree barrier to Koreans, and other measures vital to the economic rehabilitation of Korea. The Moscow agreement provided that the joint commission assist in the formation of a Provisional Korean Government. The agreement stipulated that, for this purpose, the commission should consult Korean democratic parties. When the commission convened, the Soviets refused to consult with several of the democratic parties in the American zone of Korea. The Soviet position, a clear violation of the agreement made at the Moscow Conference, led to the adjournment *sine die* of the joint commission. The Soviets have since failed to reply to requests from the American Army commander in Korea to reconvene the commission so that it may carry out the task assigned by the Moscow agreement.

It was agreed in Moscow in December that the Rumanian Government would be required to admit opposition political leaders into the cabinet and to insure free elections. These requirements have not been met. Parties in opposition to the present left-wing government are not permitted to use the radio; their leaders have been arrested, beaten or otherwise molested; their meetings have been broken up; their newspapers suppressed; their editors punished and their members otherwise subjected to an organized campaign of terrorism. The Soviet Union either through the Soviet Allied Control Commission or other agencies has done nothing to prevent this situation and has, in fact, refused to collaborate with the United States and Great Britain in the formulation of a joint note of protest to Rumania.

In Bulgaria, as in Rumania, the outstanding failure of the U.S.S.R. has been its refusal to broaden the government under the Moscow agreement.

MILITARY AGREEMENTS

In addition to the agreements which have been discussed in this chapter, a number of military agreements relating to the war against Germany and Japan were made by the United States and Soviet Union informally and without agreed written text. In general, the Soviet Union made an effort to live up to the military agreements. Performance by the Russians in many of their undertakings were not entirely satisfactory and in some cases this was due to unsatisfactory Soviet facilities, poor equipment, and poorly-trained personnel. The Soviets apparently made an effort to carry out most of the military agreements to the best of their ability.

IV

CONFLICTING VIEWS ON REPARATIONS

Reparations from the defeated Axis nations has become one of the major issues of dispute between the Soviet Union and the United States and the conflicting views on this subject illustrate clearly the conflicting foreign policies of the two nations.

At the Teheran Conference in November 1943, when Stalin spoke of reparations from Germany, Roosevelt agreed that the Soviet Union was entitled to recompense for war damage to her farmlands and industries. At Yalta in February 1945, the Three Powers agreed that reparation in kind should be exacted from Germany and that an allied commission, under a Soviet chairman, should meet in Moscow at an early date to settle the amount and nature of reparations and the share to which each Allied nation was entitled. Stalin asked for twenty billion dollars in reparations for the Soviet Union. Roosevelt said that he would willingly support any claims for reparations for the U.S.S.R. but not to the extent that the German people would starve. Churchill warmly opposed the Soviet figure of twenty billions and he and Eden argued that an excessive figure of reparations would so impoverish Germany that the Allies would have to feed and finance her later. Soviet and British debate at Yalta on reparations was bitter and acrimonious, but a protocol on reparations was finally drawn up and signed by the Three Powers. It stated that Germany must pay in kind for the losses caused by her to the Allied nations in the course of the war but it took into account British opposition and did not name a sum. General principles on reparations were outlined and the separate proposals of the British and the Soviets were set forth in detail in the protocol for the Allied Commission on Reparations to consider in Moscow.

Ambassador Edwin W. Pauley, the U.S. Representative on the Allied Commission on Reparations, arrived in Moscow early in June 1945 and began five weeks of technical discussion and argument with Soviet and British delegations. Mr. Pauley proposed eight general principles which were finally agreed to by the Soviet and British members of the Commission in mid-July. The Commission then moved to Berlin and its discussions were merged with those of the Big Three and the three Foreign Ministers who were meeting in Berlin. The agreement on principles formed the basis of the section of the Berlin Protocol dealing with reparations which was signed by President Truman, Generalissimo Stalin and Prime Minister Attlee on August 2, 1945.

U.S. aims with respect to reparations were clearly stated at Moscow and in Berlin. The United States is interested, not in getting money or goods from Germany to repay in small part the cost of the war, but in long-range security. The reparations agreements reached in Moscow and Berlin, as they are understood by Great Britain and the United States, supplement and support the economic principles for the control of Germany which were adopted by Stalin, Attlee and President Truman. These principles were devised to eliminate Germany's war potential and to decentralize her excessive concentration of economic power.

The United States upheld its views on reparations in order to avoid the mistake of the economic settlements following World War I, when reparations were obtained from current German production. Reparations from current production could not be obtained without extensive foreign credits for imports and it was necessary for Great Britain and the United States to finance German imports and the rebuilding of German industry. As the British pointed out at Yalta, Great Britain has no intention of financing such imports again and as Ambassador Pauley made abundantly clear in Moscow and in Berlin, the United States has not either.

In Moscow in June 1945, the Soviet Representative asked for reparations to the amount of ten billion dollars. Ambassador Pauley agreed to use that figure for discussion purposes only; he did not agree that the U.S.S.R. should have that amount.

The Soviet desire to set so large a figure for reparations meant that Germany could foot the bill only if her industry were rebuilt and the reparations were paid from current production over a period of years. It also meant, from the American point of view, that large imports would be necessary to maintain a high rate of productivity. If the products of the re-built German industry were drained off by the Soviet Union as reparations rather than used in normal world trade to pay for the imports, the imports probably would be paid for by the Western Allies who, in effect, would thus be paying for the reparations the Soviet Union would be getting. The Soviet demands in Moscow and Berlin of ten billion dollars appeared to the United States to have a triple aim: first, of using reparations as an excuse for the rebuilding of German industry; second, of increasing the military strength of the Soviet Union by obtaining current production from German industry for a number of years, and third, of ensuring that any central administration in Germany would be under an obligation to the U.S.S.R. which it could not meet for many years, thus making it dependent on the Kremlin's benevolent disposition.

One of the basic principles agreed to in Moscow read as follows:

"In order to avoid building up German industrial capacity and disturbing long-term stability of economies of the United Nations, long-run payment of reparations in the form of manufactured products shall be restricted to a minimum."

A second agreement was that:

"to a maximum extent, reparations shall be taken from the existing national wealth of Germany."

In addition to these two principles, fundamental in the eyes of the American delegation, it was agreed at Berlin that:

"Payment of reparations should leave enough resources to enable the German people to subsist without external assistance. In working out the economic balance of Germany the necessary means must be provided to pay for imports approved by the Control Council in Germany. The proceeds of exports from current production and stock shall be available in the first place for payment for such imports."

The last point had been repeatedly urged upon the Soviets by Ambassador Pauley, and in a letter to I. M. Maisky, Soviet Representative on the Commission, Mr. Pauley explained the matter in this fashion:

"Surely we both understand there can be no current annual reparations from Germany except as more goods are shipped out of Germany than are shipped in, i.e., there must be a large export balance. An export balance cannot be produced in Germany without some imports, such as food, alloys, cotton, etc. If these indispensable imports (without which there would be no exports of certain highly important types) are not a charge against the exports, then you, or we or some other economy will have to pay for the imports. Neither the U.S.S.R., nor the U.S.A., can think of recommending to its people a reparations plan which overlooks this elemental fact."

The United States thought that, by the written acceptance of the principles of the Moscow and Berlin agreements, the Soviet Union would abide by them and that there was a common understanding among the Three Powers on reparations, especially after Stalin himself agreed in Berlin that the figure of ten billion dollars was too high. The United States Government's hopes were ill-founded.

Although the Allied Control Council for Germany agreed on March 23, 1946 on a "Plan for Reparations and the Level of Post-war German Economy in Accordance with the Berlin Protocol" which was satisfactory to all three powers, disturbing reports reached Washington at the very time this Plan was being drawn up that the Soviets had not dismantled many of the industrial plants in their Zone of Germany but were, on the contrary, producing war materials in them. They were also believed to be confiscating the production of non-war industries without reporting the fact to the powers occupying the western zones of Germany and in direct violation of the agreement that "the proceeds of exports from current production and stock shall be available in the first place for payment of imports."

The spirit of the Berlin agreements on reparations was challenged directly on July 9, 1946 by Soviet Foreign Minister Molotov in a statement on Germany to the Council of Foreign Ministers in Paris. Molotov announced two principles as policies of the Soviet Union which, in effect, amount to a repudiation of the Berlin decisions. Molotov said:

> "The Soviet Government insists that reparations from Germany to the amount of ten billion dollars be exacted without fail because this amount is but a small portion of the enormous damage that had been done to the Soviet Union by German occupation. . . . Naturally, these reparations must include not only equipment but also commodities out of current production of Germany."

Molotov's insistence upon obtaining ten billion dollars and deriving a considerable part of it from current production is a complete reversal of the whole purpose of the Moscow agreements and the Berlin decisions. The Berlin Protocol purportedly settled the problem of reparations on the basis primarily of Allied security objectives with respect to Germany. It had been continually pointed out by the British and the Americans to the Soviet Representatives in Moscow and in Berlin that setting a specific dollar valuation on reparations was not consistent with our aim of demilitarizing Germany. Molotov is not only repudiating the spirit of the Berlin decisions but is taking a position contrary to the earlier Soviet claim that the U.S.S.R. wants to secure the economic disarmament of Germany.

The new policies announced by Molotov in Paris were followed up almost immediately on lower levels. In Berlin, Marshal Sokolovsky approached General Clay with a proposal that dismantling of factories in the Soviet Zone be postponed, perhaps as much as ten years, and current production from these plants taken as reparations.

Molotov's statement at the Paris Conference, taken with the information available on Soviet activities in Eastern Germany, indicates that the Soviet Government apparently has adopted a German policy which embodies the following points: The Soviets will press for ten billion dollars in reparations. They will take a substantial part of this ten billion dollars from the current production of industrial plants in the eastern zone of Germany for an indefinite number of years. They will contend that Soviet troops shall remain in Germany until these reparations payments have been completed. With respect to removal of industrial facilities from Germany, the Soviets can be expected to attempt to justify the retention of as large a capacity in the Soviet zone as possible, and they will oppose any effort to treat Germany as an economic unit to the extent that it means production in the eastern zone of Germany will be used to pay for imports rather than as reparations to the Soviet Union.

If the above assumptions are correct, the United States faces a situation in which it appears that the Soviets have abandoned the policy to weaken Germany but are relying instead on their belief that a reasonably strong Germany is more to their advantage than a weak Germany.

V

SOVIET ACTIVITIES AFFECTING AMERICAN SECURITY

A direct threat to American security is implicit in Soviet foreign policy which is designed to prepare the Soviet Union for war with the leading capitalistic nations of the world. Soviet leaders recognize that the United States will be the Soviet Union's most powerful enemy if such a war as that predicted by Communist theory ever comes about and therefore the United States is the chief target of Soviet foreign and military policy.

A recent Soviet shift of emphasis from Great Britain to the United States as the principle "enemy" has been made known to the world by harsh and strident propaganda attacks upon the United States and upon American activities and interests around the globe. The United States, as seen by radio Moscow and the Soviet press, is the principle architect of the "capitalistic encirclement" which now "menaces the liberty and welfare of the great Soviet masses." These verbal assaults on the United States are designed to justify to the Russian people the expense and hardships of maintaining a powerful military establishment and to insure the support of the Russian people for the aggressive actions of the Soviet Government.

The most obvious Soviet threat to American security is the growing ability of the U.S.S.R. to wage an offensive war against the United States. This has not hitherto been possible, in the absence of Soviet long-range strategic air power and an almost total lack of sea power. Now, however, the U.S.S.R. is rapidly developing elements of her military strength which she hitherto lacked and which will give the Soviet Union great offensive capabilities. Stalin has declared his intention of sparing no effort to build up the military strength of the Soviet Union. Development of atomic weapons, guided missiles, materials for biological warfare, a strategic air force, submarines of great cruising range, naval mines and mine craft, to name the most important, are extending the effective range of Soviet military power well into areas which the United States regards as vital to its security.

The Soviet Union is maintaining the strength of the Red Army by conscription along conventional lines. Large reserves are being built up and the army is so organized that it can be expanded rapidly. The mechanization of the Soviet Army has proceeded

[468]

steadily since the end of the war. The Soviets have been regrouping and modernizing their ground units to the extent that a new type of army, the "mechanized army," has been formed. This modernization, which appears to include the organic integration of tank and infantry units and the mechanization of infantry and artillery elements, is expected, in the near future, to increase materially the mobility of the Red Army. Great emphasis is placed on discipline, rigid observance of military formalities and intensified training. The Army is being maintained in a state of constant readiness for war and is placed strategically to move against any part of the Eurasian continent. The armies of Soviet satellite states are also being organized, trained and equipped along Soviet lines. A purge of anti-Soviet officers within these forces is bringing them tightly under Soviet control.

The Kremlin apparently realizes that a lack of sea power and air power was a major factor in the failure of Germany to win the first and second World Wars. This has inspired an aggressive determination to avoid the mistakes which led to the failure of Napoleon and Hitler to defeat nations possessing great sea power. The Soviet Union has begun to increase the strength and effectiveness of the Red Navy. Greatly deficient in surface ships, naval aviation and amphibious craft, the Soviet Union is now taking energetic steps to overcome these shortcomings. The U.S.S.R. is making an intensive effort to obtain an important share of German, Italian and Japanese naval vessels and she has refused to return some U.S. naval vessels which were loaned to her under Lend-Lease. The Soviet Merchant Marine is being augmented to support Soviet operations in Middle Eastern, Northern European and Far Eastern waters. Soviet naval expansion, particularly in submarine warfare, is greatly assisted by her possession of captured German shipyards, tools and technical personnel. The Soviet Union is developing as rapidly as possible a fleet of submarines designed for offensive action against sea communications, naval forces and shore installations of Great Britain and the United States. Intelligence reports indicate that the U.S.S.R. has failed to destroy captured German submarines, as she agreed to do under the Berlin Protocol, and in addition is rushing to completion submarines which were captured in an incomplete state in German shipyards. The Soviet Union is believed to be developing coastal sea communications in the Arctic areas and is striving to become efficient in Arctic operations.

The Soviet effort to develop naval power is matched by an interest in air power. Great stress is now being placed on the creation of a strategic air force, an element which the Soviet Union lacked during the recent war. Air fields are being developed in Eastern Siberia from which strategic air forces could attack the North American continent. The Soviets are expending a great deal of energy in developing electronics, guided missiles and atomic bombs.

The Soviet civil air program calls for great expansion of the air base system and the creation of a huge air transport fleet. In countries controlled by the Soviet Union, United States participation in civil air programs has been blocked, whereas the U.S.S.R. has assured the participation of its own civil air fleet by political and military pressure. Possession of a large air transport fleet will greatly strengthen the Soviet strategic position.

Although the Soviet Union at the present moment is precluded from military aggression beyond the land mass of Eurasia, the acquisition of a strategic air force, naval forces and atomic bombs in quantity would give the U.S.S.R. the capability of striking anywhere on the globe. Ability to wage aggressive warfare in any area of the world is the ultimate goal of Soviet military policy.

In addition to increasing her own military strength to a point where an attack on the United States would be possible, the Soviet Union is jeopardizing the security of the United States by her efforts to weaken the military position and to destroy the prestige of the United States in Europe, Asia and South America. Red Army troops and Red Air Force planes, maintained in combat readiness, outnumber American units in Germany, Austria and Korea in overwhelming strength, thus placing our forces literally at the mercy of the Soviet Government.

In Hungary, Rumania and Bulgaria U.S. representatives work under conditions imposed by Soviet commanders designed to make their official lives as unbearable as possible. Despite the charters under which the control councils were established, the Soviets have consistently pursued a policy of stifling all U.S. influence in these countries, demeaning U.S. representatives and the United States itself in the eyes of local populations, and letting nothing stand in the way of solidifying complete Soviet control. American representatives on Allied Control Councils have not been allowed to travel freely, discuss important matters, or question effectively the unilateral action taken by Soviet chairmen in the name of the Allied Control Councils. In general, U.S. representatives on the Councils are in complete ignorance of the manner in which Council policy is being carried out by the Soviets.

In countries where the United States enjoys a degree of equality with the Soviet Union, as in Austria and Germany, the Soviets block with the veto American efforts to bring about changes. Soviet representatives apparently follow the policy of carrying out only those agreements which are in their own interest. Soviet representatives seldom openly repudiate an agreement but they nullify it by equivocation, inertia, delay, red tape and evasion.

A number of Soviet activities in the United States zone of occupation in Germany have adversely affected American efforts to restore efficient government and maintain order. Soviet espionage activity has flourished, German scientists have been kidnapped, former German pilots now working in the United States zone have been enticed into the Soviet zone, Soviet agents have illegally entered the American zone for the purpose of collecting documents on German atomic research, and German jet propulsion experts have been recruited through German intermediaries for service with the Soviets.

Soviet activities in other areas are comparable to those in Europe. Encroachments in the Middle East are steadily weakening the British and American positions and strengthening Soviet political and military influence there. Our continued access to oil in the Middle East is especially threatened by Soviet penetration into Iran.

The U.S.S.R. has a widespread intelligence net in China covering all phases of American activity, but the Soviet propaganda program presents an even greater danger. This campaign is designed to discredit American forces in China, to convince all political groups in China that American forces should be evacuated at once and to arouse suspicion as to American post-war aims in the Far East. The Soviets, by supplying captured Japanese military material to the Communists, not only endanger the United States Marines in North China but also by prolonging the Chinese civil strife make more difficult, if not impossible, the attainment of the American aim of a unified and stable Chinese Government.

In Japan, the Soviet mission to the Allied Council, which was established under the terms of the Moscow agreement of December 1945, is over twice the size of the combined total of all other missions. Its members form an extensive espionage, subversive and sabotage net. The head of the Soviet mission to the Allied Council has shown himself completely hostile to American occupation authorities and his attitude makes it obvious that the U.S.S.R. resents the U.S. position in Japan. He and his subordinates have tried to create friction among the Japanese and to disrupt Allied plans for the democratization of Japan. He has placed subjects on the Council agenda for the purpose of criticizing the occupation, distorting General MacArthur's accomplishments, and endeavoring to demonstrate to the Japanese that he is taking the lead in necessary reforms, in order to show that the Soviet Union alone is the champion of the Japanese worker and peasant. The Soviet Council member has used the Council as a sounding board for Soviet anti-occupation and anti-American propaganda. He has sought to slow down and disrupt the repatriation program by complaining against the use of certain Japanese Navy vessels for repatriation and by demanding that some of these vessels be turned over to the Soviet Union. He has refused to consider any plan whereby the Soviet Union would assist in repatriating Japanese by using captured Japanese shipping already in its possession.

In South America the Soviet propaganda is intended to discredit the United States, break down hemispheric solidarity, and alienate the Latin republics so as to prevent the flow of essential raw materials to the United States in the event of a conflict between the United States and the Soviet Union.

Moscow is making a determined effort on all political fronts to discredit American intentions in securing bases in the Atlantic and the Pacific. Wherever possible, as in Iceland, the issue of American bases is injected by the Communists into local political disputes in such a way that the United States appears to have "aggressive, imperialistic" designs. While our interests in Iceland are being condemned, the Soviet Union has expressed an interest in establishing a base on Spitzbergen where she is ostensibly operating coal mines.

In addition to building up its own military strength and undermining U.S. influence wherever possible, the Soviet Government is actively directing espionage and subversive movements in the United States.

Two major intelligence organizations are engaged in large-scale espionage in this country. They are the groups controlled by the Soviet Ministry of Internal Affairs and the Intelligence Department of the Red Army and they operate in this country under the cover and protection of diplomatic and consular establishments. The results of espionage operations in the form of reports, photographs, films, etc., are transmitted to Moscow by diplomatic pouch carried by diplomatic couriers.

The Soviet Government has taken advantage of every opportunity to send its official representatives to the United States. Once they arrive in this country no restrictions are placed on their movements except that permission must be obtained by Soviet representatives to visit certain industrial plants having War and Navy classified contracts.

An example of a group of Soviet specialists who have entered the United States for an exhaustive survey of considerable espionage value is the case of ten engineers who are touring the principle cities of the United States at the present time. They ostensibly entered the country to receive training in the use of air compressors at a factory in Ohio. Upon their arrival in this country, the Federal Works Agency provided the Soviet engineers with letters of introduction to municipal officials in various parts of the country. They are now touring the United States taking copious notes, obtaining blue-prints, diagrams and photographs of electrical, sewage, gas and water systems, power plants, transportation terminals, bridges and other strategic points in such cities as Washington, New York, Chicago and Philadelphia. They also intend to visit the principle cities of the west coast. It is obvious that these Soviet engineering specialists are here for purpose other than to study air compressors. One of them is Senior Engineer of Gas Heating of the Moscow City Committee; one is the Chief of Water Supply of the Moscow Soviet; one is Chief of Dwelling Construction of the Moscow Soviet; one is Senior Engineer of the Moscow Gas Works, and another is Chief of the Technical Department of the Moscow Soviet.

The Soviets have been successful in getting their agents out of the United States without any record of their departure. There was a brazen disregard of United States sailing regulations when Lieutenant Colonel Nikolai Zabotin, the head of the Red Army Intelligence Activity in Canada, departed from the Port of New York on a Soviet vessel which did not file a list of the passengers aboard.

The Soviet espionage ring in this country has found it easy to load baggage aboard Soviet vessels without Customs inspection. A shortage of personnel makes it impossible for the United States Customs, without special instructions, to maintain an adequate watch on Soviet vessels for the purpose of determining who goes aboard and what luggage is placed aboard prior to sailing.

The Soviet intelligence services also operate through diplomatic and other representatives of various nations controlled by the U.S.S.R. Soviet use of diplomats of other nations for espionage purposes has been noted most frequently among the representatives of the Soviet-dominated regimes of Poland, Czechoslovakia and Yugoslavia. An example is Colonel Alexander Hess, former Assistant Military and Air Attache of the Czech Embassy in Washington, D.C. Colonel Hess was an espionage agent of the Soviet Red Army Intelligence, under the direction of Major General Ilia Saraev, recently the Soviet military attache in Washington. Use of the representatives of other governments provides not only a greater number of channels for intelligence work but also masks the operations of Soviet intelligence services.

Important elements of both the Ministry of Internal Affairs Intelligence System and the Red Army Intelligence System are found in Amtorg and in the Soviet Purchasing Commission, especially in the field of industrial and technical espionage. The Amtorg Trading Corporation was incorporated under the laws of the State of New York in 1924 but it is recognized as an official organization of the Soviet Government. Since its establishment, Amtorg has been used as a cover for espionage activities. When Lend-Lease privileges were extended to the Soviet Union, the Soviet Government Purchasing Commission was established in the United States. It has been used consistently as a cover for espionage activity. The Tass News Agency, an official Government news agency, has also been used as an espionage cover.

The Soviet Government, by utilizing the membership of the Communist Party in the United States, has thousands of invaluable sources of information in various industrial establishments as well as in the departments of the Government. In this regard it must be remembered that every American Communist is potentially an espionage agent of the Soviet Government, requiring only the direct instruction of a Soviet superior to make the potentiality a reality.

The Soviet Government depends upon the Communist Party in the United States for assistance in propaganda as well as in espionage. Use of the American Communist Party is similar to the manner in which the Soviet Government uses Communist Parties all over the world. One of the major activities of the American Communist Party at present is the dissemination of violent and widespread propaganda in favor of the foreign policy of the Soviet Union and, conversely, opposing the foreign policy of the United States. An important feature of this campaign is the propaganda urging the return to the United States of our armed forces now abroad, in order that the Soviet Union may have a free hand.

One of the objectives of the American Communist Party is the subversion of the armed forces of the United States. Important activities in this connection were the recent soldier demonstrations relating to demobilization and the recent anti-caste agitation. There is continuous Communist propaganda within the United States Army and from without to promote left-wing sentiment among soldiers. Strong and continuous efforts are being made to infiltrate the educational service of the Army and to color the material used in indoctrination and education of troops. A definite campaign, in the making at present, is being sponsored by the Communist Party to indoctrinate soldiers to refuse to act in the event the United States Army is called on to suppress domestic disturbances, to take over essential industries, or to operate public utilities.

Another objective of the Communist Party in the United States is to capture the labor movement. This would enable the Party to cripple the industrial potential of the United States by calling strikes at those times and places which would be advantageous to the Soviet Union, to prepare for sabotage in the event of war with the Soviet Union (particularly in the production of atomic weapons), and to engage in industrial espionage. The main reason for the intense Soviet activity in the World Federation of Trade Unions (with which the C.I.O. is affiliated) is to side-track the United States Government and to obtain influence directly over an important section of the American public. In this way, the Kremlin hopes to be able to exert pressure on the United States Government, so to speak, through the back door. The effort to influence U.S. action on Spain by working through this labor element is a good example of the uses to which the Soviet Government wishes to put the international labor movement.

VI

UNITED STATES POLICY TOWARD
THE SOVIET UNION

The primary objective of United States policy toward the Soviet Union is to convince Soviet leaders that it is in their interest to participate in a system of world cooperation, that there are no fundamental causes for war between our two nations, and that the security and prosperity of the Soviet Union, and that of the rest of the world as well, is being jeopardized by the aggressive militaristic imperialism such as that in which the Soviet Union is now engaged.

However, these same leaders with whom we hope to achieve an understanding on the principles of international peace appear to believe that a war with the United States and the other leading capitalistic nations is inevitable. They are increasing their military power and the sphere of Soviet influence in preparation for the "inevitable" conflict, and they are trying to weaken and subvert their potential opponents by every means at their disposal. So long as these men adhere to these beliefs, it is highly dangerous to conclude that hope of international peace lies only in "accord," "mutual understanding," or "solidarity" with the Soviet Union.

Adoption of such a policy would impel the United States to make sacrifices for the sake of Soviet-U.S. relations, which would only have the effect of raising Soviet hopes and increasing Soviet demands, and to ignore alternative lines of policy, which might be much more compatible with our own national and international interests.

The Soviet Government will never be easy to "get along with." The American people must accustom themselves to this thought, not as a cause for despair, but as a fact to be faced objectively and courageously. If we find it impossible to enlist Soviet cooperation in the solution of world problems, we should be prepared to join with the British and other Western countries in an attempt to build up a world of our own which will pursue its own objectives and will recognize the Soviet orbit as a distinct entity with which conflict is not predestined but with which we cannot pursue common aims.

As long as the Soviet Government maintains its present foreign policy, based upon the theory of an ultimate struggle between communism and capitalism, the United States must assume that the U.S.S.R. might fight at any time for the two-fold purpose of

[476]

expanding the territory under communist control and weakening its potential capitalist opponents. The Soviet Union was able to flow into the political vacuum of the Balkans, Eastern Europe, the Near East, Manchuria and Korea because no other nation was both willing and able to prevent it. Soviet leaders were encouraged by easy success and they are now preparing to take over new areas in the same way. The Soviet Union, as Stalin euphemistically phrased it, is preparing "for any eventuality."

Unless the United States is willing to sacrifice its future security for the sake of "accord" with the U.S.S.R. now, this government must, as a first step toward world stabilization, seek to prevent additional Soviet aggression. The greater the area controlled by the Soviet Union, the greater the military requirements of this country will be. Our present military plans are based on the assumption that, for the next few years at least, Western Europe, the Middle East, China and Japan will remain outside the Soviet sphere. If the Soviet Union acquires control of one or more of these areas, the military forces required to hold in check those of the U.S.S.R. and prevent still further acquisitions will be substantially enlarged. That will also be true if any of the naval and air bases in the Atlantic and Pacific, upon which our present plans rest, are given up. This government should be prepared, while scrupulously avoiding any act which would be an excuse for the Soviets to begin a war, to resist vigorously and successfully any efforts of the U.S.S.R. to expand into areas vital to American security.

The language of military power is the only language which disciples of power politics understand. The United States must use that language in order that Soviet leaders will realize that our government is determined to uphold the interests of its citizens and the rights of small nations. Compromise and concessions are considered, by the Soviets, to be evidences of weakness and they are encouraged by our "retreats" to make new and greater demands.

The main deterrent to Soviet attack on the United States, or to attack on areas of the world which are vital to our security, will be the military power of this country. It must be made apparent to the Soviet Government that our strength will be sufficient to repel any attack and sufficient to defeat the U.S.S.R. decisively if a war should start. The prospect of defeat is the only sure means of deterring the Soviet Union.

The Soviet Union's vulnerability is limited due to the vast area over which its key industries and natural resources are widely dispersed, but it is vulnerable to atomic weapons, biological warfare, and long-range air power. Therefore, in order to maintain our strength at a level which will be effective in restraining the Soviet Union, the United States must be prepared to wage atomic and biological warfare. A highly mechanized army, which can be moved either by sea or by air, capable of seizing and holding strategic areas, must be supported by powerful naval and air forces. A war with the U.S.S.R. would be "total" in a more horrible sense than any previous war and there must be constant research for both offensive and defensive weapons.

Whether it would actually be in this country's interest to employ atomic and biological weapons against the Soviet Union in the event of hostilities is a question which would require careful consideration in the light of the circumstances prevailing at the time. The decision would probably be influenced by a number of factors, such as the Soviet Union's capacity to employ similar weapons, which can not now be estimated. But the important point is that the United States must be prepared to wage atomic and biological warfare if necessary. The mere fact of preparedness may be the only powerful deterrent to Soviet aggressive action and in this sense the only sure guaranty of peace.

The United States, with a military potential composed primarily of high effective technical weapons, should entertain no proposal for disarmament or limitation of armament as long as the possibility of Soviet aggression exists. Any discussion on the limitation of armaments should be pursued slowly and carefully with the knowledge constantly in mind that proposals on outlawing atomic warfare and long-range offensive weapons would greatly limit United States strength, while only moderately affecting the Soviet Union. The Soviet Union relies primarily on a large infantry and artillery force and the result of such arms limitation would be to deprive the United States of its most effective weapons without impairing the Soviet Union's ability to wage a quick war of aggression in Western Europe, the Middle East or the Far East.

The Soviet Government's rigid controls on travellers, and its internal security measures, enable it to develop military weapons and build up military forces without our knowledge. The United States should not agree to arms limitations until adequate intelligence of events in the U.S.S.R. is available and, as long as this situation prevails, no effort should be spared to make our forces adequate and strong. Unification of the services and the adoption of universal military training would be strong aids in carrying out a forthright United States policy. In addition to increasing the efficiency of our armed forces, this program would have a salutary psychological effect upon Soviet ambitions.

Comparable to our caution in agreeing to arms limitation, the United States should avoid premature disclosure of scientific and technological information relating to war material until we are assured of either a change in Soviet policies or workable international controls. Any disclosure would decrease the advantage the United States now has in technological fields and diminish our strength in relation to that of the U.S.S.R.

In addition to maintaining our own strength, the United States should support and assist all democratic countries which are in any way menaced or endangered by the U.S.S.R. Providing military support in case of attack is a last resort; a more effective barrier to communism is strong economic support. Trade agreements, loans and technical missions strengthen our ties with friendly nations and are effective demonstrations that capitalism is at least the equal of communism. The United States can do much to ensure that economic opportunities, personal freedom and social equality are made possible in countries outside the Soviet sphere by generous financial assistance. Our policy on reparations should be directed toward strengthening the areas we are endeavoring to keep outside the Soviet sphere. Our efforts to break down trade barriers, open up rivers and international waterways, and bring about economic unification of countries, now divided by occupation armies, are also directed toward the re-establishment of vigorous and healthy non-communist economies.

The Soviet Union recognizes the effectiveness of American economic assistance to small nations and denounces it bitterly by constant propaganda. The United States should realize that Soviet propaganda is dangerous (especially when American "imperialism" is emphasized) and should avoid any actions which give an appearance of truth to the Soviet charges. A determined effort should be made to expose the fallacies of such propaganda.

There are some trouble-spots which will require diligent and considered effort on the part of the United States if Soviet penetration and eventual domination is to be prevented. In the Far East, for example, this country should continue to strive for a unified and economically stable China, a reconstructed and democratic Japan, and a unified and independent Korea. We must ensure Philippine prosperity and we should assist in the peaceful solution, along non-communistic lines, of the political problems of Southeast Asia and India.

With respect to the United Nations, we are faced with the fact that the U.S.S.R. uses the United Nations as a means of achieving its own ends. We should support the United Nations and all other organizations contributing to international understanding, but if the Soviet Union should threaten to resign at any time because it fails to have its own way, the United States should not oppose Soviet departure. It would be better to continue the United Nations as an association of democratic states than to sacrifice our principles to Soviet threats.

Since our difficulties with the Soviet Union are due primarily to the doctrines and actions of a small ruling clique and not the Soviet people, the United States should strive energetically to bring about a better understanding of the United States among influential Soviets and to counteract the anti-American propaganda which the Kremlin feeds to the Soviet people. To the greatest extent tolerated by the Soviet Government, we should distribute books, magazines, newspapers and movies among the Soviets, beam radio broadcasts to the U.S.S.R., and press for an exchange of tourists, students and educators. We should aim, through intellectual and cultural contacts, to convince Soviet leaders that the United States has no aggressive intentions and that the nature of our society is such that peaceful coexistence of capitalistic and communistic states is possible.

A long-range program of this sort may succeed where individual high-level conversations and negotiations between American and Soviet diplomats may fail in bringing about any basic change in the Soviet outlook. The general pattern of the Soviet system is too firmly established to be altered suddenly by any individual—even Stalin. Conferences and negotiations may continue to attain individual objectives but we cannot talk the Soviets into changing the character of their philosophy and society. If they can be influenced in ways beneficial to our interests, it will be primarily by what we do rather than by what we say, and it will not happen suddenly.

Our best chances of influencing Soviet leaders consist in making it unmistakably clear that action contrary to our conception of a decent world order will redound to the disadvantage of the Soviet regime whereas friendly and cooperative action will pay dividends. If this position can be maintained firmly enough and long enough the logic of it must permeate eventually into the Soviet system.

The Soviets can earn their dividends, among other ways, in

American trade. The United States Government must always bear in mind that questions as to the extent and nature of American trade should be determined by the over-all interests of this country. It should also bear in mind that, while Soviet policy can conceivably be influenced by the hope of obtaining greater economic assistance from this country, the Soviet Government will entertain no sentiments of gratitude for aid once it has been granted nor is it likely to be induced by good-will gifts to modify its general political policies. For the time being, economic aid granted to the Soviet Government or other governments within its sphere, and the fruits of private trade with persons inside these countries, will go to strengthen the entire world program of the Kremlin. This is also true of the proposals to send American engineers, scientists and technicians to share the benefits of their education and experience with Soviet counterparts. So long as Soviet industry is devoted to building up the Soviet military potential, such proposals have a direct bearing on American security.

Within the United States, communist penetration should be exposed and eliminated whenever the national security is endangered. The armed forces, government agencies and heavy industries are the principal targets for communistic infiltration at present.

Because the Soviet Union is a highly-centralized state, whose leaders exercise rigid discipline and control of all governmental functions, its government acts with speed, consistency, and boldness. Democratic governments are usually loosely organized, with a high degree of autonomy in government departments and agencies. Government policies at times are confused, misunderstood or disregarded by subordinate officials. The United States can not afford to be uncertain of its policies toward the Soviet Union. There must be such effective coordination within the government that our military and civil policies concerning the U.S.S.R., her satellites, and our allies are consistent and forceful. Any uncertainty or discrepancy will be seized immediately by the Soviets and exploited at our cost.

Our policies must also be global in scope. By time-honored custom, we have regarded "European Policy," "Near Eastern Policy," "Indian Policy" and "Chinese Policy" as separate problems to be handled by experts in each field. But the areas involved, far removed from each other by our conventional standards, all border on the Soviet Union and our actions with respect to each must be considered in the light of over-all Soviet objectives.

Only a well-informed public will support the stern policies which Soviet activities make imperative and which the United States Government must adopt. The American people should be fully informed about the difficulties in getting along with the Soviet Union, and the record of Soviet evasion, misrepresentation, aggression and militarism should be made public.

In conclusion, as long as the Soviet Government adheres to its present policy, the United States should maintain military forces powerful enough to restrain the Soviet Union and to confine Soviet influence to its present area. All nations not now within the Soviet sphere should be given generous economic assistance and political support in their opposition to Soviet penetration. Economic aid may also be given to the Soviet Government and private trade with the U.S.S.R. permitted provided the results are beneficial to our interests and do not simply strengthen the Soviet program. We should continue to work for cultural and intellectual understanding between the United States and the Soviet Union but that does not mean that, under the guise of an exchange program, communist subversion and infiltration in the United States will be tolerated. In order to carry out an effective policy toward the Soviet Union, the United States Government should coordinate its own activities, inform and instruct the American people about the Soviet Union, and enlist their support based upon knowledge and confidence. These actions by the United States are necessary before we shall ever be able to achieve understanding and accord with the Soviet Government on any terms other than its own.

Even though Soviet leaders profess to believe that the conflict between Capitalism and Communism is irreconcilable and must eventually be resolved by the triumph of the latter, it is our hope that they will change their minds and work out with us a fair and equitable settlement when they realize that we are too strong to be beaten and too determined to be frightened.

APPENDIX B

NATIONAL SECURITY AND A FREE PRESS

The Constitutional guarantee of a free press has created a dilemma for the press and for the government ever since the national charter was ratified. In time of total war, censorship in the interest of the national security has either been imposed by government or, as in the Second World War, accepted voluntarily by the press. But since government is the inevitable source of the decision that publication involves the national security, there has always been distortion or suppression of the facts under the cloak of this censorship. And on repeated occasions the press has broken through censorship to fulfill its obligation to give to the public the news to which, in the judgment of fully responsible segments of the press, the public is clearly entitled.

But the dilemma has been intensified in this age of the Limited War (as in Korea and Vietnam) and the Cold War that, was initiated by the Soviet Union immediately after the Axis powers and the Japanese laid down their arms. The new difficulty for the press and for government arises from the fact that censorship, voluntary or officially imposed, cannot be openly ventured or justified in these circumstances. Hence, government is disposed to fall back on distortion and/or suppression, and the press is disposed to take chances on risking national security in the interest of a major exclusive story.

The following material concerns an incident in the new phase of the ancient dilemma that was created by the Cold War. For though the United States military forces were not engaged on a battlefield, national security was as deeply involved as if they were. As the chief of The Washington Bureau of *The New York Times* in this period, I had to grapple with this constant issue in deciding what and what not to report for publication.

As I read the file after twenty years, it seems to me that my protestation of the *Saturday Evening Post* article was influenced, more than I admitted to myself, by the fact that the information had not been made available to *The New York Times*. But let the record speak for itself as an entry in the chronology of a perpetual major press-government issue, in this instance at the expense of a personal friendship with two colleagues whom I valued highly:

September 14, 1948

The Hon. James Forrestal
The Pentagon
Washington, D.C.

Dear Jim,

On several occasions you have discussed with me how to guard security through (1) the exercise of voluntary restraint by the press when it comes into possession of top secret facts and (2) restraints imposed by government on its own personnel with access to such facts. It seems to me that the article by the Alsops [Joseph and Stewart] in the current issue of *The Saturday Evening Post* violates both.

It informs the possible and named enemy: where and how our airplanes will strike, and with what types of airplanes; where they will be based if we can arrange it; what are the Russian targets in those areas known in detail to our intelligence groups; what are some of the Russian counter-weapons (submarines) known to us and what types they are.

I will now quote from a representation made to me by intelligence officers in the services other than the Air Force, which so obviously was the source of this published material:

"We lost lives in getting these facts, and now they can be bought for ten cents by anyone. We were instructed that almost everything published was top secret, not to be disseminated outside our group in any circumstances; and now our superiors have deliberately given it the widest publicity. If this is either sense or security, why is it?"

Frankly, I don't know whether it was wise or unwise to give the instructions which plainly were given—to release this material for the publication that was made. I think it was most unwise, and a good many people whose opinions are worth more than mine seem to agree with me. But if it was wise to make this publication, then I believe that the impact on the Russian and American people that apparently was sought would have been much greater if the material had been given to *The New York Times*. However, if it had been offered to me, I should have asked you to think again whether you really wanted it published.

I am used to requests from government officials to do constructive pieces for them and then see their real favors go elsewhere. Two of these requests came from the Pentagon within the last ten days and I granted them. This might justify me merely in saying that the material released to the Alsops should have been given to *The New York Times* as a mark of some appreciation. But that is not my point: in this instance I am discussing only the question of security.

I assume the material could not have been gathered from the source it was if you had not given instructions to furnish it. If that is incorrect, then it seems to me you have a problem of condign discipline before you.

Also, from what I hear, the cause of integration [of the Armed Services] was not well served in this instance.

Yours faithfully,
ARTHUR KROCK

MEMO (3:56 P.M., SEPTEMBER 14, 1948)

Stuart Symington, Secretary of the Air Force, phoned with respect to this letter of which I sent him a copy. He said: he thought the letter "constructive," was glad I wrote it, he had nothing to do with giving out the material, and only learned it was being published four days before it appeared.

MEMORANDUM.

Under Secretary of State Robert A. Lovett telephoned at 11:07 A.M. today to comment on my letter to Forrestal. He said he approved it highly; was glad I had written it, and was especially impressed by the point I made, that if the revelations were to be made deliberately for their public impact, it would have been more effective by far to have used such a medium as *The New York Times*. However, he agreed with me that the release should not have been made to this degree at all.

ARTHUR KROCK

Washington, D.C.
September 15, 1948

MEMORANDUM.

Hanson Baldwin's (then *Times* Military Editor) views on the Alsop article:

He does not think the plan described should have been represented as the official plan. He thinks it was bad security consciousness on the part of those who released the plan as such, and those who published it as such.

He thinks, also, it was very bad security to mention the number of proposed divisions on the Rhine—forty-five.

He thinks nearly all of the rest has been published in one form or another but not dressed up as the official master plan, which could only leave the impression that the piece had been O.K.'d by the National Military Establishment. But of all previous publications he thinks the most indiscreet were those of General Spaatz in *Life* and *Newsweek* which are repeated in this article. He does not think a former Chief of the Air Force and so recent a one should come out specifically about how we will fight a war with Russia.

ARTHUR KROCK

Washington, D.C.
September 20, 1948

THE SECRETARY OF DEFENSE
WASHINGTON

14 September 1948

Dear Arthur:

I have too much respect for your judgment, as well as appreciation of your cooperation on all matters which concern the national interest, to challenge the position you take in your letter of the 14th.

It poses a question which I think is serious enough to take up with the Chiefs of the Services—and I may ask you to attend at least part of such a meeting so that your point of view may be accurately reported.

Sincerely yours,
James Forrestal

Arthur Krock, Esq.
New York Times, Albee Bldg.
Washington, D.C.

PRIVATE MEMORANDUM.

As an outgrowth of my recent letter to Secretary Forrestal about the security questions raised in my mind by the *Saturday Evening Post* article ("If War Comes," September 11 issue) he invited me to discuss the problem at luncheon today. Others present were the Joint Chiefs of Staff—Bradley, Denfeld, Vandenberg, and Cates—and General Eisenhower. Toward the end Gen. Mark Clark came in and told us how he was integrating the services on the West Coast, including recruiting offices.

I repeated the contents of my letter and the Secretary, after first saying that he had given no "green light" for gathering the material in the article, asked for comment.

General Bradley said that while some of the figures presented as accurate were not, it was bad security for the authors and the magazine to have presented them as authoritative and the fault, in his view, lay chiefly with the magazine. It should have submitted the material to the Pentagon for guidance on the security aspects —though wholly free to disregard this—and in no event should the material have been presented as "the master plan." An editorial paragraph should have preceded it to the effect that the editors believed the material to be authentic and the broad outlines of how we would proceed to fight Russia if war came, but making no claim of presenting the master plan. Also there should have been no mention of "forty-five divisions" as the force we would use to hold at the Rhine, though he himself had never heard the figure. (This view was closely parallel to Hanson Baldwin's who gave me similar comment on the telephone with respect to my letter.)

General Eisenhower said in substance: "If it was the master plan, the Russians should not have been given it. If it was not, and there was some thought of confusing the Russians, it was equally bad because our own people would be confused also."

General Vandenberg said the Military Establishment could not be held responsible for the material in any way, since most of it was pieced together obviously from conversations with officers of all ranks and records before committees of Congress. He said he thought all publications, or nearly all, knew what information touched security and should give the Pentagon a chance to see it before publication for guidance. The other point to assure security was to inform Congress that certain explanations could not be made to it in a time like this: he had successfully used that method in asking for certain appropriations and found Congressmen reasonable when they trusted the officer who made such a request.

General Cates and Admiral Denfeld said nothing to the contrary and took about the same line.

The Secretary said politely to me that he was obliged for the intervention, that it gave them a basis for re-examination of the whole problem and that he was beginning to think there were some newspapermen he should not see intimately. He might, and General Vandenberg agreed, say one small thing, the next night someone else would say something that would make clear the full portent of the original remark, and an article or news story would result that threatened security. The trade papers knew the most technical detail and were the hardest to manage. The Russians, like ourselves, watched these publications more closely than any others.

There was much more talk—about Gen. Howland Smith's forthcoming article in *The Saturday Evening Post* on the Pacific campaign which all deplored at this time and which they had been unable to get him to cancel (though he had taken out some of his hottest attacks on the Navy and the Army), etc.

ARTHUR KROCK

Washington, D.C.
September 20, 1948

INDEX

Minton, Sherman, Associate
Justice, 269
Missile crisis, missile gap, 318 *et
ff.*
Mitchell, James J., Secretary of
Labor (Eisenhower's
presidency), 278
Mitchell, William DeWitt, At-
torney-General (Hoover's
Presidency), 138
Moley, Professor Raymond, 161,
164, 240
Molotov, V. M., 233
Monroe, James, 314
Moore, Edward, of Ohio, 152
Moore, Edward M. (Eddie),
Joseph P. Kennedy's private
secretary, 169, 335
Morgan, Gen. John, 19
Morgenthau, Henry, Jr., Sec-
retary of the Treasury
(F. D. R.'s presidency),
165, 166, 178, 185
secret errand to Quebec,
208–209
Morley, Felix, 140
Morris, Frederick (author's
uncle), 98–99
Morris, Newbold, 221, 259
Morris, "Squire" (author's
grandfather), 4 *et ff.*, 11,
98–99
Moses, George Higgins, Senator
from New Hampshire, 137
Mott, Col. Bentley, 57
Moyers, Bill M., 396
Mundelein, Cardinal George, of
Chicago, 198
Munsey, Frank A., 60
Murphy, Charles, 153, 258
Murphy, Frank, Attorney Gen-
eral (F. D. R.'s presi-
dency), 177, 184
Murphy, Frank, Governor of
Michigan, 353–354

Nasser, Gamal Abdel, 275, 320,
323, 410, 413
National Recovery Administra-
tion (NRA), 166
National Security Council, 281
Negro integration, failure of
promises resulting in agi-
tation, 277, 400
Nehru, Jawaharlal, Prime
Minister of India, 373, 410
Nelson, Donald, 202
Neuberger, Richard, 312
Nevin, John, 52
Nevins, Allen, 64
New Deal, viii, 411–412; *also see*
Roosevelt, Franklin Delano
foreign policy culminating in
war, 199 *et ff.*
New Yorker, The, 64, 66, 69
New York Evening Post, The, 60
New York Sun, The, 91
New York Times, The, 43, 56,
62, 77 *et ff.*, 124, 128, 150,
153, 157, 159, 166, 172,
173, 180, 181, 182, 183,
186, 216–217, 218, 237,
251, 269, 299, 331, 364,
366, 373, 375, 376, 389
Night Riders (1907–1908),
27–28
1925 F Street Club, 178–179,
270, 282
Nixon, Richard M., 244, 274,
287, 290, 304, 330, 388,
394
appraisal of Eisenhower's
domestic and foreign pol-
icies, 317 *et ff.*
Eisenhower's assessment of
him, 313 *et ff.*, 321
influence of TV debates with
Kennedy, 369
presidential candidate,
315–316
role during Eisenhower's illness, 304 *et ff.*